W9-BRY-613

THE COMPLETE ENCYCLOPEDIA OF

PISTOLS & REVOLVERS

THE COMPLETE ENCYCLOPEDIA OF
PISTOLS & REVOLVERS

Informative text with over 400 full-color photographs

A.E. HARTINK

CHARTWELL BOOKS, INC.

Text: A. E. Harting, The Netherlands
Pictures: Henk Reitsema, The Netherlands
Cover design: Minkowsky, Enkhuizen, The Netherlands
Editorial: Elke Doelman, TextCase, The Netherlands
Production: TextCase, The Netherlands
Typesetting: Hof&Land, The Netherlands

ISBN 0-7858-1871-5

This edition published in 2003 by
CHARTWELL BOOKS, INC.
A division of BOOK SALES, INC.
114 Northfield Avenue
Edison, New Jersey 08837

Contents

1. The development of firearms

No one knows exactly when, where, and how firearms were first developed. What is known is that the Chinese, in the eleventh century, knew the composition of what we today call blackpowder or gunpowder. However, they mainly used this to produce fireworks. It is still not known how knowledge of powder mixtures and compositions came to Europe. Some believe the formula came through trade with the Arabs. Others say Marco Polo brought the "alchemist's secret" from China to Vienna after he had made his famous voyage to China in 1271-91. Others insist that gunpowder was discovered or rediscovered in Europe itself. In this context the names of Roger Bacon and Berthold Schwarz are mentioned. The last one, a monk from Freiburg, Germany, is especially well known. "Schwarzpulver" does not originate from the black or dark-grey colour of the powder itself or from the mess caused by shooting with it but from the name of this monk.
The general composition of blackpowder is 75% saltpetre, 15% sulphur, and 10% charcoal. At some point someone discovered that, using this powder, projectiles could be shot from a tube that was closed at one side. This was the beginning of the development of firearms.

Left: Hinge locking (for more information, see Chapter 6)

Igniting the gunpowder

The basic principles of firearms technology remain the same. In the beginning, this technology was rather primitive: an iron tube was closed at one side. Then a small hole was made near the closure, which was called the ignition hole. The gunpowder was packed into this tube, through the open end.
The projectile, first made of stone or iron and later of lead, was pressed upon this powder charge. As soon as the projectile (mostly in the shape of a round ball and for that reason called a "ball") had been seated, the weapon was ready for firing. However, to shoot the ball the powder had first to be ignited and for that a fire source was necessary. In the beginning, glowing cinders or chips of wood were used.

The fuse lock

These cinders or chips were later replaced by a fuse that smouldered after it had been lit. The flash hole was filled with ground gunpowder. By means of a hinged lever, the fuse was brought into contact with the ground powder. The powder started to burn, which ignited the main powder charge in the tube.
Gases developed so quickly and these reached such high pressures that the projectile or ball was driven through the tube, back the way it had been put in. Once out of the tube (later the barrel), the high-speed bullet continued on its way through the air for quite a long distance. When the bullet hit an object, it delivered its total remaining kinetic energy. If this object happened to be a person or an animal, the delivered energy was so extensive that the victim didn't survive the collision.

As the fuse at this time was still a naked flame, the search for better systems continued, eventually giving rise to the wheel lock.

A match lock, combined with a wheel lock

Wheel lock

The wheel lock is a metal disc combined with a coil spring, which is wound up with a key and blocked. When this block is lifted by pressing the trigger, the wheel spins backwards from the tension of the spring and scrapes along a flintstone. This causes a shower of sparks, more than enough to ignite the fine gunpowder in the pan of the lock. This ignition technology is still used today in our modern cigarette lighters.

Ignition

Because the wheel lock system was complicated and expensive to make, a simpler and cheaper solution was developed. This was the flintlock ignition.

The flint was secured between the claws of a kind of hammer. This hammer or cock (as it is called) was fixed to one side of the weapon and could be drawn backwards (locked) against the pressure of a spring and, in that position, it could be secured. After pulling the trigger the flint was released. It struck a steel plate, close to the flash hole. The sparks, produced by this impact, ignited the powder in the pan, which in turn ignited the main powder charge in the barrel.

The development of the flintlock took several centuries. One of its variations is the snaphaunce lock. This system actually consisted of two kinds of hammer. The first hammer had a kind of screw claw, in which a flint was secured. This hammer could be drawn back against the pressure of the hammer spring and locked in that position. The second hammer consisted of a kind of anvil, and this was situated just above the flash hole. After pulling the trigger, the hammer with the flint struck the anvil or steel, which produced sparks that fell into the powder in the pan. As a result, the finely ground powder in the pan ignited and

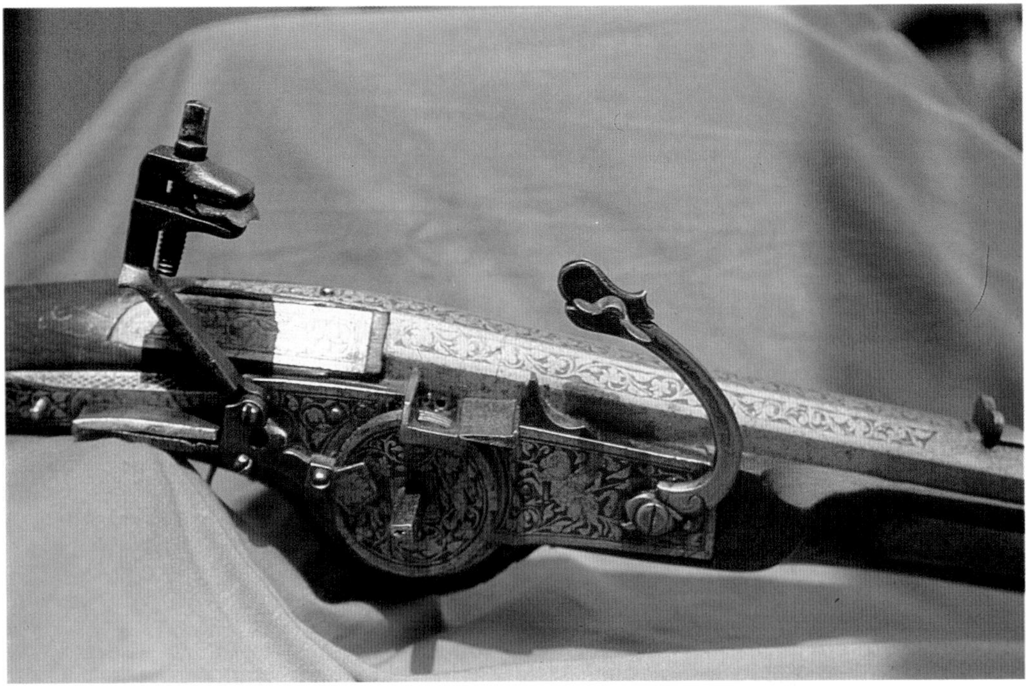

Rifle with wheel lock

Flintlock

flashed through the ignition hole to the main powder charge.
Another development was the true flintlock. Because the snaphaunce lock was rather sensitive to weather conditions, a cover was devised with which the powder pan could be closed. This vertical steel (also called frizzen) acted as a cover and as an anvil for the flint.

Percussion ignition

A real breakthrough came when the Scottish priest, Alexander Forsyth, invented the percussion primer (or at least the main principles of this system). Around 1820 a high-explosive chemical combination was developed called fulminate, which was accommodated in a small copper cup. By striking that cup with a sharp blow the fulminate detonated with a flash. The problem of using a naked flame for ignition had been solved. The chamber (or the place inside the barrel where the powder had to be fitted) still had to be loaded with powder and ball through the muzzle.
For ignition, however, a cup was placed over a kind of little chimney, screwed inside the ignition hole at the end of the chamber. This chimney is called the nipple or piston. To hit the percussion cap really hard, a kind of lock was devised based upon the shape of the flintlock hammer.
This hammer was situated directly behind or next to the barrel chamber. The hammer or cock was drawn backwards against the pressure of a spring, and locked in that position. By pulling the trigger the hammer was released, and it hit the percussion cap with force. As a result the fulminate in this cap detonated, producing a flash that, through the channel inside the nipple, ignited the powder charge in the chamber.
This percussion system was used for a long time for rifles, pistols, and later in more modern five or six-shot blackpowder revolvers.

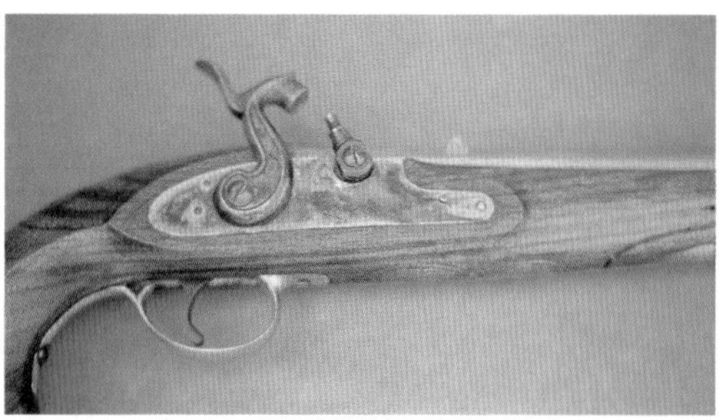

Percussion lock

Development of the cartridge

The next important step was the development of the cartridge.
At first this was made with a case of paper or cardboard, and later from brass. In the cartridge the components - projectile, powder, primer, and case - were assembled in one unit. These cartridges could not be loaded through the muzzle of the barrel, but had to be put into the chamber of the barrel through its back. This meant that the back of the "tube" had to be opened for loading the cartridge. After loading, the "tube" had to be closed securely without danger of it tearing or exploding.

Rimfire and pinfire cartridges

Variations in the development of cartridges were the rimfire cartridge and the pinfire system.
In the rimfire cartridge the means of ignition, the fulminate, is not housed in a brass cup but moulded into the inside rim of the cartridge case itself.

This rimfire ammunition is widely used for small-bore weapons, even today.
The pinfire cartridge also has its own ignition charge inside its case, which is ignited by a blow of the hammer on a protruding pin at the rear of the cartridge case. This system has only been in use for a relatively short period of time.

Another technical problem was that the chamber of the barrel had to be opened and closed repeatedly and easily. The solution to this problem is nowadays called the chamber bolt.

Pinfire revolver

The discovery of nitro-powder

The third important step in the development of weapons was the invention of the chemically formulated nitro-powder. Gas development and pressure could now be produced at much higher levels.
As a result, part of the gas pressure could now also be used to operate the closure (or bolt, slide) automatically.
This was the start of semi-automatic weapons, such as pistols, submachine-guns, rifles, and carbines.
However, as already stated, the main principles (chamber, powder, ball or bullet, ignition, and "tube" (barrel)) have not changed, although there have been tremendous developments in the technology of weapons and ammunition. These developments are, even today, still continuing, if you bear in mind such things as electronic ignition and the caseless cartridge.

Recent developments

In the early history of firearms, it took a lot of time to prepare a firearm for shooting, and dry, preferably calm, conditions were needed for a reliable ignition. Besides, the certainty of a hit was more a matter of luck than of calculation. Nowadays firearms are produced that have a cyclic rate of more than 600 shots per minute and that can be used in all weather conditions with great precision and reliability. Changing cartridge magazines is only a matter of seconds.

Today the light firearms can be roughly divided into shoulder firearms and handguns. Only roughly, because a lot of submachine-guns and (semi-)automatic rifles and carbines can also be regarded as handguns because of their small dimensions (achieved by means of folding stocks and exchangeable barrels).

Shoulder firearms

Shoulder firearms can be subdivided into the following:

- Rifles: single shots, bolt action, lever action, pump action, semi- and fully automatic.
- Shotguns: single shots, bolt action, lever action, pump action, semi- and fully automatic.
- Carbines: single shots, bolt action, lever action, pump action, semi- and fully automatic.

Handguns

Handguns can be subdivided into the following:

- Revolvers: blackpowder, small-bore rimfire, centrefire.
- Pistols: blackpowder, small-bore rimfire, centrefire.

2. Technology

Before going into details on the numerous technical aspects of pistols and revolvers, there follows a general introduction to weapons technology for those who know very little about it or for those who want to brush up their knowledge. To be able to appreciate a firearm technologically, you need to be able to appreciate how it works. For this, we need sound definitions of the various parts so that no confusion arises about their names. If, for example, one person speaks about the place to put a magazine, and another about a magazine, they sometimes mean the same thing, which is incorrect. A magazine is both a removable cartridge case in which cartridges are put and a storage depot for cartridges.

What is a pistol?

A pistol is a firearm. It does not have a definite description. According to the encyclopedia, a pistol is a (short) handgun and a semi-automatic auto-loader. The pistol's firing system is based on the following principles. The magazine, with six to twenty cartridges, is put in the pistol and, by the recoil energy of the fired cartridge on the mechanism, the empty case is automatically ejected and a new cartridge fed in.
The law is clear enough as to what a gun is: it is an object designed to shoot projectiles through a barrel, and its action is based on the production of a chemical explosion (firearms) or a physical reaction (air-weapons). Pistols can be divided into

- single-action pistols and
- double-action pistols.

Single action means that the hammer has to be cocked first before each shot. Most of the time this is done by loading the pistol, by pulling the slide backwards to introduce a cartridge into the chamber of the barrel. In this cycle the hammer is cocked automatically. Double action means that the cocking of the hammer takes place mechanically in the first stage by the pulling of the trigger. In the second stage of the trigger travel, the cock is freed again, slams forward, and the cartridge is fired. A pistol is composed of a number of parts, which are divided into the following main groups:

1 The slide group.
2 The barrel with inboard chamber, and the recoil spring/springs and recoil-spring guide.
3 The frame group, also called the grip or frame.
4 The magazine group.

Main parts of a pistol

The slide group

The slide of a pistol has broadly the same action as, for example, the breech of a rifle. The slide provides the locked action and the self-loading action. In general, the parts of a slide are:

- The slide, usually combined with the breech block.
- The firing-pin with the firing-pin spring.
- The extractor with spring, to extract the empty case out of the chamber after the shot.
- Sometimes, the ejector, to throw the fired case sideways out of the slide through the ejection port, during the reloading action. The ejector can also, in certain models, be fixed in the frame group. Sometimes the firing-pin, in combination with the extractor, acts as an ejector at the same time (for example, the FN model 1910/22 – the former Dutch Police pistol). The Colt 1911, and the models derived from it, have an ejector integrated into the frame group.
- Sometimes, the safety catch with the safety mechanism. In some models, the safety catch is on the slide, but in other types on the frame of the weapon.

The sights are fixed on the slide – the rear sight (at the back) and the front on the post near the muzzle.

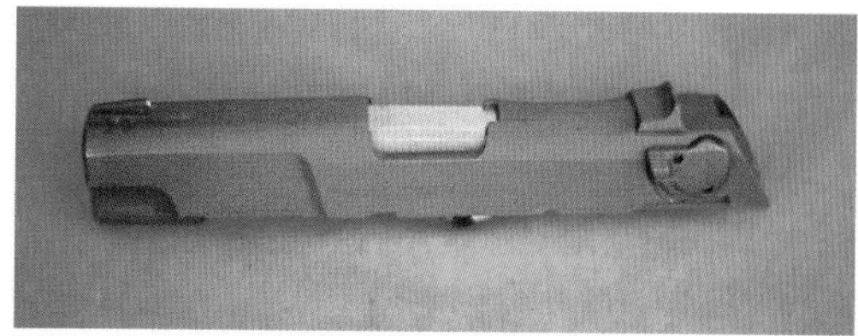

Slide group of a pistol

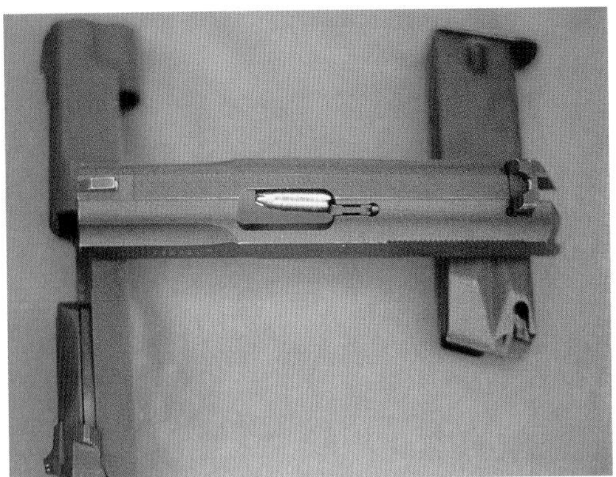

Extractor with cartridge held (seen from above) through the ejection port

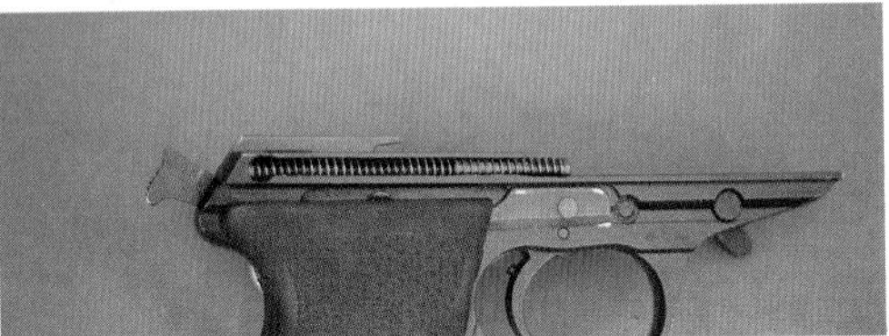

Ejector: see the pointed bar left on the top of the frame

The barrel with the cartridge chamber

The barrel consists of a (usually) round tube, into which inner side grooves or rifling (the so-called grooves and lands) have been introduced. Their function is to give the bullet (after it is fired) a rotation around the axis during its travel through the barrel. The measure or speed of this rotation is affected by the length or sharpness of the revolving grooves and lands. This rotation is also called rate of twist. For example, a twist of 250mm means that the grooves and lands make a complete rotation (360 degrees) in a length of 250mm. That is why the outside measure of the bullet is slightly larger than the inner bore (diameter) between the lands in the barrel – so the bullet is pushed through, along the lands and grooves. This rotation is necessary to give the bullet more stability in its flight trajectory. If not, the bullet would start tumbling, which could produce large deviations in trajectory. The illustrations show clearly these grooves and lands and their rotations.

The chamber is the first part of the barrel into which the dischargeable cartridge is pushed. This part is thicker than the barrel itself. It has to be, because the cartridge's ignition produces a very high gas pressure and temperature. The pressure decreases as the bullet is pushed further through the barrel (roughly speaking). If the thickness of the walls of the chamber were insufficient, the chamber could burst and the shooter could be injured by the fragments. For example, the ignition of a .45 ACP cartridge produces a gas pressure of about 1400 bar in the barrel chamber. And a 9mm Para (Luger) cartridge has a peak pressure of 2700 bar.

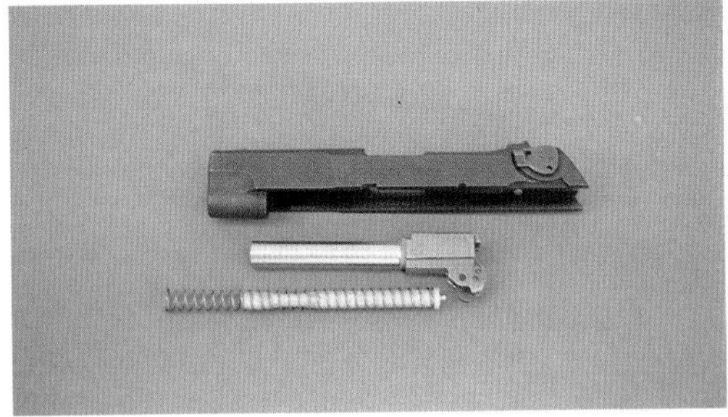

Slide, barrel with chamber block, and recoil spring with recoil-spring guide

The frame group

The frame group of a pistol is the grip, including all parts belonging to it. These parts can be as follows:

- Slide catch After the last shot, when the magazine is empty, the slide is blocked in the most rearward position. The shooter sees his or her pistol is "empty". This is convenient, because the shooter can put a new, full magazine into the pistol and can push the slide catch down. The slide slams forward and, at the same time, a fresh cartridge is pushed into the chamber. The shooter can resume firing at once.
- Magazine catch To remove the magazine out of the gun.
- Safety catch: To block the firing mechanism by means of the sear and/or the hammer and/or the trigger bar, depending on the system used.
- Trigger with trigger spring
- Trigger bar The connection between the trigger and the hammer and/or sear.
- Sear This part regulates the "launching" of the firing pin or the disconnection of the hammer, so it can strike forward to hit the firing-pin.
- Hammer with hammer or mainspring Not used in all pistols, for some models are hammerless – the firing-pin is launched directly after the trigger bar has released the sear. The firing-pin is released and strikes forward by the pressure of the firing-pin spring.
- Sometimes, the magazine safety If there is no

magazine in the gun, the sear and/or trigger bar is blocked or disconnected.

Frame of a pistol

The slide catch is mounted in the slide, above the trigger

The magazine catch is clearly visible at the rear-underside of the trigger guard

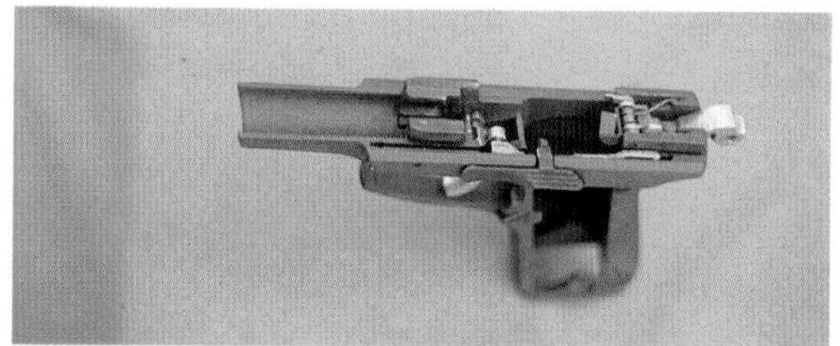
Top view of the frame of a double-action pistol.

You can see the top side of the trigger, and the trigger bar between the trigger and sear is partly visible. This trigger bar runs underneath the slide catch

The magazine group

The magazine of a pistol is very important. Everything depends on the proper feeding of the cartridges.

A magazine spring which has been mounted wrongly can cause jamming. The magazine consists of the following:

- The magazine housing.
- The follower – the plate that pushes the cartridges in the magazine upwards at a certain angle. In most cases this follower also functions as the activator of the slide catch after the last shot.
- The magazine spring.
- Sometimes, the floorplate or buttplate.

Standard magazines can contain from five to twenty-five cartridges, depending on kind, model, brand, and calibre of the gun.

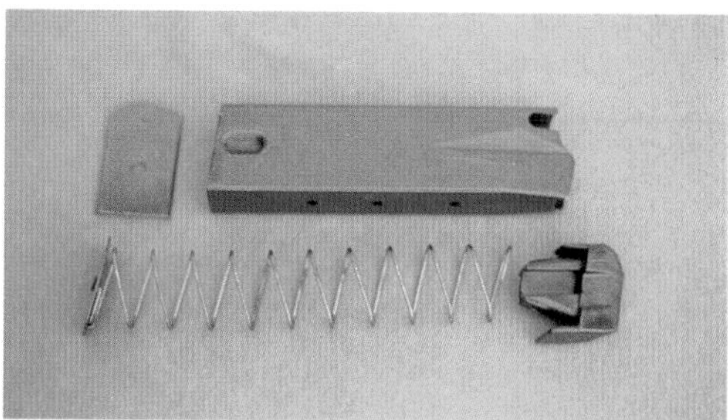
Parts of the magazine group

What is a revolver?

A revolver is also a firearm. The dictionary reads: "A light handgun with a short barrel and a revolving magazine which usually contains six cartridges".
But there is more to the revolver than that.
To begin with, revolvers can be divided into the following:

- Single-action revolvers The hammer must be cocked manually. Most of these are older models in which the cylinder cannot be hinged out of the frame. The reloading or unloading takes place through a loading gate at the back of the cylinder.
- Double-action revolvers The cocking of the

The main groups of a double-action revolver

hammer is done mechanically, by pulling the trigger. Most revolvers of this type have a hinged cylinder, to facilitate the loading and unloading. With a double-action revolver, the hammer can also be cocked manually to fire the gun in the single-action mode.

Generally, a revolver consists of the following main groups of parts:

a. The frame.
b. The barrel.
c. The cylinder.

The frame

The frame of a revolver has several combined functions. First of all, it is the grip with which you can hold the gun. Secondly, it is the housing for all mechanical movements, making sure that the trigger can be pulled, that the hammer is cocked and subsequently can strike forward, and that the cylinder rotates another chamber before the barrel.
The parts involved in this action are as follows:

- The trigger with trigger spring Generally speaking, most revolvers have a trigger group, in which several functions are combined and connected with the action of the trigger. Initially the hammer is activated, but often a cylinder hand is also activated with the movement of the trigger. The cylinder hand rotates the cylinder, so that before each shot a new chamber is revolved in front of the barrel. Secondly, usually, the cylinder stop is connected with the trigger. This cylinder stop, a cam that protrudes through the frame, blocks the cylinder after it has been rotated to the next chamber. The cylinder is blocked just before the shot is fired and cannot revolve any further (you can see this on the outside of the cylinder – the small notches near each chamber around the cylinder).

  Lastly, usually some kind of safety device is connected with the trigger. This part prevents a cartridge being fired unless the trigger is pulled completely to the rear. This mechanism is very interesting in itself. In general there are two kinds of safety principles in revolvers, namely, the transfer bar and the blocking bar. (In Chapter 5 the safety systems in revolvers are described in detail.)
- The trigger bar The connection between the trigger and the hammer. In some revolver models this function is performed by a movable trigger block or rebound slide, between the trigger and the bottom part of the hammer. Such a trigger block has a cocking cam, to cock the hammer in the double-action mode. Most Smith & Wesson revolvers have such a device, called the rebound slide assembly.
- The sear Depending on brand and model (see the preceding text), the sear has been integrated into the construction as a link

between the trigger and the hammer. This sear causes the disconnection of the cocked hammer, so that it can strike forward to fire the cartridge in the chamber.

- The hammer with hammer or mainspring When the hammer is cocked the mainspring is strained. In most revolvers this is a coiled spring, but some models have a leaf-type spring instead.
- The cylinder axis or centre pin This part makes the cylinder rotate freely and in outswinging models locks up the cylinder within the revolver frame.
- The thumb piece Allows the cylinder axis to be pushed forward, so that the lock-up of the cylinder is released. The cylinder can then be swung sideways out of the frame.
- The sights The rear sight is usually mounted at the upper rear end of the frame.

The frame of a single-action revolver (Blackhawk)

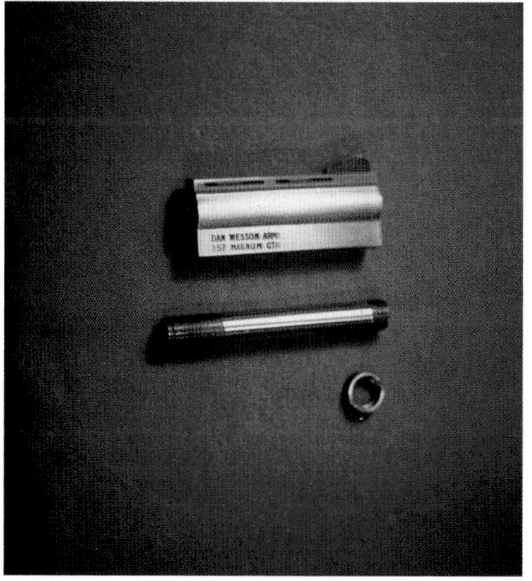

Detachable barrel of a Dan Wesson revolver, consisting of a barrel, barrel shroud, and barrel nut

The barrel

In almost all cases, the barrel is fixed to the frame. At the rear, the barrel is provided with the forcing cone. This means that the first part of the barrel is somewhat wider, so the flying bullet is caught and guided further into the lands and grooves of the barrel. This free flight of the bullet is very short, namely, in the cylinder gap between the cylinder and the barrel.
The front sight is fixed close to the muzzle end, on the upper side of the barrel. In most revolver models the ejector rod, the extension of the cylinder axis, is housed inside a barrel shroud.

The cylinder

The cylinder consists of a number of cartridge chambers, drilled in a circular pattern. For each shot the cylinder is revolved one stroke each time, so that another chamber is placed in line with the barrel. The cylinder rotates around a central axis or centre pin, in which (in most cases) the ejector rod and extractor star are fixed.

When unloading, the ejector rod is pushed backward by hand and the empty cases are extracted and ejected out of the cylinder chambers by the extractor star. That is why this rod is called the ejector rod.

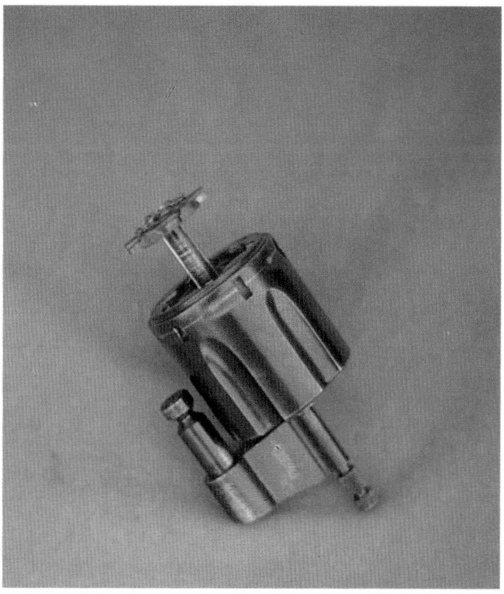

Cylinder – the extractor sticks out

3. Safety in the use of firearms

Now that the names of the main groups and the parts they contain are more familiar, before continuing with further technical systems it is important to pay some attention to safety.

For this purpose there are twelve "golden" rules:

1 *Treat each firearm as if it is loaded.* This is the most important advice. If someone hands you a gun to take a closer look and states the piece is empty, don't believe it, but check for yourself. It can save you a lot of misery.

2 *Always keep the barrel in a safe direction* and never point in a direction in which you don't want to shoot! This is especially important with handguns, because they are comparatively small. Never wave them about.

3 *Keep your finger away from the trigger and use the safety catch,* even if you are sure the gun is not loaded. Move your finger only towards the trigger on a shooting range, and only at the shooting stand, if the gun is aimed at the target you want to hit. After the shot has been fired, remove your finger from the trigger immediately. Keep your trigger finger stretched along the trigger guard.

4 *Never play with any gun.* Don't joke, for example, trying to imitate Dirty Harry in a fast draw. At best you will look a fool after having provided your house with extra ventilation in the roof.

5 *Practise loading and unloading a new gun in a safe place,* until you have perfected the drill.

6 *Never leave a loaded or unloaded gun unattended.* This is vitally important, especially in a house where there are children. Children love to imitate adults and they could be waving your gun around before you notice them.

7 *Keep your guns and ammo separately* and out of reach of children and, what is more, keep guns and ammo locked up. In this way you also prevent a burglar having a loaded gun at his or her immediate disposal.

8 *Service your guns regularly.* Before you start cleaning, check whether or not the gun is loaded. If, after not using it for some time, you are going to shoot again, you must always check if the barrel is not blocked by a wad of polishing cloth, for example. If this should prove to be the case, you will need a new gun after the first shot.

9 *Build up a certain routine in handling your gun and ammo.* Take care that different kinds of ammo remain separate. Be extremely careful when developing new hand-loaded cartridges. And bear in mind: to reload a cartridge in a "heavier" fashion, tenths of grains are used and one grain weighs only 0.0648g. Beginners in this field would be wise to ask for the advice of more experienced hand-loaders. They must also have good reference books at hand, and they should be familiar with all the theoretical "ins and outs" of hand-loading.

10 *Always wear ear protection and safety glasses.* A proportion of all shooting accidents is caused by technical defects in the guns or the ammo. Be sure your eyes are well protected against powder debris (often the case when firing a revolver, owing to the cylinder gap) or ejected pistol cases.

11 *NEVER combine shooting with alcoholic drinks* or, even worse, with drugs of any kind, or with the use of strong medicines (check the directions for use on the package). Alcohol or whatever disturbs your perception, judgement, and behaviour. Drink your beer or dram after shooting and after unloading and storing your guns safely. And, of course, after the shooting session, if you have to drive yourself home, don't drink and drive!

12 *Explain to your fellow shooter if he or she is behaving unsafely.* Beginners never learn anything until someone tells them. Try to explain the proper use of guns in a very polite way. What's more, even experienced shooters make mistakes. Avoid the company of "Mister Know-All", who thinks he or she knows better than everyone else. These people are a potential danger to life and limb.

4. Safety systems in pistols

After the previous chapters, this chapter gives more detailed information about the various technical systems which are used in pistols. Needless to say that the applied safety systems are the most important ones.

Safety systems in practice

For the sake of clarity, it is important to define the concept of a safety system. This is (usually) a manually operated system which, if it is in operation, prevents a gun being fired, either unintentionally or by means of pulling the trigger. However, there are also different automatic operating safety systems that can be lifted mechanically by pulling the trigger as, for example, an automatic firing-pin safety device.

The decocking lever

This is a mechanism which is employed most of the time on double-action pistols. It provides the means of decocking the hammer in a safe way. This perhaps needs some further explanation.
If, for example, a double-action pistol is loaded (which means a cartridge is transported out of the magazine into the chamber by means of drawing the slide to the back and then releasing it), the hammer remains cocked backwards. If the trigger should be pulled to lower the hammer, the cartridge will be fired. The use of a decocking lever will lower the hammer and thus decock it, so that no shot can be fired. Most of the time this happens by means of a firing-pin safety catch, by which, using the decocking lever, the firing-pin is pulled out of reach of the hammer.

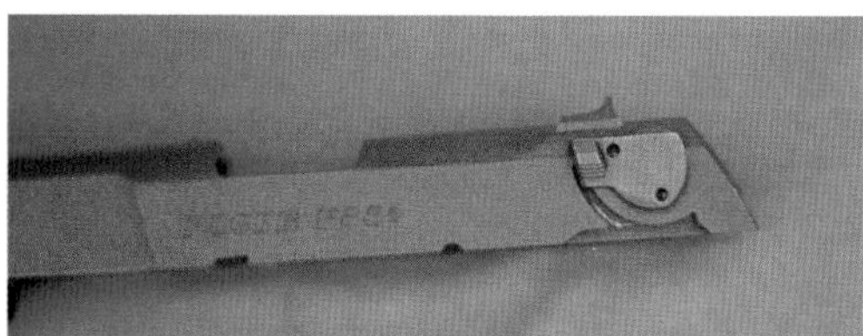

Safety catch in the firing position

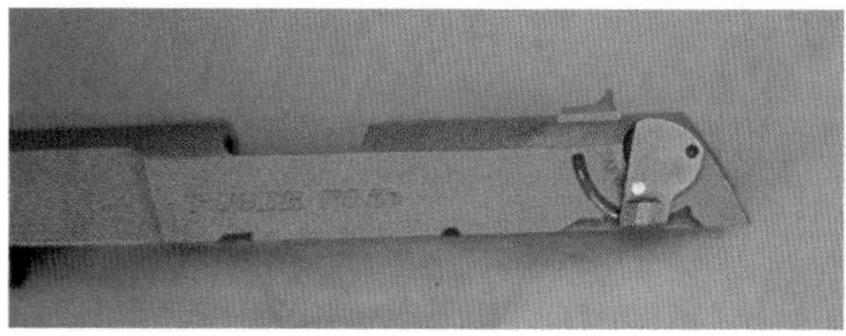

Safety catch in the safe position

The safety catch

A safety catch is operated manually. It blocks, depending on the type and model of the pistol, the hammer and/or the sear, and/or the trigger, and/or the trigger bar, and, also, sometimes the slide movement. Sometimes various combinations are employed.

Left: grip safety of a Colt pistol

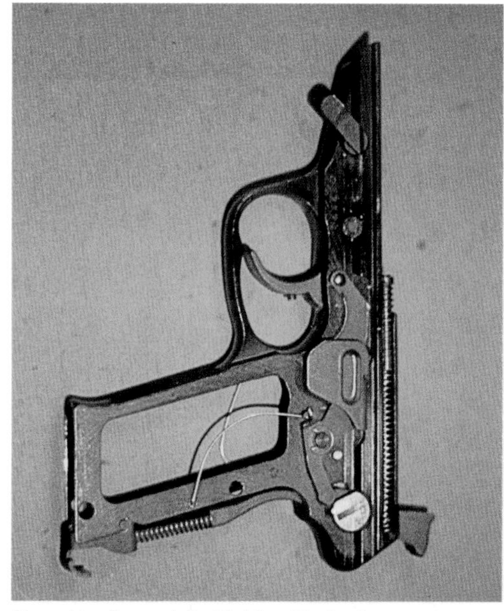

Decocking lever of the Walther P5 pistol

The grip safety

Some, often rather old-fashioned, pistol models are provided with a grip safety. This is a spring-operated part of the grip of the frame, which has to be pressed inward by clasping the grip firmly. If this safety catch is not pressed sufficiently, the gun will not fire. Most of the time this grip safety is a part of the backstrap of the grip. Its action is based on the blockage of the sear and/or the hammer. Some types of army have been equipped with such a system, to prevent unintended firing. A grip-safety system has been built into the Colt 1911, 1911-A1, the Government, and into many more brands and models derived from these pistols.

The magazine safety

Many large-bore pistols have been equipped with a magazine safety, especially pistol models without a hammer or with an internal hammer. The system is based on the principle that before the pistol is unloaded or cleaned, the magazine will be removed from the gun. Through this action the safety device is activated. In most systems the sear is blocked, so no shot can be fired by pulling the trigger. In other models the trigger bar (the connection between trigger and hammer) is disconnected.

The half-cock

Sometimes this system is used in pistols with an external hammer. If the hammer is slowly pushed backward manually, the sear catches halfway in a safety notch in the foot of the hammer. This safety position cannot be released by pulling the trigger. To achieve release, the hammer must be cocked completely into the firing position.

The slide safety

Almost all pistols have a slide safety. This system prevents a cartridge being fired if the slide is not fully home, for instance because of dirt or because of a cartridge that does not fit properly into the chamber, or whatever the reason may be. In most pistols this system functions as follows. A ridge or cam on the trigger bar has to match with a recess at the lower innerside of the slide. If this match fails, and thus the slide is not closed entirely, the trigger bar is hampered in its function and cannot reach the sear or the hammer. This means that the pistol cannot be fired.

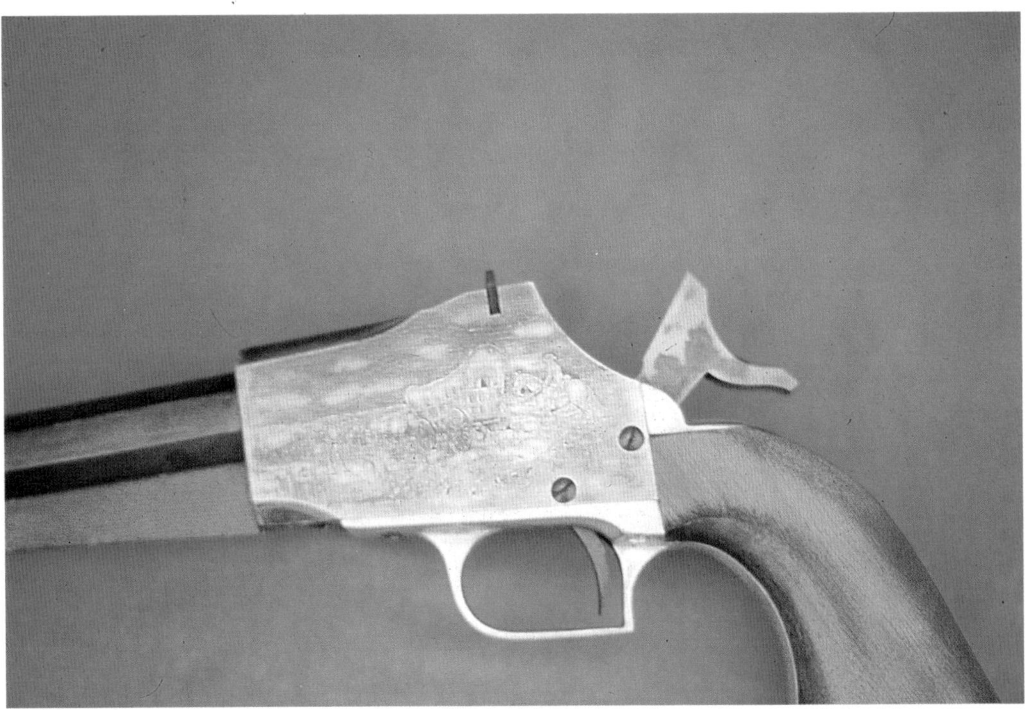

Fully cocked hammer

The loading indicator

This system has been employed in many pistols. It gives an indication of a cartridge's presence in the chamber. You can see this, for example, by means of a pin protruding on the upper or rear side of the slide.

The most widely used system is where the extractor itself serves as an indicator. If there is a cartridge in the chamber, the extractor sticks out slightly, sometimes even showing a red point on one side of it, as in Beretta and Taurus pistols.

The automatic firing-pin safety

In this system the movement of the firing-pin in the longitudinal direction is blocked. There are several systems.
One of them is the Walther system, in which the firing-pin remains in a resting position and cannot be reached by the hammer while, furthermore, the firing-pin is also protected by means of a firing-pin safety peg. By pulling the trigger, this block is lifted and the firing-pin itself is pushed upwards, so that it can be struck by the hammer.

Another system is the longitudinal blockade of the firing-pin, which is taken off by the trigger bar or by a safety lever connected with the trigger bar just before the trigger has been pulled completely to the rear.

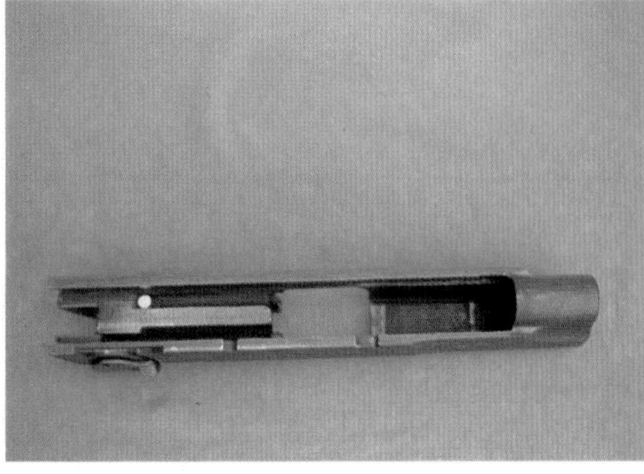

Automatic firing-pin safety. Note the light-coloured pinhead, left upper side of the slide. The trigger bar presses this pin upward, after the trigger is pulled, so the blockade of the firing-pin is cancelled

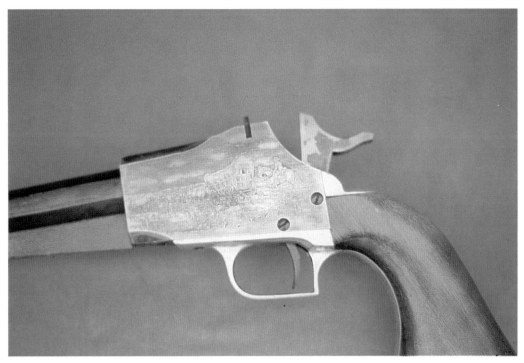

Half-cocked hammer in safety position

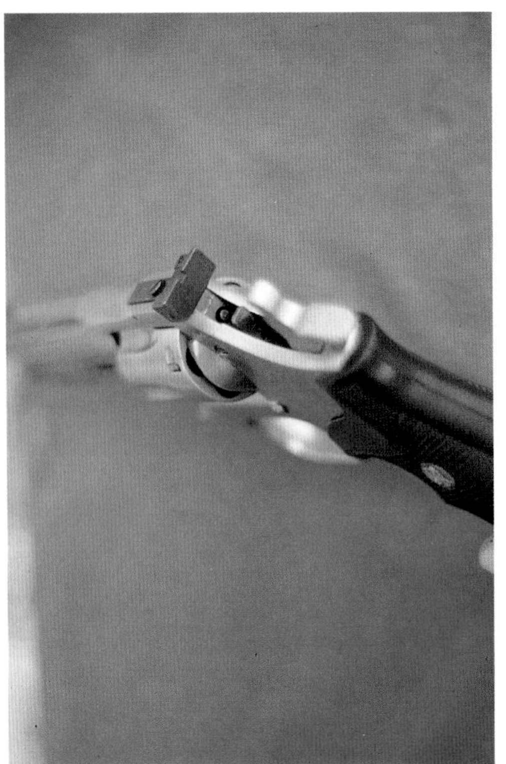

The transfer bar, just visible under/in front of the firing-pin

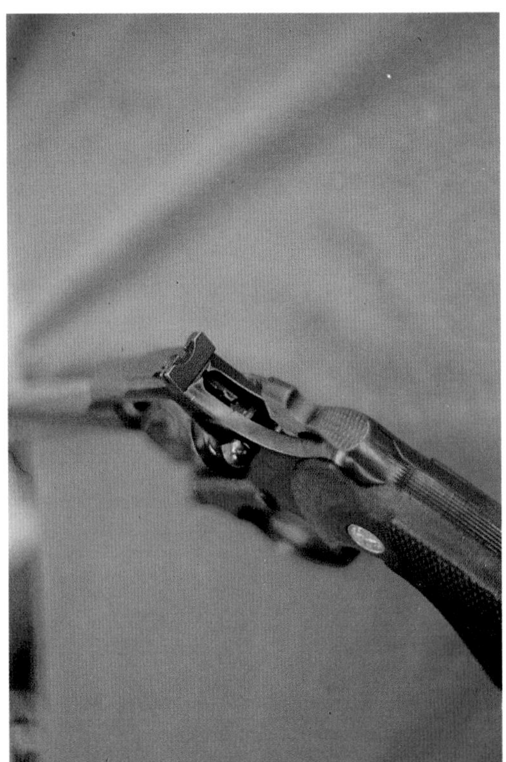

Blocking bar, difficult to see under/round the cut in the frame for the fixed firing point on the hammer nose

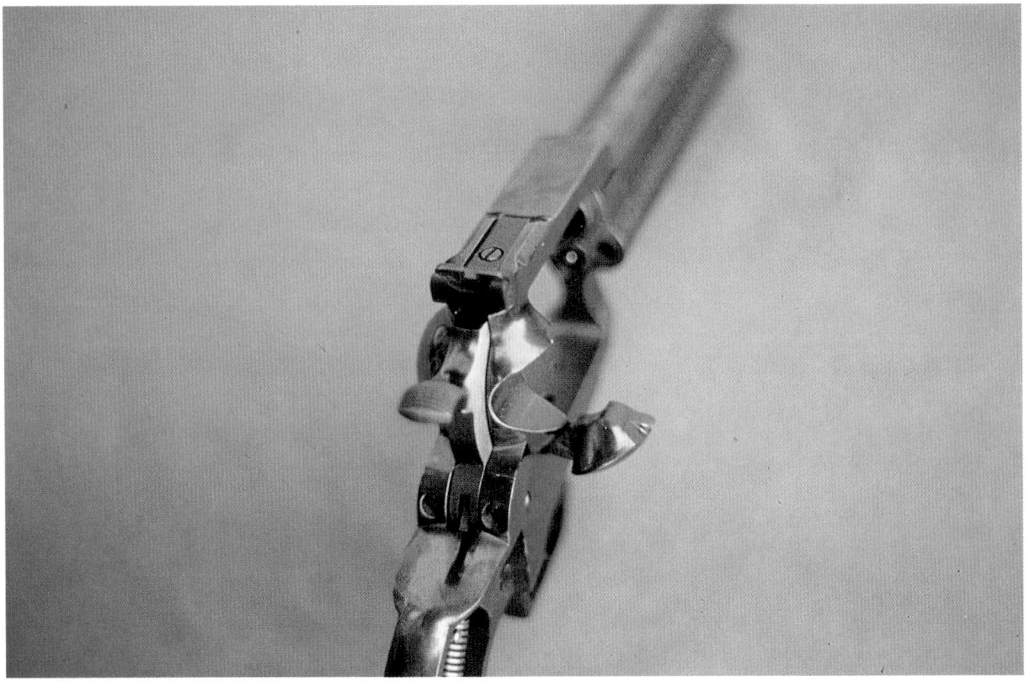

The opened leading gate. To give a clear view, part of the revolver has been dismantled

5. Safety systems in revolvers

In the previous chapter we saw that modern pistols are packed, as it were, with all kinds of more or less complicated safety devices. This is because a certain ignorance or lack of experience on the user's behalf has to be taken into account. In revolvers this is less usual. There are only a limited number of safety systems in revolvers, which are described below.

Safety systems in practice

First, however, one user's safety rule ought to be mentioned. Most revolvers have a cylinder with six chambers. When used at a shooting range, I always recommend providing only five chambers with a live round. The sixth and empty chamber is placed before the barrel when you start shooting. Whatever happens, this way no shot can ever be fired by accident, for example if the gun falls or bumps against something.

The hammer (single or double action) is cocked only when the revolver is pointed towards the target, and only then is a loaded chamber revolved before the barrel. In this way the revolver is, as it were, "fool-proof". This method dates back to the times of the old single-action revolvers of the "Wild West", which did not have any safety devices.

The mechanical safety devices with which most revolvers are equipped are as follows.

The transfer bar

The transfer bar is applied in revolvers with a "floating" firing-pin.
Normally speaking, the striking head of the hammer cannot reach this firing-pin unless a kind of bar is slipped between the hammer and the firing-pin, to pass on the blow of the hammer to the firing-pin itself. This bar slips between the hammer and the firing-pin only at the end of the stroke of the pulled trigger. The most well-known guns with this safety device are the Ruger revolvers.

The blocking bar

This system is usually employed in guns with a fixed firing-pin on the hammer nose, such as the Smith & Wesson revolvers. Normally the hammer is always blocked a little bit out of the frame, so that the hammer nose will never protrude through its slot in the frame. That way the fixed firing-pin can never reach the primer of the cartridge in the chamber. If the trigger is pulled all the way back, allowing the hammer to strike forward, this blocking bar slips down a bit, which clears the way for the hammer.

The loading gate in single-action revolvers

Many revolvers of the single-action type have to be loaded by means of a loading gate in the recoil plate of the frame. As soon as the gate is swung open, the cylinder stop is taken off, and sometimes even the hammer or trigger is blocked.
The cylinder can then be revolved around freely by hand and be loaded or unloaded, chamber after chamber.

The safety catch

Most revolvers do not have a mechanical safety lever or safety catch, as many pistols do. In the past, only some single-action revolvers were equipped with such a device – obviously without success, for modern revolvers do not have such a provision any more.

PIETRO BERETTA GARDONE V.T. - MADE IN ITALY
CAT.4343
P.B. CAL. 22 L.R. MADE IN ITALY

6. Locking systems in pistols

Since the end of the nineteenth century, semi-automatic pistols have been manufactured. Because of the complexity of their mechanisms and the technical developments that have evolved in the course of many years, the number of different locking systems has become almost impossible to summarize. I shall concentrate on the most important groups, which means the systems that are still employed in modern pistols.

Bolt action

Bolt actions are employed in pistols designed for long-distance shooting. You could compare this pistol with an extremely shortened bolt-action rifle. Depending on the system used, the manually operated bolt is equipped with a number of locking lugs at the front or rear side of the bolt. In closing or locking-up, these lugs fit into notches in the receiver of the pistol, through which the bolt and the receiver become a tight unit. A good example of such a mechanism is the Remington XP-100, which has a bolt system that resembles the Mauser rifle action. Another example (much simpler, however) is the German Anschütz Exemplar. This is a very robust and reliable locking system that can stand up to very high gas pressures and therefore also heavy ammunition.

Bolt-action lock

Blowback action. Owing to the deadweight of the breech block (upper right) and the recoil spring it contains, the pistol is functioning semi-automatically

Blowback action

Usually, this system is generally employed in pistols up to the 9mm Para or Luger calibre. One well-known exception is the Heckler & Koch VP70 pistol in 9mm Para, which is equipped with a blowback action. Because the gas pressures of pistol cartridges up to 9mm Para are not exceptionally high, such pistols do not need an absolute locked action. The lock-up of these kinds of handguns is caused by the weight (the mass) of the slide, combined with the recoil spring, which causes the slide to remain in the most forward and closed position. Because of the tension of the recoil spring the slide or breech presses against the rear side of the cartridge chamber of the barrel.

The gun's operation is as follows. When a shot is fired, this causes gas pressure. The gas pressure is responsible for driving the bullet out of the case. The bullet is then forced through the lands and grooves of the barrel towards the muzzle end. The ignition/gas pressure, the start of the bullet, and its flight along the barrel cause counter-pressure against the back inner side of the cartridge case. This case provides a gas-tight locking of the chamber. This reaction makes the case want to travel backwards, out of the chamber. This is prevented, however, by the slide or breech (depending on the model). The pressure of the recoil spring, together with the weight (mass) of the slide, have been constructed in such a way that this reaction of blowback or recoil is retarded and starts after the bullet has left the barrel. After that the system can be unlocked safely. The mass of the slide is such that when its backward movement has been started, this motion will continue until it is stopped at the end of the backward movement. So the operation occurs in this order:

1 The shot is fired.
2 With the gas pressure the slide moves backward; in combination with this action, the firing-pin (plus spring), the hammer (plus spring), and the recoil spring are pressed or cocked (as the case may be) more or less simultaneously.
3 During the blowback action of the slide, the fired case is extracted from the chamber by the extractor and ejected out of the pistol by the ejector.
4 As the recoil spring is pressed to the utmost, and after the slide is stopped at the rear position, the recoil spring wants to release again

and pushes the slide or breech forward again.

5 In its forward movement the slide strips a "fresh" cartridge out of the magazine and will ram this in the chamber of the barrel. Sometimes the recoil spring is placed around the barrel and, in other types, beneath or even above the barrel.

The Browning action

The American, John Moses Browning (1855–1926), was the inventor of the pistol locked action system that is still the most commonly used even today. This system is employed (with some variation) in, among others, pistols like the FN-High Power, the Colt Government (1911 and 1911-A1 and models derived from it), the Sig P210, and the most recent Walther P88. Compared with other systems that have yet to be discussed, it is its simplicity that is the most striking. It has, at the same time, great advantages. The system is not very sensitive to dirt, its cost of manufacture is not extremely high, and its reliability has been proven clearly by now. Generally speaking, the Browning system can be subdivided into three variations:

1. The Browning-Colt system.
2. The Browning-FN system.
3. The Browning-Petter system.

Browning-Colt system

The Browning-Colt system operates with one or two hinge points beneath the barrel, while one to three cams or lugs are mounted on the barrel, which, when the pistol is in the closed position, are locked in corresponding grooves in the inner side of the slide.

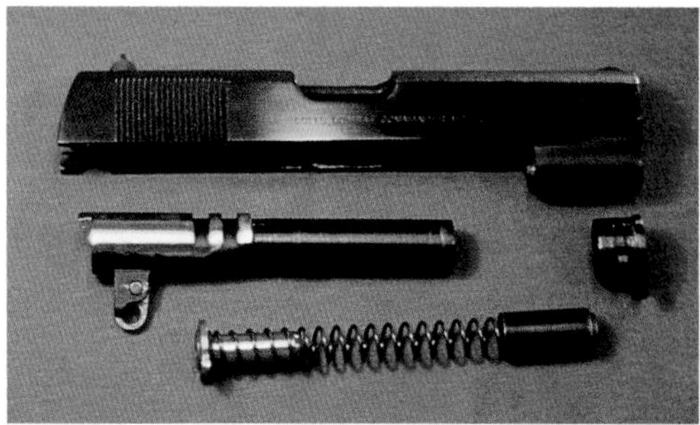

The Browning-Colt system

After the shot the slide and barrel move backwards some millimetres, under the influence of the gas pressure reaction. After this combined motion the barrel will, by means of the hinge point, drop down. The cams or lugs will then be set free from the grooves in the slide. In this way the slide and the barrel are disengaged and the slide can move backward on its own, while the barrel is stopped.

Browning-FN system

The Browning-FN system operates with one fixed barrel shank beneath the barrel instead of a hinge, and with two lugs or cams on top of the barrel, which match the corresponding grooves in the inner side of the slide. After the shot the slide and barrel, through the gas pressure reaction, move back together some millimetres and, after this, the barrel shank is stopped by a cam in the frame of the pistol. Because of the shape of the barrel shank, the barrel is forced down, through which the lugs on the barrel disengage from the grooves in the slide. The barrel stops its movement, while the slide travels further, all the way back to the rear position.

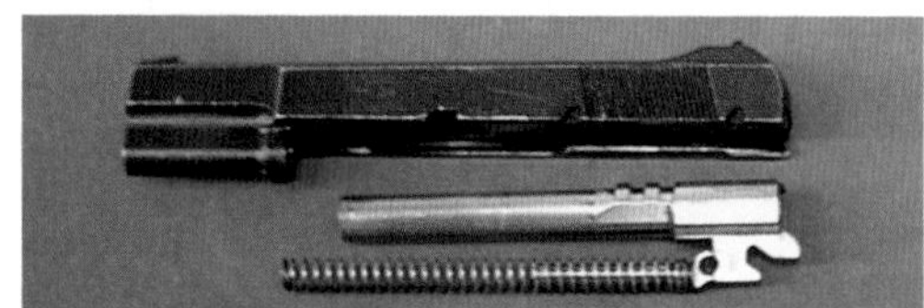

The Browning-FN system

Browning-Petter system

The Browning-Petter/Sig system operates very like the Browning-FN system, but the difference is that no lugs or cams are integrated on top of the barrel. Around the chamber a massive block has been cut out in a particular shape. This block functions as a complete lock-up, because it fits perfectly inside the slide's ejection port. This forms the lock-up between slide and barrel.

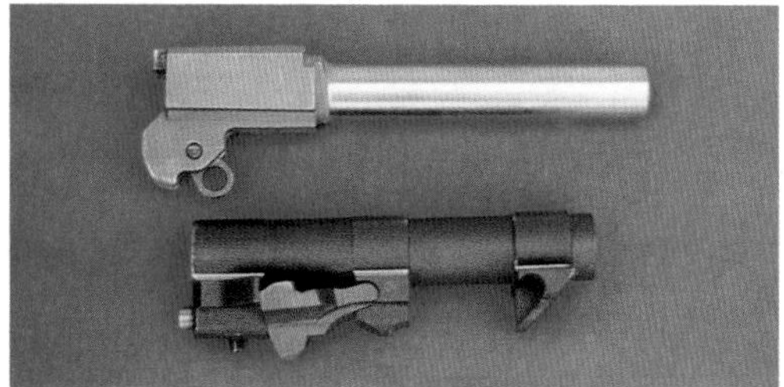

You can see the massive chamber block that locks inside the ejection port of the slide. Beneath it is a barrel with the locking-block system

The Walther block action

This locking action is employed in the Walther pistols P38/P1, P38-K, P4, and the P5 of the Dutch police. You also come across this system in Beretta pistols of the models 92 and in the Taurus pistols PT92 and PT99.

The block action operates as follows. Beneath the barrel is a small movable block of steel, which forms the connection between barrel and slide. When a shot is fired, barrel and slide glide back together for about 8mm. After this the operating pin of the locking block underneath the barrel knocks against a lug in the frame. Because of that, this pin is pushed between the under side of the barrel and the upper side of the locking block.
The wedge-shaped operating pin pivots the block downward and the lock-up between barrel and slide is removed. The slide travels further back, ejects the empty case and supplies another cartridge. Instead of one recoil spring around or beneath the barrel, two springs are mounted at the sides of the frame, which enables the slide to turn back into its locked position.

Toggle-locked action

One of the first types of locked action for a semi-automatic pistol for powerful ammo was the knee-joint or toggle action. This was employed for the first time in the Borchardt pistol and later in an improved system, the famous Luger P08 pistol.
This system, very beautiful from a technical point of view, never really came to be a "standard", as was the case with the Browning principle. The fact is, it had a number of important disadvantages.
First, it was rather complicated and required high skills in manufacture. The tolerances between the various parts had to be very small to obtain a good and reliable action. This also resulted in high manufacturing costs. Secondly, the pistol had been manufactured mainly for the army and, in the trench war of 1914–18, the gun proved to be very sensitive to sand and dirt and also to variations in ammunition.

The fact that the P08 is still such a popular handgun today can probably be put down to nostalgia. Its beautiful workmanship and characteristic appearance contribute to this as well.

The knee-joint operates by a lever that is divided into two parts and three rotation points (see illustration). In the starting position the lever is in a horizontal position, when the gun has been loaded and is ready to be fired. In the second position a cartridge is fired. Bolt B moves backward (after the bullet has left the barrel) under the influence of the gas pressure. At the same time the empty case is extracted from the chamber and the bipartite lever is pushed over (across) a slanting lever. In the third position the lever has been pushed up totally, and the fired case has been thrown out. When the action slaps forward, another cartridge is stripped from the magazine.

System lock-up is mainly achieved because the middle rotation point lies slightly lower than the total axis of the system, at least in the starting position.
Only after the bolt is forced backward will the rotation point be raised above the middle line, because the system runs along a slanting track,

Different phases of the toggle lock-up system.
In the start position (left) the lever is in the horizontal position when the weapon is through loaded. In the second position (right), the two-part lever is pushed upwards over a sloping surface

so to speak. Only then is the actual lock-up released. As already mentioned, the system is a triumph of technical skill, but from a practical point of view there are simpler and more reliable lock-up systems.

Gas-pressure locking system

In this system, which is suited to the most heavy-powered cartridges, we can also speak of a kind of blowback action. In this method, generally speaking, two systems are employed.

In the first system, the slide fits exactly around the barrel, in which a number of small holes have been drilled, and through which the gas pressure can partially escape. This gas pressure is taken up into the space between the barrel and the slide and in this way the blowback movement of the slide is retarded because of this pressure chamber. An example of this system is the Steyr GB 9mm Para pistol.

In the second system, the recoil spring (or sometimes also a separate piston or piston bar

Gas-retarded system

with spring) has been integrated into a pressure chamber. When a shot is fired, a part of the gas pressure flows into an underlying cylinder. The gas can escape from the barrel by means of a small gas hole, drilled just after the barrel chamber. In this way the pressure in this cylinder is built up against a piston, by which a kind of buffer effect is created. The unlocking of the system is retarded or delayed. After the bullet has left the barrel, so the barrel is "open",

Here the gas-retard cylinder is visible (blue tube)

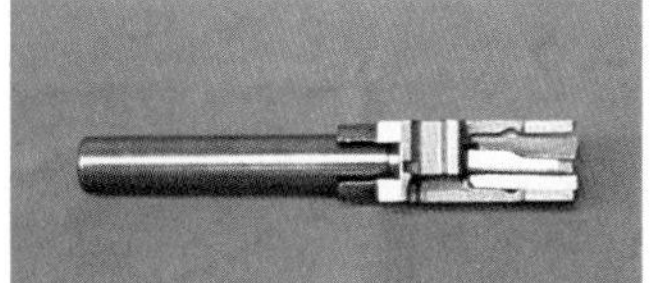
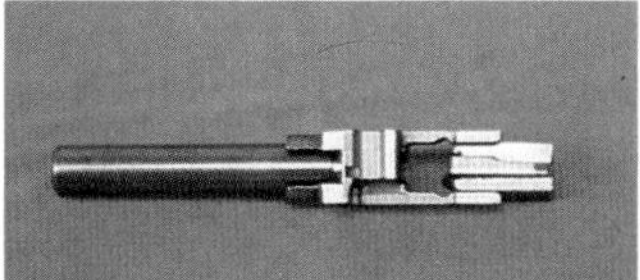
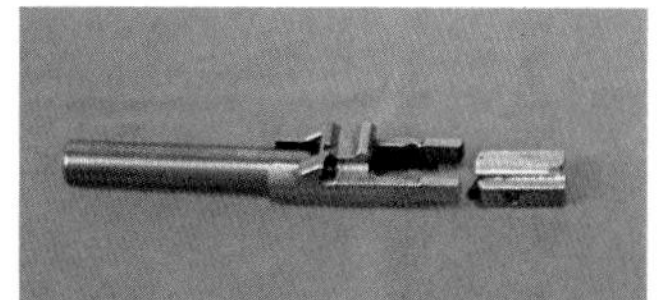

The different phases of the locking-roller system (left to right). The barrel and bolt block are locked together by the two locking rollers. In the centre picture both are unlocked, and right you see both parts separately

the gas pressure can escape through the same gas hole and the gas pressure drops to normal. Only then can the slide unlock and travel backwards. An example of this system is found in some Heckler & Koch pistols, like the P7-models (P7-M8, P7-M10, and P7-M13).

Both gas-pressure locking actions are ingenious systems with only one disadvantage: only mantle bullets can be used, because lead bullets block the indispensable little gas hole in the barrel.

Bolt-locking roller system

This system has made the German company of Heckler & Koch famous, although it did not actually invent it. This system has been applied successfully in many Heckler & Koch big-bore pistols, machine pistols, rifles, and carbines. The first firm to employ this system was the Czech company CZ, with their model CZ-52.

The operation of the roller system is as follows. Two hemispherical recesses are situated in sidelong extension pieces of the barrel. These two steel rolls, which are also fixed on the slide, can be locked by means of a kind of carriage. When the pistol is locked these two steel rolls drop into the recesses at both sides of the barrel. After firing the slide is forced backward by the gas pressure.
The two rolls swing inside and after the disconnection has been finished, the slide moves further backward. After that, the cycle of extracting, ejecting, and reloading takes place, as in other pistols.
This system has two advantages. First, the locked action (after firing the cartridge) is very stable and, secondly, the recoil is delayed because the two rolls have to swing inside their carriage. This is very comfortable for most shooters, certainly with powerful ammo. The disadvantages are the high manufacturing costs because this form of locking action demands very high precision in production. Another disadvantage is its sensitivity to variations in ammunition. At the end of the 1990s the Dutch police switched to the 9mm Para Action 3 Hollow Point cartridge, with a bullet weight very much less than that of the traditional full-mantle jacket in this calibre. As a consequence of this, the locked roller action of all police submachine-guns and semi-automatic MP-5 carbines had to be adapted.

Rotation breech-locked system

In several types of semi-automatic pistols, a rotation breech action has been employed, a system that has been derived from rifle systems. The breech or the bolt of the gun, assembled within the slide or receiver, has a number of bolt-locking lugs at the front, in the middle, or at the rear end or a combination of those. These bolt-locking lugs, after the system is locked-up (closed), engage in recesses at the rear side of the barrel or any other part of the receiver or slide, depending on the kind of construction that has been used. So, depending on the system, this is the receiver or the frame of the gun.
Because of the blowback energy of the weapon and/or the gas pressure of the fired cartridge, the breech is forced to revolve through a certain number of degrees, so that the bolt lugs on the breech or bolt are set free from the recesses in the receiver or the rear side of the barrel. With this kind of system the barrel is usually fixed to the frame and only the breech or bolt and slide are movable. The system can be compared with that of a bolt-action rifle, but in this case the operation is powered semi-automatically or even by a gas-pressured piston. Good examples of this technique are the Colt 2000 and the Desert Eagle of IMI (Israeli Military Industries).

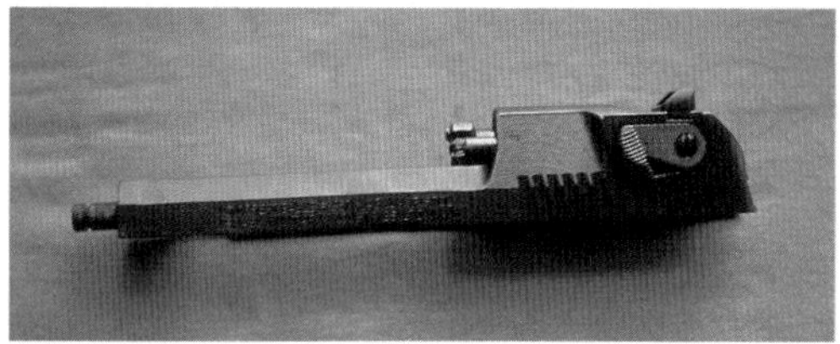

Rotation lock-up system

Webley

7. Revolver locking systems

As we saw in Chapter 5, the number of safety devices for revolvers is small compared with those of pistols. This is also the case with locking systems.

Main groups of revolvers

In the case of revolvers, there are only a few basic locking actions which have been employed from the very beginning of revolver development. First, the cylinder should not revolve unintentionally and, furthermore, it should not drop out of the frame during firing. In principle, the main groups of revolvers can be divided into three different subgroups:

1 The single-action revolver, in which the cylinder is locked up firmly in the frame. The lock-up is performed by the cylinder axis. The cylinder can only revolve around this axis.

2 The single-action or double-action revolver with the outswinging cylinder. In this type the cylinder is loaded or unloaded by swinging the cylinder sideways out of the frame. In this system, the cylinder will have to be locked on at least two sides: at the front by means of the cylinder axis, or by the lock-up of the cylinder crane into the frame, and at the rear, where a protuberance of the cylinder axis drops into a recess in the frame. As a matter of fact there have been more developments, in which the cylinder was locked in three points: at the front by the cylinder axis, through the swivel arm, and at the rear side of the cylinder.

3 The top-break revolver. In this old-fashioned revolver design, the barrel (with the cylinder attached) was hinged at the bottom of the frame. When the revolver had to be loaded this barrel/cylinder subframe hinged forward. The locking action consists of a latch at the upper side of the cylinder bridge, which runs from the barrel over the cylinder. The hook, mounted on that bridge, catches in a notch on top of the frame, next to the hammer.

There are also other, more general locking systems that are employed in different kinds of revolvers.

Left: Top-break revolver

Lock-up by the cylinder stop

At the bottom of the frame a little lug or cam is operated by the trigger movement, which locks the cylinder in a certain position. This is very important because, during firing, the top chamber has to be in line with the barrel. When moving the gun the cylinder should not be allowed to start turning again by itself. If it does so, the chamber which has to be fired will be placed out of line with the barrel. You can perhaps appreciate what the consequences would be!

You can see the lock-up very well on the outside of the cylinder. Around the cylinder, each chamber has a little notch or recess on the outside, into which the cylinder stop fits. During the cocking of the hammer this block is taken off and the cylinder revolves one chamber, until another one is put in front of the barrel. As soon as the hammer is totally cocked, this cylinder stop will drop into the notch of that new chamber.

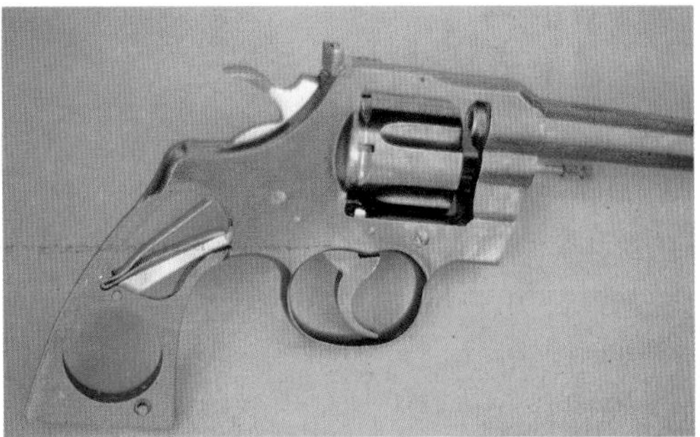

The cylinder stop can be seen in the under side of the frame, just above the trigger

The cylinder axis lock-up

The cylinder has also to be locked up in the longitudinal direction. First, the cylinder revolves around this axis. This centre pin (as it is also named) also prevents the cylinder being pushed away, out of the frame, by the enormous gas pressure, which develops during the firing. This lock-up is only taken off when the thumb piece is pushed manually forward, by which the cylinder is set free and can be swung sideways out of the frame. In most revolvers the hammer is blocked if the lock-up of the cylinder axis is disengaged. This is, of course, not the case with the single-action revolver, which has no outswinging cylinder.

In a certain type of revolver this locking action is integrated into the top-break system. These revolvers, mostly the older models, are loaded or unloaded by toppling the front part of the frame. This front part consists of the barrel, the cylinder, and the cylinder bridge, in which the latch for the lock-up between the hinged part and the rest of the frame is integrated. This is particularly the case in the Enfield and Webley (& Scott) revolvers, but also in early models of Smith & Wesson.

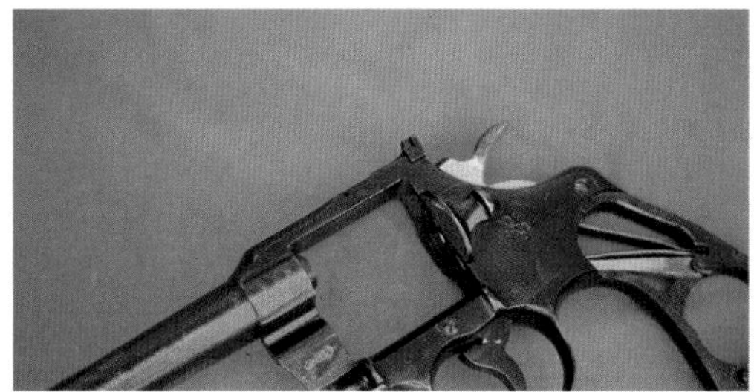

By means of the thumb piece the cylinder can swing out of the frame

Cylinder crane lock-up

In some revolvers, like the Dan Wesson and Mitchell models, the cylinder is locked at two places. First, a latch is integrated into the cylinder arm (or crane) and this latch locks into a notch in the frame. Secondly, the rear side of the cylinder axis, near the ejector star, is locked up by a ball bearing in the recoil plate of the frame. During firing, the cylinder is really locked at three places: first, at the cylinder crane; secondly, against the ejector star; and lastly, by the cylinder stop. Such a system is also called a "triple-lock".

In the rear side of the recoil lock-up plate the light-coloured notch can be seen, into which the ejector star of the cylinder fits

Cylinder crane lock-up of Dan Wesson and Mitchell revolvers

8. Ammunition for handguns

Cartridges for handguns, which means pistols and revolvers, come in many types and sizes. Depending on the bullet used, the cartridge is suitable for defence purposes, hunting, or target shooting. For each of these uses a subdivision can be made by kind, weight, and profile of the bullet. Depending on the kind of handgun, pistol cartridges can sometimes be fired from revolvers and vice versa. A good example of this is the .357 Magnum revolver cartridge. Some pistol brands can be bought in this calibre, like the Coonan pistol, the Grizzly, and the Desert Eagle. With the aid of special clips you can also use 9mm Para pistol cartridges in some revolvers.

The action of the cartridge

Almost all rifle, carbine, pistol, and revolver cartridges are made up of four different components:

- The case.
- The primer.
- The powder.
- The bullet.

Firing a cartridge happens as follows. The cartridge is ignited because the firing-pin strikes against the primer of the cartridge. In milli-seconds the little charge explodes, and the sharp flash of the flame ignites the powder charge in the case. In this way the powder is ignited, which causes a chemical reaction and the powder is converted into gas (pressure). This gas pressure can be very high, because the cartridge is enclosed on all sides. Finally, the only possible part of the cartridge that can give way gives way, the bullet, and this is pushed out of the case by the gas pressure, and reaches – in a short period of time – an accelerated speed as a result of the expanding gas. The cartridge case is often made of brass. This material is soft and elastic. As the powder is expanding during burning, and the case becomes pressed against the barrel chamber a good gas seal is achieved. This is necessary because all the gas pressure has to be used to drive the bullet. The primer is, properly speaking, a very tiny bomb in a soft metal holder. This holder contains the fulminate compound, a very highly explosive chemical mix, which can be made to explode very easily by a slight blow. This causes a sharp flash, through which the other component of the cartridge, the powder, is ignited. The powder, with which the cartridge is loaded, develops a lot of gas during burning. It does not therefore explode, as is often wrongly thought. The burning takes place so quickly that, as a matter of fact, it can be seen as a kind of explosion, at least to non-experts. In a fraction of a second

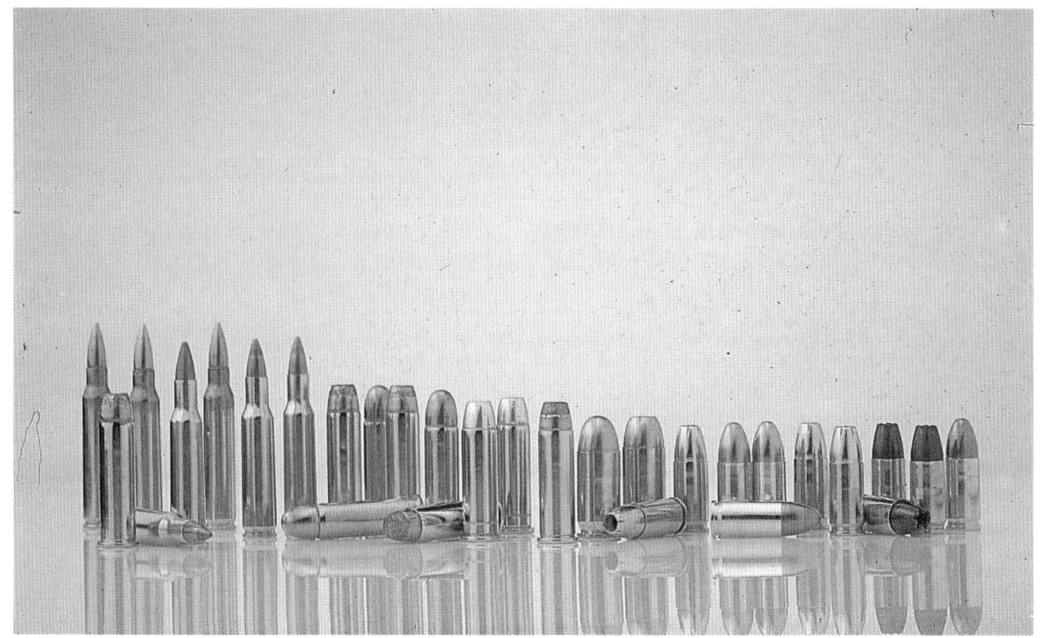

such a high pressure is developed in the small space of the case that the bullet, the fourth component of the cartridge, is very powerfully ejected from the case. The case itself is enclosed well on all sides: at the sides against the chamber wall, and at the rear against the bolt head. In a cannon this is called the breech, in a rifle the bolt, in a pistol we talk of the slide, and in a revolver this is the recoil plate, which is a part of the revolver frame. The gases, which are liberated when the powder is burnt, develop an enormous pressure: in a 9mm Para up to 2500 bar, in a rifle cartridge up to about 4000 bar, and with a powder charge that is too high this can rise to 7000 bar or more. With about 12,000 bar a good rifle will explode, and this sometimes happens. The gas pressure is exerted inside the case in all directions, and also at the bottom of the bullet. Depending on the kind of gun, the calibre, and the powder charge, the bullet will fly for hundreds or even thousands of metres. The gas pressure causes the bullet to go whistling to its target at tremendous speed.

Speed and precision

The timing is actually like this: from the moment the shooter wants to fire, it takes about 0.2 seconds before the trigger finger obeys the "brain-command". The firing-pin hits the primer of the cartridge about 0.005 seconds later. After that the powder ignites in the cartridge case within 0.0004 seconds. A total of 0.2054 seconds. The powder charge is ignited by the primer flash, and the gas pressure starts to build up. This chemical reaction continues, even after the bullet has left the barrel. After about 0.004 seconds the bullet has been pushed out of the case, and starts its trajectory through the barrel. The bullet leaves the muzzle with a "moderate" speed of about 300 metres per second (average in handguns), after it has been travelling through the barrel in about 0.0012 seconds. Depending on the rate of twist, and some other conditions, the bullet has a rotational speed of about 1000 revolutions per second. If the target is, for example, at a distance of 25 metres, the bullet will reach it in 0.1125 seconds. So, in total the firing of a cartridge will take 0.3195 seconds, before the bullet hits the target. More interesting is that the shooter feels the recoil of the gun about 0.2 seconds after the bullet has left the barrel.

Normally, a pistol or a revolver is used at distances of up to 50m, and this book describes the ammunition used for these distances. However, one exception springs to mind. Handguns in several calibres are also used for silhouette shooting. In these matches, animal shapes made of steel have to be shot down. In many countries this kind of shooting is developing rapidly as a sport. A well trained shooter with a solid gun will place all his or her hits within a circle as large as a drip pad, at a distance of 25m. Precision shooters with special "match" pistols can even shoot groups with a cross-section of 3cm. To reach this kind of precision, a lot of practice is needed, and special ammunition adapted to the gun. These two factors mean that a sporting shooter has to hand-load his or her own ammunition.

Besides the knowledge and experience of the shooter, match shooting also depends on the powder charge, the type of bullet, and the kind of weapon used. Differences in stability, trigger mechanism, cartridge feeding, the sights, the grip, the muzzle flip, the power of recoil, and the manageability between different handguns are not noticed by new shooters straight away. The experienced and more trained shooter, however, will recognize these quickly, and these factors will play an important part in choosing a new gun.

Current calibres

Below you will find a general description of most current calibres of pistol and revolver cartridges, together with illustrations of this ammunition.

Calibre .22 Long Rifle (LR)

The .22 LR has a long history. The small cartridge is used all over the world and it is being improved all the time. No other cartridge has so many variations and designs especially for target shooting, and also for vermin control. Furthermore, it has proven its usefulness in small pocket pistols, in calibre-exchange systems, or insert barrels for big-bore pistols, revolvers, and rifles.
As a sporting cartridge it has known many improvements during recent decades. To win at the Olympic Games of 1936 (Berlin) it was sufficient that every shot hit the bullseye, which then had a diameter of 30mm. Today the same precision is required with a bullseye diameter of only 12.4mm.

As this cartridge is made all over the world, there is an abundance of well-known or less well-known brands that differ in shooting

precision and price, depending on the quality. The .22 cartridge belongs to the family of rimfire cartridges. This means that the fulminate compound has been pressed inside the thin-walled case rim and ignites there by the strike of the firing-pin. There is, of course, not much compound. In the case of the RWS cartridges it is only a matter of 0.035g of the erosion-free material, 'Sinoxid'.
Cartridges like .22 Magnum (officially: .22 Winchester Magnum Rimfire) also belong to the rimfire category calibre .22, which is often used as a small-bore hunting cartridge for shooting crows and magpies. Another rimfire cartridge is the .22 Short, used for rapid-fire pistols. As well as the normal cartridges, the so-called "room ammunition" is also offered. These cartridges have a very reduced powder charge and are meant for shooting at short distances and/or in closed rooms.

The high-speed or high-velocity cartridges have a considerably higher muzzle velocity and, in combination with a hollow point bullet, a totally different effect on the target than bullets of the standard kind. For sporting shooters the use of such fast cartridges has no advantage in relation to precision. Quite the contrary has been proved for most guns in tests. Often this rimfire ammunition is called the "Flobert cartridge", which is really not correct, as the illustrations show.

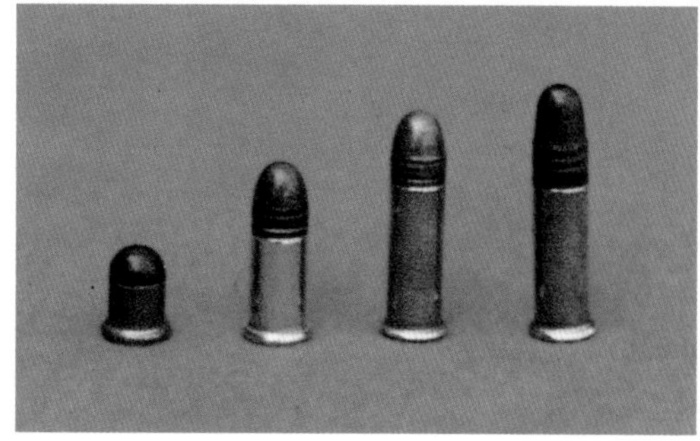

Rimfire cartridges from left to right: 6 mm Flobert, .22 Short, .22 Long en .22 LR

The table below gives the differences in bullet speed and energy.

Cartridge	Type	Bullet weight (g)	Gas pressure (bar)	V0 (m/s)	E0 (joule)
6 mm	Flobert	1,0	800	200	20
.22 Long	Z(immer)	1,8	1000	220	44
.22 Short	Standard	1,8	1800	260	61
.22 LR	Subsonic	2,6	1800	305	121
.22 LR	Standaard	2,6	1800	330	141
.22 LR	High Vel.	2,6	1800	400	208
.22 LR	Stinger	2,1	1900	510	273
.22 Magn.	WMR	2,6	1900	615	491

V0 = Velocity of the bullet at the muzzle in metres per second
E0 = Energy of the bullet at the muzzle in joules
LR = Long Rifle
WMR = Winchester Magnum Rimfire, the original name of the .22 Magnum cartridge. This is a longer rimfire cartridge which cannot be fired from guns of the calibres 6mm Flobert, .22 Short, Long, and LR.

Calibre 6 mm Flobert

The cartridge 6mm Flobert was developed in 1845 by the Parisian gunsmith, Flobert.
In fact he reshaped a copper primer case, lengthened it, and pressed a little round bullet on top of it.

Calibre .22 Short

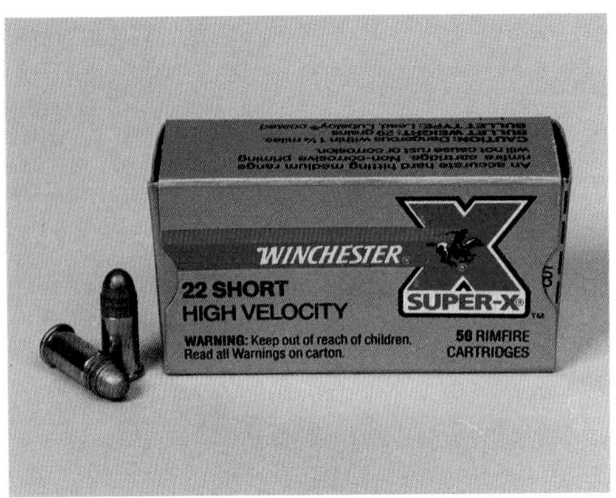

Rimfire cartridge calibre .22 Short

The .22 Short was developed in the USA from the 6mm Flobert. In 1857 Smith & Wesson introduced their first revolver with this calibre, the ‘First Model’. The gun was designed for target shooting, but was also regarded as a serious defensive weapon in those days. The original cartridge had a 1.9g bullet, and a charge of 0.26g of blackpowder.

It was only in 1927 that the Remington Company marketed a non-corrosive fulminate compound. Until that time the cartridges had been charged with a fulminate composition, which contained quicksilver, calcium chlorite, and sulphur antimony, which affected the barrels seriously because of the sulphur and chlorite. At present the .22 Short is used for a special type of target shooting, namely, rapid-fire pistol shooting, an official and Olympic discipline.

Calibre .22 Long

This cartridge can be considered, strictly speaking, as an intermediate between the .22 Short and .22 Long Rifle. This calibre was introduced in 1871. The original cartridge had a lead bullet of 1.9g and a blackpowder charge of 0.32g.

With the arrival of the .22 LR cartridge in 1887, the .22 Long was pushed into the background. As there are still guns for this calibrein use, the .22 Long ammunition is still being made. The .22 Long Z (zimmer = chamber or room) is intended for practising at short distances indoors.

Calibre .22 LR (Long Rifle)

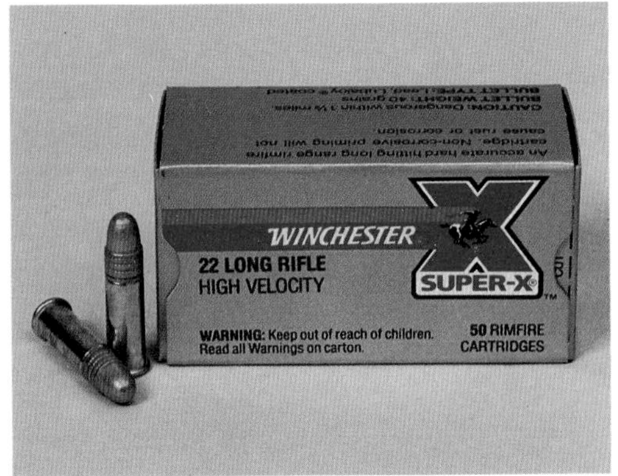

Rimfire cartridge .22 LR

The .22 LR cartridge is claimed to have been developed by the American J. Stevens Arms and Tool Company, in 1887. The original cartridge had a 2.6g bullet with 0.32g blackpowder as propellant charge. The first HV (High Velocity) cartridge in calibre .22 LR was introduced in 1930 by Remington in the bullet weights of 2.6g for a massive lead bullet, and 2.4g for a hollow point. The latter cartridge was meant for hunting small game at distances up to about 80m. In American terminology this game is indicated as "Varmint", a corruption of "vermin" which means "small harmful animals". The .22 LR is marketed under numerous brands. And almost every brand also has a large variety of types.

Calibre .22 WMR (Winchester Magnum Rimfire)

This rimfire cartridge was developed in 1959 by Winchester. Obviously, arms manufacturers immediately recognized great opportunities for this calibre, because the Ruger Company, and Smith & Wesson introduced several revolver models in this calibre shortly after it was marketed. The cartridge is meant especially for hunting small game and vermin at distances up to about 100m.

Rimfire cartridge .22 WMR

Calibre 7,65 mm (.32 ACP = Automatic Colt Pistol of .32 Auto)

Pistol cartridge calibre 7,65 mm of .32 ACP

In 1897, John Moses Browning developed this cartridge for several of his pistol designs. As a defence cartridge it obviously had a lack of power.

The penetration capacity and also the available bullet energy are poor. In spite of all this it has been a police calibre in many European countries for decades. The cartridge is effective up to about 25m. By using expanding Hornady XTP bullets the effectiveness is acceptable to some degree. The pistols in this calibre have been marketed by many arms manufacturers, but those of FN (FN-Browning) and Walther are best known. As a sporting calibre this cartridge is not very interesting. Existing pistol models are not or hardly at all suited to the use of lead bullets.

BALLISTIC DATA OF FACTORY AMMUNITION:

Bullet weight	*V0 in m/s*	*E0 in Joules*
71 grains	275	175

Calibre .32 Smith & Wesson Long

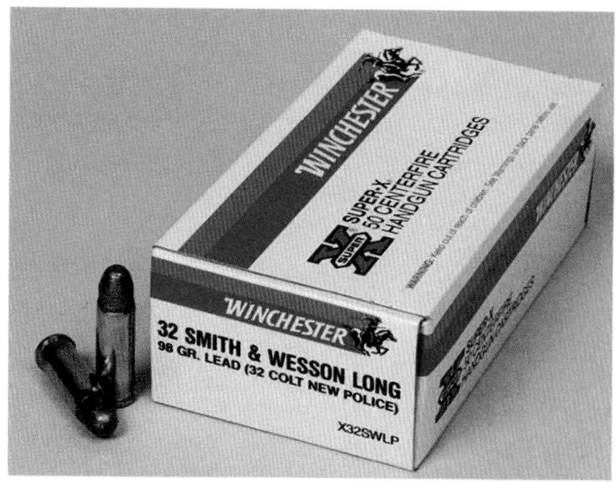

Pistol cartridge calibre .32 S&W Long

This cartridge was developed in 1903 as a revolver cartridge, based upon the .32 Smith & Wesson cartridge of 1896. For the .32 S&W Long only, the case of the old .32 S&W was lengthened. Initially this calibre was developed as a blackpowder cartridge. Later, charged with nitro-powder, this calibre has become rather popular as a match cartridge with a lead wad-cutter bullet for revolvers and pistols. Well-known sporting pistols in this calibre are, among others, the Walther GSP, and several Hammerli and Unique models. The cartridge is effective up to 25m.

BALLISTIC DATA OF FACTORY AMMUNITION:

Bullet weight	*V0 in m/s*	*E0 in Joules*
98 grains	235	140

Calibre .32 H&R-Magnum

The history of the calibre .32 Harrington & Richardson (abbreviated .32 H&R Magnum) goes back to the year 1878. In those days Smith & Wesson developed the cartridge .32 S&W for their Smith & Wesson Single-Action Model 11/2 top-break revolver. The original cartridge was loaded with blackpowder. From 1939, the .32 S&W was offered with a nitro-powder charge. Around 1902, Smith & Wesson brought out a new calibre, based upon the old .32 S&W, which was called the .32 Smith & Wesson Long. It was a revolver cartridge, especially meant for target shooting with revolvers and pistols. The difference with the old .32 S&W was only that the case of this new calibre had been lengthened by 8.1mm, so the total case length became 23.6mm. This was done to prevent the strong .32 S&W Long cartridge being fired with revolvers of the old calibre. In

1984, the case was lengthened again slightly, namely, to 27.3mm, and this cartridge, with a more powerful powder charge, was introduced as the .32 H&R Magnum. It is obvious that the ballistic properties of this new calibre are much better than those of the older cartridges. In the USA this new calibre is also used for handgun hunting small game and/or small vermin. This calibre can, of course, also be used for target shooting, but as match ammunition the calibre has as yet no official status.

The arms manufacturer Harrington & Richardson went bankrupt some years ago, but have become active again under the name New England Firearms. Charter Arms and Dan Wesson produced several revolver models for the calibre .32 H&R Magnum.

BALLISTIC DATA OF FACTORY AMMUNITION:

Calibre	*Bullet weight in grains/gram*	*V0 in m/s*	*E0 in Joules*
.32 S&W	88 grains	205	120
.32 S&W Long	100 grains	225	165
.32 H&R-Magn.	95 grains	315	308

Calibre .30-M1 (of .30 Carbine)

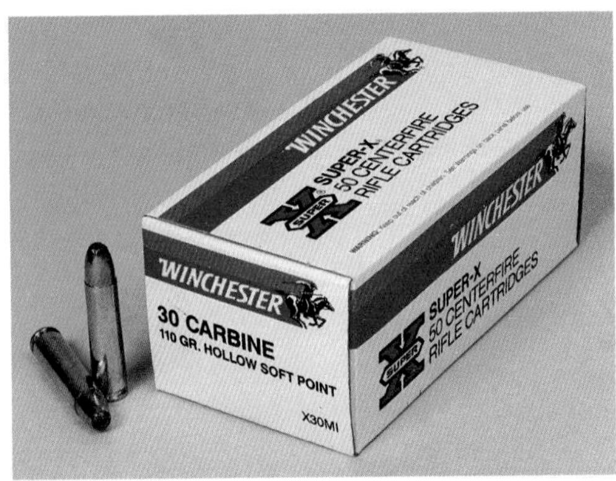

cartridge calibre .30-M1 (Carbine)

After the start of the Second World War, this cartridge was developed at great speed, on the orders of the US government, by Winchester, together with the famous .30-M1 Carbine. After the war these carbines were sold all over the world to government agencies, and later they became available for shooting sports. On the American continent as well as in Europe these carbines are very popular. In many European countries there is even an official sports discipline for the .30-M1 carbine. Only a few pistols and revolvers have been made in this special calibre. For a short period of time around 1951, Smith & Wesson produced a revolver in .30-M1. The AutoMag III and the single-shot Contender are the only handguns in this calibre at the moment. The cartridge is effective up to 200m.

BALLISTIC DATA OF FACTORY AMMUNITION:

Bullet weight	*V0 in m/s*	*E0 in Joules*
110 grains	610	1315

Calibre 9mm Short (.380 Auto or .380 Automatic)

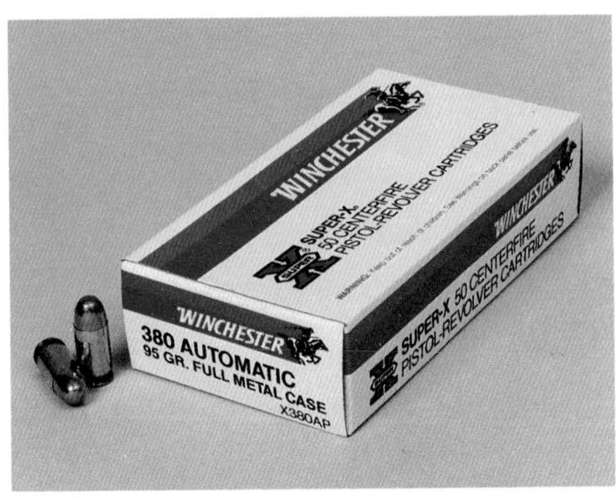

Pistol cartridge calibre 9 mm Short or .380 ACP

This calibre was developed around 1900 by the famous gun designer, John Moses Browning, in combination with one of his pistol designs. Although this cartridge was very popular in government circles until the end of the 1980s, its defensive power has always left very much to be desired. This calibre compares unfavourably with the 9mm Para cartridge. The action of this cartridge has been improved very much by the introduction of, among other things, the expanding Hornady XTP bullet. As a sporting calibre this cartridge is not of very great interest.

BALLISTIC DATA OF FACTORY AMMUNITION:

Bullet weight	*V0 in m/s*	*E0 in Joules*
90 grains	270	271

Calibre 9 mm Para(bellum), 9 mm Luger, 9x19 mm

The 9mm Parabellum, officially called the "calibre 9 x 19mm" and in North America going by the name of 9mm Luger, is the most famous and the most frequently used handgun cartridge in the world. There are hardly any army or

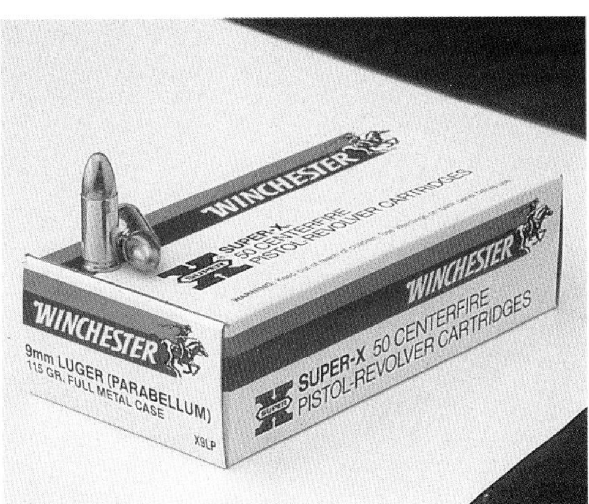

Pistol cartridge calibre 9mm Para or 9mm Luger, also known as 9 x 19mm

police units that are not equipped with guns in this calibre. Special revolvers can be loaded with 9mm Para cartridges with special clips or with an adaption of their ejector star on the cylinder. By the end of the 1980s, the American army had exchanged the calibre 9mm for their new service pistol, the Beretta model 92. This meant a great victory for this calibre, because the Americans had been wedded to their calibre .45 ACP for the old Colt model 1911-A1 since almost the beginning of this century. The 9mm Para cartridge is mainly used in semi-automatic pistols and in submachine-guns. There are also some revolver models that can fire this calibre and, furthermore, some .38 Because the diameter of the 9mm Parabullet is almost the same as that of the .38 Special calibre or .357 Magnum, you regularly see special clips for sale for use in revolvers to fire 9mm Para cartridges. The indication 'Parabellum' (abbreviated as 'Para') has been derived from the last two words of the Latin motto si vis pacem para bellum which means: "If you want peace, prepare for war". The name Luger is from the name of the original constructor Georg Luger, who had already developed the famous pistol P08 and the matching Para ammunition in the year 1902. Hugo Borchardt, too, played an important part in this event. The indication "calibre 9 x 19mm" means that the diameter of the bullet is 9mm and the length of the case 19mm. Whether or not the standard calibre 9mm Parabellum is going to be displaced by the newer calibres, such as .40 Smith & Wesson, .41 Action Express, or the 10mm Automatic, only time will tell.

BALLISTIC DATA OF FACTORY AMMUNITION:

Bullet weight	*V0 in m/s*	*E0 in Joules*
124 grains	340	462

Calibre .38 Super (.38 Super Auto)

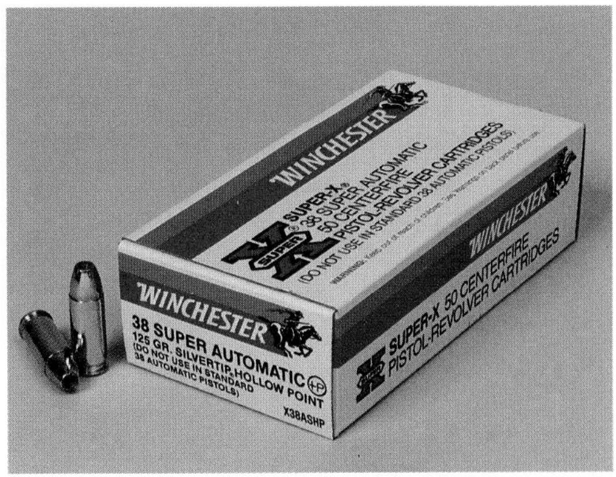

Pistol cartridge calibre .38 Super Auto

The .38 Super Auto(matic) cartridge was introduced in 1929 as an improved version of the older Colt .38 ACP cartridge. This calibre was especially designed for an adapted pistol: the Colt Government model. The case head of this cartridge has a kind of rim, a so-called semi-rim, with which the cartridge is stopped into the chamber of the barrel. This is unusual in pistol ammunition, because most of these calibres rest in the chamber with their case mouth. In old pistols the .38 Super is sometimes pushed too far into the chamber, resulting in an erratic ignition. The firing-pin cannot reach the primer in the case head. Modern pistols in this calibre have been modified in such a way that the cartridge does rest with its case-mouth rim against a ledge in the chamber of the barrel, so that this fault has been remedied. Partly because of these initial problems this calibre was never very successful. However, this calibre is often used by American match shooters in speed-event matches, because the .38 Super develops more Joules in comparison with the 9mm Para.

BALLISTIC DATA OF FACTORY AMMUNITION:

Bullet weight	*V0 in m/s*	*E0 in Joules*
125 grains	380	585

Calibre .38 Special

The .38 (Smith & Wesson) Special cartridge is one of the oldest handgun calibres, and is extremely popular all over the world. The cartridge was introduced in 1906 by Smith & Wesson, together with the first revolver in this calibre, the Military & Police Model 10. Since then this calibre has been extremely successful, because there is hardly any brand of handgun that does not have or has had a .38 Special revolver (or pistol) in its assortment. Until the introduction of the .357 Magnum cartridge and matching revolver, this calibre was widely used as a police cartridge in the USA. One of the most frequently used bullets for matches is the Wadcutter, because of its high precision. For this calibre there are also special +P (Power) cartridges for sale, which are much faster than the normally charged match cartridges. When using these it is essential to pay attention to the kind of gun being used. Old revolver models sometimes do not stand up to the maximum gas pressures of these +P cartridges. If you have your doubts, do not be ashamed to ask a good gunsmith for advice. Cartridges of this calibre can also be used in .357 Magnum revolvers without problems. The measurement of the .38 Special is rather confusing. This calibre is often indicated as about 9mm, but this is not the case because the true measure is 9.07mm or 9.1mm, while the arithmetical equivalent of .38 is 9.652mm.

BALLISTIC DATA OF FACTORY AMMUNITION:

Bullet weight	*V0 in m/s*	*E0 in Joules*
140 grains	275	345
158 grains +P	275	385

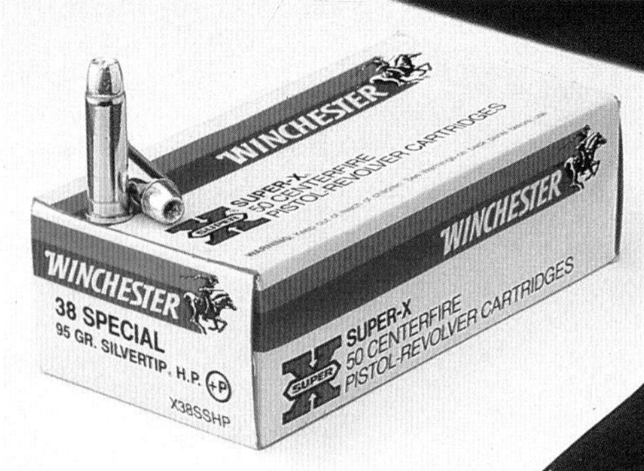

Pistol cartridge calibre .38 Special. This version is the .38 Spec. +P Silvertip

Calibre.357 Magnum

With the introduction of the .357 Magnum cartridge in 1935 by Smith & Wesson, the beginning of the "Magnum era" was ushered in. This calibre descended from the .38 Smith & Wesson Special and was initially designed as a hunting, and police cartridge. Good examples are the Smith & Wesson revolvers that were developed in this calibre, the Model 28 'Highway Patrolman' and the more luxurious Model 27, introduced in 1935. The revolver Model 27, produced until recently, is one of the oldest revolver models in this category. Shooting with this calibre is quite spectacular, most of all because of the enormous "booms" and the large muzzle blast. This cartridge is very well suited to special kinds of shooting, such as bowling pin, steel plate, silhouette matches, or recreational shooting at logs of wood, etc.

For a long time the .357 Magnum cartridge was the only Magnum, until the .44 Magnum was introduced in 1956. The .357 Magnum is, as a matter of fact, a lengthened .38 Special, namely, .135in or about 3.4mm. This lengthening of the case has been designed deliberately to prevent the Magnum cartridge being fired from .38 Special cylinders of old revolvers. As these are not adapted to the much higher gas pressures of the Magnum, this could have disastrous results. So the .357 Magnum must be fired with special .357 Magnum revolvers, in which you can also use the less powerful .38 Special cartridges. It is not possible to do the reverse. The indication .357 (Magnum) seems to suggest that this calibre would be smaller than the .38 (Special) cartridge. In spite of the strange measurements, this is not so.

BALLISTIC DATA OF FACTORY AMMUNITION:

Bullet weight	*V0 in m/s*	*E0 in Joules*
158 grains	460	1079

Revolver and Pistol cartridge calibre .357 Magnum

Calibre 10 mm Automatic

The famous American pistol specialist, Jeff Cooper, was involved in the development of this new calibre. As a police combat and arms expert, Cooper long held the opinion that the penetrating power (for which read man-stopping power) of the .45 ACP left much to be desired. After many experiments he finally ended up with a 10mm flat point bullet, which, at the velocity of about 360m per second, could develop a muzzle energy of about 840 joule. In 1979, he managed to persuade the American business company, Dornhaus & Dixon, to finance the production of a pistol, and he persuaded the ammunition manufacturer, Norma, to produce the 10mm cartridge. The final result was the 'Bren-Ten', which was eventually marketed in five different models. The name of the pistol derived from Brunner, because many technical details of the Bren had been derived from the famous CZ-75 pistol. The 'Ten' refers, of course, to the 10mm calibre. The pistol had a large magazine capacity, especially for those days, namely, 10 + 1, as it was designated in the 1980s: ten rounds in the magazine, and one in the chamber. Unfortunately, the pistol did not survive for very long and the 10mm cartridge would have been forgotten by now if no other arms manufacturers had seen any profit in this calibre. The rescue came from Colt with its Delta Elite pistol in 10mm Auto(matic). Later, other brands followed with pistols in this calibre: even Smith & Wesson, which developed a rival cartridge of that calibre – the .40 Smith & Wesson.

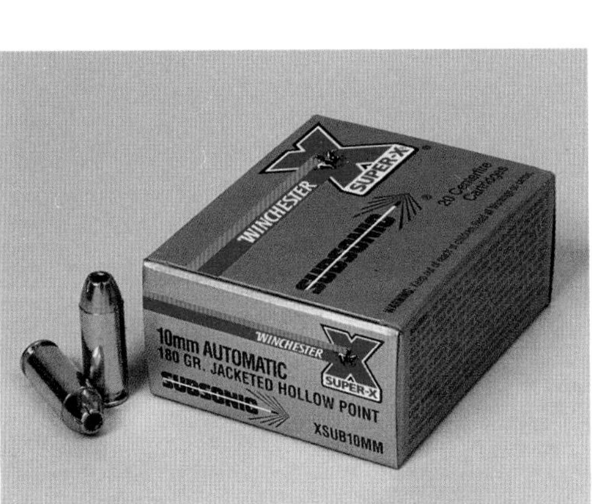

Pistol cartridge 10mm Auto

BALLISTIC DATA OF FACTORY AMMUNITION:

Bullet weight	*V0 in m/s*	*E0 in Joules*
175 grains	370	775

Calibre .40 S&W (Smith & Wesson)

The development of the .40 Smith & Wesson cartridge took place in the early 1990s. In that period more new calibres were being introduced. While Smith & Wesson was still busy improving the various pistol models in calibre 10mm Auto, they also developed a totally new calibre in co-operation with the Winchester Ammunition factories. This new cartridge was introduced at a gun show, the American Shot Show in 1990. According to Smith & Wesson, this cartridge was finally going to finish the endless debates about the ideal pistol and defence calibre, after one hundred years of discussion. Both manufacturers also predicted that other calibres, like the 9mm Para, the .45 ACP, the .41 Action Express, and even the new 10mm Auto, would soon descend into oblivion. In 1996, this cartridge has not yet reached this desired monopoly position, and this will never happen. As a matter of fact, the .40 S&W has the same dimensions as the 10mm Auto, except for its length. The recoil of the cartridge during firing is, depending on the type of handgun, more gentle than that of the 10mm Auto. This has, of course, its effect on the level of bullet energy, about 75% of the energy of the 10mm Auto. For match work and speed-shooting series like steel plate, the .40 S&W is an excellent cartridge.

BALLISTIC DATA OF FACTORY AMMUNITION:

Bullet weight	*V0 in m/s*	*E0 in Joules*
180 grains	290	492

Pistol cartridge .40 S&W

Calibre .41 AE (Action Express)

This calibre was developed in 1985 by E. Whildin, the president director of the American import company, Action Arms. Initially this cartridge was made for the Uzi submachine-gun, but later it was applied to pistols. A characteristic of this cartridge is its case head, which has the same dimensions as the 9mm Para cartridge. Because of this exchange sets are easily usable for 9mm Para pistols. After all, only barrel and magazine have to be exchanged, the slide remains the same.

BALLISTIC DATA OF FACTORY AMMUNITION:

Bullet weight	*V0 in m/s*	*E0 in Joules*
170 grains	335	620

Calibre .41 Magnum (Remington)

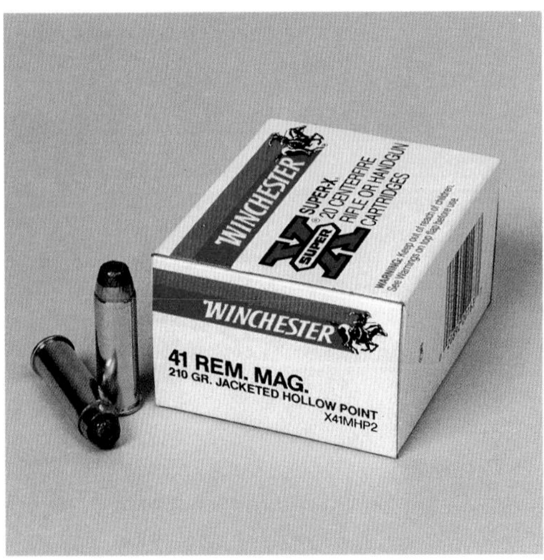

Revolver cartridge .41 Magnum

This cartridge was developed in 1964. Although Smith & Wesson was honoured for the creation of this revolver cartridge, its spiritual fathers are the gun experts Elmer Keith, Bill Jordan, and Duke Roberts (from Remington).

Smith & Wesson introduced the cartridge, together with the Model 57 revolver. This cartridge was meant to fill the gap between the .357 Magnum and the .44 Magnum calibres. The cartridge never reached the popularity it deserved, in any case not in Europe.

BALLISTIC DATA OF FACTORY AMMUNITION:

Bullet weight	*V0 in m/s*	*E0 in Joules*
210 grains	395	1065

Calibre .44 Special

The .44 Special cartridge has a long history. This calibre was introduced in 1907 by Smith & Wesson as the follow-up to the old blackpowder cartridge from the nineteenth century, namely, the .44 Russian for the old top-break revolvers. The .44 Special cartridge was rather popular, in any case until the introduction of the .44 Magnum. Today this calibre can be used as a match cartridge with a lead bullet in the heavy .44 Magnum revolvers. Furthermore, this cartridge is also applied to revolvers with very short barrels, the so-called 2in snub-nose revolvers, which are used for defence purposes.

BALLISTIC DATA OF FACTORY AMMUNITION:

Bullet weight	*V0 in m/s*	*E0 in Joules*
240 grains	245 m/s	465

Calibre .44 Magnum (.44 Remington Magnum Pistol)

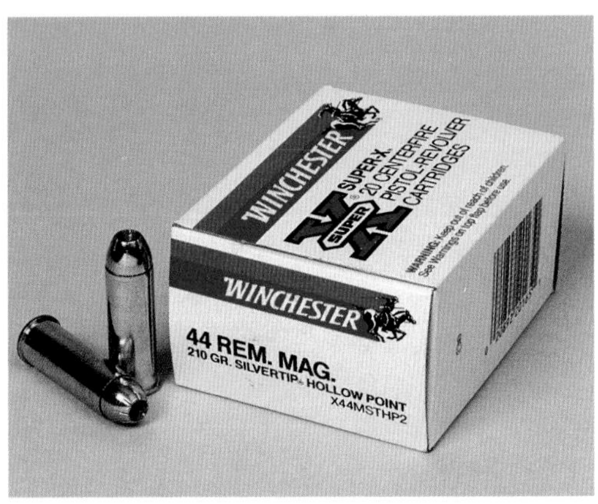

Pistol and revolver cartridge calibre .44 Magnum

The .44 Magnum has been developed by Smith & Wesson and Remington together, and was introduced in 1955, in combination with a revolver in this calibre, the Smith & Wesson Model 29.

In the creation of this cartridge the well-known American sheriff-marshal-policeman-hunter Elmer Keith played an important role. Keith was not satisfied with the results of the .357 Magnum and tried to reach a compromise between the calibres .357 Magnum and the .44 Special.

Until the introduction of special 'Super-Magnums', like those of Casull, this cartridge was the heaviest Magnum calibre. During its existence several phantasy names were coined, like 'Train-Stopper'.

The enormous recoils of the heavy charges were labelled as "kicks of a mule". For most shooters the recoil is too violent, especially with cartridges that approach the maximum loads.

That is why most shooters don't like a match series of fifty rounds. Achievements like those of "Dirty Harry" ("hitting a fly between the eyes at 100 yards"), firing from the hip, are only feasible for the happy few. This cartridge was especially developed in the USA for handgun hunting of polar bears and reindeer during the period that this was permitted in almost all or every state in North America. The story of the .44 Magnum with regard to the .44 Special is almost the same as that of the .38 Special and the .357 Magnum. For the .44 Magnum the case was also lengthened, to prevent the heavy cartridges being fired from a .44 Special handgun – not even by accident, because they don't fit in the old cylinders of the .44 Specials.

BALLISTIC DATA OF FACTORY AMMUNITION:

Bullet weight	*V0 in m/s*	*E0 in Joules*
240 grains	410	1310

Calibre .45 ACP (Automatic Colt Pistol)

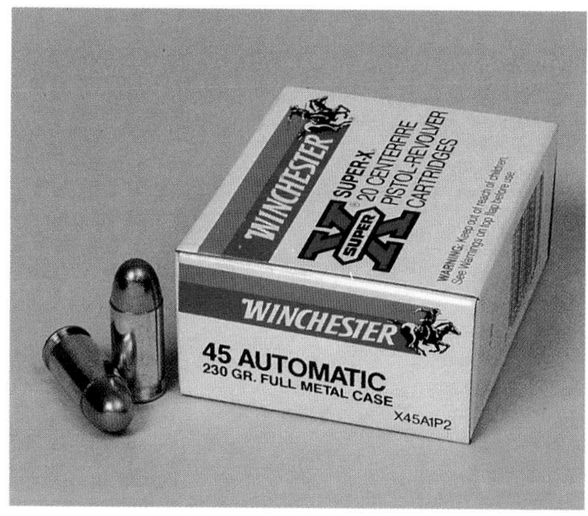

Pistol cartridge .45 ACP

In 1873, the American government decided to issue the .45 cartridge as military ammunition for rifles as well as handguns. For handguns this was the .45 Colt calibre. It could be fired from the Colt Single-Action Army revolver. Although the combination was sufficient, it was decided around 1890 to choose a smaller calibre. This became the .38 Long Colt cartridge for the new Colt Double-Action revolver. The calibre choice proved not to be practical. The .38 did not have enough stopping power and penetration capacity, which was painfully revealed in the Philippine War. Therefore the army authorities looked for a new calibre and a new gun. In those days the engineer, John Moses Browning, and the Colt Firearms Industry developed a new semi-automatic pistol, the Colt Model 1905 in calibre .45. During the initial tests the pistol and cartridge were somewhat modified and in this way the Colt pistol Model 1911 in calibre .45 ACP (Automatic Colt Pistol) emerged. This new handgun and the matching ammunition were designated as the official armament for the US army. This remained so until 1988.

The .45 ACP cartridge is very popular, especially in the USA. Because of its mild recoil and its considerable bullet energy, this calibre is very useful for sporting shooters in target, bowling pin, and steel plate events. Almost every handgun manufacturer has one or more models in this calibre and in both world wars even army revolvers were issued in this calibre.

BALLISTIC DATA OF FACTORY AMMUNITION:

Bullet weight	*V0 in m/s*	*E0 in Joules*
230 grains	260	504

Calibre .45 Long Colt (.45 Colt)

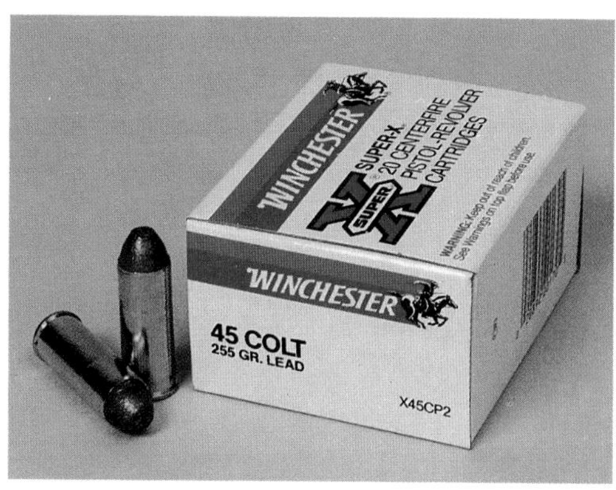

Revolver cartridge .45 Long Colt

Colt developed this cartridge in 1872 as ammunition for their Colt Peacemaker revolver, also called the Single-Action Army Model 1873. Until around 1912 this cartridge was charged with blackpowder and later with the cleaner and faster nitro-powder. Although this calibre never became very popular in Europe, it fires everyone's imagination. No real "Western" cowboy movie could exist without the legendary Colt Peacemaker. The designations .45 Long Colt and .45 Colt are often mixed up or used side by side, although the first name is correct. This calibre was a standard cartridge for the US army revolver for a long period of time (from 1873 until around 1900).

BALLISTIC DATA OF FACTORY AMMUNITION:

Bullet weight	*V0 in m/s*	*E0 in Joules*
250 grains	260	570

Calibre .45 Winchester Magnum

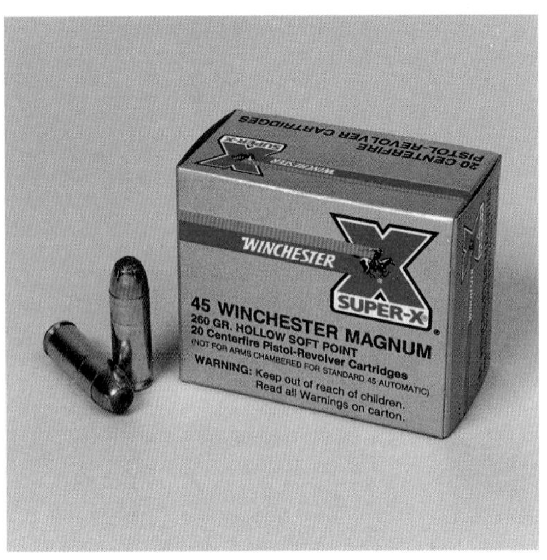

Pistol cartridge calibre .45 WM (Winchester Magnum)

This calibre was developed by Winchester, especially for a sporting Magnum pistol, the Wildey Magnum. Because of the many production problems this pistol had to endure and the great popularity of this calibre, many gun manufacturers plunged into the competitive struggle to fill the gap in this market segment. The most well-known are the Grizzly Magnum pistol, the Amt AutoMag, and the single-shot Thompson Contender. In North America this cartridge is also used for handgun hunting, which is permitted in some states. Further, this calibre is used for silhouette shooting with handguns.

In Europe this cartridge is somewhat less popular among match shooters, except for those who whant to try something different

BALLISTIC DATA OF FACTORY AMMUNITION:

Bullet weight	*V0 in m/s*	*E0 in Joules*
230 grains	425	1050

Calibre .50 AE (Action Express)

Pistol cartridge calibre .50 AE (Action Express)

In 1991 this "monster" cartridge was developed on the initiative of the American company Magnum Research Inc., together with the Israeli IMI (Israeli Military Industries), the designers and manufacturers of the Desert Eagle pistol. This semi-automatic pistol is for sale in the calibres .357 Magnum, .44 Magnum, and .50 AE. To reduce the cost of production, the diameter of the case head was reduced, namely, to the same measurements as the .44 Magnum cartridge. A similar construction was applied for the .41 AE, wich has the case head diameter of the 9mm Para. The .50 AE develops, at least for handgun calibre, an enormous amount of bullet energy, about almoust twice as much as the standard .44 Magnum can achieve, In the mean time more weapons manufacturers have started to produce handguns in this calibre, like L.A.R. with their Grizzly Magnum, th Casull M555 revolver, and Ruger with a Super Blackhawk revolver.

BALLISTIC DATA OF FACTORY AMMUNITION:

Bullet weight	*V0 in m/s*	*E0 in Joules*
325 grains	425	1905

9. Explanation of exploded drawings

Exploded drawings have nothing to do with explosions! The term means a dimensional drawing of all the parts that are assembled in a pistol or a revolver.

In this encyclopedia of pistols and revolvers, a lot of words are used that might confuse the reader. Most handguns have roughly the same design. By means of an exploded drawing, the contents and/or functioning of these weapons can be explained.

Exploded drawing of a pistol

Below you will find an exploded drawing of a Sig-Sauer pistol with a list of the names of the parts which are used in making such a pistol.

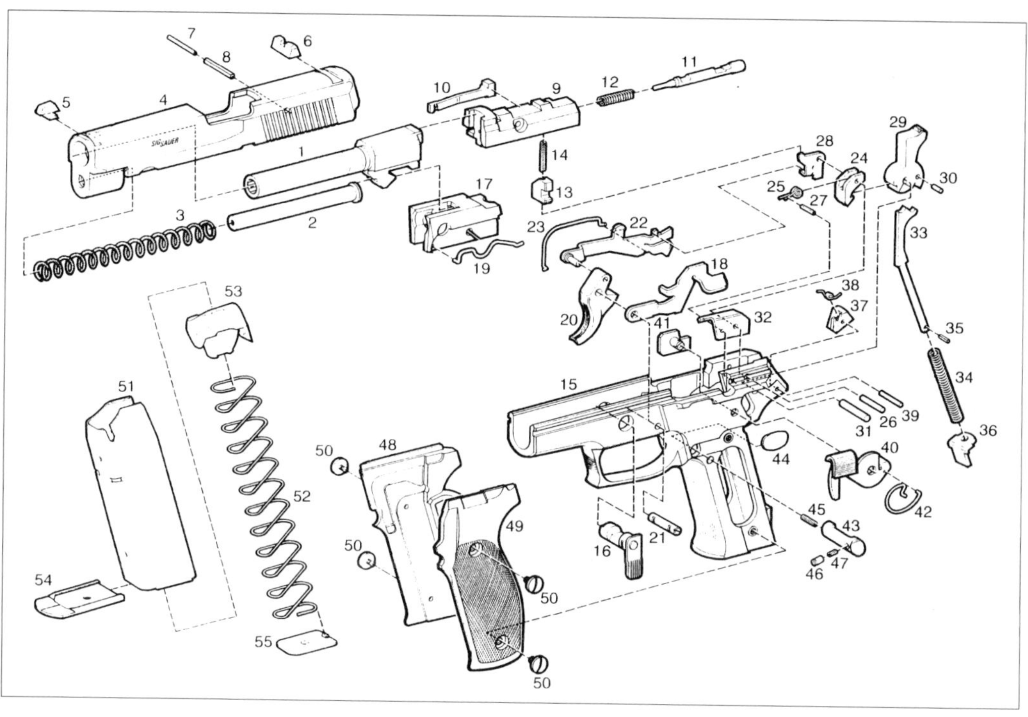

1. Barrel
2. Recoil-spring guide
3. Recoil spring
4. Slide
5. Front sight
6. Rear sight
7. Inner pin HD
8. Outer pin HD
9. Breech block
10. Extractor
11. Firing-pin
12. Firing-pin spring
13. Automatic firing-pin safety
14. Spring for firing-nr.13
15. Frame
16. Take-down lever
17. Locking-system insert
18. Slide catch
19. Slide-catch spring
20. Trigger
21. Trigger axis
22. Trigger bar
23. Trigger-bar spring
24. Sear
25. Sear spring
26. Sear axis
27. Sear-spring pin HD
28. Safety lever (of firing-pin safety)
29. Hammer
30. Hammer-strut pin
31. Hammer axis
32. Ejector
33. Hammer-spring guide
34. Hammer or mainspring
35. Hammer-spring pin
36. Mainspring seat
37. Hammer stop
38. Hammer-stop spring or reset spring
39. Axis for nr. 37/38
40. Decocking lever
41. Decocking-lever axis
42. Decocking-lever spring
43. Magazine catch
44. Right side plate for magazine catch
45. Magazine-catch spring
46. Magazine-catch stop
47. Magazine-stop spring
48. Grip plate right side
49. Grip plate left side
50. Screws
51. Magazine housing
52. Magazine spring
53. Magazine follower
54. Magazine-floor plate
55. Magazine insert

Exploded drawing of a revolver

For the exploded drawing of a revolver, a drawing of a Smith & Wesson revolver is used. With it you have to keep in mind that, with most Smith & Wesson revolvers, the firing-pin is fixed to the hammer. There are revolvers where this firing-pin is "floating" (tensioned by a firing-pin spring) within the frame.
An exploded drawing of those will look somewhat different (see the chapter about safety).

1. Extractor rod
2. Centre pin
3. Centre-pin spring
4. Extractor-rod collar
5. Extractor spring
6. Gas ring
7. Cylinder
8. Extractor centring pins
9. Extractor (star)
10. Rear-sight leaf
11. Rear-sight plunger
12. Rear-sight plunger spring
13. Rear-sight elevation nut
14. Rear-sight windage nut
15. Rear-sight spring clip
16. Rear-sight elevation stud
17. Rear-sight slide
18. Rear-sight windage screw
19. Rear-sight leaf screw
20. Thumb-piece nut
21. Thumb piece
22. Cylinder bolt
23. Bolt-plunger spring
24. Bolt plunger
25. Frame
26. Rebound slide stud
27. Hammer stud
28. Trigger stud
29. Frame lug
30. Hammer-nose bushing
31. Yoke
32. Sideplate
33. Plate screw (crowned)
34. Plate screw (flat)
35. Stock pin
41. Grip plate left
42. Escutcheon
43. Grip-plate screw
44. Scutcheon nut
45. Grip plate right
46. Hammer
47. Hammer-nose spring
48. Hammer nose (fixed firing-pin)
49. Sear
50. Sear spring
51. Hammer-nose rivet
52. Sear axis
53. Stirrup
55. Mainspring strain screw
56. Barrel
64. Locking-bolt pin
65. Locking-bolt spring
66. Locking bolt
67. Cylinder stop
68. Cylinder-stop spring
69. Trigger
70. Trigger bar
71. Cylinder-hand torsion spring
72. Cylinder hand
73. Cylinder-hand pin
74. Trigger stop
75. Rebound slide
76. Rebound-slide pin
77. Rebound-slide spring
78. Blocking bar (safety)
82. Cylinder-stop stud
83. Stirrup pin
84. Cylinder-hand pin
85. Cylinder-hand torsion pin
86. Trigger-bar pin
87. Trigger-stop screw
88. Main (hammer) spring

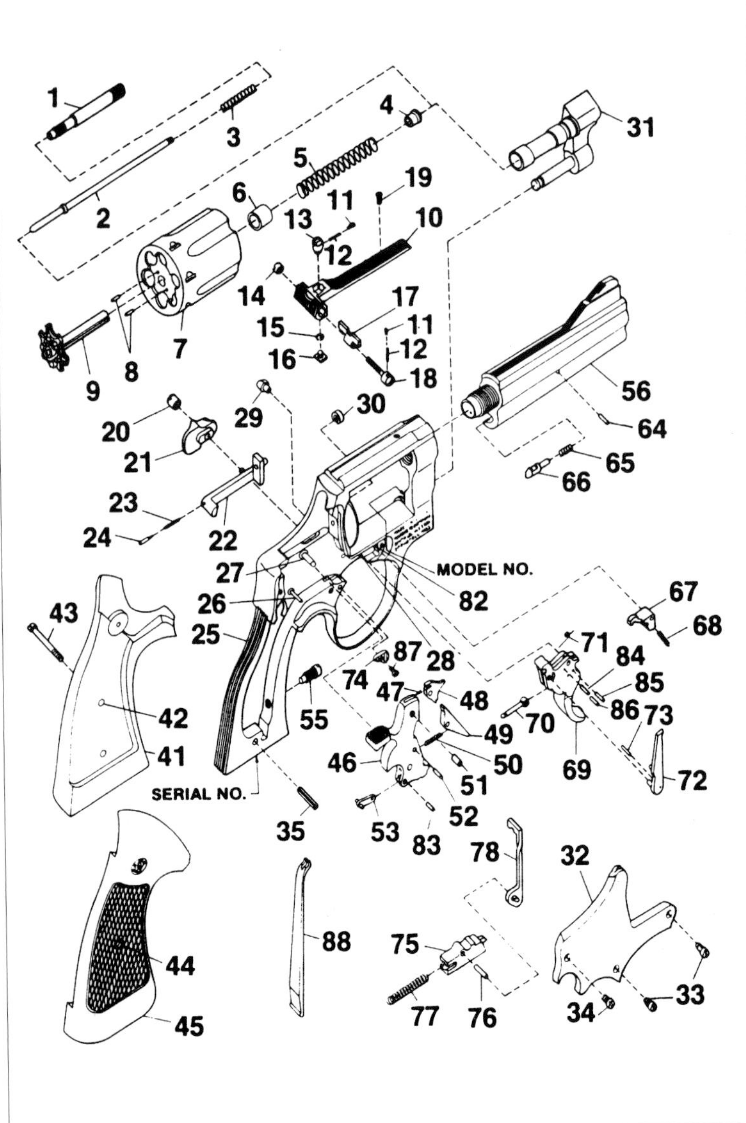

Guide to the symbols for use or purpose

In this encyclopedia you will find symbols under each handgun. This will give you a quick reference of the purpose of each individual weapon. However, this is not some kind of "law". A pistol, for instance designed as a service gun for the police, like the Walther P5 calibre 9mm Para, might be used as a target gun (even quite satisfactorily with the right reload), but it was never intended or designed that way. On the other hand, a special parcours or "race" pistol, designed and built for fast shooting at bowling pin or falling plate, is certainly useful as a defence pistol but it was not intended that way.Things can sometimes be combined: a double-action match revolver with a 4in barrel and adjustable sights is very useful as a defensive handgun. If a red-dot sight is mounted on such a revolver, you are capable of joining in a falling plate match.

More generally, the reader will understand that with a fixed-sight 3in barrelled revolver you can't get the same results at 25m as you would with a 6in barrel revolver with micrometric sights. You must view the symbols in the light of this. In short, the symbols are concerned with general applications for the average handgunner (including the author of this book).

Service handgun

These handguns are mostly provided with fixed sights and are destined for the police, army, and other civil services. For general defence purposes, these weapons are very useful. They are not really intended for target shooting.

Parcours or combat handguns

These guns are intended for fast shooting. They are mostly provided with special combat sights and have a large magazine capacity. Parcours or combat shooting consists of a special walking/running and shooting circuit, in which all kinds of shooting exercises are done at high speed. Included are all kinds of barricades from/on/after/under which the shooter has to shoot at the target.

Target shooting

The pistols and revolvers for match or target shooting are all provided with an adjustable rear sight. In this way the handgun can be adjusted to the standard or special ammunition the shooter wants to use. "Rapid fire" shooting, which means firing at clapboard targets in calibre .22 Short, is included in this category.

Action shooting

These guns are intended for fast shooting. The discipline of bowling pin shooting gives most shooters a real kick, if the heavy "pins" tumble from the table, shot after shot. These handguns can be provided with compensators and almost always with adjustable sights or red-dot scopes. This type of handgun is also used for other shooting matches, like "falling plate" With the latter kind of shooting, a number of little round (or square) steel plates are hinged to a table in a row. The intention is to shoot them down in as little time as possible. The same time limit applies for bowling shooting, as a matter of fact. These matches are often called pin shooting, steel event, speed event, etc.

Silhouette shooting

For silhouette shooting, special guns are used. After all, the heavy-steel animal-shaped targets are standing at distances of up to 200m. Because of this, big and heavy calibres have to be used. Handguns in calibre .357 Magnum are the bottom-line in this discipline. There are, however, special matches for small-bore handguns, like the .22 LR.

10. An A-Z of pistols and revolvers

AMT-pistols

In 1969 the designer Harry W. Sanford introduced a big and heavy pistol in a completely new calibre: the .44 AMP (AutoMag Pistol). This AutoMag semi-automatic pistol has a rotating bolt with six locking cams, whereby the system resembles that of the Colt M16 army rifle. The small Sanford gun shop was expanded into the AutoMag Corporation (AMC) and special ammunition was made by a Mexican subsidiary of Remington, called the CDM (Cartouches Deportivos de Mexico SA).

Hand-loaders can create their own cases by shortening .308 Winchester cases. In 1971 the pistol came on to the market in stainless steel, named the Pasadena AutoMag. Partly because the manufacture of several parts was subcontracted (which led frequently to delays), the total production rate was affected. The company went bankrupt in May 1967. The Thomas Oil Company bought the machinery and parts in stock in order to assemble a number of complete pistols. For this purpose the Trust Deed Estates Corporation (TDE) was founded. Sanford was hired to manage the assembly line. The TDE was initially situated in North Hollywood, but later on it moved to El Monte in the State of California. There the production of new pistols started again, and a new pistol in a new calibre was introduced, the .357 AMP. In the mean time, several special series were made, which have a high collectors' value today. The last series, the 'C-Series', are being made by the newly founded AMT (Arcadia Machine & Tool Inc.) in Covina, California. The AutoMag is still produced in small quantities from time to time. Furthermore, AMT and IAI are manufacturing stainless-steel pistols, like the AutoMag II (.22 WMR), AutoMag III (.30-M1 Carbine), AutoMag IV (.45 WM and 10mm Auto), and AutoMag V (.50 Action Express).

In 1985, the semi-automatic pistol, the AutoMag II, was designed by the founder of the company, Harry W. Sanford and his factory manager, Larry Grossman. It is a series-made pistol in calibre .22 WMR (Winchester Magnum Rimfire). In 1987 the pistol was launched. After its introduction, several modifications were applied to later versions, such as a half-cock hammer.

The pistol has a unique locking system, which operates as follows. Immediately after the chamber of the barrel, four gas holes are drilled. In the chamber block, surrounding the chamber, two circular groups of six holes each are drilled. Because of this the gas pressure from the fired cartridge presses straight at the outside of the cartridge case in the chamber. As a result, the case is retained in the chamber by the force, until the pressure has decreased to a safe level. Directly after the bullet has left the barrel, the gas pressure in the chamber block can escape through the four front holes. After that the slide can travel its normal way to the rear, as any other semi-automatic weapon. The security catch, in the left rear side of the slide, blocks the firing-pin in the "safe" position, and a massive bar is rotated before the hammer as well. That way the hammer can never reach the firing-pin.
The pistol is manufactured in three versions: the Standard (152mm barrel), the Modified Model (115mm barrel), and the Compact (86mm barrel).

The AutoMag III in the carbine calibre .30-M1 was a new venture of the designer, Harry Sanford, the spiritual father of all AutoMags. First of all he experimented with several kinds of locking systems, based on the AutoMag II concept. Ultimately the Browning system was chosen. The AutoMag III in calibre .30-M1 Carbine is not particularly new. During the Second World War, Smith & Wesson developed a revolver for this calibre, but the project was not successful. In 1955 the Kimball Company introduced a pistol in calibre .30-M1, but this effort also failed, owing to the high pressure level of the cartridge. Around 1965 Ruger released a version of their Blackhawk revolver in calibre .30-M1. This combination was not a great success either, but the revolver is still in production. Furthermore, Thompson has an interchangeable barrel for its single-shot Contender in this calibre. In 1990 the model AutoMag IV was introduced by IAI in the calibres .45 WM (Winchester Magnum) and

10mm Magnum, a lengthened 10mm Auto cartridge with much more "power". As a matter of fact, AMT is the only supplier for the 10mm Magnum cases at the moment.The functioning and lock-up system of the AutoMag IV are identical to that of the AutoMag III. The pistol is mainly intended for handgun hunting (not permitted in Europe), and for silhouette shooting up to ranges of 200m. Again under the old company name of AMT (Arcadia Machine & Tool Inc.) Harry W. Sanford produced another pistol in the AMT line in 1993, the AutoMag V in the "giant" calibre .50 AE (Action Express). The functioning and locking mechanism are identical to the previous model, the AutoMag IV. The gun is made of stainless steel. The AMT Government is a Colt clone, but completely of stainless steel. This model was designed for police units. The gun has fixed sights. Under the AMT name three versions are available:

- AMT Government in calibre .45 ACP.
- AMT Hardballer in calibre .45 ACP.
- AMT Longslide Hardballer in calibre .45 ACP.

One of the new models, derived from the Colt 1911, is the IAI Javelina in calibre 10mm Auto. The AMT Hardballer was intended as a target pistol. It has adjustable sights, an enlarged combat-style safety and slide catch, a wide and adjustable trigger, a bevelled magazine, and a loading indicator.
The AMT Longslide Hardballer has the same features. This pistol has a lengthened barrel and slide by 5.5cm, which increases the sight radius. The IAI Javelina in calibre 10mm Auto is available in two versions: a target pistol with a 7in barrel and a hunting model with the standard 5in barrel. The AMT and IAI pistols are provided with the adjustable Millet rear sight, except the AMT Government.

Automag II Standard Model

TECHNICAL SPECIFICATIONS:

Calibre	: .22 WMR (Winchester Magnum Rimfire)
Trigger action	: single action
Magazine capacity	: 9 rounds
Locking mechanism	: blowback system with gas-assisted action
Weight	: 910g
Length	: 235mm
Height	: 133mm
Barrel length	: 152mm
Trigger stop	: none
Sights	: adjustable Millet rear sight
Sight radius	: 200 mm
External safety	: safety catch on left side of slide
Internal safety	: half-cock, slide safety

FEATURES:

• slide catch	: on left side frame
• magazine catch	: in heel of grip
• material	: stainless steel
• finish	: stainless
• grips	: black synthetics

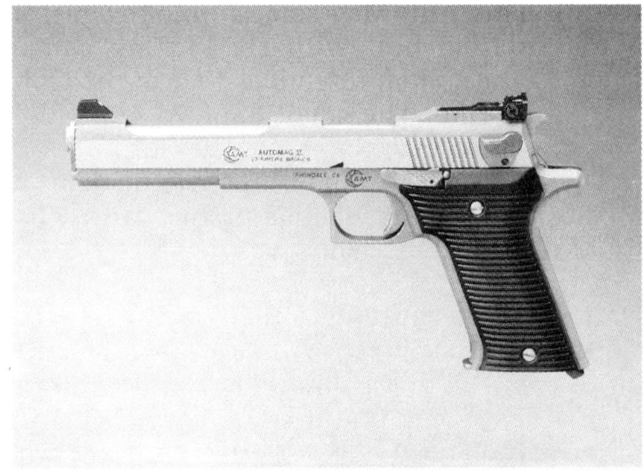

Automag II Modified Model

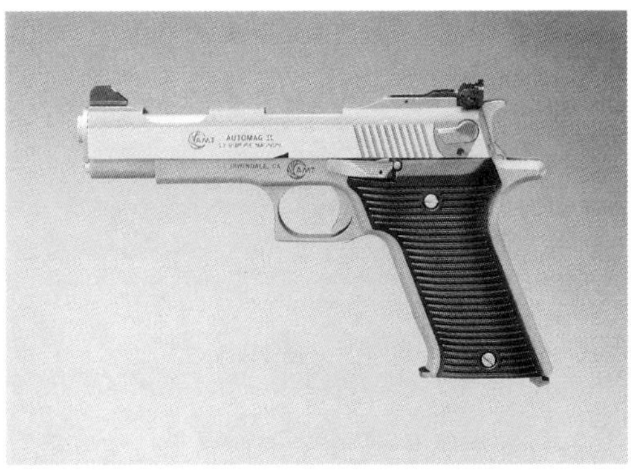

TECHNICAL SPECIFICATIONS:

Calibre	: .22 WMR (Winchester Magnum Rimfire)
Trigger action	: single action
Magazine capacity	: 9 rounds
Locking mechanism	: blowback system with gas-assisted action
Weight	: 850g
Length	: 203mm
Height	: 133mm
Barrel length	: 114mm

Trigger stop : none
Sights : adjustable Millet rear sight
Sight radius : 190mm
External safety : safety catch on left side of slide
Internal safety : half-cock, slide safety

FEATURES:

- slide catch : on left side frame
- magazine catch : in heel of grip
- material : stainless steel
- finish : stainless
- grips : black synthetics

Automag II Compact

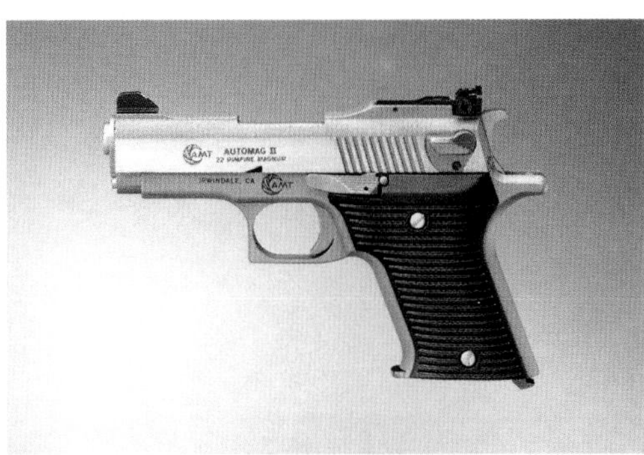

TECHNICAL SPECIFICATIONS:

Calibre : .22 WMR (Winchester Magnum Rimfire)
Trigger action : single action
Magazine capacity : 7 rounds
Locking mechanism : blowback system with gas-assisted action
Weight : 680g (Standard)
Length : 172mm
Height : 102mm
Barrel length : 86mm
Trigger stop : no
Sights : adjustable Millet rear sight
Sight radius : 142mm
External safety : safety catch on left side of slide
Internal safety : half-cock, slide safety

FEATURES:

- slide catch : on left side frame
- magazine catch : in heel of grip
- material : stainless steel
- finish : stainless
- grips : black synthetics

Automag III

TECHNICAL SPECIFICATIONS:

Calibre : .30-M1 Carbine
Trigger action : single action
Magazine capacity : 8 rounds
Locking mechanism : Browning lock-up
Weight : 1219g
Length : 267mm
Height : 131mm
Barrel length : 172mm
Trigger stop : no
Sights : adjustable 3-punts Millet rear sight
Sight radius : 225mm
External safety : safety catch on left side of slide
Internal safety : slide safety

FEATURES:

- slide catch : on left side frame
- magazine catch : on left side frame, behind trigger guard
- material : stainless steel
- finish : stainless
- grips : black synthetics

Automag IV

TECHNICAL SPECIFICATIONS:

Calibre : .45 WM (Winchester Magnum), 10 mm Magnum
Trigger action : single action
Magazine capacity : 7 rounds
Locking mechanism : Browning/FN-system
Weight : 1304g
Length : 267mm
Height : 135mm
Barrel length : 165mm
Trigger stop : no
Sights : adjustable 3-punts Millet rear sight
Sight radius : 225mm

External safety : safety catch on left side of slide
Internal safety : slide safety

FEATURES:

- slide catch : on left side frame
- magazine catch : on left side frame, behind trigger guard
- material : stainless steel
- finish : stainless
- grips : black synthetics

Automag V

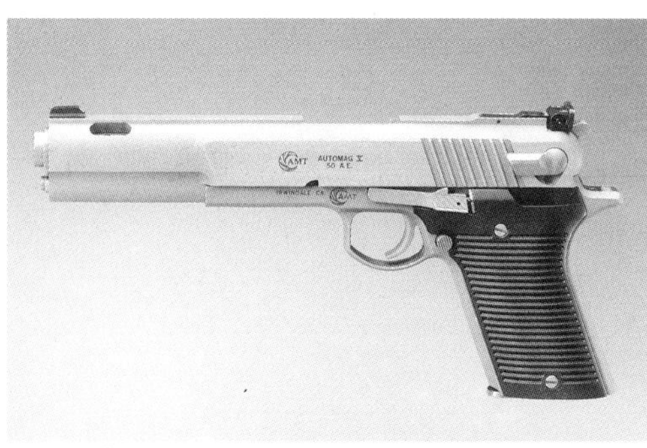

TECHNICAL SPECIFICATIONS:

Calibre : .50 Action Express
Trigger action : single action
Magazine capacity : 7 rounds
Locking mechanism : Browning/SIG/Petter system
Weight : 1305g
Length : 273mm
Height : 135mm
Barrel length : 165mm
Trigger stop : yes
Sights : adjustable Millet rear sight
Sight radius : 230mm
External safety : safety catch on left side of slide
Internal safety : slide safety

FEATURES:

- slide catch : on left side frame
- magazine catch : on left side frame, behind trigger guard
- material : stainless steel
- finish : stainless
- grips : black synthetics

This pistol was produced as part of a 'One of 3000' series. A similar series might possibly be repeated in the future.

AMT Back Up – .380 ACP pistol

TECHNICAL SPECIFICATIONS:

Calibre : .380 ACP (9 mm Short)
Trigger action : only double-action
Magazine capacity : 5 rounds
Locking mechanism : Browning lock-up
Weight : 510g
Length : 127mm
Height : 103mm
Barrel length : 64mm
Trigger stop : no
Sights : fixed
Sight radius : 115mm
External safety : none
Internal safety : slide safety, automatic firing-pin safety

FEATURES:

- slide catch : none
- magazine catch : in heel of grip
- material : stainless steel
- finish : stainless
- grips : black synthetics

AMT Back Up – 9 mm Para pistol

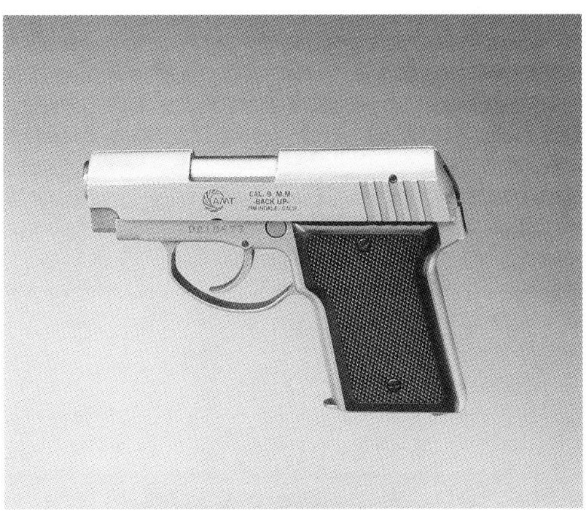

TECHNICAL SPECIFICATIONS:

Calibre : 9 mm Para
Trigger action : only double action
Magazine capacity : 6 rounds
Locking mechanism : Browning lock-up
Weight : 709g
Length : 146mm
Height : 103mm
Barrel length : 76mm
Trigger stop : no
Sights : fixed
Sight radius : 128mm
External safety : safety catch on left side frame
Internal safety : slide safety, automatic firing-pin safety

FEATURES:

- slide catch : none
- magazine catch : in heel of grip
- material : stainless steel
- finish : stainless
- grips : black synthetics

AMT Back Up – .38 Super Auto-pistol

TECHNICAL SPECIFICATIONS:

Calibre : .38 Super Auto
Trigger action : only double action
Magazine capacity : 6 rounds
Locking mechanism : Browning lock-up
Weight : 680g
Length : 146mm
Height : 103mm
Barrel length : 76mm
Trigger stop : no
Sights : fixed
Sight radius : 128mm
External safety : none
Internal safety : slide safety, automatic firing-pin safety

FEATURES:

- slide catch : none
- magazine catch : in heel of grip
- material : stainless steel
- finish : stainless
- grips : black synthetics

AMT Back Up – .40 S&W pistol

TECHNICAL SPECIFICATIONS:

Calibre : .40 Smith & Wesson
Trigger action : only double action
Magazine capacity : 5 rounds
Locking mechanism : Browning lock-up
Weight : 709g
Length : 146mm
Height : 103mm
Barrel length : 76mm
Trigger stop : no
Sights : fixed
Sight radius : 128mm
External safety : none

Internal safety : slide safety, automatic firing-pin safety

FEATURES:

- slide catch : none
- magazine catch : in heel of grip
- material : stainless steel
- finish : stainless
- grips : black synthetics

AMT Back Up – .45 ACP pistol

TECHNICAL SPECIFICATIONS:

Calibre : .45 ACP
Trigger action : only double action
Magazine capacity : 5 rounds
Locking mechanism : Browning lock-up
Weight : 652g
Length : 146mm
Height : 103mm
Barrel length : 76mm
Trigger stop : no
Sights : fixed
Sight radius : 128mm
External safety : none
Internal safety : slide safety, automatic firing-pin safety

FEATURES:

- slide catch : none
- magazine catch : in heel of grip
- material : stainless steel
- finish : stainless
- grips : black synthetics

AMT Government

TECHNICAL SPECIFICATIONS:

Calibre : .45 ACP
Trigger action : single action
Magazine capacity : 7 rounds
Locking mechanism : Browning lock-up
Weight : 1770g
Length : 220mm
Barrel length : 127mm
Trigger stop : adjustable
Sights : fixed
Sight radius : 170mm
External safety : safety catch, half-cock, grip safety
Internal safety : load indicator, slide safety

FEATURES:

- slide catch : enlarged slide catch on left side frame
- magazine catch : left side frame, behind trigger guard
- material : stainless steel
- finish : stainless
- grips : black neoprene synthetics

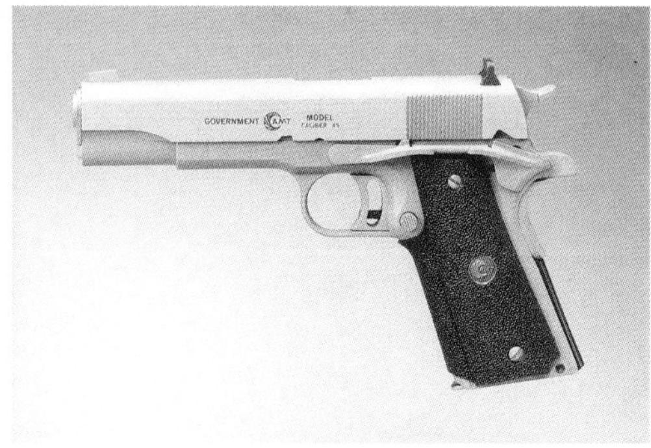

AMT Hardballer

TECHNICAL SPECIFICATIONS:

Calibre : .45 ACP
Trigger action : single action
Magazine capacity : 7 rounds
Locking mechanism : Browning lock-up
Weight : 1770g
Length : 220mm
Barrel length : 127mm
Trigger stop : adjustable
Sights : adjustable Millet rear sight
Sight radius : 170mm
External safety : safety catch, half-cock, grip safety
Internal safety : load indicator, slide safety

FEATURES:

- slide catch : enlarged slide catch on left side frame
- magazine catch : on left side frame, behind trigger guard

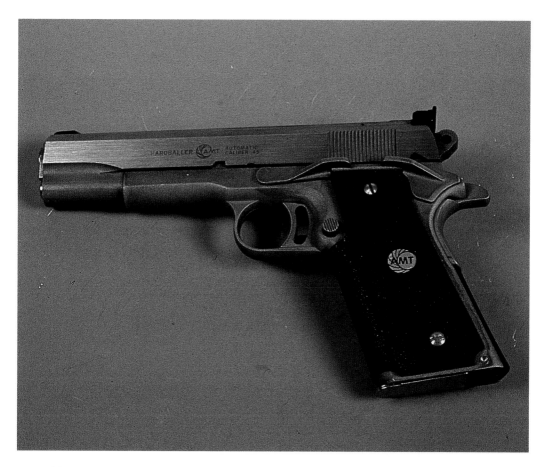

• material	:	stainless steel
• finish	:	stainless
• grips	:	black neoprene synthetics

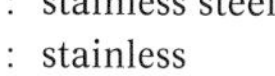

AMT Hardballer Long Slide

TECHNICAL SPECIFICATIONS:

Calibre	:	.45 ACP
Trigger action	:	single action
Magazine capacity	:	7 rounds
Locking mechanism	:	Browning lock-up
Weight	:	1900g
Length	:	266mm
Barrel length	:	177mm
Trigger stop	:	adjustable
Sights	:	adjustable Millet-sights
Sight radius	:	220mm
External safety	:	safety catch, half-cock, grip safety
Internal safety	:	load indicator, slide safety

FEATURES:

• slide catch	:	enlarged slide catch left side frame
• magazine catch	:	left side frame, behind trigger guard
• material	:	stainless steel
• finish	:	stainless
• grips	:	black neoprene synthetics

Anschütz

Until about ten years ago, Anschütz were known only for their superior small-bore match rifles and carbines. In 1987 at the yearly Shot Show in the USA, this German company introduced its first bolt-action pistol, called Exemplar. This pistol is regarded as one of the most accurate long-range handguns in the world, although it is not so well known in Western Europe. This is largely because silhouette shooting is in its infancy owing to the lack of appropriate shooting ranges, and handgun hunting is not allowed in most European countries. This is not the case in the USA.

The Exemplar was first marketed in calibre .22 LR, but at the Shot Show of 1988 in Las Vegas it was also introduced in calibre .22 Hornet. A year later a calibre .222 Remington was launched, but this disappeared shortly afterwards from the catalogue. Both centre-fire calibres are typical of the 'Varmint' class, which is best described as the collective name for all sorts of rodents such as cotton-tails (rabbits), prairie dogs, etc. These are very accurate calibres: the .22 Hornet up to 100m and the .222 Remington up to 200m. The Exemplar in calibre .22 Hornet is capable of shooting a five-shot group with a diameter of 25mm at 100m and in calibre .222 Remington of 65mm at 200m. These centre-fire pistols are sold without iron sights, but several scope mounts can be attached immediately. The Exemplar can be regarded as a shortened match rifle. Its technique is derived from the famous Anschütz Match-54 system, with the Anschütz 5099 trigger system. The factory-installed trigger pressure is around 560g, but is fully adjustable. The Exemplars are available in the following models:

- Exemplar Standard with a micrometric rear sight in calibre .22 LR.
- Exemplar Hornet, in calibre .22 Hornet, without sights and intended for a scope.
- Exemplar XIV in calibre .22 LR with an extra-long barrel of 356mm and an overall length of 587mm.
- Exemplar Kurz (short) in calibre .22 LR with a barrel length of 176mm and an overall length of 405mm.

From top to bottom: Anschütz Exemplar calibre .22 LR, Anschütz Exemplar XIV calibre .22 LR, Anschütz Exemplar calibre .22 Hornet

Anschütz Exemplar

TECHNICAL SPECIFICATIONS:

Calibre	: .22 Hornet, .222 Remington an .22 LR
Trigger action	: bolt-action pistol
Magazine capacity	: 5 rounds (.22 Hornet/.22 LR), 3 rounds (.222 Remington)
Locking mechanism	: Anschütz-(rifle)locking mechanism
Weight	: 1980g
Length	: 485mm
Height	: 177mm
Barrel length	: 250mm
Trigger stop	: yes
Sights	: target rear sight
Sight radius	: 390mm
External safety	: wing safety on rear side of bolt, slide safety
Internal safety	: load indicator by protruding pin at rear side of bolt

FEATURES:

• slide catch	: not relevant
• magazine catch	: underside, in front of trigger guard
• material	: steel
• finish	: blued
• stock	: walnut

Arminius revolvers

Weihrauch, a German company, has produced firearms since 1899, at first in the town of Zella-Mehlis (Thuringen) and since 1948 in Mellrichstadt. Apart from the well-known Weihrauch (HW) airguns, the company also manufactures a number of revolvers under the name of Arminius.
The Arminius HW-9ST is the best known from this series. It has been modified with the course of time. The first type had a ventilated barrel with a removable shroud as an extra barrel weight. The cylinder was swung out by pulling the ejector rod forward.
The second type was provided with a thumb piece, behind the recoil plate, with which the cylinder could be unlocked, to swing out the cylinder. The third type also has a removable barrel shroud as extra weight. However, without this shroud the revolver cannot be fired, because the front post is mounted on the shroud. The gun has a trigger stop and a wide trigger shoe, which can be removed. Furthermore, the revolver has a blocking-bar safety system. It has a special match grip with an adjustable palm rest. The HW-9ST is also available with a 10in barrel, specially for small-bore silhouette shooting.

Since 1993, this silhouette model, with hooded rear sight and front post, has also been produced in stainless steel. Other models of the Arminius series are the Windicator in calibre .38 Special and .357 Magnum, and the HW-357 Match in calibre .357 Magnum. The Arminius HW38 in calibre .38 Special is available as a standard model as HW38 or in a match version as the HW38T. The standard model has fixed sights and the HW38T (Target) has a fully adjustable rear sight. It is made with 21/2in, 4in, or 6in barrel. The match model has barrel lengths of 3in, 4in, or 6in and has a wooden target grip.

The revolver HW357 was developed in 1977 and has similar versions, designated the HW357 and HW357T. The barrel lengths of the standard model are 21/2in, 4in, or 6in and of the target model 3in, 4in, or 6in. Furthermore, Weihrauch has a special match model with a heavy barrel and adjustable rear sight with a 6in barrel. This match revolver has an adjustable trigger pressure and extra-wide trigger shoe, and an optional grip with adjustable palm rest. And all this at reasonable prices.

The Arminius Windicator, also called the Vindicator, was developed for the fast-shooting Practical Revolver Parcours. It has an extra-heavy barrel and flattened barrel shroud, and is only available with a 4in barrel in the calibres .38 Special or .357 Magnum.

Arminius HW357 Target

TECHNICAL SPECIFICATIONS:

Calibre	: .357 Magnum
Trigger action	: double action
Magazine capacity	: 6 rounds
Locking mechanism	: rearside centre pin
Weight	: 935g
Length	: 286mm
Barrel length	: 6"
Trigger stop	: only Match-finish
Sights	: Target and Match: adjustable
Sight radius	: 202mm
External safety	: none

Internal safety : transfer bar, cylinder blocks with cocked hammer

FEATURES:

- thumb piece : on left side frame
- material : steel
- finish : blued of chrome plated
- grips : wood or synthetics; Match model: target grip

Arminius HW38 (2½")

TECHNICAL SPECIFICATIONS:

Calibre : .38 Special
Trigger action : double action
Magazine capacity : 6 rounds
Locking mechanism : rearside centre pin
Weight : 725g
Length : 197mm
Barrel length : 63mm
Trigger stop : no
Sights : fixed; HW38T: adjustable
Sight radius : 114mm
External safety : none
Internal safety : transfer bar, cylinder blocks with cocked hammer

FEATURES:

- thumb piece : on left side frame
- material : steel barrel and cylinder, alloy frame
- finish : blued or chrome plated
- grips : wood or synthetics

Arminius HW38 (4")

TECHNICAL SPECIFICATIONS:

Calibre : .38 Special
Trigger action : double action
Magazine capacity : 6 rounds
Locking mechanism : rearside centre pin
Weight : 815g
Length : 235mm
Barrel length : 102mm
Trigger stop : no
Sights : fixed; HW38T: adjustable
Sight radius : 152mm
External safety : none
Internal safety : transfer bar, cylinder blocks with cocked hammer

FEATURES:

- thumb piece : on left side frame
- material : steel barrel and cylinder, alloy frame
- finish : blued or chrome plated
- grips : wood or synthetics

Arminius HW-7S

TECHNICAL SPECIFICATIONS:

Calibre	: .22 LR
Trigger action	: double action
Magazine capacity	: 8 rounds
Locking mechanism	: rearside centre pin
Weight	: 865g
Length	: 265mm
Height	: 146mm
Barrel length	: 152mm (6"-barrel)
Trigger stop	: no
Sights	: windage adjustable rear notch
Sight radius	: 195mm
External safety	: none
Internal safety	: blocking bar, cylinder blocks with cocked hammer

FEATURES:

• thumb piece	: left side
• material	: steel barrel and cylinder, alloy frame
• finish	: blued
• grips	: wooden match

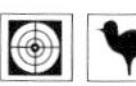

Arminius HW-9ST

TECHNICAL SPECIFICATIONS:

Calibre	: .22 LR
Trigger action	: double action
Magazine capacity	: 6 rounds
Locking mechanism	: rearside centre pin
Weight	: 1020g
Length	: 290mm
Height	: 146mm
Barrel length	: 152mm (6"-barrel)
Trigger stop	: adjustable
Sights	: adjustable
Sight radius	: 183mm
External safety	: none
Internal safety	: blocking bar, cylinder blocks with cocked hammer

Arminius HW-9ST

FEATURES:

• thumb piece	: on left side
• material	: steel (alloy barrel shroud)
• finish	: blued
• grips	: special target

Arminius Windicator

TECHNICAL SPECIFICATIONS:

Calibre	: .38 Special of .357 Magnum
Trigger action	: double action
Magazine capacity	: 6 rounds
Locking mechanism	: rearside centre pin
Weight	: 900g
Length	: 220mm
Barrel length	: 102mm
Trigger stop	: no
Sights	: fixed
Sight radius	: 135mm
External safety	: none
Internal safety	: transfer bar, cylinder blocks with cocked hammer

FEATURES:

• thumb piece	: on left side frame
• material	: steel
• finish	: blued
• grips	: synthetics or wood (combat grip)

Astra

The Astra Company, that is, the Unceta Y Compañía (Unceta & Co.) from Guernica in the north of Spain, has manufactured firearms since the beginning of this century. The Spanish factory, first situated in Eibar and later moved to Guernica, has never made pistols heavier than the calibre 9mm Parabellum, until the model A-80. The pistols varied in calibre from .22 Short (Astra Camper) up to 9mm Para (Model 600 or Model Militar). Until the turn of the century Astra manufactured many guns under the name 'Victoria', mostly Smith & Wesson revolver clones and Colt pistol clones. Furthermore, Astra produced copies of the famous Mauser C-96 pistol, under the name of Astra 900, 901, 902, and 903, of which the model 901 was fully automatic. The Astra A-80 was developed in 1981 and looks at first sight very much like the Sig-Sauer pistols. The magazine catch is not situated at the most likely spot, i.e. at the rear underside (the heel) of the grip.
In the later model A-90, a 9mm Para intended as an army pistol, the magazine catch was moved to the left side of the frame, behind the trigger guard. A very ingenius feature is the extractor, which doubles as a loading indicator.
If a cartridge is in the chamber of the barrel, the extractor projects from the slide and shows a red dot. This new pistol has, strangely enough, a kind of hotchpotch of safety systems. In the model A-90 an ambidextrous safety catch is mounted on the slide. The firing-
pin of the A-90 consists of two parts. The safety catch pivots the rear part of the firing-pin upwards, outside the reach of the hammer, if that catch is on "safe".
Apart from this, the decocking lever of the A-80 was retained, and the pistol is also provided with an automatic firing-pin safety. In 1993, at the International Arms Exhibition at Neurenberg (Germany), the new Astra A-100 was introduced.

Astra has lost out at gun-replacement trials in various countries. The Astra A-100 was developed to increase market potential in the service pistol sector.
The Astra was also given a phantasy name: 'Panther'. It is available in the calibres 9mm Para, .40 S&W, and .45 ACP. Some years ago Astra succeeded in gaining a foothold in the domestic market because of its issue to some units of the Spanish police. The pistol is

provided with a decocking lever and has no separate safety catch. Because of the decocking device and the firing-pin safety, the gun can be carried loaded with a live round in the chamber and with a decocked hammer. Consequently, a first double-action shot can be fired rapidly.

Astra A-70

TECHNICAL SPECIFICATIONS:

Calibre	: 9mm Para
Trigger action	: single action
Magazine capacity	: 8 rounds
Locking mechanism	: Browning lock-up
Weight	: 830g
Length	: 166mm
Height	: 120mm
Barrel length	: 89mm
Trigger stop	: no
Sights	: fixed
Sight radius	: 124mm
External safety	: safety catch on left side frame
Internal safety	: slide safety

FEATURES:

• slide catch	: on left side frame, above trigger guard
• magazine catch	: on left side frame, behind trigger guard
• material	: steel
• finish	: blued
• grips	: black synthetics

Astra A-75 Firefox

TECHNICAL SPECIFICATIONS:

Calibre	: 9mm Para
Trigger action	: double-action
Magazine capacity	: 8 rounds
Locking mechanism	: modified Browning lock-up
Weight	: 880g
Length	: 166mm
Height	: 120mm
Barrel length	: 89mm
Trigger stop	: no
Sights	: fixed
Sight radius	: 128mm
External safety	: combination decock/safety catch
Internal safety	: slide safety, half-cock safety, automatic firing-pin safety

FEATURES:

• slide catch	: on left side frame, above trigger guard
• magazine catch	: on left side frame, behind trigger guard
• material	: steel
• finish	: blued
• grips	: black synthetics

Astra A-75 L(ight) Firefox

TECHNICAL SPECIFICATIONS:

Calibre	: 9mm Para
Trigger action	: double action
Magazine capacity	: 8 rounds
Locking mechanism	: modified Browning lock-up
Weight	: 760g
Length	: 166mm
Height	: 125mm
Barrel length	: 89mm
Trigger stop	: no
Sights	: fixed
Sight radius	: 128mm
External safety	: combined decock/safety catch
Internal safety	: slide safety, half-cock safety, automatic firing-pin safety

FEATURES:

• slide catch	: on left side frame, above trigger guard
• magazine catch	: on left side frame, behind trigger guard
• material	: alloy frame, steel slide
• finish	: matt frame, blued slide
• grips	: black synthetics

Astra A-90

TECHNICAL SPECIFICATIONS:

Calibre	: 9mm Para, .38 Super and .45 ACP
Trigger action	: double action
Magazine capacity	: 15 rounds (9mm Para/.38 Super); 9 rounds (.45 ACP)
Locking mechanism	: Browning/Sig-system
Weight	: 985g (9mm Para) 955g (.45 ACP)
Length	: 180mm
Height	: 142mm
Barrel length	: 97mm
Trigger stop	: no
Sights	: windage adjustable rear sight
Sight radius	: 152mm
External safety	: decock lever, load indicator, separate ambidextrous safety catch on slide
Internal safety	: slide safety, automatic firing-pin safety

FEATURES:

• slide catch	: on left side frame
• magazine catch	: on left side frame, behind trigger guard
• material	: steel
• finish	: blued
• grips	: black synthetics

Astra A-100 Panther

TECHNICAL SPECIFICATIONS:

Calibre	: 9mm Para, .40 S&W, .45 ACP
Trigger action	: double action
Magazine capacity	: 15 rounds (9mm Para)
Locking mechanism	: Browning lock-up with one locking cam
Weight	: 985g (9mm Para)
Length	: 180mm
Height	: 143mm
Barrel length	: 97mm
Trigger stop	: no
Sights	: windage adjustable
Sight radius	: 136mm
External safety	: decock lever
Internal safety	: slide safety, automatic firing-

pin safety

FEATURES:

- slide catch : on left side frame
- magazine catch : left, behind trigger guard
- material : steel
- finish : bluede or chrome frame and blued slide
- grips : black synthetics

Astra A-100 Duo Panther

TECHNICAL SPECIFICATIONS:

Calibre	: 9 mm Para
Trigger action	: double action
Magazine capacity	: 15 rounds
Locking mechanism	: Browning lock-up with one lug
Weight	: 985g
Length	: 180mm
Height	: 143mm
Barrel length	: 97mm
Trigger stop	: no
Sights	: windage adjustable
Sight radius	: 136mm
External safety	: decocking lever
Internal safety	: slide safety, automatic firing-pin safety

FEATURES:

- slide catch : on left side frame
- magazine catch : left behind trigger guard
- material : steel
- finish : blued slide, chrome plated frame
- grips : black synthetics

Astra A-100 Inox Panther

TECHNICAL SPECIFICATIONS:

Calibre	: 9mm Para, .40 S&W, .45 ACP
Trigger action	: double action
Magazine capacity	: 15 rounds (9mm Para)
Locking mechanism	: Browning lock-up with one locking cam
Weight	: 995g (9mm Para)
Length	: 180mm
Height	: 143mm
Barrel length	: 97mm
Trigger stop	: no
Sights	: windage adjustable
Sight radius	: 136mm
External safety	: decocking lever
Internal safety	: slide safety, automatic firing-pin safety

FEATURES:

- slide catch : on left side frame
- magazine catch : left behind trigger guard
- material : stainless steel
- finish : satin (matt)
- grips : black synthetics

Astra A-100 L(ight) Panther

TECHNICAL SPECIFICATIONS:

Calibre	: 9mm Para, .40 S&W, .45 ACP
Trigger action	: double-action
Magazine capacity	: 15 rounds (9mm Para)
Locking mechanism	: Browning lock-up with one locking cam
Weight	: 865g (9mm Para)
Length	: 180mm
Height	: 143mm
Barrel length	: 97mm
Trigger stop	: no
Sights	: windage adjustable
Sight radius	: 136mm
External safety	: decocking lever
Internal safety	: slide safety, automatic firing-pin safety

FEATURES:

• slide catch	: on left side frame
• magazine catch	: left behind trigger guard
• material	: alloy frame, steel slide
• finish	: satin frame, blued slide
• grips	: black synthetics

Astra Model Falcon (400)

TECHNICAL SPECIFICATIONS:

Calibre	: .32 ACP, .380 ACP
Trigger action	: singleaction
Magazine capacity	: 8 rounds (.32), 8 rounds (.380)
Locking mechanism	: blowback system
Weight	: 670g
Length	: 164mm
Height	: 112mm
Barrel length	: 99mm
Trigger stop	: none
Sights	: fixed
Sight radius	: 125mm
External safety	: safety catch on left side frame
Internal safety	: slide safety, magazine safety

FEATURES:

• slide catch	: none
• magazine catch	: in bottom left grip
• material	: alloy frame, steel slide
• finish	: blued
• grips	: black synthetics

Astra TS-22

TECHNICAL SPECIFICATIONS:

Calibre	: .22 LR
Trigger action	: single action
Magazine capacity	: 10 rounds
Locking mechanism	: blowback system
Weight	: 1000g
Length	: 233mm
Height	: 136mm
Barrel length	: 152mm
Trigger stop	: none
Sights	: adjustable match sight
Sight radius	: 175mm
External safety	: safety catch on left side frame
Internal safety	: slide safety, magazine safety

FEATURES:

• slide catch	: on left side frame, above trigger guard
• magazine catch	: on left side frame, behind trigger guard
• material	: alloy frame, steel slide
• finish	: blued
• grips	: wooden target stock

Auto-Ordnance

The American Auto-Ordnance Corporation from West Hurley in the State of New York is primarily known for its Thompson ('Tommy Gun') submachine-guns in calibre .45 ACP. These are still in production, in full or semi-automatic versions, as the models 1927 A-5, Model 1927 M1, 1927 A-1, 1927 A-1C, Model 1928, and Model 1928 M1.
A lot of accessories are available for these submachine guns and carbines, and, among others, is a real violin carrying case which can be used as a gun case.
During the Second World War, the company was situated in Bridgeport, Connecticut. The Auto-Ordnance Corp. is a subsidiary company of the well-known Gun Parts Corporation, specializing in gun parts. Since its foundation, Auto Ordnance has manufactured all kinds of variations of the colt M1911-A1 pistol under the name of Thompson.
A compact model, introduced in 1989, is the ZG-51 or 'Pitbull'.
Auto-Ordnance also has an extensive range of parts, which enables the shooter to adapt his or her M1911-A1 to his or her individual needs. These parts are different types of lengthened back straps (the socalled beaver tail), special sights, compensators, lengthened magazine wells, enlarged ejectors, safety and magazine catches, etc. The company also produces special "custom" parts for other kinds of firearms, like the .30-M1 Carbine, the Ruger Mini-14, the M1 Garand rifle, and others.

Auto-Ordnance Thompson Model 1911 A1

The pistol shown here is a deluxe version with three-dot sights

TECHNICAL SPECIFICATIONS:

Calibre	: .45 ACP, 9 mm Para, .38 Super
Trigger action	: single action
Magazine capacity	: 7 rounds (.45), 9 rounds (9mm/.38)
Locking mechanism	: Browning/Colt system
Weight	: 1105g
Length	: 216mm
Height	: 140mm
Barrel length	: 127mm
Trigger stop	: none
Sights	: fixed
Sight radius	: 166mm
External safety	: safety catch, grip safety
Internal safety	: slide safety, half-cock-safety

FEATURES:

• slide catch	: on left side frame, above trigger guard
• magazine catch	: on left side frame, behind trigger guard
• material	: steel
• finish	: blued
• grips	: black rubber monogrip or standard rubber grips

Auto-Ordnance Thompson Model 1911 A1 Satin Nickel

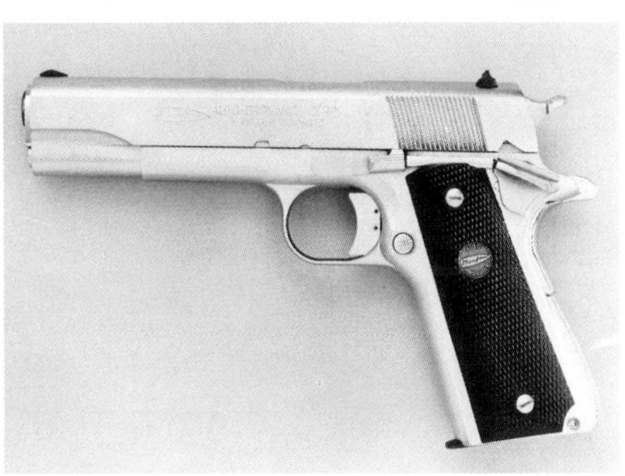

TECHNICAL SPECIFICATIONS:

Calibre	: .45 ACP
Trigger action	: single action
Magazine capacity	: 7 rounds
Locking mechanism	: Browning/Colt system
Weight	: 1110g
Length	: 216mm
Height	: 140mm
Barrel length	: 127mm
Trigger stop	: none
Sights	: fixed

Sight radius : 166mm
External safety : safety catch, grip safety
Internal safety : slide safety, half-cock-safety

FEATURES:

- slide catch : on left side frame, above trigger guard
- magazine catch : on left side frame, behind trigger guard
- material : steel
- finish : satin nickel
- grips : black rubber

Auto-Ordnance Thompson Model 1911 A1 Duo Tone

TECHNICAL SPECIFICATIONS:

Calibre : .45 ACP
Trigger action : single action
Magazine capacity : 7 rounds
Locking mechanism : Browning/Colt system
Weight : 1110g
Length : 216mm
Height : 140mm
Barrel length : 127mm
Trigger stop : none
Sights : fixed three-dot sights
Sight radius : 166mm
External safety : safety catch, grip safety
Internal safety : slide safety, half-cock safety

FEATURES:

- slide catch : on left side frame, above trigger guard
- magazine catch : on left side frame, behind trigger guard
- material : steel
- finish : matt, blued slide nickel frame
- grips : black rubber monogrip

Auto-Ordnance Thompson Model 1911 A1 WWII

TECHNICAL SPECIFICATIONS:

Calibre : .45 ACP
Trigger action : single action
Magazine capacity : 7 rounds
Locking mechanism : Browning/Colt system
Weight : 1110g
Length : 216mm
Height : 140mm
Barrel length : 127mm
Trigger stop : none
Sights : fixed
Sight radius : 166mm
External safety : safety catch, grip safety
Internal safety : slide safety, half-cock-safety

FEATURES:

- slide catch : on left side frame, above trigger guard
- magazine catch : on left side frame, behind trigger guard
- material : steel
- finish : matt black, with lanyard loop
- grips : black rubber

Auto-Ordnance Thompson Model ZG-51 'Pit Bull' (Compact)

TECHNICAL SPECIFICATIONS:

Calibre : .45 ACP

Trigger action	: single action
Magazine capacity	: 7 rounds
Locking mechanism	: Browning/Colt system
Weight	: 1020g
Length	: 184mm
Height	: 140mm
Barrel length	: 89mm
Trigger stop	: none
Sights	: fixed three-dot sights
Sight radius	: 138mm
External safety	: safety catch, grip safety
Internal safety	: slide safety, half-cock-safety

FEATURES:

• slide catch	: on left side frame, above trigger guard
• magazine catch	: on left side frame, behind trigger guard
• material	: steel
• finish	: blued
• grips	: black rubber

Auto-Ordnance Thompson Model 1911 A1 General

TECHNICAL SPECIFICATIONS:

Calibre	: .45 ACP
Trigger action	: single action
Magazine capacity	: 7 rounds
Locking mechanism	: Browning/Colt system
Weight	: 1050g
Length	: 197mm
Height	: 140mm
Barrel length	: 114mm
Trigger stop	: none
Sights	: fixed three-dot sights
Sight radius	: 144mm
External safety	: safety catch, grip safety
Internal safety	: slide safety, half-cock-safety

FEATURES:

• slide catch	: on left side frame, above trigger guard
• magazine catch	: on left side frame, behind trigger guard
• material	: steel
• finish	: blued
• grips	: black rubber monogrip

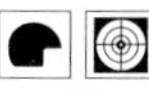

Auto-Ordnance Thompson Model 1911 A1 10 mm

TECHNICAL SPECIFICATIONS:

Calibre	: 10 mm Auto
Trigger action	: single action
Magazine capacity	: 8 rounds
Locking mechanism	: Browning/Colt system
Weight	: 1105g
Length	: 216mm
Height	: 140mm
Barrel length	: 127mm
Trigger stop	: none
Sights	: fixed three-dot sights

Sight radius	: 166mm
External safety	: safety catch, grip safety
Internal safety	: slide safety, half-cock-safety

FEATURES:

• slide catch	: on left side frame, above trigger guard
• magazine catch	: on left side frame, behind trigger guard
• material	: steel
• finish	: blued
• grips	: black rubber monogrip

Auto-Ordnance Thompson 1911 A1 Competition Model

TECHNICAL SPECIFICATIONS:

Calibre	: .45 ACP,
Trigger action	: single action
Magazine capacity	: 7 rounds
Locking mechanism	: Colt-Browning lock-up
Weight	: 1255g
Length	: 256mm (inc. compensator)
Height	: 150mm
Barrel length	: 130mm
Trigger stop	: adjustable
Sights	: fixed three-dot sights
Sight radius	: 166mm
External safety	: safety catch, grip safety
Internal safety	: slide safety, half-cock-safety

FEATURES:

• slide catch	: on left side frame, above trigger guard
• magazine catch	: on left side frame, behind trigger guard
• material	: steel
• finish	: blued
• grips	: black rubber monogrip

This match pistol has an enlarged slide catch, magazine catch, and beaver tail.

Benelli

The Italian Benelli Company, founded at the beginning of the twentieth century by Filippo and Giovanni Benelli, is situated in Urbino. The company is primarily known as a manufacturer of motorcycles, but also produces machinery, tools, and, since 1967, firearms. At first it mainly manufactured shotguns. In 1980 Benelli introduced a new eight-round 9mm Para double-action pistol.

Benelli described this handgun in its brochure as a rugged army and police pistol with the accuracy of a match pistol. Nevertheless, the Benelli B-76 did not score in several government trials in various countries, because the pistol did not meet with technical requirements. This was, in the main, because the handgun lacked a decocking lever and an automatic firing-pin safety.

To take advantage of the gun's double-action mode, it had to be decocked by means of the trigger, which is not desirable. The most interesting part of this pistol is that its barrel is fixed into a subframe, which is attached to the frame itself.

The lock-up is made by a bolt block, which connects the slide and the subframe. One of the pistol's great advantages is that the parts which are affected by powder gases are chrome plated. Furthermore, the firing-pin is made of stainless steel.

The pistol is made in a number of calibres: 9mm Para, 7.65 Luger, .32 ACP, .32 S&W-Long and 9mm Ultra (9 x 18mm). A variation of this model is the B-80. This pistol has a magazine catch behind the trigger guard, but is otherwise almost identical to its predecessor. The Benelli MP3-S was introduced in 1984. It is a match version of the Benelli B-76 and the B-80. With this pistol, the barrel is also fixed into a subframe.

The unusual Benelli lock-up is achieved by a movable bolt which connects the slide and the subframe during firing. The magazine catch is, fortunately, in the correct place, i.e. behind the trigger guard.

The MP3-S has a single-action trigger and is available in 9mm Para and .32 S&W-Long.

There is also a conversion set to convert from 9mm Para to calibre .32 S&W-Long. The special Target model has a lengthened barrel with an extra barrel weight, on which the front post is fixed.

With the new MP90-S pistol, Benelli is trying to capture a share of the market in sporting or match pistols. It is available in calibre .22 LR, .32 S&W-Long, and as a rapid-fire pistol in calibre .22 Short.
There are no conversion sets to convert from one calibre to another. The magazine is situated in front of the trigger. The trigger mechanism is removable as a unit, and can easily be adjusted. The trigger is adjustable in length and angle. The trigger pressure and trigger travel are fully adjustable.
A small synthetic block can be fitted into the gun for dry-training. With this system in place, the firing-pin is protected against excessive wear. An extra barrel weight of 65g can be placed in the frame, underneath the barrel. The pistol is provided with an ergonomic grip with an adjustable palm rest. The barrel is made of chrome-nickel steel.

Benelli B-76

TECHNICAL SPECIFICATIONS:

Calibre	: 9 mm Para
Trigger action	: double action
Magazine capacity	: 8 rounds
Locking mechanism	: retarded blowback (Benelli patent)
Weight	: 970g
Length	: 205mm
Height	: 139mm
Barrel length	: 108mm
Trigger stop	: none
Sights	: fixed sight with low-light markings
Sight radius	: 140 mm
External safety	: safety catch on left side frame
Internal safety	: load indicator (extractor), slide safety, half-cock safety

FEATURES:

• slide catch	: on left side frame
• magazine catch	: on left side frame, behind trigger guard
• material	: steel slide, alloy frame
• finish	: blued
• grips	: wood or synthetics

Benelli B-80S/B-82S

TECHNICAL SPECIFICATIONS:

Calibre	: 9mm Para, 9x18mm Ultra, 7.65mm Para
Trigger action	: double action
Magazine capacity	: 8 rounds
Locking mechanism	: retarded blowback (Benelli patent)
Weight	: 930g
Length	: 205mm
Height	: 139mm
Barrel length	: 108mm
Trigger stop	: none
Sights	: adjustable rear sight
Sight radius	: 140mm
External safety	: safety catch on left side frame
Internal safety	: load indicator (extractor), slide safety, half-cock safety

FEATURES:

• slide catch	: on left side frame
• magazine catch	: on left side frame, behind trigger guard
• material	: steel slide, alloy frame
• finish	: blued
• grips	: wood or synthetics

Benelli MP3-S

TECHNICAL SPECIFICATIONS:

Calibre	: 9mm Para, .32 S&W Long, assembly
Trigger action	: single action
Magazine capacity	: 6 rounds
Locking mechanism	: retarded blowback (Benelli-patent)
Weight	: 1175g
Length	: 237mm
Height	: 142mm
Barrel length	: 143mm
Trigger stop	: adjustable
Sights	: adjustable rear sight
Sight radius	: 178mm
External safety	: safety catch on left side frame
Internal safety	: load indicator (extractor), slide safety

FEATURES:

• slide catch	: on left side frame
• magazine catch	: backside of frame heel
• material	: steel
• finish	: blued
• grips	: wood or synthetics; Target model with adjustable stock and extended barrel

Benelli MP90-S

TECHNICAL SPECIFICATIONS:

Calibre	: .22 LR, .32 S&W Long
Trigger action	: single action
Magazine capacity	: 5 rounds
Locking mechanism	: blowback action
Weight	: 1110g
Length	: 300mm
Height	: 132mm
Barrel length	: 110mm
Trigger stop	: adjustable, adjustable trigger
Sights	: adjustable rear sight
Sight radius	: 218mm
External safety	: ambidextrous safety catch
Internal safety	: slide safety, magazine safety

FEATURES:

• slide catch	: none
• magazine catch	: front of magazine, before trigger
• material	: steel slide, alloy trigger group
• finish	: blued
• grips	: adjustable walnut grip with palm rest

Benelli MP95-E Nera

TECHNICAL SPECIFICATIONS:

Calibre	: .22 LR, .32 S&W Long
Trigger action	: single action
Magazine capacity	: 6 rounds (.22), 5 rounds (.32)
Locking mechanism	: blowback action
Weight	: 1000g
Length	: 300mm
Height	: 132mm
Barrel length	: 110mm
Trigger stop	: adjustable trigger

Sights : adjustable rear sight
Sight radius : 218mm
External safety : ambidextrous safety catch
Internal safety : slide safety, magazine safety

FEATURES:

- slide catch : none
- magazine catch : front of magazine, before trigger
- material : steel slide, alloy trigger group
- finish : blued
- grips : anatomical walnut grip with adjustable palm rest

Benelli MP95-E Kromo

TECHNICAL SPECIFICATIONS:

Calibre : .22 LR, .32 S&W Long
Trigger action : single action
Magazine capacity : 6 rounds (.22), 5 rounds (.32)
Locking mechanism : blowback action
Weight : 1000g
Length : 300mm
Height : 132mm
Barrel length : 110mm
Trigger stop : adjustable trigger
Sights : adjustable rear sight
Sight radius : 218mm
External safety : ambidextrous safety catch
Internal safety : slide safety, magazine safety

FEATURES:

- slide catch : none
- magazine catch : front of magazine, before trigger
- material : steel slide, alloy trigger group
- finish : matt chrome plated
- grips : anatomical walnut grip with adjustable palm rest

Beretta-pistols

The history of the Italian company, Pietro Beretta from Brescia, goes back to the fifteenth century. The company mainly manufactures rifles and shotguns but, around the turn of this century, started to produce pistols, mostly for the military market. In 1976 Beretta introduced the original pistol models 81 and 84. Later, the 83, 84, 85, and 87 Cheetah were developed from these. The Beretta 92 was created in 1976. The great breakthrough came in 1977, when the US army organized trials to replace the old Colt 1911-A1 service pistol. As a result of several tests conducted by the US air force between 1978 and 1980, the research committee recommended in 1980 the adoption of the Italian Beretta M92S-1 pistol in calibre 9mm Para. The Pentagon wanted a full-scale trial, in which as many 9mm Para pistols as possible would be tested. For this, a standard specification was drawn up in June 1981 called the JSOR (Joint Service Operational Requirement), in which the chosen pistol was designated as the PDW-XM9 (Personal Defence Weapon). The list of technical requirements contained fifty attributes the pistols had to comply with. These were called the AQRs (Absolute Quantitative Requirements). At the end of 1981 the race began. Participants included, among others, Beretta, Heckler & Koch, Smith & Wesson, and Sig-Sauer. The testing programme was broken off quite suddenly in February 1982, because none of the pistols on trial could meet all the requirements.
In 1982 a new list was published, in which less rigid requirements were demanded. In November 1983 a formal request was issued to all gun manufacturers to put test guns at the government's disposal. The participating manufacturers had to deliver thirty test pistols to the test committee, free of charge. Eight companies supplied test guns:

- Beretta, with the M92SB-F pistol.
- Sig-Sauer, with the P226.
- Steyr, with their GB pistol.
- Colt, with a new SSP pistol (Stainless Steel Pistol).
- FN-Browning, with a newly developed double-action pistol.
- Heckler & Koch, with their P7-M13.
- Walther, with the P88 pistol.
- Smith & Wesson, with the model 459.

The first to lose was the Steyr GB. FN-Browning withdrew from the contest, followed by Colt. For technical reasons the Walther P88, the HK P7-M13, and the S&W M459 disappeared from the scene. Consequently, only two pistols remained in the race: the Sig-Sauer P226 and the Beretta M92SB-F. Both companies made an offer for the delivery of 305,580 pistols, to be produced in five years' time. Sig-Sauer asked US$176.33 per item, while Beretta came to a price of US$178.50. Eventually, Beretta received the order, because the overall price, including spare parts, was around US$3,000,000 – below the Sig-Sauer offer.
So the Beretta M92SB-F was adopted as the official service handgun for the joint US armed forces under the name of M9. Later, the order was increased to a total of 320,030 pistols. Protests followed.
The US manufacturers, in particular, could not bear the fact that a foreign pistol had been chosen. Furthermore Smith & Wesson, Heckler & Koch, and Sig-Sauer filed a complaint, which was turned down. Smith & Wesson went a step further and started a lawsuit against the Department of Defense, on the grounds of, according to S&W, incorrect test procedures. This lawsuit was also rejected. Smith & Wesson did not sit down in despair. Through a great deal of lobbying in the US Congress, they were able to initiate a new test programme. The decision was made in June 1988. The former contract with Beretta had to stand, but a new trial, the XM-10, had to be developed for a second and additional supply series of 142,292 pistols. The new contestants were Beretta, Sig-Sauer, Ruger (the P85 pistol), and Smith & Wesson. The others were not successful. On 24 May 1989, the Pentagon announced that Beretta had again won the trials, and was being granted the second order for 142,292 pistols. To meet American complaints about the choice of a foreign-made army pistol, Beretta founded a separate company, Beretta USA Corporation, in Accokeek, Maryland.

Beretta Model 76

TECHNICAL SPECIFICATIONS:

Calibre	: .22 LR
Trigger action	: single action
Magazine capacity	: 10 rounds
Locking mechanism	: blowback action
Weight	: 930g
Length	: 233mm

Height	: 143mm
Barrel length	: 150mm
Trigger stop	: none
Sights	: adjustable
Sight radius	: 176mm
External safety	: safety catch on left side frame
Internal safety	: slide safety

FEATURES:

• slide catch	: on left side frame, above trigger guard
• cartridge holder catch	: in left grip plate
• material	: alloy barrel housing, steel frame
• finish	: blued
• grips	: wooden target grips

Beretta Model 84

TECHNICAL SPECIFICATIONS:

Calibre	: .32 ACP(7.65 mm), 9mm Short
Trigger action	: double action
Magazine capacity	: 13 rounds (M84); 8 rounds (M85)
Locking mechanism	: blowback action
Weight	: 690g
Length	: 172mm
Height	: 122mm
Barrel length	: 97mm
Trigger stop	: none
Sights	: fixed
Sight radius	: 127mm
External safety	: ambidextrous safety catch
Internal safety	: slide safety, firing-pin safety, half-cock safety, magazine safety, load indicator

FEATURES:

• slide catch	: on left side frame
• magazine catch	: on left side frame, behind trigger guard (reversible for left-handed shooters)
• material	: alloy frame, steel slide
• finish	: matt blued (Bruniton) or nickel plated
• grips	: wood or synthetics

Beretta Model 92 F

TECHNICAL SPECIFICATIONS:

Calibre	: 9mm Para
Trigger action	: double action
Magazine capacity	: 15 rounds
Locking mechanism	: pivoting block mechanism (Beretta/Walther system)
Weight	: 964g
Length	: 217mm
Height	: 137mm
Barrel length	: 125mm
Trigger stop	: no
Sights	: fixed

Sight radius	: 155mm
External safety	: combined decock/safety catch on slide
Internal safety	: slide safety, load indicator, automatic firing-pin safety

FEATURES:

• slide catch	: on left side frame
• magazine catch	: on left side frame, behind trigger guard
• material	: alloy frame, steel slide
• finish	: blued
• grips	: wood or synthetics

Beretta Model 92 FS

TECHNICAL SPECIFICATIONS:

Calibre	: 9mm Para
Trigger action	: double action
Magazine capacity	: 15 rounds
Locking mechanism	: pivoting block mechanism (Beretta/Walther-system)
Weight	: 975g
Length	: 217mm
Height	: 137mm
Barrel length	: 125mm
Trigger stop	: none
Sights	: fixed
Sight radius	: 155mm
External safety	: ambidextrous decock/safety catch on slide
Internal safety	: slide safety, load indicator, automatic firing-pin safety

FEATURES:

• slide catch	: on left side frame
• magazine catch	: on left side frame, behind trigger guard
• material	: alloy frame, steel slide
• finish	: blued
• grips	: wood or synthetics

Beretta Model 92 FS Inox

TECHNICAL SPECIFICATIONS:

Calibre	: 9 mm Para
Trigger action	: double action
Magazine capacity	: 15 rounds
Locking mechanism	: pivoting block mechanism (Beretta/Walther system)
Weight	: 975g
Length	: 217mm
Height	: 137mm
Barrel length	: 125mm
Trigger stop	: no
Sights	: fixed
Sight radius	: 155mm
External safety	: ambidextrous decock/safety catch on slide
Internal safety	: slide safety, load indicator, automatic firing-pin safety

FEATURES:

• slide catch	: on left side frame
• magazine catch	: on left side frame, behind trigger guard
• material	: alloy frame, steel slide
• finish	: matt nickel plated
• grips	: black synthetic

Beretta Model 92 S

TECHNICAL SPECIFICATIONS:

Calibre	: 9 mmPara
Trigger action	: double action
Magazine capacity	: 15 rounds
Locking mechanism	: pivoting block mechanism (Beretta/Walther system)
Weight	: 975g
Length	: 217mm
Height	: 137mm
Barrel length	: 125mm
Trigger stop	: none

Sights	: fixed
Sight radius	: 155mm
External safety	: combined decock/safety catch on slide
Internal safety	: slide safety, load indicator, automatic firing-pin safety

FEATURES:

• slide catch	: on left side frame
• magazine catch	: on left side frame, behind trigger guard
• material	: alloy frame, steel slide
• finish	: blued
• grips	: wood or synthetics

The Beretta M92 S pistol is a modification of the model 92 from 1978, and it is in use with the Italian police.

Beretta Model 92 SB

TECHNICAL SPECIFICATIONS:

Calibre	: 9mm Para
Trigger action	: double action
Magazine capacity	: 15 rounds
Locking mechanism	: pivoting block mechanism (Beretta/Walther system)
Weight	: 970g
Length	: 217mm
Height	: 137mm
Barrel length	: 125mm
Trigger stop	: none
Sights	: fixed
Sight radius	: 155mm
External safety	: ambidextrous combined decock/safety catch on slide
Internal safety	: slide safety, load indicator, automatic firing-pin safety

FEATURES:

• slide catch	: on left side frame
• magazine catch	: on left side frame, behind trigger guard
• material	: alloy frame, steel slide
• finish	: blued
• grips	: wood or synthetics

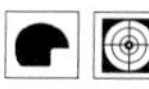

Beretta Model 92 SB Compact

TECHNICAL SPECIFICATIONS:

Calibre	: 9mm Para
Trigger action	: double action
Magazine capacity	: 13 rounds
Locking mechanism	: pivoting block mechanism (Beretta/Walther system)
Weight	: 885g
Length	: 197mm
Height	: 129mm
Barrel length	: 109mm
Trigger stop	: none
Sights	: fixed
Sight radius	: 135mm

External safety	:	ambidextrous decock /safety catch on slide
Internal safety	:	slide safety, load indicator, automatic firing-pin safety

FEATURES:

• slide catch	:	on left side frame
• magazine catch	:	on left side frame, behind trigger guard
• material	:	alloy frame, steel slide
• finish	:	blued
• grips	:	wood or synthetics

Beretta Model 92 Stock

TECHNICAL SPECIFICATIONS:

Calibre	:	9mm Para
Trigger action	:	double action
Magazine capacity	:	15 rounds
Locking mechanism	:	pivoting block mechanism (Beretta/Walther system)
Weight	:	1000g
Length	:	217mm
Height	:	140mm
Barrel length	:	125mm
Trigger stop	:	no
Sights	:	fixed
Sight radius	:	161mm
External safety	:	safety catch on frame: blocks trigger, sear and slide
Internal safety	:	slide safety, load indicator

FEATURES:

• slide catch	:	on left side frame
• magazine catch	:	on left side frame, behind trigger guard
• material	:	alloy frame, steel slide
• finish	:	blued
• grips	:	black synthetics

Beretta Model 93R (Automatic)

TECHNICAL SPECIFICATIONS:

Calibre	:	9 mm Para
Trigger action	:	semi-automatic or full automatic in controlled bursts of three shots
Magazine capacity	:	20 rounds
Locking mechanism	:	pivoting block mechanism (Beretta/Walther system)
Weight	:	1170g
Length	:	240mm
Height	:	170mm
Barrel length	:	156mm (inc. compensator)
Trigger stop	:	none
Sights	:	fixed
Sight radius	:	160mm
External safety	:	safety catch on left side frame, also acts as fire selector
Internal safety	:	slide safety, load indicator, magazine safety

FEATURES:

• slide catch	:	on left side frame
• magazine catch	:	on left side frame, behind trigger guard
• material	:	steel
• finish	:	blued
• grips	:	black synthetics

This fully automatic pistol can be fitted with a folding stock with a total length of 368mm. The pistol is a special model for security departments and is not for sale to civilians.

Beretta Model 96 G Centurion

TECHNICAL SPECIFICATIONS:

Calibre	: .40 S&W
Trigger action	: double action
Magazine capacity	: 10 rounds
Locking mechanism	: pivoting block mechanism (Beretta/Walther system)
Weight	: 975g
Length	: 217mm
Height	: 137mm
Barrel length	: 125mm
Trigger stop	: none
Sights	: fixed
Sight radius	: 155mm
External safety	: ambidextrous decocking lever on slide
Internal safety	: slide safety, load indicator, automatic firing-pin safety

FEATURES:

• slide catch	: on left side frame
• magazine catch	: on left side frame, behind trigger guard
• material	: alloy frame, steel slide
• finish	: blued
• grips	: synthetics

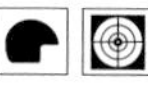

Beretta Model 8000 Cougar-G

TECHNICAL SPECIFICATIONS:

Calibre	: 9mm Para
Trigger action	: double action
Magazine capacity	: 15 rounds
Locking mechanism	: rotating lock mechanism
Weight	: 950g
Length	: 180mm
Height	: 140mm
Barrel length	: 92mm
Trigger stop	: none
Sights	: fixed three-dot sights
Sight radius	: 132mm
External safety	: ambidextrous decocking lever on slide
Internal safety	: slide safety, automatic firing-pin safety

FEATURES:

• slide catch	: on left side frame
• magazine catch	: on left side frame, behind trigger guard
• material	: alloy frame, steel slide
• finish	: matt black Bruniton-coating
• grips	: black synthetics

Beretta Model 8000 Cougar-G Inox

TECHNICAL SPECIFICATIONS:

Calibre	: 9mm Para
Trigger action	: double action
Magazine capacity	: 15 rounds
Locking mechanism	: rotating lock mechanism
Weight	: 950g
Length	: 180mm

Height	: 140mm
Barrel length	: 92mm
Trigger stop	: no
Sights	: fixed three-dot sights
Sight radius	: 132mm
External safety	: ambidextrous decocking lever on slide
Internal safety	: slide safety, automatic firing-pin safety

FEATURES:

• slide catch	: on left side frame
• magazine catch	: on left side frame, behind trigger guard
• material	: alloy frame, stainless slide
• finish	: matt stainless steel
• grips	: wood

Beretta Model 8000 Cougar-G Combo

TECHNICAL SPECIFICATIONS:

Calibre	: 9x21 IMI, .41AE
Trigger action	: double action
Magazine capacity	: 15 rounds (9 mm), 10 rounds (.41)
Locking mechanism	: rotating lock mechanism
Weight	: 950g
Length	: 180mm
Height	: 140mm
Barrel length	: 92mm
Trigger stop	: none
Sights	: fixed three-dot sights
Sight radius	: 132mm
External safety	: ambidextrous decocking lever on slide
Internal safety	: slide safety, automatic firing-pin safety

FEATURES:

• slide catch	: on left side frame
• magazine catch	: on left side frame, behind trigger guard
• material	: alloy frame, steel slide
• finish	: matt black Bruniton-coating
• grips	: black synthetics

For the model 8000 Cougar-G Combo, an interchangeable set is available for the calibre .41 AE (Action Express).

Beretta Model 8040 Cougar-G

TECHNICAL SPECIFICATIONS:

Calibre	: .40 S&W
Trigger action	: double action
Magazine capacity	: 11 rounds
Locking mechanism	: rotating lock mechanism
Weight	: 950g
Length	: 180mm
Height	: 140mm
Barrel length	: 92mm
Trigger stop	: none
Sights	: fixed three-dot sights
Sight radius	: 132mm
External safety	: ambidextrous decocking lever on slide
Internal safety	: slide safety, automatic firing-pin safety

FEATURES:

• slide catch	: on left side frame
• magazine catch	: on left side frame, behind trigger guard
• material	: alloy frame, steel slide
• finish	: matt black Bruniton-coating
• grips	: black synthetics

Beretta Model 84 Cheetah

TECHNICAL SPECIFICATIONS:

Calibre	: .380 ACP (9mm Short)
Trigger action	: double action
Magazine capacity	: 13 rounds
Locking mechanism	: blowback mechanism
Weight	: 660g
Length	: 172mm
Height	: 122mm
Barrel length	: 97mm
Trigger stop	: fixed
Sights	: fixed
Sight radius	: 124mm
External safety	: ambidextrous combined decock/safety catch
Internal safety	: slide safety, automatic firing-pin safety, load indicator

FEATURES:

• slide catch	: on left side frame
• magazine catch	: on left side frame, behind trigger guard (reversible for left-handed shooters)
• material	: alloy frame, steel slide
• finish	: blued
• grips	: wood or synthetics

Beretta Model 85 Cheetah

TECHNICAL SPECIFICATIONS:

Calibre	: .380 ACP (9mm Short)
Trigger action	: double action
Magazine capacity	: 8 rounds
Locking mechanism	: blowback mechanism
Weight	: 620g
Length	: 172mm
Height	: 122mm
Barrel length	: 97mm
Trigger stop	: fixed
Sights	: fixed
Sight radius	: 124mm
External safety	: ambidextrous combined decock/safety catch
Internal safety	: slide safety, automatic firing-pin safety, load indicator

FEATURES:

• slide catch	: on left side frame
• magazine catch	: on left side frame, behind trigger guard
• material	: alloy frame, steel slide
• finish	: blued
• grips	: black synthetics

Beretta Model 85 Cheetah Nickel

TECHNICAL SPECIFICATIONS:

Calibre	: .380 ACP (9mm Short)
Trigger action	: double action
Magazine capacity	: 8 rounds
Locking mechanism	: blowback mechanism
Weight	: 620g
Length	: 172mm
Height	: 122mm
Barrel length	: 97mm
Trigger stop	: fixed
Sights	: fixed
Sight radius	: 124mm
External safety	: ambidextrous combined decock/safety catch
Internal safety	: slide safety, automatic firing-pin safety, load indicator

FEATURES:

• slide catch	: on left side frame
• magazine catch	: on left side frame, behind trigger guard
• material	: alloy frame, steel slide

• finish	:	matt nickel plated
• grips	:	wood

Beretta Model 86 Cheetah

TECHNICAL SPECIFICATIONS:

Calibre	:	.380 ACP (9mm Short)
Trigger action	:	double action
Magazine capacity	:	8 rounds
Locking mechanism	:	blowback mechanism
Weight	:	660g
Length	:	186mm
Height	:	123mm
Barrel length	:	111mm
Trigger stop	:	fixed
Sights	:	fixed
Sight radius	:	124mm
External safety	:	embidextrous safety catch on frame
Internal safety	:	slide safety, automatic firing-pin safety, load indicator

FEATURES:

• slide catch	:	on left side frame
• magazine catch	:	on left side frame, behind trigger guard
• material	:	alloy frame, steel slide
• finish	:	matt black coating
• grips	:	wood

Beretta Model 87 Cheetah

TECHNICAL SPECIFICATIONS:

Calibre	:	.22 LR
Trigger action	:	double action
Magazine capacity	:	8 rounds
Locking mechanism	:	blowback mechanism
Weight	:	570g
Length	:	172mm
Height	:	120mm
Barrel length	:	97mm
Trigger stop	:	none

Sights	:	fixed
Sight radius	:	124mm
External safety	:	ambidextrous safety catch on frame
Internal safety	:	slide safety, automatic firing-pin safety, load indicator

FEATURES:

• slide catch	:	on left side frame
• magazine catch	:	on left side frame, behind trigger guard
• material	:	alloy frame, steel slide
• finish	:	matt black coating
• grips	:	wood

Beretta Model 87 Cheetah Long Barrel

TECHNICAL SPECIFICATIONS:

Calibre	:	.22 LR
Trigger action	:	double action
Magazine capacity	:	8 rounds
Locking mechanism	:	blowback mechanism
Weight	:	660g
Length	:	225mm
Height	:	120mm
Barrel length	:	150mm
Trigger stop	:	none
Sights	:	fixed
Sight radius	:	124mm
External safety	:	ambidextrous safety catch on frame
Internal safety	:	slide safety, automatic firing-pin safety, load indicator

FEATURES:

• slide catch	:	on left side frame
• magazine catch	:	on left side frame, behind trigger guard
• material	:	alloy frame, steel slide
• finish	:	matt black coating
• grips	:	wood

Beretta Model 89 Gold Standard

TECHNICAL SPECIFICATIONS:

Calibre	:	.22 LR
Trigger action	:	single action
Magazine capacity	:	8 rounds
Locking mechanism	:	blowback mechanism
Weight	:	1160g
Length	:	240mm
Height	:	135mm
Barrel length	:	152mm
Trigger stop	:	adjustable
Sights	:	adjustable
Sight radius	:	185mm
External safety	:	safety catch on left side frame
Internal safety	:	slide safety

FEATURES:

• slide catch	:	on left side frame
• magazine catch	:	on left side frame, behind trigger guard
• material	:	alloy frame, steel slide
• finish	:	matt black coating
• grips	:	wooden target grip or match stock with adjustable palm rest

Bernardelli-pistolen

The Italian company of Bernardelli from Gardone, founded in 1865, is mainly known for its shotguns. But before the Second World War the factory produced pocket pistols, mostly copies, like those from the Walther Model 9.

From the beginning of the 1960s Bernardelli marketed a series of small-bore pistols. In 1984 the company introduced a big-bore pistol, by the name of P-018/9 in calibre 9mm Para, and in calibre 7.65 Para by the name of P-018. The latter (not a common calibre in northern Europe) was necessary because, in several countries, the 9mm Para cartridge is not permitted for civilian use.

The gun was designed as a service arm for army and police, but did not play any important role in that capacity. The gun can be regarded as "super-safe", because several safety devices are combined:

a safety catch blocks the slide, the hammer, and the trigger bar.

The latter connects the trigger with the sear. The second safety is the automatic firing-pin safety, and the third the hammer, which can be half-cocked with a notch on the hammer foot. And then, of course, the pistol has the usual slide safety.

The big fault with this pistol is that the magazine catch is situated in the heel of the grip. Fortunately this was corrected in 1989 when the magazine catch was moved on the newer models to the left side of the frame, behind the trigger guard. Other versions of this pistol are the P-018 Combat, the P-018 Match, and the P-018 Compact (the 15-round short model with a 102mm barrel).

At the International Arms Exhibition in 1992, a sports model was introduced, the 'Practical VB', with a two-chamber compensator and adjustable rear sight in the calibres 9mm Para, .40 S&W, and 9 x 21mm IMI. Bernardelli also made a series of small-bore pistols.

First was the Model 69, introduced in 1969. This pistol was succeeded by the Model P010, also in .22 LR. This is a complete steel single-action match pistol with a nickel-chrome barrel. The slide of the pistol is divided into two parts. The rear part forms the massive lock-up for the blowback action.

The front part, connected to the frame, serves as a barrel weight, on which the barrel rib is fixed. The rear sight is adjustable and the front post is exchangeable for other colours and heights. The trigger is adjustable for trigger pressure and trigger stop. The one-piece wooden grip can be changed for a match grip with an adjustable palm rest. The pistol is highly accurate and, quite wrongly, rarely seen at shooting-ranges. Unfortunately, Bernardelli has caused confusion with its policy on names. In several countries some model variations are known by different names. The older model is the 69, later called the Model 100. A later modification bears the name P010.

Bernardelli P018/9

TECHNICAL SPECIFICATIONS:

Calibre	: 9 mm Para
Trigger action	: double action
Magazine capacity	: 16 rounds
Locking mechanism	: Browning locking mechanism
Weight	: 1010g
Length	: 213mm
Height	: 145mm
Barrel length	: 122mm
Trigger stop	: fixed
Sights	: fixed; on match model adjustable
Sight radius	: 160mm
External safety	: safety catch
Internal safety	: slide safety, automatic firing-pin safety, half-cock safety

FEATURES:

• slide catch	: on left side frame
• magazine catch	: on left side frame, behind trigger guard (older model: in heel of grip)
• material	: steel
• finish	: blued
• grips	: standard: black synthetic; match: wood

Bernardelli P018

TECHNICAL SPECIFICATIONS:

Calibre	: 7.65mm Para
Trigger action	: double action
Magazine capacity	: 16 rounds
Locking mechanism	: Browning locking mechanism
Weight	: 1010g
Length	: 213mm
Height	: 145mm
Barrel length	: 122mm
Trigger stop	: fixed
Sights	: fixed; match model adjustable
Sight radius	: 160mm
External safety	: safety catch
Internal safety	: slide safety, automatic firing-pin safety, half-cock safety

FEATURES:

• slide catch	: on left side frame
• magazine catch	: on left side frame, behind trigger guard (older model: in heel of grip)
• material	: steel
• finish	: blued
• grips	: standard: black synthetic; match: wood

Bernardelli Model 60 (Model U.S.A. Automatic)

TECHNICAL SPECIFICATIONS:

Calibre	: .22 LR (also in calibre .380 ACP and .32 ACP)
Trigger action	: single action
Magazine capacity	: 10 rounds
Locking mechanism	: blowback action
Weight	: 700g
Length	: 165mm
Height	: 123mm
Barrel length	: 90mm
Trigger stop	: none
Sights	: fixed
Sight radius	: 110mm
External safety	: safety catch on left side frame, behind trigger quard
Internal safety	: slide safety, magazine safety

FEATURES:

• slide catch	: none, but slide stays open after last shot
• magazine catch	: in heel of grip
• material	: steel
• finish	: blued
• grips	: wood or black synthetic

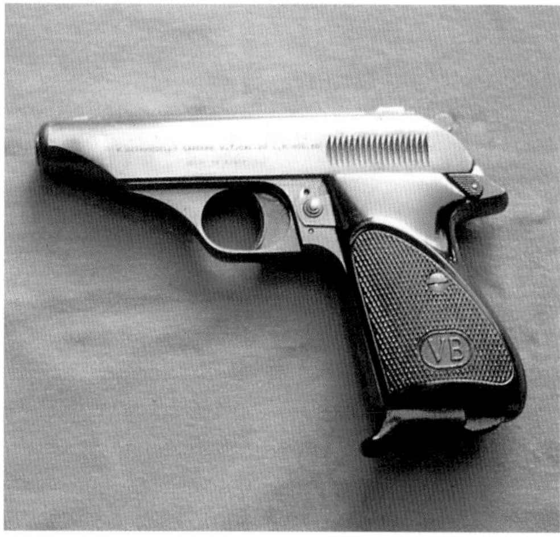

Bernardelli Model 69

TECHNICAL SPECIFICATIONS:

Calibre	: .22 LR
Trigger action	: single action

Magazine capacity : 10 rounds
Locking mechanism : blowback action
Weight : 1130g
Length : 248mm
Height : 140mm
Barrel length : 150mm
Trigger stop : adjustable
Sights : adjustable
Sight radius : 190mm
External safety : safety catch on left side frame, behind trigger quard
Internal safety : slide safety, magazine safety

FEATURES:

- slide catch : on right side frame
- magazine catch : in heel of grip
- material : steel
- finish : blued
- grips : wood

Bersa

The Argentinian arms factory of Bersa is not very well known in Europe, which is a pity for the Europeans. Formerly, Bersa concentrated mainly on the South and North American markets.
Traditionally Bersa produces good, small pistols.
In 1984 Bersa introduced two new pistols, the model 223 in calibre .22 LR and the model 383 in .380 ACP (9mm Short).
In 1985 and 1986 Bersa again marketed two new pistols, the Model 85 and Model 86 in calibre .380 ACP, which is derived externally from the Walther PP and PPK. Both pistols have a capacity of 13 rounds.
All Bersa pistols are double action. At the American Shot Show of 1993 in Houston, Texas, Bersa announced a completely new pistol concept. This new pistol, with the appropriate name 'Thunder-9', is a modern handgun in calibre 9mm Para. It appears that Bersa has tried to combine all kinds of technical specialities into one pistol model.

Bersa Thunder-9

TECHNICAL SPECIFICATIONS:

Calibre : 9 mm Para
Trigger action : double action
Magazine capacity : 15 rounds
Locking mechanism : modified Browning/Petter system
Weight : 870g
Length : 192mm
Height : 140mm
Barrel length : 108mm
Trigger stop : adjustable
Sights : adjustable
Sight radius : 152mm
External safety : ambidextrous decock and safety catch
Internal safety : slide safety, automatic firing-pin safety

FEATURES:

- slide catch : ambidextrous on frame
- magazine catch : enlarged catch on left side frame, behind trigger guard. Can be reversed to right side
- material : steel
- finish : matt blued
- grips : black synthetic

Browning-pistolen

The Browning High-Power HP-35 pistol – in French known as the Grand Puissance (GP-35) – was developed by John Moses Browning in 1926, and the Belgian firearms factory, Fabrique Nationale (National Factory), in Liège, obtained the licence rights. Because the pistol was issued in 1935 to the Belgian army, the figures "35" were added. For some decades several variations of the model were introduced. These were, among others,

adjustable rear sights, a combined holster/carbine stock, and several kinds of finishes. When the German army occupied Belgium in 1940, production continued. A number of FN technicians escaped to England, and they were sent to Canada in 1942 to organize the production of this pistol for the Allied forces in the factory of John Inglis. The most striking difference between the Belgian and Canadian Browning is the changed shape of the sights. Furthermore, the Canadian Browning MK has a barrel with four lands and grooves instead of the Belgian six. After 1945, production at FN in Belgium was continued under the name of H-Power. The pistol has been used as an army and police handgun in many countries. Besides this, the gun is, after some modifications, very suitable for target shooting. Quite a number of manufacturers have made clones or copies of this model. The HP-MK II is a modernized version of the old model HP-35. This pistol has an ambidextrous safety catch on the frame. Moreover, the design of the grip and plates has been given a sporting appearance. From the serial number 245-PR-03101 the pistols are provided with an automatic firing-pin safety. A variation of this model, the MK II-Sport, has a lengthened barrel with an extra barrel weight at the muzzle end. The HP-MK III is primarily adapted to modern times by its appearance. Specifically, the stainless frame with its blued slide looks attractive. The technology is mostly equal to that of the HP-MK II. There are several sports versions derived from this model, among them a type with a longer barrel and compensator. This pistol was also available in the double-action mode.
Because of technical problems, this model was taken out of production. The factory plays an important part in the field of small-bore pistols. Older pistol models like the 'Concours' and the 'Tire' were succeeded by new pistol models, the 'International', later renamed the 'International II', because of a modified rear sight, and the 'Practice 150'. Both pistols are almost equal, only the grips are different.
The American trading company, the Browning Arms Company, introduced a new kind of small-bore pistol at the Shot Show in 1985 in Atlanta. This is called the Browning Buck Mark .22. It was the successor not only to the Challenger pistols but also to the International pistol models. The Buck Mark attracts attention with its heavy, square barrel. In the mean time, several variations of the basic model have been marketed, namely, the Buck Mark Plus with wooden grip plates. In 1987 the Buck Mark Varmint followed, a model with a 250mm long rounded barrel, without sights, suitable for scope mounting. In 1990 the Buck Mark Target 5.5 was shown to the public at the yearly Shot Show. This handgun, also with a round barrel, has hooded sights, so the shooter is not bothered by light falling on the sights. The pistol line was extended in 1992 with a silhouette version with a 14in barrel.
The Target, Varmint, and Silhouette have a wide grooved barrel band on top of their heavy barrels. These are suitable for mounting a scope. The trigger is adjustable for pressure from around 1100g up to 2300g. The most recent models of Browning are the BDA (Browning Double Action) and the BDM (Browning Double Mode), following the current trend in big-bore pistols.

Browning BDA (Browning Double Action)

TECHNICAL SPECIFICATIONS:

Calibre	: 9mm Para
Trigger action	: double action
Magazine capacity	: 13 rounds
Locking mechanism	: FN Browning locking mechanism
Weight	: 870g
Length	: 200mm
Height	: 132mm
Barrel length	: 118mm
Trigger stop	: none
Sights	: fixed

Sight radius : 160mm
External safety : ambidextrous decocking lever on the frame
Internal safety : slide safety, automatic firing-pin safety

FEATURES:
- slide catch : on left side frame
- magazine catch : on left side frame, behind trigger guard
- material : alloy frame, steel slide
- finish : blued
- grips : black synthetic

Browning BDAO (Browning Double Action Only)

TECHNICAL SPECIFICATIONS:
Calibre : 9mm Para
Trigger action : double action
Magazine capacity : 13 rounds
Locking mechanism : Browning locking mechanism
Weight : 870g
Length : 200mm
Height : 132mm
Barrel length : 118mm
Trigger stop : none
Sights : fixed
Sight radius : 160mm
External safety : none
Internal safety : slide safety, automatic firing-pin safety

FEATURES:
- slide catch : on left side frame
- magazine catch : on left side frame, behind trigger guard
- material : alloy frame, steel slide
- finish : blued
- grips : black synthetic

Browning BDM (Browning Double Mode)

TECHNICAL SPECIFICATIONS:
Calibre : 9mm Para
Trigger action : switchable from double action to double-action only
Magazine capacity : 13 rounds
Locking mechanism : Browning locking mechanism
Weight : 880g
Length : 200mm
Height : 140mm
Barrel length : 120mm
Trigger stop : no
Sights : fixed
Sight radius : 160mm
External safety : ambidextrous selector on frame for DA of DAO
Internal safety : slide safety, automatic firing-pin safety

FEATURES:
- slide catch : on left side frame
- magazine catch : on left side frame, behind trigger guard
- material : alloy frame, steel slide
- finish : blued
- grips : black synthetics

Browning Buck Mark Gold

TECHNICAL SPECIFICATIONS:
Calibre : .22 LR
Trigger action : single action
Magazine capacity : 10 rounds
Locking mechanism : blowback action
Weight : 1030g
Length : 245mm
Height : 137mm
Barrel length : 140mm

Trigger stop	: none
Sights	: adjustable
Sight radius	: 205mm
External safety	: safety catch on left side frame
Internal safety	: slide safety

FEATURES:

• slide catch	: on left side frame
• magazine catch	: on left side frame, behind trigger guard
• material	: steel
• finish	: blued barrel and bolt, gold-coated frame and barrel band
• grips	: wood

Browning Buck Mark Gold Target

TECHNICAL SPECIFICATIONS:

Calibre	: .22 LR
Trigger action	: single action
Magazine capacity	: 10 rounds
Locking mechanism	: blowback action
Weight	: 1030g
Length	: 245mm
Height	: 137mm
Barrel length	: 140mm
Trigger stop	: yes
Sights	: adjustable (with front and rear sight caps)
Sight radius	: 205mm
External safety	: safety catch on left side frame
Internal safety	: slide safety

FEATURES:

• slide catch	: on left side frame
• magazine catch	: on left side frame, behind trigger guard
• material	: steel
• finish	: blued barrel and bolt, gold-coated frame and barrel band
• grips	: wood

Browning Buck Mark Plus

TECHNICAL SPECIFICATIONS:

Calibre	: .22 LR
Trigger action	: single action
Magazine capacity	: 10 rounds
Locking mechanism	: blowback action
Weight	: 900g
Length	: 240mm
Height	: 137mm
Barrel length	: 140mm
Trigger stop	: none
Sights	: adjustable
Sight radius	: 203mm
External safety	: safety catch on left side frame
Internal safety	: slide safety

FEATURES:

• slide catch	: on left side frame
• magazine catch	: on left side frame, behind trigger guard

• material	: steel
• finish	: blued with golden trigger
• grips	: wood

Browning Buck Mark Silhouette

TECHNICAL SPECIFICATIONS:

Calibre	: .22 LR
Trigger action	: single action
Magazine capacity	: 10 rounds
Locking mechanism	: blowback action
Weight	: 1500g
Length	: 355mm
Height	: 137mm
Barrel length	: 250mm
Trigger stop	: none
Sights	: adjustable
Sight radius	: 310mm
External safety	: safety catch on left side frame
Internal safety	: slide safety

FEATURES:

• slide catch	: on left side frame
• magazine catch	: on left side frame, behind trigger guard
• material	: steel
• finish	: blued blued with golden trigger
• grips	: wood

Browning Buck Mark Target

TECHNICAL SPECIFICATIONS:

Calibre	: .22 LR
Trigger action	: single action
Magazine capacity	: 10 rounds
Locking mechanism	: blowback action
Weight	: 1030g
Length	: 245mm
Height	: 137mm
Barrel length	: 140mm
Trigger stop	: yes
Sights	: adjustable (with front and rear sight caps)
Sight radius	: 205mm
External safety	: safety catch on left side frame
Internal safety	: slide safety

FEATURES:

• slide catch	: on left side frame
• magazine catch	: on left side frame, behind trigger guard

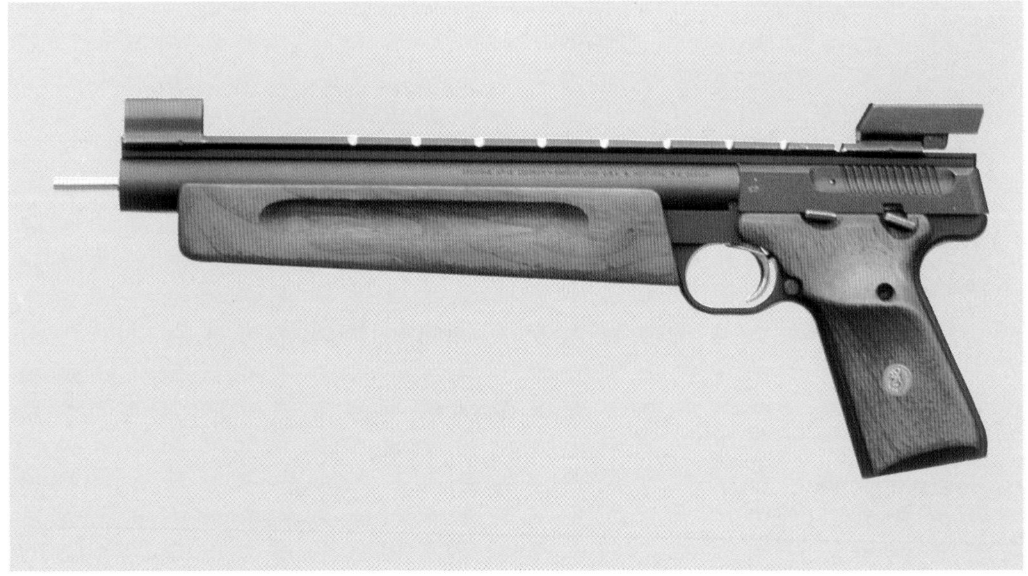

• material	: steel
• finish	: blued with golden trigger
• grips	: wood

Browning Buck Mark Varmint

TECHNICAL SPECIFICATIONS:

Calibre	: .22 LR
Trigger action	: single action
Magazine capacity	: 10 rounds
Locking mechanism	: blowback action
Weight	: 1360g
Length	: 355mm
Height	: 137mm
Barrel length	: 250mm
Trigger stop	: none
Sights	: without sight (on picture with scope)
Sight radius	: not relevant
External safety	: safety catch on left side frame
Internal safety	: slide safety

FEATURES:

• slide catch	: on left side frame
• magazine catch	: on left side frame, behind trigger guard
• material	: steel
• finish	: blued with golden trigger
• grips	: wood

Browning High Power (HP-35)

TECHNICAL SPECIFICATIONS:

Calibre	: 9mm Para
Trigger action	: single action
Magazine capacity	: 13 rounds
Locking mechanism	: FN Browning system
Weight	: 910g
Length	: 200mm
Height	: 132mm
Barrel length	: 118mm
Trigger stop	: no
Sights	: fixed
Sight radius	: 160mm
External safety	: safety catch on left side frame
Internal safety	: slide safety, half-cock safety, magazine safety

FEATURES:

• slide catch	: on left side frame
• magazine catch	: on left side frame, behind trigger guard
• material	: steel
• finish	: blued
• grips	: synthetic or wood

Browning High Power (HP-35) Competition

TECHNICAL SPECIFICATIONS:

Calibre : 9mm Para
Trigger action : single action
Magazine capacity : 13 rounds
Locking mechanism : FN Browning system
Weight : 990g
Length : 235mm
Height : 132mm
Barrel length : 152mm
Trigger stop : no
Sights : adjustable
Sight radius : 195mm
External safety : safety catch on left side frame
Internal safety : slide safety, half-cock safety, magazine safety

FEATURES:

- slide catch : on left side frame
- magazine catch : on left side frame, behind trigger guard
- material : steel
- finish : blued
- grips : synthetic

At the muzzle of this pistol the slide is lengthened with a barrel weight. Because of this, the sight radius is also extended. Browning also has a model with compensator holes in the slide extension (Model MK II Competition).

Browning MK II .40 S&W

TECHNICAL SPECIFICATIONS:

Calibre : .40 S&W
Trigger action : single action
Magazine capacity : 10 rounds
Locking mechanism : FN Browning system
Weight : 935g
Length : 200mm
Height : 132mm
Barrel length : 118mm
Trigger stop : none
Sights : fixed (sport: adjustable)
Sight radius : 160mm
External safety : ambidextrous safety catch on frame
Internal safety : slide safety, automatic firing-pin safety

FEATURES:

- slide catch : on left side frame
- magazine catch : on left side frame, behind trigger guard
- material : alloy frame, steel slide
- finish : blued
- grips : black synthetic

Browning MK II

TECHNICAL SPECIFICATIONS:

Calibre : 9mm Para
Trigger action : single action
Magazine capacity : 13 rounds
Locking mechanism : FN Browning system
Weight : 930g
Length : 200mm
Height : 132mm
Barrel length : 118mm
Trigger stop : none
Sights : fixed (sport: adjustable)
Sight radius : 160mm
External safety : ambidextrous safety catch on frame
Internal safety : slide safety, automatic firing-pin safety (after serial no. 245PR03101), magazine safety

FEATURES:

- slide catch : on left side frame
- magazine catch : on left side frame, behind trigger guard
- material : steel
- finish : blued
- grips : synthetic

Browning MK II Capitan

TECHNICAL SPECIFICATIONS:

Calibre : 9mm Para
Trigger action : single action
Magazine capacity : 13 rounds
Locking mechanism : FN Browning system
Weight : 980g
Length : 200mm
Height : 132mm
Barrel length : 118mm
Trigger stop : none
Sights : adjustable ladder sight for 50-500m
Sight radius : 160mm
External safety : ambidextrous safety catch on frame
Internal safety : slide safety, automatic firing-pin safety

FEATURES:

- slide catch : on left side frame
- magazine catch : on left side frame, behind trigger guard
- material : steel
- finish : blued
- grips : synthetic

Most Browning MKII-Capitan pistols have a slot in the rearside of the grip, into which a wooden carbine stock (annex holster) can be fitted.

Browning MK II Capitan Normandy Model 'June 6, 1944'

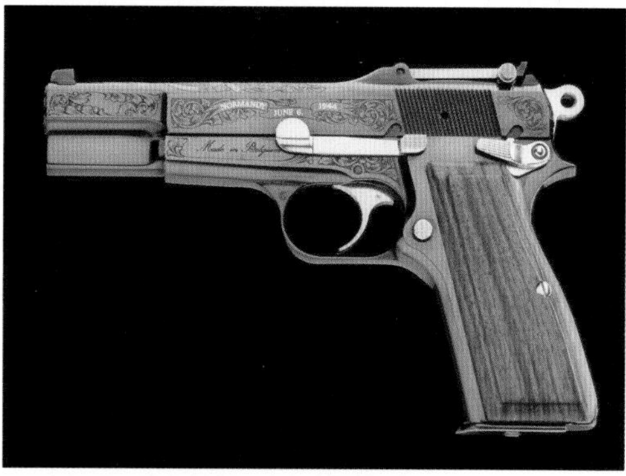

TECHNICAL SPECIFICATIONS:

Calibre : 9mm Para
Trigger action : single action
Magazine capacity : 13 rounds
Locking mechanism : FN Browning system
Weight : 980g
Length : 200mm
Height : 132mm
Barrel length : 118mm
Trigger stop : none
Sights : adjustable ladder sight for 50-500m
Sight radius : 160mm
External safety : ambidextrous safety catch on frame
Internal safety : slide safety, automatic firing-pin safety

FEATURES:

- slide catch : on left side frame
- magazine catch : on left side frame, behind trigger guard
- material : steel
- finish : blued, engraved, and with gold-plated operating elements
- grips : walnut

This pistol is a so-called "commemorative" model, with which the Allied landing on "D-Day" (Decision-Day: 6 June 1944) is commemorated.

Browning MK II Capitan 'Omaha Beach'

TECHNICAL SPECIFICATIONS:

Calibre : 9mm Para
Trigger action : single action
Magazine capacity : 13 rounds

Locking mechanism : FN Browning system
Weight : 980g
Length : 200mm
Height : 132mm
Barrel length : 118mm
Trigger stop : no
Sights : adjustable ladder sight for 50-500m
Sight radius : 160mm
External safety : ambidextrous safety catch on frame
Internal safety : slide safety, automatic firing-pin safety

FEATURES:

- slide catch : on left side frame
- magazine catch : on left side frame, behind trigger guard
- material : steel
- finish : nickel plated, engraved, and with gold-plated operating elements
- grips : walnut

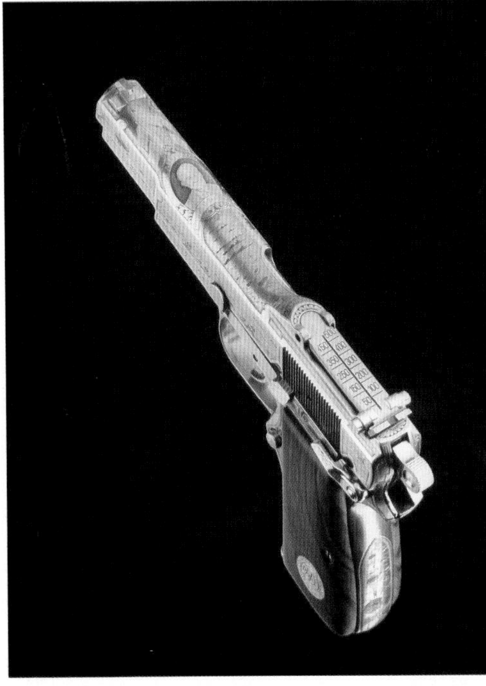

The portrait on top of the slide is of Dwight Eisenhower, combined with an overview of the battlefield at Omaha Beach (Normandy). On the grip is an engraving of the airborne troops

This pistol is a so-called "commemorative" model, with which the Allied landing of "D-Day" (Decision-Day: 6 June 1944) on Omaha Beach is commemorated.

Browning MK II Capitan Victory Model 'May 8, 1945'

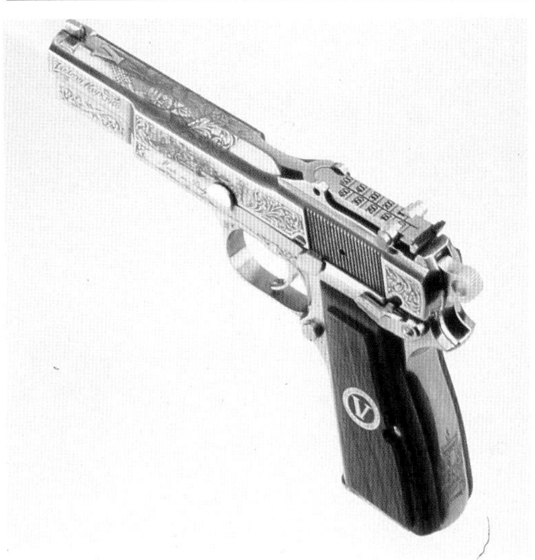

TECHNICAL SPECIFICATIONS:

Calibre : 9mm Para
Trigger action : single action
Magazine capacity : 13 rounds
Locking mechanism : FN Browning system
Weight : 980g
Length : 200mm
Height : 132mm
Barrel length : 118mm
Trigger stop : none
Sights : adjustable ladder sight for 50-500m
Sight radius : 160mm
External safety : ambidextrous safety catch on the frame
Internal safety : slide safety, automatic firing-pin safety

FEATURES:

- slide catch : on left side frame
- magazine catch : on left side frame, behind trigger guard
- material : stainless steel
- finish : stainless, engraved, and with gold-plated operating elements
- grips : walnut with angled "V" medallion

This pistol is a "commemorative" model, with which the end of the Second World War is commemorated.

Browning HP-MK II Practical

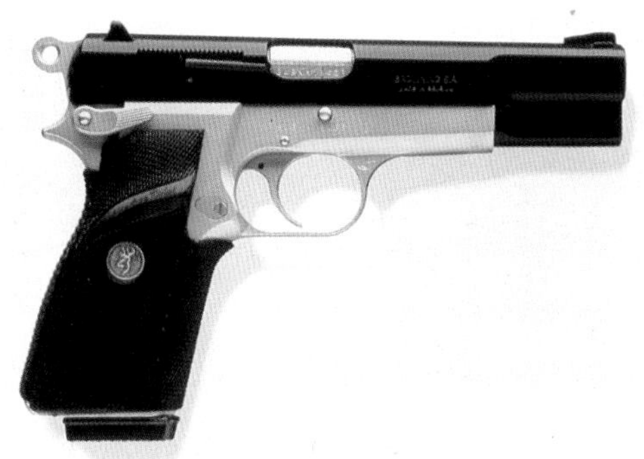

TECHNICAL SPECIFICATIONS:

Calibre	: 9mm Para
Trigger action	: single action
Magazine capacity	: 13 rounds
Locking mechanism	: FN Browning system
Weight	: 950g
Length	: 200mm
Height	: 132mm
Barrel length	: 118mm
Trigger stop	: none
Sights	: fixed
Sight radius	: 160mm
External safety	: ambidextrous safety catch on the frame
Internal safety	: slide safety, automatic firing-pin safety

FEATURES:

• slide catch	: on left side frame
• magazine catch	: left side, behind trigger guard
• material	: alloy frame, steel slide
• finish	: frame matt nickel plated, slide blued
• grips	: rubber Pachmayr or Browning

Browning MK II GP Renaissance

TECHNICAL SPECIFICATIONS:

Calibre	: 9 mm Para
Trigger action	: single action
Magazine capacity	: 13 rounds
Locking mechanism	: FN Browning system
Weight	: 930g
Length	: 200mm
Height	: 132mm
Barrel length	: 118mm
Trigger stop	: none
Sights	: fixed
Sight radius	: 160mm
External safety	: ambidextrous safety catch on the frame
Internal safety	: slide safety, automatic firing-pin safety (after serial no: 245PR03101), magazine safety

FEATURES:

• slide catch	: on left side frame
• magazine catch	: on left side frame, behind trigger guard
• material	: alloy frame, steel slide
• finish	: nickel plated and engraved with gold-plated trigger
• grips	: walnut

Browning MK II GP Silver Chrome Sport

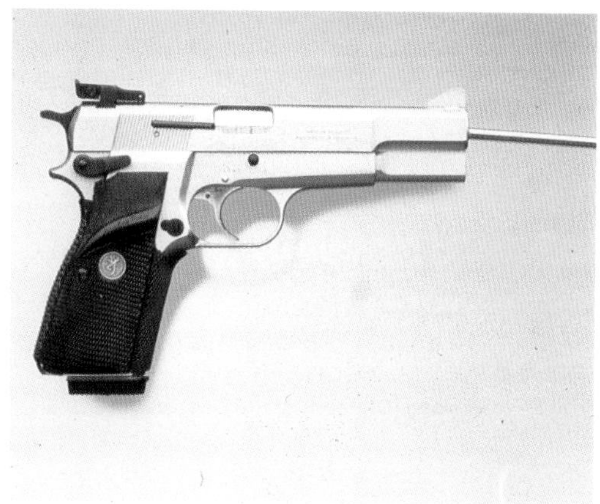

TECHNICAL SPECIFICATIONS:

Calibre	: 9mm Para
Trigger action	: single action

Magazine capacity : 13 rounds
Locking mechanism : FN Browning system
Weight : 950g
Length : 200mm
Height : 132mm
Barrel length : 118mm
Trigger stop : none
Sights : adjustable
Sight radius : 170mm
External safety : ambidextrous safety catch on the frame
Internal safety : slide safety, automatic firing-pin safety

FEATURES:

- slide catch : on left side frame
- magazine catch : on left side frame, behind trigger guard
- material : alloy frame, steel slide
- finish : matt, chrome plated
- grips : black rubber

Browning GP-MK III

TECHNICAL SPECIFICATIONS:

Calibre : 9mm Para
Trigger action : single action
Magazine capacity : 13 rounds
Locking mechanism : FN Browning system
Weight : 950g
Length : 200mm
Height : 132mm
Barrel length : 118mm
Trigger stop : neen
Sights : fixed
Sight radius : 160mm
External safety : ambidextrous safety catch on the frame
Internal safety : slide safety, automatic firing-pin safety

FEATURES:

- slide catch : on left side frame
- magazine catch : on left side frame, behind trigger guard
- material : alloy frame, steel slide
- finish : blued or in two-tone finish
- grips : black synthetic

Browning GP-MK III Sport

TECHNICAL SPECIFICATIONS:

Calibre : 9mm Para
Trigger action : single action
Magazine capacity : 13 rounds
Locking mechanism : FN Browning system
Weight : 950g
Length : 200mm
Height : 132mm
Barrel length : 118mm
Trigger stop : adjustable
Sights : adjustable
Sight radius : 165mm
External safety : ambidextrous safety catch on the frame
Internal safety : slide safety, automatic firing-pin safety

FEATURES:

- slide catch : on left side frame
- magazine catch : on left side frame, behind trigger guard
- material : alloy nickel-plated frame, stainless steel slide
- finish : stainless steel
- grips : Pachmayr 'Signature'

Calico pistols

The American California Instrument Company was founded in 1982 in Bakersfield, California. At first it designed and produced specialized tools for the oil industry. In 1985 the Calico gun line was introduced. Calico concentrates particularly on light automatic and semi-automatic guns with an unusually high magazine capacity. In 1985 the first prototype of a .22 LR carbine with a magazine capacity of 100 rounds was developed. This was followed in 1989 by a 50-round and a 100-round 9mm Para pistol and submachine-gun. The large magazine capacity is achieved by the use of a multi-row helical box magazine that is fixed on top of the gun.
The rows of cartridges are pushed forward by a spring and the rotating movements of the magazine axis.
The cartridges are pushed one by one inside the chamber of the barrel at the underside of the magazine.
During firing the helical rows with cartridges are pushed forward, because of the resulting space. This special feature has not yet been applied in firearms. It is true that Ruger has a similar magazine for its small-bore carbine, but that is only a rotating 10-round magazine and has no feeding movement towards the front. Unfortunately, Calico is the victim of the recent stricter gun laws in the USA.
Firearms with a magazine capacity of more than 10 rounds are not permitted on the civilian market. Calico is dependent on the orders of governmental services and on the export possibilities, because in most of Europe these guns are not restricted.

Calico .22 LR

TECHNICAL SPECIFICATIONS:

Calibre	: .22 LR
Trigger action	: single action
Magazine capacity	: 100 rounds
Locking mechanism	: blowback action
Weight	: 1700g
Length	: 455mm
Height	: 175mm
Barrel length	: 155mm
Trigger stop	: none
Sights	: rear flip sight, adjustable front post (windage and elevation)
Sight radius	: 290mm
External safety	: ambidextrous safety catch
Internal safety	: slide safety
FEATURES:	
• slide catch	: bolt catch on left side of trigger housing
• magazine catch	: none
• material	: stock, grip, and magazine made of high-impact composition, barrel and action made of steel
• finish	: black coating
• grips	: integrated

Calico 9 mm

TECHNICAL SPECIFICATIONS:

Calibre	: 9mm Para
Trigger action	: single action
Magazine capacity	: 50 of 100 rounds
Locking mechanism	: blowback action
Weight	: 2100g
Length	: 530mm
Height	: 178mm
Barrel length	: 155mm
Trigger stop	: none
Sights	: rear flip sight, adjustable front post (windage and elevation)
Sight radius	: 170mm
External safety	: ambidextrous safety catch
Internal safety	: slide safety
FEATURES:	
• slide catch	: bolt catch on left side of trigger housing
• magazine catch	: none

- material : stock, grip, and magazine made of high-impact composition, barrel and action made of steel
- finish : black coating
- grips : integrated

Casull revolvers

Until 1956 the .44 Magnum revolver was the heaviest handgun in the world. Around 1956, the young American gunsmith, Dick Casull from Utah, experimented with Colt Single-Action and Bisley revolvers. From these guns he developed a number of new calibres, like the .454 Casull. To begin with, he mostly converted Ruger Super Blackhawks to a five-round revolver in this heavy calibre.
Later on he produced complete revolvers in stainless steel. After some business failures, he founded the Freedom Arms Company in 1980, together with another gunsmith, in the town of Freedom in the State of Wyoming. His huge revolvers are used in the USA for hunting and silhouette shooting.
Freedom Arms produces several small and big revolver models, including a .22 LR revolver (introduced in 1990: the model 252 Casull) and a .357 Magnum: the .353 Casull, which was introduced in 1991.
The accuracy of both models surpasses many rifles or carbines. For the .454 Casull, a conversion cylinder is available in the calibres .45 Long Colt, .45 ACP, and .45 WM (Winchester Magnum). Casull also manufactures revolvers in calibre .44 Magnum, especially the silhouette model with a 10in barrel. The Freedom Arms range includes several models and finishes, such as the Casull Varmint Class, a .22 LR revolver with a 71/2in barrel and a total weight of 1550g, and the Casull Premiergrade in the calibres .357 Magnum, .44 Magnum, and .454 Casull-Magnum, as this calibre is now known. Furthermore, there is the Casull Fieldgrade in calibre .454 Casull-Magnum, especially built for hunting. In 1993 the Casull 555 model was introduced in the special pistol calibre .50 AE (Action Express).

Casull Fieldgrade

TECHNICAL SPECIFICATIONS:

Calibre	: .454 Casull-Magnum
Trigger action	: single action
Magazine capacity	: 5 rounds
Locking mechanism	: centre pin
Weight	: 1465g
Length	: 356mm
Height	: 135mm
Barrel length	: 190mm (71/2" barrel)
Trigger stop	: none
Sights	: adjustable micrometer rear sight

Sight radius	: 220mm
External safety	: none
Internal safety	: half-cock safety, loading-gate blocks with cocked hammer

FEATURES:

• thumb piece	: none
• material	: stainless steel
• finish	: matt stainless
• grips	: black composition or Pachmayr

Casull Premiergrade

TECHNICAL SPECIFICATIONS:

Calibre	: .454 Casull-Magnum, .44 Magnum of .357 Magnum
Trigger action	: single action
Magazine capacity	: 5 rounds
Locking mechanism	: centre pin
Weight	: 1465-1500g
Length	: 356mm
Height	: 135mm
Barrel length	: 190mm (71/2") or 120 mm (43/4")
Trigger stop	: no
Sights	: adjustable micrometer rear sight
Sight radius	: 230mm (71/2")
External safety	: none
Internal safety	: half-cock safety, loading-gate blocks with cocked hammer

FEATURES:

• thumb piece	: none
• material	: stainless steel
• finish	: stainless, matt, or high gloss
• grips	: wood or Pachmayr

Colt-pistolen

The American company, Colt, has been producing firearms for more than 160 years. To begin with, they only manufactured revolvers, but later they also produced semi-automatic pistols. John Moses Browning (1854-1926), from the State of Utah, was the designer of the locking mechanism that would come to be used all over the world. The famous Colt 1911 .45 ACP pistol was his design. The improved model, the Colt 1911-A1, had a service life of seventy years. Its successor is the Beretta model 92-F pistol in calibre 9mm Para. The Colt 1911-

A1 always performed, even under the most extreme circumstances. The operation levers are in the correct place for comfortable handling. In the models of the 'Series 80', Colt introduced an automatic firing-pin safety. The Colt 1911-A1 is known for its large number of variants, among them the Colt Government, Model MK I up to IV, and the models in 'Series 70' and 'Series 80'. In the first series a modified barrel bushing was used, and the firing-pin safety already mentioned was integrated into the latter. In 1991 Colt reintroduced the old army pistol in a newer version under the name of Colt 1991-A1. This pistol has the automatic firing-pin safety. Other models, derived from the Colt 1911-A1, can be roughly divided into three main types: the large Government model, the smaller Commander pistol-type, and the handy pocket model Officer's ACP. The main calibre of Colt has always been the .45 ACP cartridge, although the gun was made in other calibres as well, such as .455 (in the Second World War for Canada and other countries), 9mm Para, .38 Super, .41 Action Express, 10mm Auto, .40 S&W, .38 Special-Wadcutter (with a lengthened slide), and in a number of lesser known calibres for export purposes, such as the .30 Luger, 9mm Steyr, etc. The Colt Commander was introduced in 1949 and, since 1970, it has been known as the Colt Combat Commander. The Combat Commander also has a lightweight version, with a very strong alloy frame. This lightweight is only available in calibre .45 ACP and weighs only 765g. Around 1970, Colt brought out the Government with the model 'MK IV Series 70'. The original model had been given a number of improvements, among other things a new barrel bushing. Furthermore, the pistol was also produced in other calibres, such as the .38 Super and 9mm Parabellum.

Colt dominated a large part of the pistol market. Many shooters wanted special modifications of their Colt pistols to their own

specifications. Because Colt could not meet these demands, opportunities were created for numerous small and specialist gun shops which could provide such modifications. Among these were Swenson, Wilson, and Devel. In 1983, the next series of Colt pistols was announced, with the indication 'MK IV Series 80'. In these models not only was the rear sight improved but Colt also used the automatic firing-pin safety. Other Commander versions are the Commanding Officer and the Gold Cup Commander with an adjustable rear sight.
The National Match .45 ACP pistol was introduced by Colt in 1932. In 1933, Colt manufactured this pistol (derived from the Model 1911-A1) in calibre .45 ACP and called it the 'National Match'. In 1935, this gun was also produced in calibre .38 Super. Because of the pressures of the war effort during this time the National Match Model was pushed into the background, but was relaunched in 1957 under the name of the Colt Gold Cup National Match. The specific features of this Gold Cup model are the wide match trigger, with an adjustable trigger stop, a very good adjustable Colt-Elliason target rear sight, an enlarged ejection port in the slide, and a straight mainspring housing. Initially the postwar model was only available in calibre .45 ACP, but in 1961 the pistol was also introduced in calibre .38 Special-Wadcutter-Midrange. The different types within the National Match concept are designated as the Mark I, Mark II, etc. The Mark I was the "old" National Match, produced from 1933 until 1942. The National Match Mark II was manufactured by Colt in the period from 1957 to 1960. In 1960 its successor, the Mark III, was marketed in calibre .39 Special-Wadcutter. The production of the Gold Cup National Match 'Mark IV/Series 70' began in 1970, but the calibre was limited to .45 ACP. With this model the barrel bushing was changed, which led to improved accuracy. The Gold Cup was available in the blued Colt Blue or the high-polish nickel-
plated finish. Since the introduction of the Gold Cup National Match Mark IV/Series 80, the pistol has also been available in stainless steel (in either matt or high-gloss finish). Pistols from the Series 80 are provided with an automatic firing-pin safety.
Colt marketed a 10mm Auto pistol in 1987, derived from the .45 ACP Government, called the Colt Delta Elite. Another pistol of the Elite line is the Combat Elite, a fine-looking handgun with a stainless frame and a deep-blued slide. The match model in this series is the Colt Delta Gold Cup, with an adjustable rear sight and an adjustable trigger stop. In 1984 the Colt Firearms Company from Hartford, Connecticut, introduced its Colt Officer's ACP Mark IV/80. This is a compact version of the Colt 1911-A1, shortened in length and height. The pistol is provided with plenty of safety devices: the grip safety, a slide safety (the pistol cannot be fired if the slide is not closed completely), naturally, the safety catch, and an automatic firing-pin safety, which is lifted only if the trigger is pulled.
In 1988, Colt made a quantity of Officer's Match conversion sets. Such a set consisted of a stainless slide, a barrel, recoil springs and recoil-spring guide, and an Officer's ejector. If these parts were exchanged with those of the Gold Cup, the owner had an Officer's ACP on top of a Gold Cup frame and therefore still a cartridge capacity of seven rounds. Nowadays these sets are true collectors' items. Colt also made several versions of the Officer's ACP in blue and in a stainless finish. Colt even supplied a lightweight model with an alloy frame, which weighed only 680g. In 1990, a high-polish stainless Officer's ACP was introduced as the 'Ultimate Stainless'. In 1991, the Colt Double Eagle Officer's Model .45 ACP appeared. This is a compact Officer's version of the Double Eagle, which was introduced in 1990. The word "Double" stands for the double-action trigger system. This type has no traditional safety catch, but a decocking lever at the left side of the frame, just beneath the slide catch.
Colt also has a long history in small-bore pistols in calibre .22 LR. After the Second World War, Colt introduced the Colt Woodsman, later followed by the Targetsman, Challenger, and Huntsman. Furthermore, Colt built a .22 LR model of the Colt 1911-A1 pistol, called the Colt Ace. All pistols have long since disappeared from Colt's range of products. At the Shot Show 1994 in Dallas, Texas, Colt introduced a new .22 LR pistol by the name of Colt Cadet. Later this name was changed to Colt .22. This is a stainless steel pistol with a heavy ventilated barrel. The grip on which the trigger guard is attached is made by Pachmayr from a synthetic rubber. The location of the safety catch is somewhat unusual. It is placed at the rear of the frame. The push button must be pushed from right to left, through the frame, to secure the gun, and to shoot it is naturally pushed the other way. The magazine catch is situated at the right side of the frame, above the trigger guard. Furthermore, the pistol is provided with a slide catch. In 1995, Colt introduced a Colt .22 Target, with an adjustable rear sight.

Colt M1991 A-1

This Colt Model M1991-A1 is an original Colt 1911-A1, which since 1991 has again been produced by Colt

TECHNICAL SPECIFICATIONS:

Calibre	: .45 ACP
Trigger action	: single action
Magazine capacity	: 7 rounds
Locking mechanism	: Browning system
Weight	: 1077g
Length	: 216mm
Height	: 135mm
Barrel length	: 127mm
Trigger stop	: no
Sights	: fixed
Sight radius	: 165mm
External safety	: grip safety and safety catch
Internal safety	: slide safety, half-cock-safety, automatic firing-pin safety

FEATURES:

• slide catch	: on left side frame
• magazine catch	: on left side frame, behind trigger guard
• material	: steel
• finish	: matt blued
• grips	: hard rubber

Colt M1991 A1 Compact

TECHNICAL SPECIFICATIONS:

Calibre	: .45 ACP
Trigger action	: single action
Magazine capacity	: 6 rounds
Locking mechanism	: Browning system
Weight	: 964g
Length	: 184mm
Height	: 134mm
Barrel length	: 89mm
Trigger stop	: none
Sights	: fixed
Sight radius	: 133mm
External safety	: grip safety and safety catch
Internal safety	: slide safety, half-cock-safety, automatic firing-pin safety

FEATURES:

• slide catch	: on left side frame
• magazine catch	: on left side frame, behind trigger guard
• material	: steel
• finish	: matt blued
• grips	: hard rubber

Colt M1991 A1 Commander

TECHNICAL SPECIFICATIONS:

Calibre	: .45 ACP
Trigger action	: single action

Magazine capacity	:	7 rounds
Locking mechanism	:	Browning system
Weight	:	1021 gram
Length	:	197 mm
Height	:	135 mm
Barrel length	:	114 mm
Trigger stop	:	no
Sights	:	fixed
Sight radius	:	146 mm
External safety	:	grip safety and safety catch
Internal safety	:	slide safety, half-cock-safety, automatic firing-pin safety

FEATURES:

• slide catch	:	on left side frame
• magazine catch	:	left side frame, behind trigger guard
• material	:	steel
• finish	:	matt blued
• grips	:	hard rubber

Colt All American Model 2000

TECHNICAL SPECIFICATIONS:

Calibre	:	9 mm Para
Trigger action	:	double-action
Magazine capacity	:	15 rounds
Locking mechanism	:	Colt-rotating lock mechanism
Weight	:	935 gram
Length	:	191 mm
Height	:	147 mm
Barrel length	:	114 mm
Trigger stop	:	none
Sights	:	fixed, with low-light sights
Sight radius	:	162 mm
External safety	:	none
Internal safety	:	slide safety, automatic firing-pin safety

FEATURES:

• slide catch	:	on left side frame
• magazine catch	:	on left side frame, behind trigger guard
• material	:	steel slide, alloy or composition frame
• finish	:	blued
• grips	:	black composition

Colt .22

TECHNICAL SPECIFICATIONS:

Calibre	:	.22 LR
Trigger action	:	single-action
Magazine capacity	:	10 rounds
Locking mechanism	:	blowback action
Weight	:	950 gram
Length	:	219 mm
Height	:	122 mm
Barrel length	:	114 mm
Trigger stop	:	no
Sights	:	fixed
Sight radius	:	191 mm
External safety	:	push safety button on backstrap of frame
Internal safety	:	slide safety

FEATURES:

• slide catch	:	on left side frame, above centre of grip
• magazine catch	:	under frontside of grip
• material	:	stainless steel
• finish	:	stainless
• grips	:	monostock of black composition with integrated trigger guard

Colt .22 Target

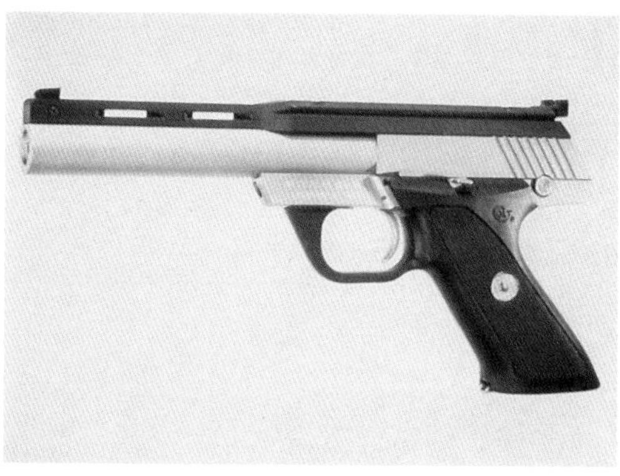

TECHNICAL SPECIFICATIONS:

Calibre : .22 LR
Trigger action : single action
Magazine capacity : 10 rounds
Locking mechanism : blowback action
Weight : 1148g
Length : 270mm
Height : 122mm
Barrel length : 152mm
Trigger stop : none
Sights : adjustable
Sight radius : 235mm
External safety : push safety button on backstrap of frame
Internal safety : slide safety

FEATURES:

- slide catch : on left side of frame, above centre of grip
- magazine catch : under front of grip
- material : stainless steel
- finish : stainless
- grips : monostock of black composition with integrated trigger guard

Colt Combat Commander Blue

TECHNICAL SPECIFICATIONS:

Calibre : .45 ACP
Trigger action : single action
Magazine capacity : 8 rounds
Locking mechanism : Browning/Colt system
Weight : 1020g
Length : 197mm
Height : 140mm
Barrel length : 108mm
Trigger stop : none
Sights : fixed
Sight radius : 146mm
External safety : safety catch on left side frame, grip safety
Internal safety : slide safety, half-cock-safety and from Series 80 with automatic firing-pin safety

FEATURES:

- slide catch : on left side frame
- magazine catch : on left side frame, behind trigger guard
- material : steel
- finish : blued
- grips : hard rubber

Colt Combat Commander Stainless

TECHNICAL SPECIFICATIONS:

Calibre : .45 ACP
Trigger action : single action
Magazine capacity : 8 rounds
Locking mechanism : Browning/Colt system
Weight : 1020g
Length : 197mm
Height : 140mm

Barrel length	:	108mm
Trigger stop	:	none
Sights	:	fixed
Sight radius	:	146mm
External safety	:	safety catch on left side frame, grip safety
Internal safety	:	slide safety, half-cock-safety and from Series 80 with automatic firing-pin safety

FEATURES:

• slide catch	:	on left side frame
• magazine catch	:	on left side frame, behind trigger guard
• material	:	stainless steel
• finish	:	matt stainless
• grips	:	hard rubber

Colt Combat Commander Double Eagle Stainless

TECHNICAL SPECIFICATIONS:

Calibre	:	.45 ACP
Trigger action	:	double action
Magazine capacity	:	8 rounds
Locking mechanism	:	Browning/Colt system
Weight	:	1020g
Length	:	197mm
Height	:	140mm
Barrel length	:	108mm
Trigger stop	:	none
Sights	:	fixed
Sight radius	:	146mm
External safety	:	safety catch on left side frame, grip safety
Internal safety	:	slide safety, half-cock-safety, automatic firing-pin safety

FEATURES:

• slide catch	:	on left side frame
• magazine catch	:	on left side frame, behind trigger guard
• material	:	stainless steel
• finish	:	matt stainless
• grips	:	hard rubber

Colt Combat Elite

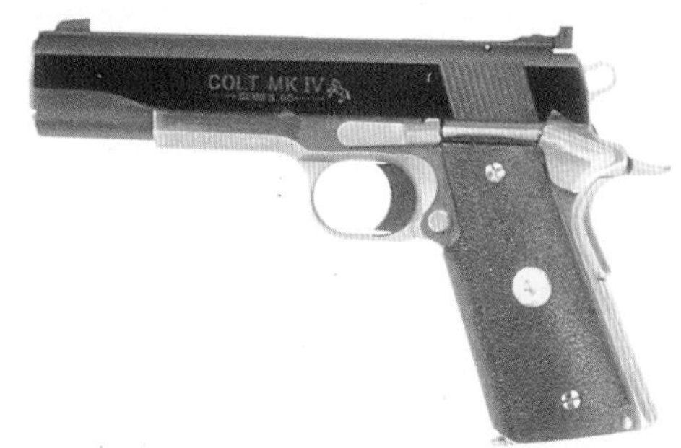

TECHNICAL SPECIFICATIONS:

Calibre	:	.45 ACP, .38 Super
Trigger action	:	single action
Magazine capacity	:	8 rounds (.38 Super: 9 rounds)
Locking mechanism	:	Browning/Colt system
Weight	:	1077g
Length	:	216mm
Height	:	134mm
Barrel length	:	127mm
Trigger stop	:	none
Sights	:	Accro adjustable sights
Sight radius	:	172mm
External safety	:	safety catch on left side frame, grip safety in backstrap of frame
Internal safety	:	slide safety, half-cock safety, automatic firing-pin safety

FEATURES:

• slide catch	:	on left side frame
• magazine catch	:	on left side frame, behind trigger guard
• material	:	steel or stainless steel
• finish	:	blued (Blue Elite), stainless (Delta Elite Stainless) or in "two-tone"-finish with blued slide and stainless frame
• grips	:	black hard rubber

Colt Delta Elite Blue

TECHNICAL SPECIFICATIONS:

Calibre	: 10mm Auto
Trigger action	: single action
Magazine capacity	: 8 rounds
Locking mechanism	: Browning/Colt system
Weight	: 1077g
Length	: 216mm
Height	: 135mm
Barrel length	: 127mm
Trigger stop	: no
Sights	: fixed three-dot combat sights
Sight radius	: 165mm
External safety	: safety catch on left side frame, grip safety in backstrap of frame
Internal safety	: slide safety, half-cock-safety, automatic firing-pin safety

FEATURES:

• slide catch	: on left side frame
• magazine catch	: on left side frame, behind trigger guard
• material	: steel
• finish	: blued
• grips	: black hard rubber

Colt Delta Elite Stainless

TECHNICAL SPECIFICATIONS:

Calibre	: 10mm Auto
Trigger action	: single action
Magazine capacity	: 8 rounds
Locking mechanism	: Browning/Colt system
Weight	: 1077g
Length	: 216mm
Height	: 135mm
Barrel length	: 127mm
Trigger stop	: none

Sights: fixed three-dot combat sights
Sight radius: 165 mm
External safety: safety catch on left side frame, grip safety in backstrap of frame
Internal safety: slide safety, half-cock-safety, automatic firing-pin safety

FEATURES:
- slide catch: on left side frame
- magazine catch: on left side frame, behind trigger guard
- material: stainless steel
- finish: stainless
- grips: black hard rubber

Colt Delta Elite Gold Cup Stainless

TECHNICAL SPECIFICATIONS:
Calibre: 10mm Auto
Trigger action: single action
Magazine capacity: 8 rounds
Locking mechanism: Browning/Colt system
Weight: 1106g
Length: 216mm
Height: 135mm
Barrel length: 127mm
Trigger stop: adjustable
Sights: Accro adjustable rear sight
Sight radius: 172mm
External safety: safety catch on left side frame, grip safety in backstrap of frame
Internal safety: slide safety, half-cock-safety, automatic firing-pin safety

FEATURES:
- slide catch: on left side frame
- magazine catch: on left side frame, behind trigger guard
- material: stainless steel
- finish: matt stainless slide top
- grips: black hard rubber

Colt Delta Elite Blue Laser

TECHNICAL SPECIFICATIONS:
Calibre: 10 mm Auto
Trigger action: single action
Magazine capacity: 8 rounds
Locking mechanism: Browning/Colt system
Weight: 1077g
Length: 216mm
Height: 135mm
Barrel length: 127mm
Trigger stop: none
Sights: fixed three-dot combat sights, on front side of trigger guard, and extra ALS-Laser aiming system
Sight radius: 165mm
External safety: safety catch on left side frame, grip safety in backstrap of frame
Internal safety: slide safety, half-cock-safety, automatic firing-pin safety

FEATURES:
- slide catch: on left side frame
- magazine catch: on left side frame, behind trigger guard
- material: steel
- finish: blued
- grips: black hard rubber

Colt Double Eagle

TECHNICAL SPECIFICATIONS:

Calibre	: .45 ACP
Trigger action	: double action
Magazine capacity	: 8 rounds
Locking mechanism	: Browning/Colt system
Weight	: 1106g
Length	: 216mm
Height	: 133mm
Barrel length	: 127mm
Trigger stop	: no
Sights	: fixed
Sight radius	: 165mm
External safety	: decocking lever on left side frame
Internal safety	: slide safety, automatic firing-pin safety

FEATURES:

• slide catch	: on left side frame
• magazine catch	: on left side frame, behind trigger guard
• material	: stainless steel
• finish	: stainless
• grips	: black Xenoy composition

Colt Gold Cup National Match

TECHNICAL SPECIFICATIONS:

Calibre	: .45 ACP
Trigger action	: single action
Magazine capacity	: 8 rounds
Locking mechanism	: Browning/Colt system
Weight	: 1106g
Length	: 216mm
Height	: 136mm
Barrel length	: 127mm
Trigger stop	: adjustable
Sights	: Colt Elliason microsights
Sight radius	: 172mm
External safety	: safety catch on left side frame, grip safety
Internal safety	: slide safety, automatic firing-pin safety, half-cock-safety

FEATURES:

• slide catch	: on left side frame
• magazine catch	: on left side frame, behind trigger guard
• material	: stainless steel
• finish	: high-gloss 'Ultimate' finish
• grips	: hard rubber

The Colt Gold Cup National Match pistol is also available in a matt stainless steel or in a blued finish.

Colt Government Model Blue Series 80 (1911 A1)

TECHNICAL SPECIFICATIONS:

Calibre	: .45 ACP
Trigger action	: single action
Magazine capacity	: 8 rounds
Locking mechanism	: Browning/Colt system
Weight	: 1077g
Length	: 216mm
Height	: 140mm
Barrel length	: 127mm
Trigger stop	: none
Sights	: fixed
Sight radius	: 165mm
External safety	: grip safety and safety catch
Internal safety	: slide safety, half-cock-safety, automatic firing-pin safety

FEATURES:

• slide catch	: on left side frame
• magazine catch	: on left side frame, behind trigger guard
• material	: steel
• finish	: blued
• grips	: hard rubber

Colt Government Model Bi-Tone Series 80 (1911 A1)

TECHNICAL SPECIFICATIONS:

Calibre	: .45 ACP
Trigger action	: single action
Magazine capacity	: 8 rounds
Locking mechanism	: Browning/Colt system
Weight	: 1077g
Length	: 216mm
Height	: 140mm
Barrel length	: 127mm
Trigger stop	: none
Sights	: fixed
Sight radius	: 165mm
External safety	: grip safety and safety catch
Internal safety	: slide safety, half-cock-safety, automatic firing-pin safety

FEATURES:

• slide catch	: on left side frame
• magazine catch	: on left side frame, behind trigger guard
• material	: steel slide, stainless steel frame
• finish	: blued slide, stainless frame
• grips	: hard rubber

Colt Government Model MK IV Compensator

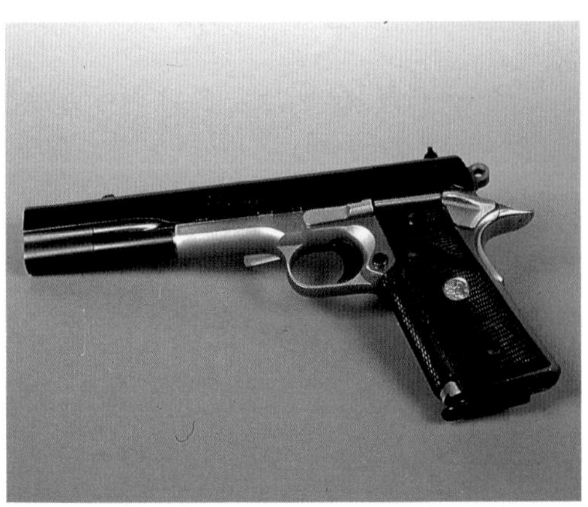

The model shown here has a compensator for reduction of the recoil and muzzle jump during fast-shooting sessions. Very often these models have an adjustable rear sight, which is not the case with this example.

TECHNICAL SPECIFICATIONS:

Calibre	: .45 ACP
Trigger action	: single action
Magazine capacity	: 8 rounds
Locking mechanism	: Browning/Colt system
Weight	: 1165g
Length	: 251 mm inc. compensator
Height	: 140mm
Barrel length	: 127mm
Trigger stop	: none
Sights	: fixed
Sight radius	: 165mm
External safety	: grip safety and safety catch
Internal safety	: slide safety, half-cock-safety, automatic firing-pin safety

FEATURES:

- slide catch : on left side frame
- magazine catch : on left side frame, behind trigger guard
- material : frame stainless steel, slide steel
- finish : bluede slide, stainless frame
- grips : hard rubber

Colt Government Model Stainless

TECHNICAL SPECIFICATIONS:

Calibre	: .45 ACP
Trigger action	: single action
Magazine capacity	: 8 rounds
Locking mechanism	: Browning/Colt system
Weight	: 1077g
Length	: 216mm
Height	: 140mm
Barrel length	: 127mm
Trigger stop	: none
Sights	: fixed three-dot sights
Sight radius	: 165mm
External safety	: grip safety and safety catch
Internal safety	: slide safety, half-cock-safety, automatic firing-pin safety

FEATURES:

- slide catch : on left side frame
- magazine catch : on left side frame, behind trigger guard
- material : stainless steel
- finish : matt stainless
- grips : hard rubber

This model is also available in high-gloss 'Ultimate' or blued finish.

Colt Government Model 38 Super Ultimate

TECHNICAL SPECIFICATIONS:

Calibre	: .38 Super
Trigger action	: single action
Magazine capacity	: 9 rounds
Locking mechanism	: Browning/Colt system
Weight	: 1106g
Length	: 216mm
Height	: 140mm
Barrel length	: 127mm
Trigger stop	: none
Sights	: fixed three-dot sights
Sight radius	: 165mm
External safety	: grip safety and safety catch
Internal safety	: slide safety, half-cock-safety, automatic firing-pin safety

FEATURES:

- slide catch : on left side frame
- magazine catch : on left side frame, behind trigger guard
- material : stainless steel
- finish : high-gloss 'Ultimate' stainless steel
- grips : hard rubber

This model is also available in a matt stainless or blued finish.

Colt 380 Government Model Stainless

TECHNICAL SPECIFICATIONS:

Calibre	: .380 ACP (9mm Short)
Trigger action	: single action
Magazine capacity	: 7 rounds
Locking mechanism	: Browning/Colt system
Weight	: 617g
Length	: 152mm
Height	: 115mm
Barrel length	: 83mm
Trigger stop	: none
Sights	: fixed
Sight radius	: 108mm
External safety	: safety catch on left side frame
Internal safety	: slide safety, automatic firing-pin safety

FEATURES:

• slide catch	: on left side frame
• magazine catch	: on left side frame, behind trigger guard
• material	: stainless steel
• finish	: matt stainless
• grips	: hard rubber

This model is also available in blues finish.

Colt Mustang Pocketlite Blue

TECHNICAL SPECIFICATIONS:

Calibre	: .380 ACP (9mm Short)
Trigger action	: single action
Magazine capacity	: 6 rounds
Locking mechanism	: Browning/Colt system
Weight	: 354g
Length	: 140mm
Height	: 110mm
Barrel length	: 70mm
Trigger stop	: none
Sights	: fixed
Sight radius	: 95mm
External safety	: safety catch on left side frame
Internal safety	: slide safety, automatic firing-pin safety

FEATURES:

• slide catch	: on left side frame
• magazine catch	: on left side frame, behind trigger guard
• material	: steel slide, alloy frame
• finish	: matt blued
• grips	: black hard rubber

Colt Mustang Pocketlite Stainless

TECHNICAL SPECIFICATIONS:

Calibre	: .380 ACP (9mm Short)
Trigger action	: single action
Magazine capacity	: 6 rounds
Locking mechanism	: Browning/Colt system
Weight	: 354g

Length	:	140mm
Height	:	110mm
Barrel length	:	70mm
Trigger stop	:	none
Sights	:	fixed
Sight radius	:	95mm
External safety	:	safety catch on left side frame
Internal safety	:	slide safety, automatic firing-pin safety

FEATURES:

• slide catch	:	on left side frame
• magazine catch	:	on left side frame, behind trigger guard
• material	:	steel slide, alloy frame
• finish	:	matt stainless slide, alloy frame with stainless Teflon coating
• grips	:	black hard rubber

Colt Mustang Stainless

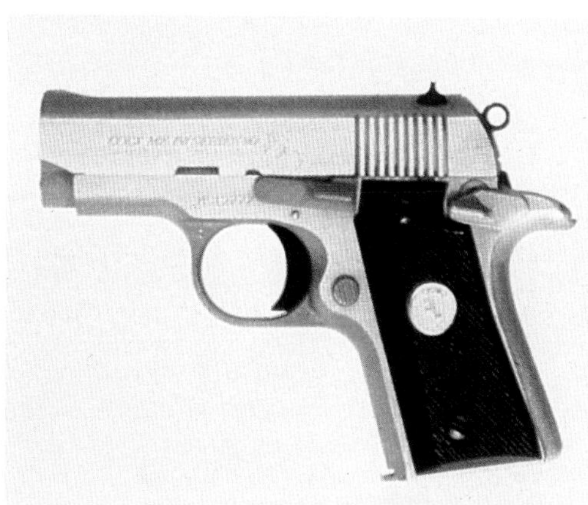

TECHNICAL SPECIFICATIONS:

Calibre	:	.380 ACP (9mm Short)
Trigger action	:	single action
Magazine capacity	:	6 rounds
Locking mechanism	:	Browning/Colt system
Weight	:	525g
Length	:	140mm
Height	:	110mm
Barrel length	:	70mm
Trigger stop	:	no
Sights	:	fixed
Sight radius	:	95mm
External safety	:	safety catch on left side frame
Internal safety	:	slide safety, automatic firing-pin safety

FEATURES:

• slide catch	:	on left side frame
• magazine catch	:	on left side frame, behind trigger guard
• material	:	stainless steel
• finish	:	matt stainless
• grips	:	black hard rubber

The Colt Mustang is also available with a blued finish.

Colt Officer's ACP Blue

TECHNICAL SPECIFICATIONS:

Calibre	:	.45 ACP
Trigger action	:	single action
Magazine capacity	:	6 rounds
Locking mechanism	:	Browning/Colt system
Weight	:	964g
Length	:	184mm
Height	:	131mm
Barrel length	:	89mm
Trigger stop	:	none
Sights	:	fixed three-dot low-light sights
Sight radius	:	133mm
External safety	:	safety catch, grip safety
Internal safety	:	slide safety, automatic firing-pin safety

FEATURES:

• slide catch	:	on left side frame
• magazine catch	:	on left side frame, behind trigger guard
• material	:	steel
• finish	:	blued
• grips	:	hard rubber

Colt Officer's ACP Stainless

TECHNICAL SPECIFICATIONS:

Calibre	: .45 ACP
Trigger action	: single action
Magazine capacity	: 6 rounds
Locking mechanism	: Browning/Colt system
Weight	: 964g
Length	: 184mm
Height	: 131mm
Barrel length	: 89mm
Trigger stop	: none
Sights	: fixed three-dot low-light sights
Sight radius	: 133mm
External safety	: safety catch, grip safety
Internal safety	: slide safety, automatic firing-pin safety

FEATURES:

• slide catch	: on left side frame
• magazine catch	: on left side frame, behind trigger guard
• material	: stainless steel
• finish	: high-gloss 'Ultimate' finish
• grips	: hard rubber

Colt-revolvers

The Colt Peacemaker dates from the year 1873, from the time of the "Wild West". Other names for the same gun are the Colt 1873 or the Single-Action Army. The firearms industry in America was already by that time dominated by Colt and Smith & Wesson. The latter was more particularly concerned with foreign military orders and Colt addressed itself more to the domestic market. The Peacemaker was designed for the American army and specifically for the cavalry. That is the origin of the name Single-Action Army. But this revolver (under the name of Peacemaker) was also very popular with the American public. The Colt was produced from 1873 until 1941, when Colt had to switch to war work. Up to that year, Colt had produced more than 357,000 pieces of this gun. After the Second World War, Colt received many requests to restart production, which eventually it did, partly under pressure from competition. From 1955, Colt produced about 250,000 Peacemakers. Colt has maintained production of this model, with some interruptions.
The gun is available in a high-polish nickel-plated finish and in a blued version. This revolver was made in about twenty-nine different calibres, from .22 LR up to .476 Eley. There are also some variations in the barrel length, such as the very long barrel of the so-called 'Buntline', the Frontier Six-Shooter, the Sheriff's Model, Frontier Scout, Storekeepers Model, Bisley Model, and many others. Nowadays this revolver is only available in the calibres .45 Long Colt and .44-40. The latter is actually an old carbine cartridge.

The Peacemaker still appeals to people's imagination. No Western movie can ever be made without this faithful six-shooter. This revolver was replicated many times by other manufacturers, with or without a licence. The Colt Officer's Model revolver was produced by Colt from 1904 until 1972, with interruptions during both world wars. Then the production capacity had to be used for more urgently needed weapons. Several versions of this model are made, including the Officer's Model Match, featured in this book, which is a special match model for target practice. The Officer's Model was made with barrel lengths of 4in, 4-1/2in, 5in, 6in, and even with a 7-1/2in barrel. The calibres varied from .22 LR, .22 WMR, .32 Colt, .38 Special, and .38 Short or Long Colt. The small-bore .22 LR model, which has only a 6in barrel and was produced from 1950, shoots very accurately, mainly because of the special attention each part has received during the production process. Because this model was never made in large numbers, they have a high collectors' value. Other names for the same model are: Colt Officer's Model, Colt Officer's Model Special, and Colt Officer's Model Target. After the Second World War, Colt had to rearrange its factories for the peacetime production of civil arms. After the war the costs of labour had risen, so that the management had to search for savings by cost-cutting means of production. In the 1960s, Colt decided to design a new revolver, based on the idea of economy. This became the Colt Trooper III,

introduced in 1969. This model was the replacement for the old Trooper model, that was in production from 1953 until 1967.
The Trooper Mark III was initially marketed in calibre .357 Magnum, but later other calibres followed, such as .22 LR, .22 WMR, and .38 Special. Derived models were the Lawman Mark III with a fixed rear sight, the Official Police and the Officer's Model Mark III, both in calibre .38 Special, and the Metropolitan revolver. The trigger system was derived from the Colt Python, except that, for this new model, a coiled mainspring was used in place of the Python leaf spring. These revolvers were available in several finishes, including blued, nickel plated, and, in a special version by the name of Colt Guard, a high-
gloss nickel. The Colt Trooper Mark V was introduced in 1982 as a replacement for the Mark III. The gun has the same design to a large extent, but Colt made some changes as regards technology. The most striking is the ventilated barrel rib. Moreover, the angle of the mainspring has been changed, so that the angle of impact of the hammer on the firing-pin is altered, namely, from 54 to 46 degrees. Because of this, the trigger pressure for the double-action mode was much improved.
The Colt Python occupies a special place as far as double-action revolvers are concerned. The Python is regarded as the 'Rolls-Royce' of American double-action revolvers. Anyone who has ever fired this handgun knows what is meant by this. As well as having a superior trigger action, the workmanship of this revolver is flawless. Colt introduced the Python in 1955 and it is the brainchild of Bill Henry, a Colt representative. The name of the revolver was in keeping with the Colt trend in those days. The first "snake" revolver dates back to 1951, the Cobra .38 Special. This tradition was continued in the later revolver models, such as the King Cobra and the Anaconda.

At first the Python was available in one barrel length only: 6in, but Colt had to diversify. Some years later Colt introduced a 4in Python Police model, followed by a 2-1/2in barrelled model, and for hunters an 8in barrel version was marketed in 1980. During the period of production, from 1955 up to the present, there have been several calibre experiments, which were put on hold after a while owing to a lack of success. In connection with this, there once was a Python in calibre .38 Special and even one in calibre .22 LR. Other changes mainly concern the exterior of the gun. The standard finish of the Python is in high-polished royal blue, but a nickel-plated model is also available, as well as a stainless-steel model, in a matt or high-gloss finish. The latter is, very appropriately, called the Colt Python Ultimate. These days the Python can be bought in the barrel lengths of 2_, 4, 6, and 8in.

At the end of 1985 Colt announced a new revolver model, the Colt King Cobra. Production should have started at the beginning of 1986, but Colt was affected by a strike, which caused great delay in manufacture. This was especially painful because Colt was celebrating its 150 years' jubilee. The revolver is made of stainless steel. As for the technology, this revolver resembles the Trooper MK V, but has its own shape. The barrel has an integrated barrel weight and in this way looks rather like the new Smith & Wesson revolvers, such as the Model 686. The King Cobra is available with a 2-1/2, 4, 6, and 8in barrel. The double-action gun has a special and adjustable Colt-Accro rear sight. Furthermore, the gun has a standard hard-rubber Pachmayr 'Gripper' grip. The cylinder is locked into the frame at the back. The mainspring is coiled instead of the old leaf type, like the Python and the Trooper MK III.

Strangely enough, Colt did not manufacture a revolver in the well-known calibre .44 Magnum. This was the case until 1990, about thirty-five years after the birth of the .44 Magnum cartridge, when the Colt Anaconda was introduced in this calibre. The market for this type of heavy revolver was previously dominated by Smith & Wesson, Ruger, and Dan Wesson. The Anaconda can be regarded as an enlarged version of the Colt Python. In 1993 the Anaconda also became available in calibre .45 Long Colt. This calibre goes back to the early days of Colt. The first Colt revolver in this old calibre was the Lightning in 1877. The Anaconda looks beautiful with its integrated barrel weight under the barrel itself and the ventilated barrel rib on top of it. The designation of this revolver is very striking, and in line with the Colt tradition. All the names of the modern Colt revolvers refer to snakes: the Python, the King Cobra, and now also the Anaconda, the biggest snake in the world. The grip, more like a hard-rubber stock of the Pachmayr type, but with the Colt logo (the rearing horse), has finger grooves to improve control of the gun during heavy recoil. At the end of 1992 Colt implemented a modification, which is not reflected in the serial number sequence or model designation. In the first series a specific depth of the lands and fields created an excessive lead contamination of the barrel. For the newer series this was modified.

Colt .38 SF-VI

TECHNICAL SPECIFICATIONS:

Calibre	: .38 Special
Trigger action	: double action
Magazine capacity	: 6 rounds
Locking mechanism	: centre pin, cylinder crane
Weight	: 595g
Length	: 178mm
Height	: 120mm
Barrel length	: 51mm
Trigger stop	: none
Sights	: fixed
Sight radius	: 102mm
External safety	: none
Internal safety	: transfer bar, cylinder blocks with cocked hammer

FEATURES:

• thumb piece	: on left side frame
• material	: stainless steel
• finish	: matt stainless
• grips	: hard rubber combat

Colt Anaconda Stainless 4"

TECHNICAL SPECIFICATIONS:

Calibre	: .44 Magnum
Trigger action	: double action
Magazine capacity	: 6 rounds
Locking mechanism	: rearside centre pin, cilinder crane
Weight	: 1333g
Length	: 245mm
Height	: 149mm
Barrel length	: 102mm
Trigger stop	: none
Sights	: adjustable rear sight
Sight radius	: 146mm
External safety	: none
Internal safety	: transfer bar, cylinder blocks with cocked hammer

FEATURES:

• cilinderpal	: on left side frame
• material	: stainless steel
• finish	: stainless
• grips	: hard rubber combat

Colt Anaconda Stainless 6"

TECHNICAL SPECIFICATIONS:

Calibre	: .44 Magnum, .45 Long Colt
Trigger action	: double action
Magazine capacity	: 6 rounds
Locking mechanism	: rearside centre pin, cylinder crane
Weight	: 1503g
Length	: 295mm
Height	: 149mm
Barrel length	: 152mm
Trigger stop	: none
Sights	: adjustable
Sight radius	: 197mm
External safety	: none
Internal safety	: transfer bar, cylinder blocks with cocked hammer

FEATURES:

• thumb piece	: on left side frame
• material	: stainless steel
• finish	: stainless
• grips	: hard rubber combat

Colt Anaconda Stainless 8"

TECHNICAL SPECIFICATIONS:

Calibre	: .44 Magnum, .45 Long Colt
Trigger action	: double action
Magazine capacity	: 6 rounds
Locking mechanism	: rearside centre pin, cylinder crane
Weight	: 1673g
Length	: 346mm
Height	: 149mm
Barrel length	: 203mm
Trigger stop	: no
Sights	: adjustable
Sight radius	: 248mm
External safety	: none
Internal safety	: transfer bar, cylinder blocks with cocked hammer

FEATURES:

• thumb piece	: on left side frame
• material	: stainless steel
• finish	: stainless
• grips	: hard rubber combat

 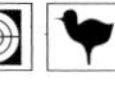

Colt Detective Special

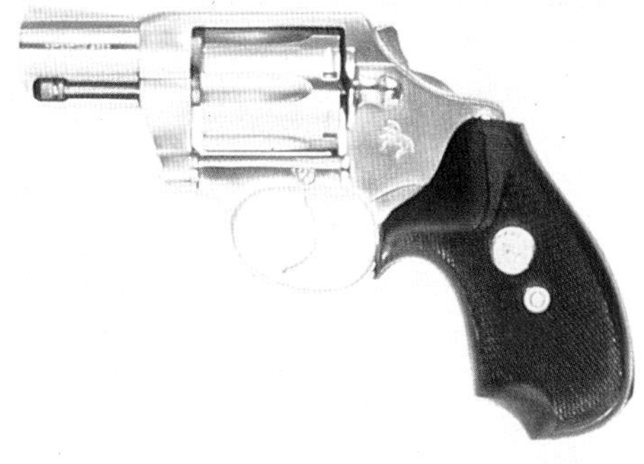

The Colt Detective Special revolver shown here is a custom model in DAO (Double-Action Only) with a hard-chrome finish

TECHNICAL SPECIFICATIONS:

Calibre	: .38 Special
Trigger action	: double action
Magazine capacity	: 6 rounds
Locking mechanism	: rearside centre pin, cylinder crane
Weight	: 595g
Length	: 178mm
Height	: 120mm
Barrel length	: 51mm
Trigger stop	: none
Sights	: fixed
Sight radius	: 95mm
External safety	: none

Internal safety : transfer bar, cylinder blocks with cocked hammer

FEATURES:

- thumb piece : on left side frame
- material : steel
- finish : blued
- grips : hard rubber combat

Colt King Cobra 4"

TECHNICAL SPECIFICATIONS:

Calibre : .357 Magnum
Trigger action : double action
Magazine capacity : 6 rounds
Locking mechanism : rearside of cylinder
Weight : 1191g
Length : 229mm
Height : 144mm
Barrel length : 102mm
Trigger stop : adjustable
Sights : adjustable Colt-Accro sight
Sight radius : 140mm
External safety : none
Internal safety : transfer bar, cylinder blocks with cocked hammer

FEATURES:

- thumb piece : on left side frame
- material : stainless steel
- finish : matt stainless
- grips : hard rubber combat

Colt King Cobra Ultimate 4"

TECHNICAL SPECIFICATIONS:

Calibre : .357 Magnum
Trigger action : double action
Magazine capacity : 6 rounds
Locking mechanism : rearside centre pin, cylinder crane
Weight : 1191g
Length : 229mm
Height : 144mm
Barrel length : 102mm
Trigger stop : adjustable
Sights : adjustable Colt-Accro sight
Sight radius : 140mm
External safety : none
Internal safety : transfer bar, cylinder blocks with cocked hammer

FEATURES:

- thumb piece : on left side frame
- material : stainless steel
- finish : high-gloss stainless
- grips : hard rubber combat

Colt King Cobra 6"

TECHNICAL SPECIFICATIONS:

Calibre : .357 Magnum
Trigger action : double action
Magazine capacity : 6 rounds
Locking mechanism : rearside centre pin, cylinder crane
Weight : 1304g
Length : 279mm

Height	: 144mm
Barrel length	: 152mm
Trigger stop	: adjustable
Sights	: adjustable
Sight radius	: 191mm
External safety	: none
Internal safety	: transfer bar, cylinder blocks with cocked hammer

FEATURES:

• thumb piece	: on left side frame
• material	: stainless steel
• finish	: matt stainless
• grips	: hard rubber combat

Colt Officer's Model Match

TECHNICAL SPECIFICATIONS:

Calibre	: .22 LR, .22 WMR, .38 Special/Colt, .32 Colt
Trigger action	: double action
Magazine capacity	: 6 rounds
Locking mechanism	: centre pin and cylinder crane
Weight	: 1075g (.22 LR)
Length	: 286mm (6")
Height	: 145mm
Barrel length	: 153mm
Trigger stop	: none
Sights	: adjustable
Sight radius	: 181mm
External safety	: none
Internal safety	: blocking bar, cylinder blocks with cocked hammer

FEATURES:

• thumb piece	: on left side frame
• material	: steel
• finish	: blued
• grips	: walnut

Colt Police Positive

TECHNICAL SPECIFICATIONS:

Calibre	: .38 Special
Trigger action	: double action
Magazine capacity	: 6 rounds
Locking mechanism	: backside centre pin, cylinder crane
Weight	: 709g
Length	: 229mm
Height	: 120mm
Barrel length	: 102mm
Trigger stop	: none
Sights	: fixed
Sight radius	: 140mm
External safety	: none
Internal safety	: transfer bar, cylinder blocks with cocked hammer

FEATURES:

• thumb piece	: on left side frame
• material	: steel
• finish	: blued
• grips	: hard rubber combat

Colt Python 4"

TECHNICAL SPECIFICATIONS:

Calibre	: .357 Magnum
Trigger action	: double action
Magazine capacity	: 6 rounds
Locking mechanism	: rearside centre pin, cylinder crane
Weight	: 1077g
Length	: 241mm
Height	: 140mm
Barrel length	: 102mm
Trigger stop	: none
Sights	: adjustable rear sight
Sight radius	: 140mm
External safety	: none
Internal safety	: transfer bar, cylinder blocks with cocked hammer

FEATURES:

- thumb piece : on right side frame
- material : steel, stainless steel
- finish : blued, nickel, matt or high-gloss stainless
- grips : hard rubber, Hogue Monogrip or walnut

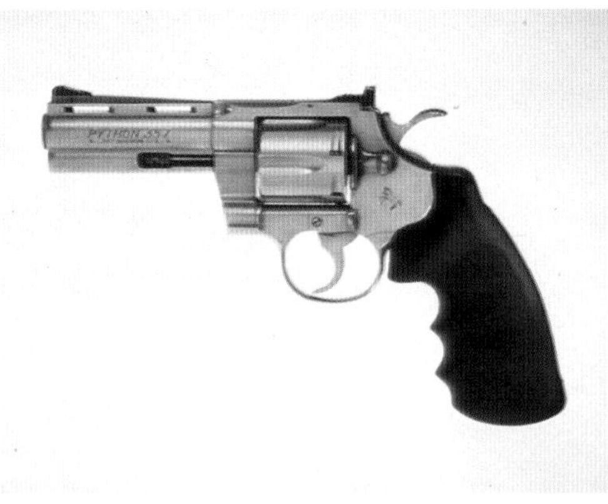

Colt Python 6"

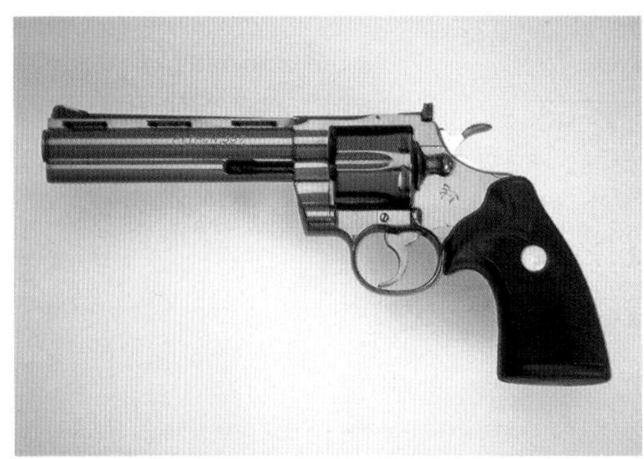

TECHNICAL SPECIFICATIONS:

Calibre	: .357 Magnum
Trigger action	: double action
Magazine capacity	: 6 rounds
Locking mechanism	: rearside centre pin, cylinder crane
Weight	: 1233g
Length	: 292mm
Height	: 140mm
Barrel length	: 152mm
Trigger stop	: none
Sights	: adjustable rear sight
Sight radius	: 191mm
External safety	: none
Internal safety	: transfer bar, cylinder blocks with cocked hammer

FEATURES:

- thumb piece : on right side frame
- material : steel, stainless steel
- finish : blued, nickel, matt or high-gloss stainless
- grips : match grips in wood or hard rubber

Colt Python 8"

TECHNICAL SPECIFICATIONS:

Calibre	: .357 Magnum
Trigger action	: double action
Magazine capacity	: 6 rounds
Locking mechanism	: back(side) centre pin, cylinder crane
Weight	: 1361g
Length	: 343mm
Height	: 140mm
Barrel length	: 203mm
Trigger stop	: none
Sights	: adjustable
Sight radius	: 241mm
External safety	: none
Internal safety	: transfer bar, cylinder blocks with cocked hammer

FEATURES:

- thumb piece : on right side frame
- material : steel, stainless steel
- finish : blued, nickel, matt or high-gloss stainless
- grips : match grip of wood or hard rubber

Colt Single Action Army (Peacemaker)

TECHNICAL SPECIFICATIONS:

Calibre	: .44-40
Trigger action	: single action
Magazine capacity	: 6 rounds
Locking mechanism	: fixed centre pin
Weight	: 1191g
Length	: 279mm
Height	: 130mm
Barrel length	: 140mm
Trigger stop	: none
Sights	: fixed
Sight radius	: 165mm
External safety	: none
Internal safety	: half-cock safety, blocking bar, loading gate blocks if hammer is cocked

FEATURES:

• thumb piece	: none: loading port in right side of frame
• material	: steel
• finish	: blued with flame-hardened frame or nickel
• grips	: wood or hard rubber 'Eagle' grips

Colt Single Action Army revolvers are very valuable collectors' items, even when they are of recent manufacture.

Colt Single Action Army (Peacemaker)

TECHNICAL SPECIFICATIONS:

Calibre	: .45 Long Colt
Trigger action	: single action
Magazine capacity	: 6 rounds
Locking mechanism	: fixed centre pin
Weight	: 1134g
Length	: 260mm
Height	: 130mm
Barrel length	: 121mm
Trigger stop	: none
Sights	: fixed
Sight radius	: 141mm
External safety	: none
Internal safety	: half-cock safety, blocking bar, loading gate blocks if hammer is cocked

FEATURES:

• thumb piece	: none: loading port in right side of frame
• material	: steel
• finish	: nickel or blued
• grips	: wood or hard rubber 'Eagle' grips

Coonan pistol

The Coonan .357 Magnum pistol was the first semi-automatic pistol to be introduced in this calibre. It was marketed in 1983 by the American Coonan Arms Company from St Paul in Minnesota. It is quite clear from the appearance of the gun that it was derived from the Colt 1911-A1 or Government. The most striking difference is that the Coonan was made of stainless steel from the start, whilst Colt was not yet producing stainless guns at that time. In the first model, later called Model A, the locking mechanism used is of the reliable Browning/Colt type. There is only one locking lug on top of the barrel, just before the chamber. Underneath the chamber of the barrel a movable hinged barrel link is attached, which enables the barrel (after the shot, after it travels backwards a little together with the slides) to drop, in order to abolish the lock-up between the barrel and slide. The Model B, introduced in 1986, is, according to Coonan itself, an improved model. For this pistol the Browning/FN locking system was used (like the High Power), which involves a fixed locking lug beneath the barrel, with only one lug on top of the barrel, which locks inside the corresponding locking grooves inside the slide. The pistol is adapted to the high gas pressure of the .357 Magnum cartridge. This can be seen, among other things, in the presence of a pin at the upper-rear side of the chamber, which locks into an extra cut-out in the slide. This prevents the bullet's rotation being passed on to the barrel. Coonan also thought of the comfort of the shooter. The short round hammer is small, whilst the rear side of the grip safety, the so-called beaver-tail, is deepened. Because of this the hammer head comes down neatly into this cut-out if it is cocked. In 1992 a shorter model was introduced, the Coonan Cadet, also in calibre .357 Magnum. This stainless pistol has a total length of 198mm and weighs around 1120g. For legal reasons the name Cadet was changed, shortly after introduction, to Coonan .357 Baby.

Coonan .357 Magnum

TECHNICAL SPECIFICATIONS:

Calibre	: .357 Magnum (exchangeable set for calibre .38 Special is available - no Wadcutters)
Trigger action	: single action
Magazine capacity	: 7 rounds
Locking mechanism	: Browning/FN-system
Weight	: 1190g (empty)
Length	: 226mm
Height	: 150mm
Barrel length	: 125mm
Trigger stop	: none
Sights	: adjustable Bo-Mar sights
Sight radius	: 182mm
External safety	: safety catch on left side frame
Internal safety	: slide safety, half-cock safety, grip safety (Colt system)

FEATURES:

• slide catch	: on left side frame
• magazine catch	: on left side frame, behind trigger guard
• material	: stainless steel; special model with alloy frame is available
• finish	: combined matt/high-gloss stainless
• grips	: walnut

CZ-pistols

The former Czechoslovakia has a long tradition in the field of firearms. In 1952 the bolt-locking roller system was already being used in the VZ/52 pistol, long before the well-known Heckler & Koch introduced this system into the free world. This type of locking mechanism was designed by the Czech gunsmith Budichowsky, the same man who developed the famous Korriphila HSP-701 pistol. The CZ-75 was introduced in 1975 and is derived from the High Power design of FN-Browning, although the CZ designers rebuilt the system into a double-action pistol.
In the times of the "Cold War" and the "Iron Curtain", this handgun was responsible for a lot of foreign currency, even though the gun could not be imported into the USA at that time. As a weapon of the Warsaw Pact, this pistol did not play a large role because the handguns of those armies were based upon the calibre 9mm Makarov, 7.62mm Tokarev, and 5.45mm Russian.
The pistol has several submodels, such as the CZ-75-Compact. This thirteen-shot compact pistol has an overall length of 182mm and a height of 129mm. Furthermore, there is a fully automatic version with a lengthened barrel with integrated compensator.
Several years ago another model was added, the CZ-75 Semi-Compact, with dimensions between the standard and compact versions. This latest model is a fifteen-round pistol. Some years ago a number of special finishes of the CZ-75 were marketed, mainly by the German wholesale and retail firearms company of Frankonia. These models have adjustable rear sights, chrome-plated frames, and there is even a special match model. The CZ-factory has a

consistent way of naming their pistols. This name is mainly linked to the year of introduction. This indicates that the CZ-85 pistol was marketed for the first time in 1985.

This is also a double-action pistol, with a strong resemblance to its predecessor, the CZ-75, which is still in production. The differences compared with the CZ-75 are

- an ambidextrous safety catch;
- an ambidextrous slide catch; and
- an automatic firing-pin safety.

The CZ-85 is produced in some submodels, the CZ-85 Standard and the CZ-85 Combat. The latter has a fully adjustable rear sight. The latest models are the CZ-100 and the compact CZ-101. The frame of these pistols is made of a high-impact synthetic material.
The CZ-100 has a double-stack magazine for thirteen rounds of 9mm Para, whilst the magazine of the CZ-101 has a single row of seven rounds.

CZ 75

TECHNICAL SPECIFICATIONS:

Calibre	: 9mm Para, 9x21 IMI or .40 S&W
Trigger action	: double action
Magazine capacity	: 15 rounds
Locking mechanism	: Browning system
Weight	: 1000g
Length	: 206mm
Height	: 138mm
Barrel length	: 120mm
Trigger stop	: none
Sights	: fixed or adjustable
Sight radius	: 161mm

External safety	: safety catch on left side frame
Internal safety	: slide safety, half-cock safety,
FEATURES:	
• slide catch	: on left side frame, behind trigger guard
• magazine catch	: ambidextrous behind trigger guard
• material	: steel
• finish	: blued, matt black coating or mattnickel slide or frame
• grips	: black composition or wood

CZ 75 Compact

TECHNICAL SPECIFICATIONS:

Calibre	: 9 mm Para
Trigger action	: double action
Magazine capacity	: 13 rounds (Compact); 15 rounds (SC)
Locking mechanism	: Browning system
Weight	: 920g (C); 960g (SC)
Length	: 186mm
Height	: 128mm (C); 138mm (SC)
Barrel length	: 100mm
Trigger stop	: no
Sights	: fixed
Sight radius	: 141mm
External safety	: safety catch on left side frame
Internal safety	: slide safety, half-cock safety, automatic firing-pin safety (special order)

FEATURES:

• slide catch	: left side frame, behind trigger guard
• magazine catch	: on left side frame, behind trigger guard
• material	: steel
• finish	: blued or matt-black coating
• grips	: black composition or wood

CZ 75 Semi-Compact

TECHNICAL SPECIFICATIONS:

Calibre	: 9mm Para
Trigger action	: double action
Magazine capacity	: 15 rounds
Locking mechanism	: Browning system
Weight	: 960g
Length	: 186mm
Height	: 138mm
Barrel length	: 100mm
Trigger stop	: none
Sights	: fixed
Sight radius	: 141mm
External safety	: safety catch on left side frame
Internal safety	: slide safety, half-cock safety, automatic firing-pin safety (special order)

FEATURES:

• slide catch	: left side frame, behind trigger guard
• magazine catch	: on left side frame, behind trigger guard
• material	: steel
• finish	: blued or matt-chrome frame
• grips	: black composition or wood

CZ 83

TECHNICAL SPECIFICATIONS:

Calibre	: .380 ACP or .32 ACP (as model CZ-82 also available in calibre 9 mm Makarov)
Trigger action	: double action
Magazine capacity	: 12 rounds (.380); 15 rounds (.32)
Locking mechanism	: blowback action
Weight	: 800g
Length	: 172mm
Height	: 127mm
Barrel length	: 96mm
Trigger stop	: none
Sights	: fixed
Sight radius	: 123mm
External safety	: ambidextrous safety catch on frame
Internal safety	: slide safety, automatic firing-pin safety

FEATURES:

• slide catch	: on left side frame
• magazine catch	: ambidextrous, behind trigger guard
• material	: steel
• finish	: blued
• grips	: walnut

CZ 85

TECHNICAL SPECIFICATIONS:

Calibre	: 9mm Para
Trigger action	: double action
Magazine capacity	: 15 rounds
Locking mechanism	: Browning system

Weight : 1000g
Length : 206mm
Height : 138mm
Barrel length : 120mm
Trigger stop : none (available on CZ 85 Combat)
Sights : fixed or adjustable (Combat model)
Sight radius : 161mm
External safety : ambidextrous safety catch on frame
Internal safety : slide safety, automatic firing-pin safety

FEATURES:

- slide catch : ambidextrous on frame
- magazine catch : left side frame, behind trigger guard
- material : steel
- finish : blued or two-tone finish
- grips : black composition or wood

The special model, the CZ 85 Champion, is available in the calibres 9mm Para or .40 S&W, has a factory compensator and a special single-action match (tuned) trigger.

CZ 100/CZ 101

TECHNICAL SPECIFICATIONS:

Calibre : 9mm Para, .40 S&W
Trigger action : double-action-only (DAO)
Magazine capacity : CZ 100: 13 rounds (9mm Para); 10 rounds (.40 S&W); CZ 101: 7 rounds (9mm Para); 6 rounds (.40 S&W)
Locking mechanism : Browning system
Weight : CZ 100: 680g; CZ 101: 670g
Length : 177mm
Height : 126mm
Barrel length : 95mm
Trigger stop : no
Sights : fixed
Sight radius : 148mm
External safety : none
Internal safety : slide safety, automatic firing-pin safety

FEATURES:

- slide catch : on left side frame
- magazine catch : ambidextrous, behind trigger guard
- material : composition frame, steel slide
- finish : matt-black coating
- grips : integrated composition frame/stock

On top of the slide, just behind the ejection port, a characteristically shaped hook is attached, with which the pistol can be cocked and loaded against a solid object, single-handed.

CZ Grand revolver

TECHNICAL SPECIFICATIONS:

Calibre : .22 LR
Trigger action : double action
Magazine capacity : 6 rounds
Locking mechanism : centre pin
Weight : 870g
Length : 265mm
Height : 146mm
Barrel length : 152mm (6"-barrel)
Trigger stop : no
Sights : windage adjustable rear sight
Sight radius : 195mm
External safety : none

Internal safety	:	blocking bar, cylinder blocks with cocked hammer

FEATURES:

• thumb piece	:	on left side frame
• material	:	alloy frame, steel barrel and cylinder
• finish	:	blued
• grips	:	walnut

Daewoo-pistolen

Daewoo (pronounced "Dayoo") is an extremely large Asian conglomerate. The concern includes automobiles, shipping, mining, electronics, machinery, and weapons. The Daewoo pistols have been produced for several years by the Korean factory, Daewoo Precision Industries Ltd in Seoul. The DP-51, a thirteen-shot pistol in calibre 9mm Para, has a somewhat strange trigger system, described by the manufacturer as the 'Tri-Action'.
The pistol can be fired in three different modes. The first is the normal double-action technique. The gun is not cocked, and there is a cartridge in the chamber. By pulling the trigger the hammer is first cocked, subsequently released, and the gun is fired. The second method is the usual single-action mode for continuous shooting.

The pistol will recycle after the first shot, so the hammer stays in a cocked position. With this pistol there is also a third mode. First of all the gun is loaded and cocked. Then the hammer can be lowered with the thumb to a rest position.

The hammer is uncocked, but the mainspring stays under tension. If the gun has to be fired, only a light trigger pull will be necessary to topple the hammer over again and fire the pistol. This system is also called the Fast Action or Selective Action by some other manufacturers.

The barrel of this pistol is throated, which enables a good fit within the slide and this will assist accuracy. The pistol is sold with a second magazine and a magazine loader to facilitate the loading of the magazine. In 1993 a compact thirteen-round version of the DP-51, the DP-51 Compact, was introduced. That same year another calibre was introduced, the .40 S&W, and the Daewoo pistol DH-40.

Daewoo DP-51

TECHNICAL SPECIFICATIONS:

Calibre	: DP-51: 9mm Para; DH-40: .40 S&W
Trigger action	: FA (Fast-Action)
Magazine capacity	: 13 rounds
Locking mechanism	: FN-Browning system
Weight	: 800g
Length	: 190mm
Height	: 133mm
Barrel length	: 105mm
Trigger stop	: no
Sights	: windage adjustable
Sight radius	: 142mm
External safety	: ambidextrous safety catch on frame
Internal safety	: slide safety, automatic firing-pin safety

FEATURES:

• slide catch	: on left side frame
• magazine catch	: on left side frame, behind trigger guard
• material	: steel slide, alloy frame
• finish	: black parkerized
• grips	: black synthetic material

Erma

The German company Erma, short for Erfurther Maschinenfabrik (Machinery Factory Erfurth) from Dachau, was founded in 1949. Erma owes its success mainly to producing copies of famous pistols. In this connection the company manufactures small-bore versions of the Luger P08 pistol in several models and also of the Walther PP and PPK pistols. Moreover, Erma has an excellent small-bore .22 LR conversion system for the Luger/Mauser P08 pistol. Erma is also doing good business in the field of carbines, such as the .22 LR version of the Winchester, the .30-M1 Carbine, Model EM-1, and several models of the Winchester lever-action "Wild-West" carbines (model EG-712). In the course of time, Erma has produced a great number of revolver models in blued and stainless steel in the calibres .22 LR up to .357 Magnum. Their special match revolver in the calibres .22 LR, .32 S&W Long, and .357 Magnum – complete with ergonomic grip with adjustable palm rest – and the models ER-773-Match and ER-772-Match are quite famous, at least in northern Europe. At the beginning of 1980, a match pistol was developed, which was eventually marketed in 1985.

This pistol, called the ESP-85A, can be obtained with a conversion kit for calibre .32 S&W Long. In 1989, a second and shorter model followed as a so-called hunting model. In the mean time the basic pistol has had a couple of modifications, following comments from shooters and hunters.

The first involved the adjustability of the trigger. The appearance of the gun was modified, too, from a high polish to a more matt finish.

The butt plate of the magazine was provided with a slant synthetic buffer and the trigger was reshaped. In 1994 the ESP-85 Junior was introduced. This model is a simple version of the standard match pistol. The muzzle end is rounded. For that reason the extra muzzle weights, suitable for the standard model, cannot be fitted to the junior model.

Erma EP 882

TECHNICAL SPECIFICATIONS:

Calibre	: .22 LR
Trigger action	: double action
Magazine capacity	: 8 rounds
Locking mechanism	: blowback action
Weight	: 800g (Sport)
Length	: 227mm (Sport)
Height	: 122mm
Barrel length	: 152mm
Trigger stop	: none
Sights	: adjustable (Sport)
Sight radius	: 165mm
External safety	: safety catch on left side of slide
Internal safety	: slide safety, magazine safety

FEATURES:

• slide catch	: on left side frame
• magazine catch	: in heel of grip
• material	: steel
• finish	: blued
• grips	: black composition

Erma ESP-85 A-HV Sport

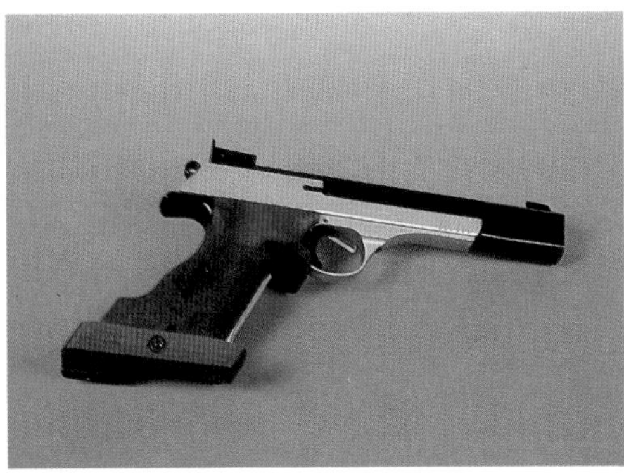

TECHNICAL SPECIFICATIONS:

Calibre	: .22 LR (exchange set for calibre .32 S&W Long)
Trigger action	: single action
Magazine capacity	: 8 rounds
Locking mechanism	: blowback action
Weight	: 1140g (ESP-85 A)
Length	: 255mm
Height	: 142mm
Barrel length	: 153mm
Trigger stop	: adjustable (1000-1360g)
Sights	: adjustable micrometer rear sight
Sight radius	: 165mm
External safety	: safety catch on left side of slide
Internal safety	: slide safety, magazine safety

FEATURES:

• slide catch	: on left side frame
• magazine catch	: in heel of grip
• material	: steel
• finish	: matt hard-chrome frame, blued steel slide
• grips	: ergonomic stock

Erma ESP-85 A Sport

TECHNICAL SPECIFICATIONS:

Calibre	: .22 LR (exchange set for calibre .32 S&W Long)
Trigger action	: single action
Magazine capacity	: 8 rounds
Locking mechanism	: blowback action
Weight	: 1140g (ESP-85 A)
Length	: 255mm
Height	: 142mm
Barrel length	: 153mm
Trigger stop	: adjustable (1000-1360 g)
Sights	: adjustable micrometer rear sight
Sight radius	: 165mm
External safety	: safety catch on left side of slide
Internal safety	: slide safety, magazine safety

FEATURES:

• slide catch	: on left side frame
• magazine catch	: in heel of grip
• material	: steel
• finish	: blued
• grips	: ergonomic stock

At the moment the ESP-85A pistol is available in three different models:

- ESP-85A Standard: blued finish with wooden match grip;
- ESP-85A Hunting: simple finish with simple adjustable rear sight;

- ESP-85A Sport: micrometer rear sight and ergonomic stock with adjustable palm rest.

Fas

Over the years the Italian company, Fabbrica Armi Sportivi, FAS for short, has produced several match pistols, at first under the name of Igi Domino and later under their own brand: FAS. As a matter of fact, FAS is not a single arms factory, but a joint venture between small arms businesses and gunsmiths from the Italian region of Brescia.

From 1986, FAS manufactured the model 602 in calibre .22 LR and the same pistol in calibre .32 S&W Long as the model 603. A new model, the 607 in calibre .22 LR, was introduced at the end of 1993.

The FAS handguns are typical small-bore match pistols and come into the same category as the Walther GSP, the Unique, and others. The models have an extremely low line of sight, which means the weapon system hardly sticks up above the shooting hand. The recoil during firing does not produce any muzzle flip, but only a backward effect. The most striking feature of the FAS pistols is the fact that the magazine is loaded into the pistol from the top of the slide.

Fas Model SP 602

TECHNICAL SPECIFICATIONS:

Calibre	: .22 LR
Trigger action	: single action
Magazine capacity	: 5 rounds
Locking mechanism	: blowback action
Weight	: 1050g
Length	: 285mm
Height	: 135mm
Barrel length	: 142mm
Trigger stop	: adjustable
Sights	: adjustable
Sight radius	: 220mm
External safety	: safety catch on left side frame
Internal safety	: slide safety

FEATURES:

• slide catch	: only manual
• magazine catch	: left side frame, behind trigger guard
• material	: steel
• finish	: blued
• grips	: match grip with adjustable palm rest

FEG pistols

For decades the FEG company has manufactured a number of pistol models in Budapest, Hungary.
FEG stands for Fegyver es Gazkeszuelekgyara, an arms and machinery factory. The FEG model FP9 bears a strong resemblance to the FN-Browning High Power HP35 pistol. The FP9 has a ventilated rib on top of the slide, into which the sights are integrated. Another model, the FP, is not identical to the High Power. There are some differences, the main one being that the FP has a double-action trigger system. Instead of designing a completely new pistol, the Hungarians combined the technique of Smith & Wesson with that of the High Power. Another variation, compared with the HP35, is the differently shaped hammerspur, which is somewhat rounded. Furthermore, the FP9 has a shortened slide catch. The latest FEG pistol, the P9R model, looks like a combination of the High Power and the Smith & Wesson model 59 pistol.
The safety/decock lever of the P9R is situated at the left side of the slide. The pistol was developed and produced for the Hungarian army in calibre 9mm Para, a remarkable calibre for a then Warsaw Pact force. In the USA the gun was marketed under the name of MBK-9HP.
The pistol is provided with a combined safety and decocking lever which blocks the firing-pin and decocks the hammer. The P9R was introduced in 1985 and is sold in Western Europe by Mauser as the Mauser 90-DA.

At the end of 1993 FEG introduced a similar double-action pistol in calibre .45 ACP, especially for the North and South American markets under the model name of GKK45.

FEG 22LR DA

TECHNICAL SPECIFICATIONS:

Calibre	: .22 LR
Trigger action	: double action
Magazine capacity	: 6 rounds
Locking mechanism	: blowback action
Weight	: 530g
Length	: 157mm
Height	: 110mm
Barrel length	: 86mm
Trigger stop	: no
Sights	: fixed
Sight radius	: 115mm
External safety	: combined decock/safety catch on left side of slide
Internal safety	: slide safety

FEATURES:

• slide catch	: on left side frame
• magazine catch	: on frame, above trigger guard
• material	: alloy frame, steel slide
• finish	: blued
• grips	: black composition

FEG 45ACP DA

TECHNICAL SPECIFICATIONS:

Calibre	: .45 ACP
Trigger action	: double action
Magazine capacity	: 8 rounds
Locking mechanism	: improved Browning system
Weight	: 1120g
Length	: 210mm
Height	: 147mm
Barrel length	: 119mm
Trigger stop	: no
Sights	: fixed
Sight radius	: 165mm
External safety	: combined decock/safety catch on slide
Internal safety	: combined decock/safety catch on slide, half-cock safety

FEATURES:

• slide catch	: on left side frame
• magazine catch	: on left side frame, behind trigger guard
• material	: steel
• finish	: blued
• grips	: wood

FEG BR61 DA

TECHNICAL SPECIFICATIONS:

Calibre	: .380 ACP (9mm Short)
Trigger action	: double action
Magazine capacity	: 6 rounds
Locking mechanism	: Browning action
Weight	: 530g
Length	: 157mm
Height	: 104mm
Barrel length	: 86mm
Trigger stop	: none
Sights	: fixed
Sight radius	: 115mm
External safety	: combined decock/safety catch on left side of slide
Internal safety	: slide safety

FEATURES:

• slide catch	: on left side frame
• magazine catch	: on frame, above trigger guard
• material	: steel slide, alloy frame
• finish	: blued
• grips	: black composition or wood

FEG B9R DA

TECHNICAL SPECIFICATIONS:

Calibre	: .380 ACP (9mm Short)
Trigger action	: double action
Magazine capacity	: 15 rounds
Locking mechanism	: Browning system
Weight	: 700g
Length	: 174mm
Height	: 133mm
Barrel length	: 101mm
Trigger stop	: none
Sights	: fixed
Sight radius	: 133mm
External safety	: combined decock/safety catch on left side of slide
Internal safety	: slide safety

FEATURES:

• slide catch	: on left side frame
• magazine catch	: on left side frame, behind trigger guard
• material	: steel slide, alloy frame
• finish	: blued
• grips	: wood

FEG FP9: the Hungarian Hi-Power

TECHNICAL SPECIFICATIONS:

Calibre	: 9 mm Para
Trigger action	: double action
Magazine capacity	: 13 rounds
Locking mechanism	: Browning system
Weight	: 950g
Length	: 198mm
Height	: 138mm
Barrel length	: 118mm
Trigger stop	: no
Sights	: fixed
Sight radius	: 160 mm
External safety	: safety catch on left side of slide
Internal safety	: slide safety

FEATURES:

• slide catch	: on left side frame
• magazine catch	: on left side frame, behind trigger guard
• material	: steel
• finish	: blued
• grips	: wood

FEG P9M SA

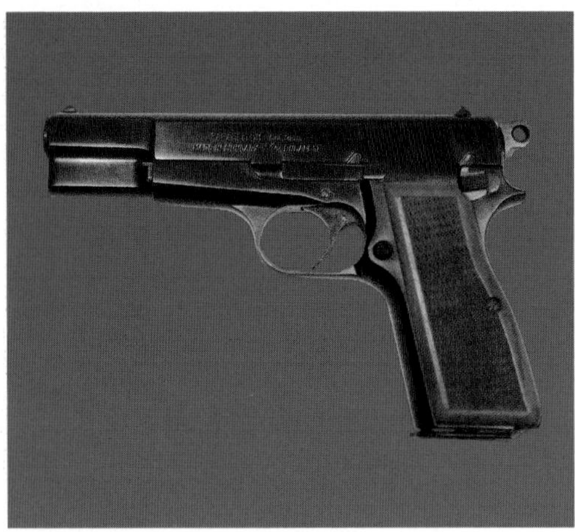

TECHNICAL SPECIFICATIONS:

Calibre	: 9mm Para
Trigger action	: single action
Magazine capacity	: 13 rounds
Locking mechanism	: Browning system
Weight	: 910g
Length	: 198mm
Height	: 126mm
Barrel length	: 118mm
Trigger stop	: none
Sights	: fixed
Sight radius	: 158mm
External safety	: safety catch on left side frame
Internal safety	: slide safety, half-cock safety

FEATURES:

• slide catch	: on left side frame
• magazine catch	: on left side frame, behind trigger guard
• material	: steel
• finish	: blued
• grips	: wood

FEG P9R DA

TECHNICAL SPECIFICATIONS:

Calibre	: 9mm Para
Trigger action	: double action
Magazine capacity	: 14 rounds
Locking mechanism	: Browning system
Weight	: 1000g
Length	: 203mm
Height	: 134mm
Barrel length	: 119mm
Trigger stop	: none
Sights	: fixed
Sight radius	: 162mm
External safety	: combined decock/safety catch on left side of slide
Internal safety	: slide safety

FEATURES:

• slide catch	: on left side frame
• magazine catch	: on left side frame, behind trigger guard
• material	: steel
• finish	: blued
• grips	: wood

FEG P9RK DA Compact

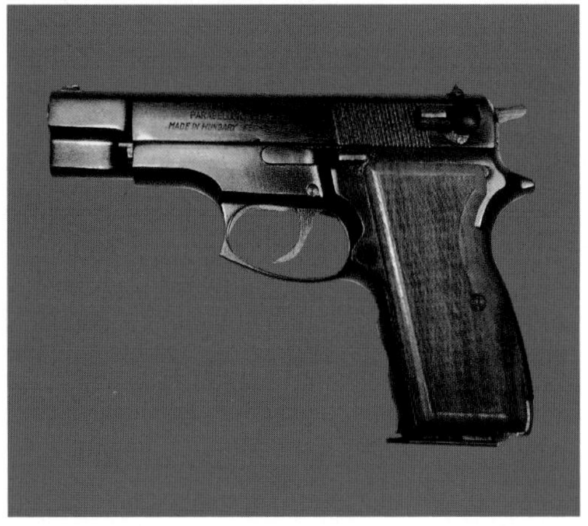

TECHNICAL SPECIFICATIONS:

Calibre	: 9mm Para
Trigger action	: double action
Magazine capacity	: 14 rounds

Locking mechanism	:	Browning system
Weight	:	970g
Length	:	190mm
Height	:	134mm
Barrel length	:	106mm
Trigger stop	:	none
Sights	:	fixed
Sight radius	:	145mm
External safety	:	combined decock/safety catch on left side of slide
Internal safety	:	slide safety
FEATURES:		
• slide catch	:	on left side frame
• magazine catch	:	on left side frame, behind trigger guard
• material	:	steel
• finish	:	blued
• grips	:	wood

Feinwerkbau

The German arms manufacturer Feinwerkbau (FWB), actually Feinwerkbau Westinger & Altenburger KG, is located in Oberndorf on the River Neckar. Since the foundation of the company in 1949, precision instruments have been made and it was not until 1961 that FWB became involved with the production of match airguns and match airpistols. Their range of these is extensive. FWB manufactures everything from light airguns up to the most sophisticated match guns. The company is particularly famous in the field of match airguns. First of all they introduced the Model 65 airpistol, followed by the models 80 and 90. The last model is even provided with an electronic trigger system. Furthermore, FWB was one of the first manufacturers to introduce a CO2 airpistol, the Model 2. In 1992 a new line of airpistols was developed, namely, the models 102 and C25. At the beginning of the 1990s, FWB began cautiously with a production programme of rifles in calibre .22 LR. At the International Waffen (Arms) Exhibition of 1994, FWB introduced a prototype of their first small-calibre sporting pistol. The design of this pistol was by Edwin Wöhrstein and Bernhard Knaeble, both designers of FWB. In the development of this gun, extreme care was taken with the pistol's point of balance which is exactly on the trigger guard. It was specially designed that way, because the magazine is situated in the grip of the gun and not, as with many competitive match pistols, in front of the trigger group. Furthermore, the line of fire is so deeply set inside the anatomic and ergonomic target grip that the line of sight and bore axis are nearly above the shooting hand. For match pistols of this kind, this fact is extremely important.

Feinwerkbau AW 93

Feinwerkbau AW 93

TECHNICAL SPECIFICATIONS:

Calibre	: .22 LR
Trigger action	: single action
Magàzine capacity	: 5 rounds
Locking mechanism	: blowback system
Weight	: 1210g
Length	: 278mm
Height	: 145mm
Barrel length	: 152mm
Trigger stop	: adjustable
Sights	: adjustable micrometer rear sight
Sight radius	: 217mm
External safety	: safety catch near rear-sight base
Internal safety	: slide safety, magazine safety

FEATURES:

• slide catch	: on left side frame, just above trigger
• magazine catch	: in heel of grip
• material	: stainless steel
• finish	: stainless
• grips	: anatomic stock with adjusable palm rest

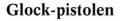

Glock-pistolen

In 1980 the Glock pistol was developed by the Austrian engineer, Gaston Glock. It is known worldwide as the "plastic pistol". It got its nickname because of the large number of parts made of special high-impact synthetic material. The Glock's construction is simple and ultra-modern. On the outside the gun has no manual safety devices. Moreover, the gun has no external hammer. The internal safeties work automatically, on the basis of the trigger action. The Glock 17 is issued to the Austrian army and police under the name of P80. Norway and Sweden also bought this gun for their armed forces. Furthermore, other countries have issued this pistol to army, police, or special security units. In the USA the introduction of this gun on the civilian market led to hysterical outbursts from journalists, except in the specialist press. The general opinion was that this "plastic pistol" could not be detected at airport security, and the gutter press had a field-day with the "terrorist special". Tests clearly proved that this was nonsense. Besides, most leading manufacturers have followed the Glock example in the last fifteen years with "ultra-modern" pistols with a synthetic frame. The Glock 17 is the standard model, as it was introduced in 1980.
As an optional accessory, Glock can provide extra-long magazines, with which the cartridge capacity can be enlarged by two extra rounds. Glock has extended its model 17 to a complete pistol range.
The recent Glock series consists of the following types:

- Glock 17 : 9mm Para (standard model),
- Glock 17 L : 9mm Para (competition model),
- Glock 18 : 9mm Para (fully automatic pistol),
- Glock 19 : 9mm Para Compact model
- Glock 20 : 10mm Auto
- Glock 21 : .45 ACP,
- Glock 22 : .40 S&W,
- Glock 23 : .40 S&W,
- Glock 24 : .40 S&W,
- Glock 25 : compact.380 ACP (9mm Short)

Glock 17

TECHNICAL SPECIFICATIONS:

Calibre	: 9mm Para
Trigger action	: safe action
Magazine capacity	: 17 rounds
Locking mechanism	: Browning-Petter system
Weight	: 703g
Length	: 186mm
Height	: 138mm
Barrel length	: 114mm
Trigger stop	: no
Sights	: fixed or adjustable
Sight radius	: 165mm

External safety	: none
Internal safety	: slide safety, trigger safety, firing-pin safety, drop safety (trigger bar is always blocked, unless the trigger is completely pulled)

FEATURES:

• slide catch	: on both sides of frame
• magazine catch	: on left side frame, behind trigger guard
• material	: steel-reinforced high-impact Polymer frame, steel slide
• finish	: matt Tenifer coating
• grips	: integral composition frame

Glock-17 L

TECHNICAL SPECIFICATIONS:

Calibre	: 9 mm Para
Trigger action	: safe action
Magazine capacity	: 17 rounds
Locking mechanism	: Browning-Petter system
Weight	: 748g
Length	: 225mm
Height	: 138mm
Barrel length	: 153mm
Trigger stop	: none
Sights	: adjustable
Sight radius	: 205mm
External safety	: none
Internal safety	: slide safety, trigger safety, firing-pin safety, drop safety (trigger bar is always blocked, unless the trigger is completely pulled)

FEATURES:

• slide catch	: on both sides of frame
• magazine catch	: on left side frame, behind trigger guard
• material	: steel-reinforced high-impact Polymer frame, steel slide
• finish	: matt Tenifer coating
• grips	: integral black composition frame

Glock-18 C

TECHNICAL SPECIFICATIONS:

Calibre	: 9 mm Para
Trigger action	: safe action
Magazine capacity	: 17 rounds
Locking mechanism	: Browning-Petter system
Weight	: 620g
Length	: 183mm
Height	: 131mm
Barrel length	: 114mm
Trigger stop	: no
Sights	: fixed
Sight radius	: 165mm
External safety	: none
Internal safety	: slide safety, trigger safety, firing-pin safety, drop safety (trigger bar is always blocked, unless the trigger is completely pulled)

FEATURES:

• slide catch	: on both sides of frame
• magazine catch	: on left side frame, behind trigger guard
• material	: steel-reinforced high-impact Polymer frame, steel slide

• finish	: matt Tenifer coating
• grips	: integral black composition frame

This fully automatic Glock Model 18 has a fire selector at the left side of the slide to switch the gun to semi- or fully automatic. In most countries this version cannot be owned legally by civilians, except possibly with a special licence.

Glock 19

TECHNICAL SPECIFICATIONS:

Calibre	: 9 mm Para
Trigger action	: safe action
Magazine capacity	: 15 rounds
Locking mechanism	: Browning-Petter system
Weight	: 665g
Length	: 174mm
Height	: 127mm
Breedte	: 30mm
Barrel length	: 102mm
Trigger stop	: no
Sights	: adjustable
Sight radius	: 152mm
External safety	: none
Internal safety	: slide safety, trigger safety, firing-pin safety, drop safety (trigger bar is always blocked, unless the trigger is completely pulled)

FEATURES:

• slide catch	: on both sides of frame
• magazine catch	: on left side frame, behind trigger guard
• material	: steel-reinforced high-impact Polymer frame, steel slide
• finish	: matt Tenifer coating
• grips	: integral black composition frame

Glock 20

TECHNICAL SPECIFICATIONS:

Calibre	: 10 mm Auto
Trigger action	: safe action
Magazine capacity	: 15 rounds
Locking mechanism	: Browning-Petter system
Weight	: 860g
Length	: 193mm
Height	: 139mm
Barrel length	: 117mm
Trigger stop	: no
Sights	: fixed
Sight radius	: 172mm
External safety	: none
Internal safety	: slide safety, trigger safety, firing-pin safety, drop safety (trigger bar is always blocked, unless the trigger is completely pulled)

FEATURES:

• slide catch	: on both sides of frame
• magazine catch	: on left side frame, behind trigger guard
• material	: steel-reinforced high-impact Polymer frame, steel slide
• finish	: matt Tenifer coating
• grips	: integral black composition frame

Glock 21

TECHNICAL SPECIFICATIONS:

Calibre	: .45 ACP
Trigger action	: safe action
Magazine capacity	: 13 rounds
Locking mechanism	: Browning-Petter system
Weight	: 833g
Length	: 193mm
Height	: 139mm
Barrel length	: 117mm
Trigger stop	: none
Sights	: fixed
Sight radius	: 172mm
External safety	: none
Internal safety	: slide safety, trigger safety, firing-pin safety, drop safety (trigger bar is always blocked, unless the trigger is completely pulled)

FEATURES:

• slide catch	: on both sides of frame
• magazine catch	: on left side frame, behind trigger guard
• material	: steel-reinforced high-impact Polymer frame, steel slide
• finish	: matt Tenifer coating
• grips	: integral black composition frame

Glock 22

TECHNICAL SPECIFICATIONS:

Calibre	: .40 S&W
Trigger action	: safe action
Magazine capacity	: 15 rounds
Locking mechanism	: Browning/Petter-system
Weight	: 728g
Length	: 186mm
Height	: 138mm
Barrel length	: 114mm
Trigger stop	: none
Sights	: fixed
Sight radius	: 165mm
External safety	: none
Internal safety	: slide safety, trigger safety, firing-pin safety, drop safety (trigger bar is always blocked, unless the trigger is completely pulled)

FEATURES:

• slide catch	: on both sides of frame
• magazine catch	: on left side frame, behind trigger guard
• material	: steel-reinforced high-impact Polymer frame, steel slide
• finish	: matt Tenifer coating
• grips	: integral black composition frame

Glock 23

TECHNICAL SPECIFICATIONS:

Calibre	: .40 S&W
Trigger action	: safe action
Magazine capacity	: 13 rounds
Locking mechanism	: Browning-Petter system
Weight	: 670g
Length	: 174mm
Height	: 127mm
Barrel length	: 102mm
Trigger stop	: none
Sights	: fixed
Sight radius	: 152mm
External safety	: none
Internal safety	: slide safety, trigger safety,

firing-pin safety, drop safety (trigger bar is always blocked, unless the trigger is completely pulled)

FEATURES:

• slide catch	: on both sides of frame
• magazine catch	: on left side frame, behind trigger guard
• material	: steel-reinforced high-impact Polymer frame, steel slide
• finish	: matt Tenifer coating
• grips	: integral black composition frame

Glock 24-C

TECHNICAL SPECIFICATIONS:

Calibre	: .40 S&W
Trigger action	: safe-action
Magazine capacity	: 15 rounds
Locking mechanism	: Browning-Petter system
Weight	: 835g
Length	: 225mm
Height	: 138mm
Barrel length	: 153mm
Trigger stop	: none
Sights	: fixed
Sight radius	: 205mm
External safety	: none
Internal safety	: slide safety, trigger safety, firing-pin safety, drop safety (trigger bar is always blocked, unless the trigger is completely pulled)

FEATURES:

• slide catch	: on both sides of frame
• magazine catch	: on left side frame, behind trigger guard
• material	: steel-reinforced high-impact Polymer frame, steel slide
• finish	: matt Tenifer coating
• grips	: integral black composition frame

Grizzly Magnum pistol

Until 1979 the "Dirty Harry" Smith & Wesson .44 Magnum was considered to be the most powerful handgun calibre ever made, but in that year this calibre was surpassed with the introduction of the .45 Winchester Magnum cartridge, originally designated for the semi-automatic Wildey pistol. At the same time another special calibre was developed: the 9mm Winchester Magnum. Because the Wildey was experiencing considerable production difficulties, the single-shot Thompson Center Contender pistol was the only standard pistol that could fire the .45 Win. Magnum. This new cartridge led a twilight existence because of the lack of choice in handguns for this giant calibre. In 1983, the ammunition manufacturer, Winchester, was even considering ceasing production. At the end of 1983 the Grizzly Winchester Magnum in calibre .45 Win. Magnum was introduced, by the LAR Manufacturing Company from West Jordan in the State of Utah.
The LAR Manufacturing Inc., founded in 1968, had until then been mainly a supply company for other arms manufacturers. The company

made, among other things, tripods for machine-guns on behalf of the American army, and parts for the M16 rifle.

The Grizzly looks of an enlarged Colt 1911-A1 and, as a matter of fact, it is. From a total of 49 parts, 39 of them are interchangeable with a normal Colt pistol. The other 10 parts, such as grips, magazine, slide, barrel, barrel bushing, firing-pin, recoil spring, and extractor, are not, because they are limited by calibre. The takedown procedure is also identical to that of a Colt, and so is the locking mechanism.

This mechanism is basically a Browning lock-up, applied in numerous old and most modern types of handguns. Compared with other locking systems this Browning mechanism is notable for its simplicity. The system is hardly affected by dirt, the production costs are reasonable, and its reliability has been proven thousands of times. The first models of the Grizzly were provided with a barrel, which had two gas outlets cut out at the muzzle end to control the recoil and muzzle flip of the gun. For experts, a kind of Magna-Porting. The Grizzly has three safety systems. The ambidextrous enlarged safety catch, so very useful for left-handers, blocks the hammer as well as the sear. Furthermore, the pistol has a grip safety in the backstrap of the grip and, finally, the slide safety. The magazine well is bevelled at the base in the so-called "combat-style", in order to facilitate quick changes of magazines. The most interesting part of the Grizzly is the opportunity to use calibre-exchange kits. The pistol can be converted (in next to no time) from .357 Magnum to, for instance, .45 ACP or .45 Win. Magnum. Originally these conversion kits were also made in the calibre 9mm Win. Magnum, but the production of this cartridge has ceased and with it the conversion kit. If you own one, hang on to it! The newest model of the Grizzly family is the pistol in calibre .50 AE or .50 Magnum, as it is also known.

Grizzly Magnum pistol

TECHNICAL SPECIFICATIONS:

Calibre	: .45 Winchester Magnum, .357 Magnum, 10mm Auto, .45 ACP (9 mm Winchester Magnum), .50 AE (Magnum)
Trigger action	: single action
Magazine capacity	: 7 rounds
Locking mechanism	: Browning system
Weight	: 1490g
Length	: 262mm
Height	: 143mm
Barrel length	: 158mm
Trigger stop	: adjustable
Sights	: adjustable Millet rear sight
Sight radius	: 194mm
External safety	: ambidextrous safety catch, grip safety
Internal safety	: slide safety

FEATURES:

• slide catch	: on left side frame, above trigger guard
• magazine catch	: on left side frame, behind trigger guard
• material	: steel or stainless steel
• finish	: blued, nickel plated, or stainless
• grips	: Pachmayr

Hämmerli sportpistols

The Swiss Hämmerli Company was founded in 1863 and, until the turn of the century, was mainly engaged in the production of rifle barrels for the Swiss army. At the end of the last century the name of Hämmerli was linked with match shooting, when in 1897 the world championship was won with Martini rifles that had been rebuilt by Hämmerli. In the period 1897–1914, 17 out of the 18 world championships were won by the Swiss Hämmerli-Martini team.
After that Hämmerli specialized in sporting weapons. In 1933, the first free pistol, called the

33MP in calibre .22 Extra-Long, was introduced and the Swiss Hämmerli team was very successful with it for many years. During both world wars the Hämmerli production capacity was devoted to arms for the defence of the neutral Swiss State.

In 1952 Hämmerli introduced its first rapid-fire pistol in calibre .22 Short. The company started a subsidiary company in the German town of Waldshut-Tiengen in 1956, where mainly high-quality airguns were produced and, from 1961, large-bore match rifles under the name of Hämmerli-Tanner.

The world championship for the 300m match rifle was won with these rifles in 1962 in Cairo. The Swiss concern, SIG, bought a majority shareholding in the Hämmerli company in 1971. SIG is short for Schweizerische Industrie Gesellschaft (Swiss Industrial Company), and it produces, together with a number of subsidiaries, arms, trains, electronics, industrial robots, ores, timber products, and packaging (in the broadest sense).

In the arms business the company manufactures pistols with the name of Sig-Sauer, match pistols under the Hämmerli brand, hunting rifles with the name of Sauer, and army and police guns under the name of Sig and Sig-Sauer.
Hämmerli has a wide range of match pistols, such as the so-called "free pistols" and the semi-automatic small-bore pistols in calibre .22 LR. Both types are used by top shooters for the Olympic Games and world championships. In the course of time the Hämmerli pistols have undergone several modifications. For instance, the free pistols Model 150 from 1972 and the 152-Electronic from 1980 were replaced by the Hämmerli 160 and 162-Electronic in 1992. The semi-automatic models 211, 212, and 215 are no longer produced. From 1972, Hämmerli manufactured a special large-bore match pistol, the Hämmerli P240 in the calibres .32 S&W-Long and even in .38 Special-Wadcutter.
In 1988, the newest pistol model was introduced, the P280 in the calibres .22 LR and .32 S&W-Long. This pistol is mainly made of high-impact carbon synthetics.

Hämmerli 160

TECHNICAL SPECIFICATIONS:

Calibre	: .22 LR
Trigger action	: single action
Magazine capacity	: none: single shot
Locking mechanism	: falling block system
Weight	: 1330g
Length	: 445mm
Height	: 145mm
Barrel length	: 287mm

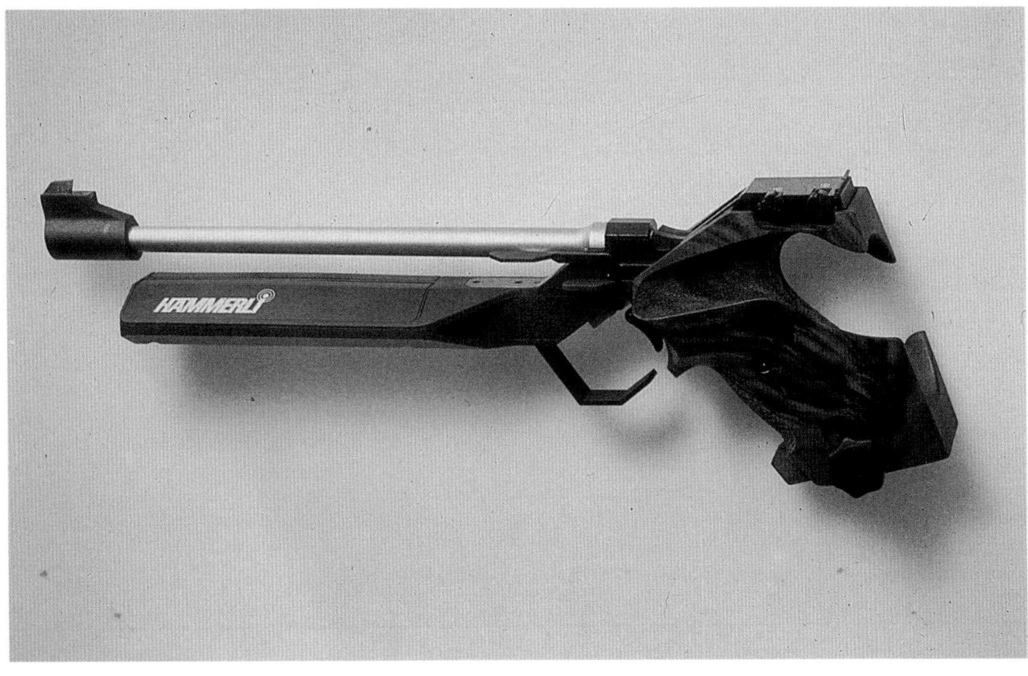

Trigger stop	: adjustable
Sights	: micrometer rear sight
Sight radius	: 370mm
External safety	: none
Internal safety	: slide safety

FEATURES:

• slide catch	: not relevant
• magazine catch	: not relevant
• material	: steel
• finish	: blued
• grips	: anatomic stock with adjustable palm rest

The 162 model has an electronic firing system.

Hämmerli 208

TECHNICAL SPECIFICATIONS:

Calibre	: .22 LR
Trigger action	: single action
Magazine capacity	: 8 rounds
Locking mechanism	: blowback action
Weight	: 1065g
Length	: 255mm
Height	: 150mm
Barrel length	: 150mm
Trigger stop	: adjustable
Sights	: micrometer rear sight
Sight radius	: 208mm
External safety	: safety catch on left side frame
Internal safety	: slide safety, magazine safety

FEATURES:

• slide catch	: none (slide stays open after last shot)
• magazine catch	: in heel of grip
• material	: steel
• finish	: blued
• grips	: wooden stock with adjustable palm rest

Hämmerli 280

TECHNICAL SPECIFICATIONS:

Calibre	: .22 LR, .32 S&W Long
Trigger action	: single action
Magazine capacity	: 6 rounds (.22); 5 rounds (.32)
Locking mechanism	: blowback action
Weight	: 990g (.32 S&W Long: 1200 g)
Length	: 300mm
Height	: 150mm
Barrel length	: 116mm
Trigger stop	: adjustable
Sights	: micrometer rear sight
Sight radius	: 220mm
External safety	: safety catch
Internal safety	: slide safety

FEATURES:

• slide catch	: none (slide stays open after last shot)
• magazine catch	: underneath trigger guard
• material	: frame, magazine of carbon composition
• finish	: black
• grips	: wooden stock with adjustable palm rest

Heckler & Koch pistols

The P9 pistol in calibre 9mm Para was introduced by the German company Heckler & Koch in 1970. Later the calibre models .45 ACP and 7.65mm Para were added with an eye to foreign markets. The pistol is very striking technologically, mainly because of the bolt-locking roller system and the polygonal barrel (see Chapter 2). Another remarkable feature is the cocking lever at the left side of the frame, behind the trigger guard. Because of the position, that lever can easily be mistaken for a magazine catch. That, however, is situated in the heel of the grip. This cocking lever serves as a cocking device for the firing system. The pistol can be fired in double-action mode, but by cocking the cocking lever the pistol can also be fired, even for the first shot, in a single-action mode.

The first model, the P9, was a single-action only pistol, but was replaced rapidly by the P9S, a double-action model. The addition "S" stands for the German word Spann-abzug (double-action).

In 1973, the third variant was introduced, the P9S-Sport, with a lengthened barrel, on which a barrel weight, complete with front post, is attached at the muzzle end. This sports model has an adjustable rear sight. The extractor also serves as a loading indicator, if a cartridge is loaded into the chamber of the barrel. When the system is cocked an indicator pin protrudes from the rear side of the slide.

In 1981, Heckler & Koch introduced a completely new pistol concept, the PSP (Police Self-loading Pistol), which shortly afterwards became known as the P7. In this new pistol a great many technical innovations were introduced, at least for that time. First of all, the pistol had a polygonal barrel. Instead of lands and fields, the barrel is edged with many (poly) small corners which have a certain twist to give the passing bullet a rotation. Furthermore, the gun has a squeeze cocking grip instead of the more usual double- or single-action trigger system.

The pistol is always decocked until the squeeze grip at the front strap of the grip is pressed. Then the firing-pin is tensioned and can be released by the trigger.

The pistol has a gas-retarded locking system (see Chapter 2). The gun has no slide catch, but the slide stays open after the last shot. In order to close the slide again, the squeezer has to be pressed.

A variation model of the P7 is the P7-K3, a special sports model, for which exchange kits are available in the calibres .22 LR, .25 ACP (635mm), .32 ACP (765mm), and .380 ACP (9mm Short).

The Heckler & Koch P7-M8 is largely a further development of the P7 pistol. In the P7 the magazine catch was located in the heel of the grip.

For the civilian market, this raised objections from customers. For fast shooting and magazine changes, such a magazine catch at the rear side of the heel of the grip is not very practical.

The P7-M8 has a magazine catch at the left side of the frame, behind the trigger guard. The other technical specifications are identical to the older P7. For countries where government or army calibres are not permitted for civilian use, such as Italy and some parts of Latin America, the pistol is also produced in the calibre 9 x 21mm.

The Heckler & Koch P7-M13 was derived from the P7-M8, and specially designed for the US army trials that were held to investigate replacing the old Colt 1911-A1 army pistol. It is a thirteen-round gun with an ambidextrous magazine catch behind the trigger guard.

Other technical details are the same as for the P7-M8. The P7-M13 did not make it as the US service pistol, so Heckler & Koch had to try the civilian market.

Because of that the company also made a version in calibre .40 S&W, named the P7-M10. The P7-M10 is more heavily built, because of the heavier calibre. Strangely enough, the M10 does not have the polygonal barrel but the more conventional fields and lands.

Because of some miscalculations (with, among other models, the futuristic G-11 military assault rifle with caseless ammo), this German company ended up in financial difficulties at the end of 1990. In March 1991, the company was taken over by the British Royal Ordnance, a subsidiary of the Aerospace holding company. In view of the competition, HK wanted to design a modern pistol model but lacked the necessary financial resources. In the summer of 1991 the company received a development task from the Pentagon. For special units of the army, navy, and airforce, the Pentagon wanted a special .45 ACP handgun for the SOCOM (Special Operations Command).

The SOCOM modular pistol can, if so desired, be provided with a laser sight, infra-red or white light sight, as well as a sound suppressor.

In 1994 HK introduced a civilian model, derived from this SOCOM design, the USP (Universal Selbstlade Pistole = Universal Self-loading Pistol).

Because of the American development aid, the pistol is nicknamed the 'United States Pistol'.

Heckler & Koch HK P7 M8

TECHNICAL SPECIFICATIONS:

Calibre	: 9mm Para
Trigger action	: squeeze cocker
Magazine capacity	: 8 rounds
Locking mechanism	: gas-retarded blowback system
Weight	: 785g
Length	: 171mm
Height	: 127mm
Barrel length	: 105mm
Trigger stop	: none
Sights	: fixed
Sight radius	: 148mm
External safety	: none
Internal safety	: slide safety, squeeze cocker, automatic firing-pin safety

FEATURES:

• slide catch	: by squeeze cocker
• magazine catch	: on left side frame, behind trigger guard
• material	: steel
• finish	: blued or matt nickel plated
• grips	: composition

Heckler & Koch HK P7 M13

TECHNICAL SPECIFICATIONS:

Calibre	: 9mm Para
Trigger action	: squeeze cocker
Magazine capacity	: 13 rounds
Locking mechanism	: gas-retarded blowback system
Weight	: 785g
Length	: 169mm
Height	: 135mm
Barrel length	: 105mm
Trigger stop	: none
Sights	: fixed
Sight radius	: 148mm
External safety	: none
Internal safety	: slide safety, squeeze cocker, automatic firing-pin safety

FEATURES:

• slide catch	: by squeeze cocker
• magazine catch	: ambidextrous, behind trigger guard
• material	: steel
• finish	: blued of matt nickel plated
• grips	: composition

Heckler & Koch HK P7 M13 Compensator

TECHNICAL SPECIFICATIONS:

Calibre	: 9mm Para
Trigger action	: squeeze cocker
Magazine capacity	: 13 rounds
Locking mechanism	: gas-retarded blowback system
Weight	: 885g
Length	: 237mm, inc. compensator
Height	: 135mm
Barrel length	: 125mm
Trigger stop	: no
Sights	: fixed
Sight radius	: 185mm
External safety	: none
Internal safety	: slide safety, squeeze cocker, automatic firing-pin safety

FEATURES:

• slide catch	: by squeeze cocker
• magazine catch	: ambidextrous, behind trigger guard
• material	: steel
• finish	: blued of matt nickel plated
• grips	: composition

Heckler & Koch HK P9S

TECHNICAL SPECIFICATIONS:

Calibre	: 9mm Para, .45 ACP, 7.65 Para
Trigger action	: double action
Magazine capacity	: 9 rounds (9mm Para); 7 rounds (.45 ACP)
Locking mechanism	: HK roller-locked action
Weight	: 875g
Length	: 192mm
Height	: 141mm
Barrel length	: 102mm
Trigger stop	: adjustable
Sights	: fixed (P9S Sport: adjustable)
Sight radius	: 147mm
External safety	: safety catch on left side of slide
Internal safety	: slide safety, cocking lever

FEATURES:

• slide catch	: left side frame, just above cocking lever
• magazine catch	: in heel or grip
• material	: steel
• finish	: blued
• grips	: composition

Heckler & Koch USP

TECHNICAL SPECIFICATIONS:

Calibre	: .40 S&W, 9mm Para
Trigger action	: by choice single action, double action, or DAO(double-action only)
Magazine capacity	: 15 rounds (9mm), 13 rounds (.40)
Locking mechanism	: improved Browning-Petter system
Weight	: 835g
Length	: 194mm
Height	: 136mm
Barrel length	: 108mm
Trigger stop	: none
Sights	: three-dot sights, windage adjustable
Sight radius	: 158mm
External safety	: by choice: safety catch, decocking lever, or combined, can be mounted either left or right side of frame
Internal safety	: slide safety, automatic firing-pin safety

FEATURES:

• slide catch	: on left side frame
• magazine catch	: ambidextrous, behind trigger guard
• material	: composition frame, steel slide
• finish	: black coating
• grips	: integrated with frame

Heckler & Koch HK VP70 Z(ivil)

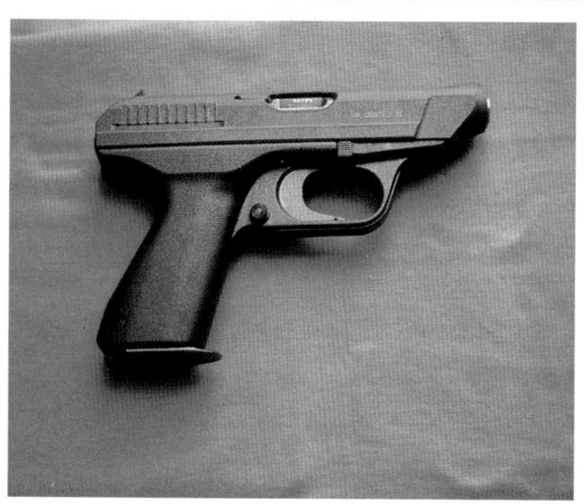

TECHNICAL SPECIFICATIONS:

Calibre	: 9 mm Para
Trigger action	: DAO (double-action only)
Magazine capacity	: 18 rounds
Locking mechanism	: blowback system
Weight	: 820g
Length	: 204mm
Height	: 142mm
Barrel length	: 116mm
Trigger stop	: none
Sights	: fixed
Sight radius	: 175mm
External safety	: safety catch on left side frame, behind trigger guard
Internal safety	: slide safety

FEATURES:

• slide catch	: none
• magazine catch	: in heel of grip
• material	: steel slide, composition frame
• finish	: black
• grips	: black composition stock

The HK VP70-Z (Civil) pistol is the civilian version of the fully automatic Volks Pistole (People's Pistol), on which a carbine stock can be mounted. This is one of the first pistols with a composition frame, long before other manufacturers made this a trend. The same applies to the DAO (double-action only) design – at least for a pistol. The safety catch of this pistol is situated in the place where normally the magazine catch is mounted. Furthermore, this gun is one of the few pistols in calibre 9mm Para that can make do with the simple blowback action.

High Standard-sport pistols

The High Standard Company had a glorious history until, some years ago, they had to bow to competition and ceased production. The first pistol models of High Standard were manufactured in the period 1939–41 and were called Model A and Model B. They were fitted with fixed rear sights and a 6in barrel. At the same time the same pistol was introduced with a heavy barrel as model HB. Model B had an internal hammer, whilst model HB (Heavy Barrel) was provided with an external hammer. From 1942 to 1945, the pistol, although only suitable for the civilian market, was marked with the inscription "Property of the US." From 1945 to 1950, High Standard introduced a small-bore pistol with an adjustable rear sight. During these years several small modifications were implemented for the standard models. To indicate these modifications, certain characters were used, like model HD, HA, D, etc. The most well-known model from that period was the model HD (Military) with a heavy barrel, external hammer, and a rear sight that was only windage adjustable. This HD model was also used as a training and match pistol in the US army. In 1951, the company started with the model Duramatic, with a tapered barrel of 61/2in, fixed sights, and internal hammer. That same year the pistol line of the Supermatic, Field King, Sport King, and Military Trophy was set up. These new models were provided with a barrel-locking plunger (or takedown plunger) at the front of the trigger guard. Other models produced by High Standard over the years were as follows:

- The Sport King, a ten-round pistol with a 41/2 or 63/4in standard barrel.
- The model Sharpshooter with a 51/2in heavy barrel.
- The Supermatic Citation Military with a 71/4 in fluted barrel to reduce weight and the 51/2in heavy barrel.
- The Supermatic Trophy with a 51/2in heavy barrel or a 71/4in tapered barrel, with a gilded safety catch, trigger, magazine catch (in the front lower side of the grip), and slide catch.
- The Victor Military Model Target, with a ventilated barrel.

- The 10X, a Trophy model with a 51/2in heavy barrel. The last gun mentioned was hand-fitted and was the parade horse of High Standard: their first-class match pistol.

In 1984 the company went bankrupt and the production licences were bought by the American company, Mitchell, founded by the last manager of High Standard. Since 1995, the High Standard pistols have also been produced by the American firm, New England Arms. In 1993, however, the High Standard Manufacturing Company Inc. was founded in Houston, Texas. The assets, like the High Standard name and trademarks, as well as the patent rights, formerly owned by an arms wholesaler, Gordon Elliot, were incorporated into this new High Standard company and from 1995 the new High Standard products were produced. The pistols shown here are from that new company.

High Standard Supermatic Trophy

TECHNICAL SPECIFICATIONS:

Calibre	: .22 LR
Trigger action	: single action
Magazine capacity	: 10 rounds
Locking mechanism	: blowback action
Weight	: 1320g
Length	: 250mm
Height	: 142mm
Barrel length	: 139mm
Trigger stop	: adjustable
Sights	: adjustable
Sight radius	: 218mm
External safety	: safety catch
Internal safety	: slide safety and magazine safety

FEATURES:

• slide catch	: on left side frame
• magazine catch	: lower front side of grip
• material	: steel
• finish	: blued
• grips	: walnut

High Standard The Victor

TECHNICAL SPECIFICATIONS:

Calibre	: .22 LR
Trigger action	: single action
Magazine capacity	: 10 rounds
Locking mechanism	: blowback action
Weight	: 1305g
Length	: 241mm
Height	: 143mm
Barrel length	: 140mm
Trigger stop	: adjustable
Sights	: adjustable
Sight radius	: 218mm
External safety	: safety catch on left side frame
Internal safety	: slide safety, magazine safety

FEATURES:

• slide catch	: none; slide stays open after last shot
• magazine catch	: lower front side of grip
• material	: steel
• finish	: blued
• grips	: walnut match grip

I.M.I.-pistols

Immediately after the foundation of the independent State of Israel, the country had to cope with a lot of serious problems. Not only had the state to deal with, to put it mildly, rather hostile neighbours, but it was also isolated politically. Because the nation suffered from a shortage of foreign currency, it had to depend for the most part on its own facilities.

In 1949, the Israeli army colonel, Uziel Gal, a well-known arms expert, designed the famous Uzi submachine-gun, derived from the Czech

submachine-gun CZ-23. Israel's own, initially modest, arms industry, called IMI (Israel Military Industries) offered great advantages and the Uzi was specially designed to keep the costs of production very low.
In the Israeli–Arab War of 1948, which broke out directly after the proclamation of the independent State of Israel on 14 May 1948, it soon turned out that Israel was short of submachine-guns and had only the old British sten guns. In 1951, the Uzi was issued in bulk to the Israeli army. It was to become the most reliable submachine-gun in the world. It was produced by the hundred thousands, and was for quite some time manufactured under licence by the FN Browning Company at Herstal-Liège in Belgium and at the Hembrug factory in The Netherlands. A number of countries in Western Europe, like The Netherlands, Belgium, and other Nato countries, have or had the Uzi in use. Furthermore, the Uzi was the official army submachine-gun in Iran, South Africa, Venezuela, and Surinam. Later on the Uzi "family" was completed with the Mini-Uzi and the Micro-Uzi. The latest is a fully automatic version of the Uzi and was specially designed for security units.
The Uzi pistol is a semi-automatic and specifically suited for fans of the "military look". Because of the large magazine capacity of twenty rounds, it is a very handy weapon, although the pistol is not exactly suitable as a holster gun.
IMI has also been very busy in the civilian arms field. An excellent range of sporting pistols has been developed with the American company, Magnum Research from Minneapolis. The Israeli drive for efficiency took control again, because the standard models are superb army or police handguns. Their first design was the Desert Eagle.
The gun has a unique locking system, at least for a handgun, with a rotating bolt. At first the Desert Eagle was only available in calibre .357 Magnum, but later on also in .41 and .44 Magnum, and recently in calibre .50 AE (Action Express or Magnum). A little later this was followed by a compact version, the Baby Eagle, which also has the name Jericho 941.
Other branches of shooting were not forgotten, which can be seen from the introduction, some years ago, of the single-shot silhouette pistol Lone Eagle, available in fourteen different calibres, from .22-250 Remington up to .444 Marlin.
For the small-bore market, IMI developed the ten-round Mountain Eagle, a very modern handgun with a synthetic frame, magazine, and barrel shroud. Only the bolt, bolt housing, and inner barrel are made of steel.

Desert Eagle .357M

TECHNICAL SPECIFICATIONS:

Calibre	: .357 Magnum
Trigger action	: single action
Magazine capacity	: 9 rounds (.357 Magnum)
Locking mechanism	: gas-operated rotating bolt
Weight	: 1766g (.357 Magnum)
Length	: 270mm (with standard 6"-barrel)
Height	: 145mm
Barrel length	: 152mm (6")
Trigger stop	: none
Sights	: fixed
Sight radius	: 215mm
External safety	: ambidextrous safety catch on slide
Internal safety	: slide safety

FEATURES:

• slide catch	: on left side frame, above trigger guard
• magazine catch	: on left side frame, behind trigger guard
• material	: steel, stainless steel or with alloy frame
• finish	: black coating, high-gloss chrome, nickel plated, matt chrome, high-gloss blued, gold plated, etc.
• grips	: black composition, wood or Hogue

Interchangeable barrels are available in 10in (254mm) and 14in (356mm) in normal or Magna-Port version: close to the muzzle several gas-vent ports are cut, to reduce recoil and muzzle flip. Interchangeable calibre sets are available for the conversion from .357 Magnum to .41 Magnum, and/or .44 Magnum, and/or .50 AE (Magnum), and backwards.

Desert Eagle .41M

TECHNICAL SPECIFICATIONS:

Calibre	: .41 Magnum
Trigger action	: single action
Magazine capacity	: 9 rounds (.357 Magnum)
Locking mechanism	: gas-operated rotating bolt
Weight	: 1766g (.357 Magnum)
Length	: 270mm (with standard 6"-barrel)
Height	: 145mm
Barrel length	: 152mm (6")
Trigger stop	: none
Sights	: fixed
Sight radius	: 215mm
External safety	: ambidextrous safety catch on slide
Internal safety	: slide safety
FEATURES:	
• slide catch	: on left side frame, above trigger guard
• magazine catch	: on left side frame, behind trigger guard
• material	: steel, stainless steel or with alloy frame
• finish	: black coating, high-gloss chrome, nickel plated, matt chrome, high-gloss blued, gold plated, etc.
• grips	: black composition, wood or Hogue

Interchangeable barrels are available in 10in (254mm) and 14in (356mm) in normal or Magna-Port version: close to the muzzle several gas-vent ports are cut, to reduce recoil and

muzzle flip. Interchangeable calibre sets are available for the conversion from .357 Magnum to .41 Magnum, and/or .44 Magnum, and/or .50 AE (Magnum), and backwards.

Desert Eagle .44M

TECHNICAL SPECIFICATIONS:

Calibre	: .44 Magnum, .50 AE ((Action Express or Magnum
Trigger action	: single action
Magazine capacity	: 9 rounds (.44 Magnum)
Locking mechanism	: gas-operated rotating bolt
Weight	: 1897g
Length	: 270mm (with standard 6"-barrel)
Height	: 145mm
Barrel length	: 152mm (6")
Trigger stop	: none
Sights	: fixed
Sight radius	: 215mm
External safety	: ambidextrous safety catch op de slide
Internal safety	: slide safety
FEATURES:	
• slide catch	: on left side frame, above trigger guard
• magazine catch	: on left side frame, behind trigger guard
• material	: steel, stainless steel or with alloy frame
• finish	: black coating, high-gloss chrome, nickel plated, matt chrome, high-gloss blued, gold plated, etc.
• grips	: black composition, wood or Hogue

Interchangeable barrels are available in 10in (254mm) and 14in (356mm) in normal or Magna-Port version: close to the muzzle several gas-vent ports are cut, to reduce recoil and muzzle flip. Interchangeable calibre sets are available for the conversion from .357 Magnum to .41 Magnum, and/or .44 Magnum, and/or .50 AE (Magnum), and backwards.

  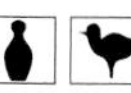

Jericho 941 (Baby Eagle)

TECHNICAL SPECIFICATIONS:

Calibre	: 9mm Para, .40 S&W, .41 AE
Trigger action	: double action
Magazine capacity	: 16 rounds (9mm Para)
Locking mechanism	: improved Browning system
Weight	: 1090g
Length	: 207mm
Height	: 140mm
Barrel length	: 112mm polygonal
Trigger stop	: none
Sights	: fixed
Sight radius	: 150mm
External safety	: ambidextrous decocking lever on slide
Internal safety	: slide safety, retracted firing-pin, automatic firing-pin safety (941F series), disconnected trigger (in safe position: Series 941)

FEATURES:

• slide catch	: on left side frame
• magazine catch	: on left side frame, behind trigger guard
• material	: steel
• finish	: matt blued, matt chrome plated,or two-tone finish
• grips	: black composition

Jericho 941F HV (Baby Eagle)

TECHNICAL SPECIFICATIONS:

Calibre	: 9mm Para, .40 S&W, .41 AE
Trigger action	: double action
Magazine capacity	: 16 rounds (9mm Para)
Locking mechanism	: improved Browning system
Weight	: 1090g
Length	: 207mm
Height	: 140mm
Barrel length	: 112mm polygonal
Trigger stop	: none
Sights	: fixed
Sight radius	: 150mm
External safety	: ambidextrous safety catch on frame
Internal safety	: slide safety, retracted firing-pin,automatic firing-pin safety

FEATURES:

• slide catch	: on left side frame
• magazine catch	: on left side frame, behind trigger guard
• material	: steel
• finish	: matt blued, matt chrome plated,or two-tone finish
• grips	: black composition

Jericho 941FB HV(Baby Eagle)

TECHNICAL SPECIFICATIONS:

Calibre	: 9mm Para, .40 S&W, .41 AE
Trigger action	: double action
Magazine capacity	: 16 rounds (9mm Para)
Locking mechanism	: improved Browning system
Weight	: 945g
Length	: 184mm

Height	: 125mm
Barrel length	: 90mm polygonal
Trigger stop	: none
Sights	: fixed
Sight radius	: 134mm
External safety	: ambidextrous safety catch on the frame
Internal safety	: slide safety, automatic firing-pin safety

FEATURES:

• slide catch	: on left side frame
• magazine catch	: on left side frame, behind trigger guard
• material	: steel
• finish	: matt blued, matt chrome plated or two-tone finish
• grips	: black composition

Jericho 941FS(Baby Eagle)

TECHNICAL SPECIFICATIONS:

Calibre	: 9mm Para, .40 S&W, .41 AE
Trigger action	: double-action
Magazine capacity	: 16 rounds (9mm Para)
Locking mechanism	: improved Browning system
Weight	: 990g
Length	: 184mm
Height	: 140mm
Barrel length	: 90mm polygonal
Trigger stop	: none
Sights	: fixed
Sight radius	: 134mm
External safety	: ambidextrous safety catch on the frame
Internal safety	: slide safety, automatic firing-pin safety

FEATURES:

• slide catch	: on left side frame
• magazine catch	: on left side frame, behind trigger guard
• material	: steel
• finish	: matt blued, matt chrome plated or two-tone finish
• grips	: black composition

Lone Eagle Silhouette

TECHNICAL SPECIFICATIONS:

Calibre	: wide range of calibres (see list below)
Trigger action	: single action
Magazine capacity	: none: single shot
Locking mechanism	: manually rotated bolt
Weight	: depending on calibre, between 1899 and 2013g
Length	: 385mm
Height	: 140mm
Barrel length	: 337mm
Trigger stop	: none
Sights	: adjustable (barrel is drilled and

	tappedfor scope mounts)
Sight radius	: 280mm
External safety	: safety catch above trigger
Internal safety	: bolt-closure safety

FEATURES:

• slide catch:	: not relevant
• magazine catch:	: not relevant
• material:	: steel
• finish:	: black oxide
• grips:	: black composition or wooden stock

AVAILABLE CALIBRES

- .22/250 Remington
- .223 Remington
- .22 Hornet
- .243 Winchester
- 7mm-08 (option: with integrated muzzle break)
- 7mm Bench Rest
- .30-30 Winchester
- .30-06 Springfield (option: with integrated muzzle break)
- .308 Winchester (option: with integrated muzzle break)
- .358 Winchester
- .357 Maximum
- .35 Remington
- .44 Magnum
- .444 Marlin

This pistol is marketed as the Magnum Research SSP 91 in the USA.

Mountain Eagle

TECHNICAL SPECIFICATIONS:

Calibre	: .22 LR
Trigger action	: single action
Magazine capacity	: 15 rounds
Locking mechanism	: blowback action
Weight	: 595g
Length	: 269mm
Height	: 152mm
Barrel length	: 152mm
Trigger stop	: none
Sights	: adjustable
Sight radius	: 230mm
External safety	: safety catch on left side frame
Internal safety	: slide safety

FEATURES:

• slide catch	: on left side frame
• magazine catch	: on left side frame, behind trigger guard
• material	: composition frame, alloy barrel sleeve and receiver
• finish	: black
• grips	: composition stock

Another model which is available is the special target version with an 8in barrel. Magazines are made from transparant high-grade polycarbonate.

ITM

The Swiss company ITM in Solothurn has been producing pistols, based on the Czech CZ-75 design, since the 1980s. To begin with, pistol parts of the CZ-75 were imported and assembled in Solothurn, but later the AT pistol was produced entirely by ITM itself. The AT-84 is available in a compact version, the AT-84P, with a smaller cartridge capacity than the bigger model, namely, thirteen rounds instead of the fifteen rounds of the AT-84. The overall length of the AT-84P is 195mm, with a barrel length of 92mm. A difference compared with the CZ-75 is the long slide-spring guidance.
With the introduction of three new models within the AT-84 design, introduced in 1988, and the addition of a new calibre, the pistol range of ITM became much more interesting. The older AT-84 was available as the AT-84S (standard model) and the AT-84P (the compact model). The new line consists of the AT-88S, the standard full-size pistol; AT-88P, the newer compact model; and the AT-88H, an even more compact combat-style pistol. The three types are available in the calibres 9mm Para and .41 Action Express (.41 AE). The models are still clear copies of the CZ-75, but with a number of interesting modifications. The most interesting innovation is the interchangeability of calibres. To switch from 9mm Para to .41 AE, the shooter only has to change the barrel.

The magazine remains the same, because this can contain 9mm Para cartridges as well as the .41 AE rounds. Furthermore, all three models are provided with an automatic firing-pin safety and can safely be carried loaded (with a cartridge in the chamber) for the first quick shot. The locking mechanism of the AT-88 models has also been modified. The older AT-84 had a locking system based on the typical Browning lock-up, although with some Sig characteristics. The new locking system is completely in accordance with the Sig style, which means that the shape of the breech or chamber block locks the barrel with the slide within the ejection port, instead of having the Browning locking lugs on top of the barrel. Because of this the ejection port has been enlarged. The AT-88S is the standard model with a full-size length of 204mm. It is interesting to know that the guidance rails for the slide (along which the slide runs over the top of the frame) are of full frame length. This feature improves accuracy. The AT-88P is the compact model of the AT-88S, with an overall length of 190mm. In other respects the gun is the same as the AT-88S. The AT-88H varies somewhat in appearance. With this model the guidance rails do not extend the complete length of the frame top. Also, the trigger guard is of typical combat style, which means it is square and serrated at the front. This pistol has an overall length of only 168mm. The gun is available in a beautiful combat finish, with a satin nickel-plated frame and a blued slide. ITM is also doing good business with their frame production. A lot of prominent race-gun builders use frames from ITM as a basis for their special products.

ITM AT 84S

TECHNICAL SPECIFICATIONS:

Calibre	: 9mm Para
Trigger action	: double action
Magazine capacity	: 15 rounds
Locking mechanism	: Browning system
Weight	: 950g
Length	: 204mm
Height	: 138mm
Barrel length	: 113mm
Sight radius	: 160mm
Trigger stop	: none
Sights	: fixed
External safety	: safety catch on left side frame
Internal safety	: slide safety, automatic firing-pin safety

FEATURES:

• slide catch	: on left side frame
• magazine catch	: on left side frame, behind trigger guard
• material	: steel
• finish	: blued
• grips	: wood

Kel-Tec

The American company Kel-Tec CNC Industries Inc., from Cocoa in Florida, is quite a newcomer to the arms business. In 1995 a 9mm Para pistol was introduced with a trigger system for double action only.
The handgun is the smallest and lightest 9mm Para pistol ever designed. It weighs only 400g and it has an overall length of only 140mm. The pistol has been completely designed with the aid of a computer for plain- clothes police personnel, or as a back-up handgun for regular police and army use.
The pistol is of high quality because of the excellent materials that are used in manufacture. The barrel is made from SAE-4140 steel and hardened up to 50-Rockwell. The slide, firing-pin, and extractor are made of the same steel. The separate bolt housing is machined out of a solid block of 7075-T6 alloy. The grip has been produced from a high-impact synthetic, DuPont ST-800. The magazine well and trigger guard are integrated in the grip. Because of the special construction and placement of the firing-pin, the gun does not need a separate firing-pin safety. The firing-pin remains free of (spring) tension, until it is hit by the hammer. The gun will also operate with the double-stack magazines from Smith & Wesson 9mm Para pistols.

Kel-Tec P11

TECHNICAL SPECIFICATIONS:

Calibre	: 9mm Para
Trigger action	: double-action-only (DAO)
Magazine capacity	: 10 rounds
Locking mechanism	: Browning-Petter system
Weight	: 400g
Length	: 142mm
Height	: 109mm
Barrel length	: 78mm
Trigger stop	: no
Sights	: fixed
Sight radius	: 116mm
External safety	: none
Internal safety	: slide safety, inertia (free-floating) lightweight firing-pin

FEATURES:

• slide catch	: on left side frame
• magazine catch	: on left side frame, behind trigger guard
• material	: steel slide, alloy receiver, composition frame/stock (DuPont ST-800)
• finish	: black
• grips	: integrated composition stock

Korth

The German company Korth from Ratzeburg was founded in 1956 and produces pistols and revolvers. In those four decades of its existence, Korth has became famous for its high-quality revolvers, known as the "Rolls-Royces" of revolvers.
The Korth revolvers are made of a special kind of steel. The barrels are cold hammered, which produces a very dense steel structure. In the lockwork of these revolvers, a small wheel is attached to the trigger bar instead of the usual cam.
The pressure point of the trigger action can be adjusted by changing this wheel. Furthermore, the trigger weight can be regulated between 1000 and 2500g, by a screw.
The Korth pistol in calibre 9mm Para was introduced in 1987. The gun was designed by Willi Korth. This ten-round double-action pistol has a very interesting locking system. Korth used a falling-block mechanism in the front side of a barrel block around the muzzle end of the barrel. This unusual location of the lock-up system has a reducing effect on the muzzle flip of the gun during the actual shooting.
The pistol has no external safety catch.
Korth's opinion is that such a device is unnecessary for a defence handgun and can only result in operational mistakes during moments of stress.
The gun is the last word in technology, workmanship, and finish, which is of course reflected in its price. All parts are machined out of massive steel.

Korth pistol

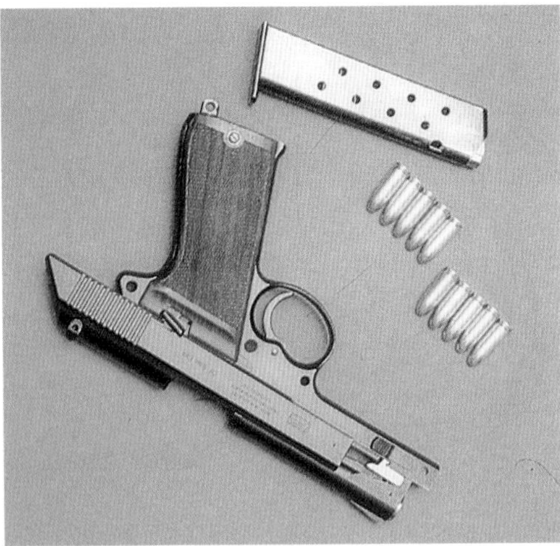

TECHNICAL SPECIFICATIONS:

Calibre	: 9mm Para, 7.65 mm Para, .45 ACP
Trigger action	: double action
Magazine capacity	: 10 rounds (9mm Para)
Locking mechanism	: Korth falling-block patented system
Weight	: 1240g
Length	: 206mm
Height	: 148mm
Barrel length	: 102mm
Trigger stop	: none
Sights	: adjustable
Sight radius	: 154mm
External safety	: none
Internal safety	: slide safety, half-cock safety
FEATURES:	
• slide catch	: on left side frame
• magazine catch	: on left side frame, behind trigger guard
• material	: steel
• finish	: blued
• grips	: walnut

Korth Stainless pistol

TECHNICAL SPECIFICATIONS:

Calibre	: 9mm Para, 7.65mm Para, .45 ACP
Trigger action	: double action
Magazine capacity	: 10 rounds (9mm Para)
Locking mechanism	: Korth falling-block patented system
Weight	: 1240g
Length	: 206mm
Height	: 148mm
Barrel length	: 102mm
Trigger stop	: none
Sights	: adjustable
Sight radius	: 154mm
External safety	: none
Internal safety	: slide safety, half-cock safety
FEATURES:	
• slide catch	: on left side frame
• magazine catch	: on left side frame, behind trigger guard
• material	: stainless steel
• finish	: stainless
• grips	: walnut

Korth Combat Stainless revolver

TECHNICAL SPECIFICATIONS:

Calibre	: .357 Magnum
Trigger action	: double action
Magazine capacity	: 6 rounds
Locking mechanism	: front/rear-side centre pin
Weight	: 950g
Length	: 208mm

Height	144mm
Barrel length	76mm
Trigger stop	adjustable
Sights	fixed
Sight radius	125mm
External safety	none
Internal safety	cylinder blocks with cocked hammer

FEATURES:

• thumb piece	rearside of frame, next to hammer
• material	stainless steel
• finish	stainless
• grips	wood

Korth Combat revolver

TECHNICAL SPECIFICATIONS:

Calibre	.357 Magnum with interchangeable cylinder for calibre 9mm Para
Trigger action	double action
Magazine capacity	6 rounds
Locking mechanism	front/rear-side centre pin
Weight	1020g
Length	233mm
Height	144mm
Barrel length	102mm
Trigger stop	adjustable
Sights	fixed
Sight radius	150mm
External safety	none
Internal safety	cylinder blocks with cocked hammer

FEATURES:

• thumb piece	rearside of frame, next to hammer
• material	steel
• finish	blued
• grips	wood

Korth Sport Stainless revolver

TECHNICAL SPECIFICATIONS:

Calibre	.357 Magnum
Trigger action	double action
Magazine capacity	6 rounds
Locking mechanism	front/rear-side centre pin
Weight	1020g
Length	233mm
Height	144mm
Barrel length	102mm
Trigger stop	adjustable
Sights	adjustable micrometer rear sight
Sight radius	150mm
External safety	none
Internal safety	cylinder blocks with cocked hammer

FEATURES:

• thumb piece	rearside of frame, next to hammer
• material	stainless steel
• finish	high-gloss stainless, gold-plated trigger and hammer
• grips	wood

Korth Sport revolver

TECHNICAL SPECIFICATIONS:

Calibre	.357 Magnum
Trigger action	double action
Magazine capacity	6 rounds
Locking mechanism	front/rear-side centre pin
Weight	1100g
Length	320mm

Height	:	145mm
Barrel length	:	152mm
Trigger stop	:	adjustable
Sights	:	adjustable micrometer rear sight
Sight radius	:	230mm
External safety	:	none
Internal safety	:	cylinder blocks with cocked hammer

FEATURES:

• thumb piece	:	rearside of frame, next to hammer
• material	:	steel
• finish	:	blued
• grips	:	wood

The Korth revolver shown here is a specially engraved commemorative model in honour of the thirty years of the Korth Company

Korth Sport revolver

TECHNICAL SPECIFICATIONS:

Calibre	:	.38 Special
Trigger action	:	double action
Magazine capacity	:	6 rounds
Locking mechanism	:	front/rear-side centre pin
Weight	:	1020g
Length	:	233mm
Height	:	144mm
Barrel length	:	102mm
Trigger stop	:	adjustable
Sights	:	adjustable micrometer rear sight
Sight radius	:	150mm
External safety	:	none
Internal safety	:	cylinder blocks with cocked hammer

FEATURES:

• thumb piece	:	rearside of frame, next to hammer
• material	:	steel
• finish	:	blued
• grips	:	wood

Korth Sport revolver

TECHNICAL SPECIFICATIONS:

Calibre	:	.357 Magnum
Trigger action	:	double action
Magazine capacity	:	6 rounds
Locking mechanism	:	front/rear-side centre pin
Weight	:	1020g
Length	:	233mm
Height	:	144mm
Barrel length	:	102mm
Trigger stop	:	adjustable
Sights	:	adjustable micrometer rear sight
Sight radius	:	150mm

External safety	: none
Internal safety	: cylinder blocks with cocked hammer

FEATURES:

• thumb piece	: rearside of frame, next to hammer
• material	: steel
• finish	: high-gloss blued and engraved
• grips	: imitation ivoor

Les Baer sport pistols

In 1992 Les Baer, manager of the Springfield Custom Shop, decided to start up in business himself. He founded his company, Les Baer Custom Inc., in Hillsdale, Illinois. At first he specialized in rebuilding all kinds of pistol types to the specific wishes of each customer. This service has been extended considerably to a large range of special products, all based on the original Colt Model 1911-A1 pistol.
The Les Baer programme consists of special frames, slides, barrels, barrels with fixed compensators, scope mounts, special recoil buffers, special firing-pins, extractors, ejectors, magazine extensions, triggers, etc.
Besides this programme Les Baer has a wide range of pistols, also derived from the Colt 1911-A1.
Furthermore, it is very interesting that Les Baer developed a special pistol, ordered by the FBI, called the Baer SRP (Swift Response Pistol) for special Hostage Rescue Teams. This pistol was tested extensively, together with pistols from other competitors, and Baer won that test.
For the "normal" Les Baer pistols, frames of Baer's own design are used or, if desired, Para-Ordnance frames. The Les Baer pistols have a blued, stainless, or two-tone finish to order.

Les Baer Euro Master

TECHNICAL SPECIFICATIONS:

Calibre	: .38 Super Auto
Trigger action	: single action
Magazine capacity	: 20 rounds
Locking mechanism	: improved Browning system
Weight	: 1610g
Length	: 264mm
Height	: 150mm
Barrel length	: 127mm
Trigger stop	: adjustable

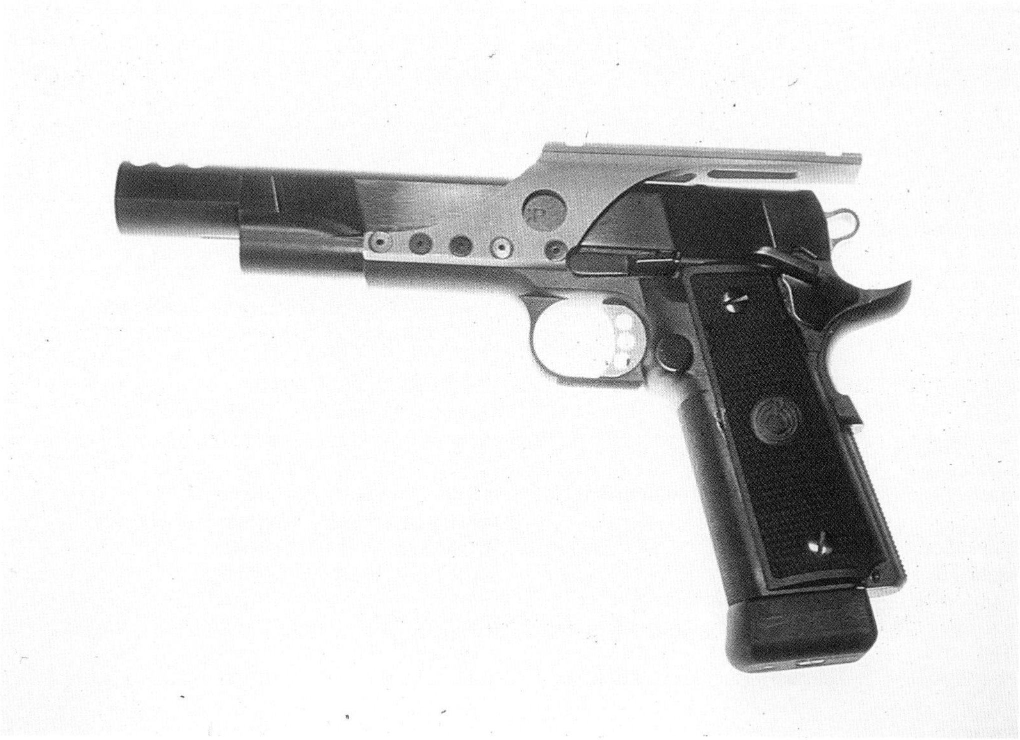

Sights	: none: special scope mount on slide
Sight radius	: not relevant
External safety	: safety catch on left side frame, grip safety
Internal safety	: slide safety

FEATURES:

• slide catch	: on left side frame
• magazine catch	: left side frame, behind trigger guard
• material	: steel or stainless steel
• finish	: blued steel or stainless
• grips	: special rubber Para-Ordnance

Les Baer Premier II

TECHNICAL SPECIFICATIONS:

Calibre	: .45 ACP
Trigger action	: single action
Magazine capacity	: 8 rounds
Locking mechanism	: improved Browning system
Weight	: 1100g
Length	: 216mm
Height	: 140mm
Barrel length	: 127mm
Trigger stop	: adjustable
Sights	: adjustable BoMar micro-rear sight
Sight radius	: 172mm
External safety	: ambidextrous safety catch on the frame, grip safety
Internal safety	: slide safety, half-cock safety

FEATURES:

• slide catch	: on left side frame
• magazine catch	: on left side frame, behind trigger guard
• material	: steel
• finish	: blued
• grips	: rosewood

This pistol is factory equipped with an enlarged ejection port, tuned trigger mechanism, special match trigger, bevelled magazine well, polished feeding ramp, throated barrel, and recoil buff.

Les Baer Prowler

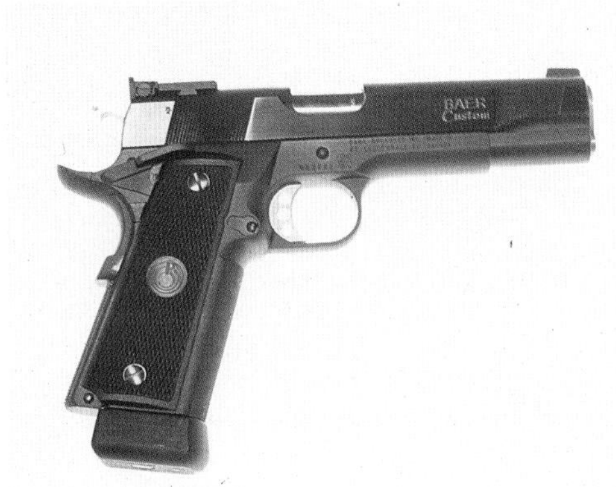

TECHNICAL SPECIFICATIONS:

Calibre	: .45 ACP
Trigger action	: single action
Magazine capacity	: 8 rounds
Locking mechanism	: improved Browning system
Weight	: 1100g
Length	: 216mm
Height	: 140mm
Barrel length	: 127mm
Trigger stop	: adjustable
Sights	: adjustable BoMar micro-rear sight
Sight radius	: 175mm
External safety	: ambidextrous safety catch on the frame, grip safety
Internal safety	: slide safety, half-cock safety

FEATURES:

• slide catch	: on left side frame
• magazine catch	: on left side frame, behind trigger guard
• material	: steel
• finish	: blued
• grips	: rosewood

This pistol is factory equipped with an enlarged ejection port, tuned trigger mechanism, special match trigger, bevelled magazine well, polished feeding ramp, throated barrel, and recoil buff.

Les Baer Ultimate Master 'Para'

TECHNICAL SPECIFICATIONS:

Calibre : .45 ACP
Trigger action : single action
Magazine capacity : 14 rounds
Locking mechanism : improved Browning system
Weight : 1610g
Length : 216mm
Height : 140mm
Barrel length : 127mm
Trigger stop : adjustable
Sights : adjustable BoMar micro-rear sight
Sight radius : 175mm
External safety : ambidextrous safety catch on frame, grip safety
Internal safety : slide safety, half-cock safety

FEATURES:

- slide catch : on left side frame
- magazine catch : on left side frame, behind trigger guard
- material : stainless steel
- finish : stainless
- grips : special rubber Para-Ordnance

This special IPSC pistol (Limited Class) is completely tuned. It is guaranteed to shoot 65mm (21/2in) at 50 yards (45m).

Les Baer Ultimate Master Racegun

TECHNICAL SPECIFICATIONS:

Calibre : .38 Super Auto
Trigger action : single action
Magazine capacity : 20 rounds
Locking mechanism : improved Browning system
Weight : 1610g
Length : 264mm
Height : 150mm
Barrel length : 127mm
Trigger stop : adjustable
Sights : none: special scope mount on slide
Sight radius : not relevant
External safety : ambidextrous safety catch on frame, grip safety
Internal safety : slide safety, half-cock safety

FEATURES:

- slide catch : on left side frame
- magazine catch : on left side frame, behind trigger guard
- material : stainless steel
- finish : stainless
- grips : rubber

This pistol is factory tuned.

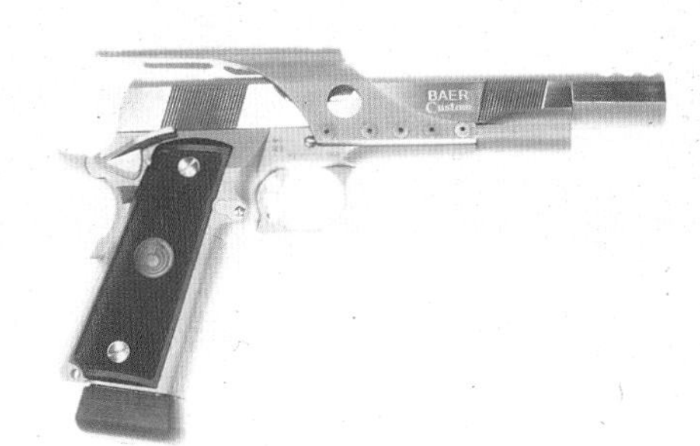

Les Baer Ultimate Master STI

TECHNICAL SPECIFICATIONS:

Calibre : .38 Super Auto
Trigger action : single action
Magazine capacity : 17 rounds
Locking mechanism : improved Browning system
Weight : 1190g
Length : 275mm (inc. compensator)
Height : 220mm (inc. scope)
Barrel length : 135mm
Trigger stop : adjustable
Sights : scope mount
Sight radius : none
External safety : ambidextrous safety catch on frame, grip safety

Internal safety	:	slide safety, half-cock safety

FEATURES:

• slide catch	:	on left side frame
• magazine catch	:	on left side frame, behind trigger guard
• material	:	stainless steel slide, alloy frame
• finish	:	stainless
• grips	:	special rubber

This pistol is factory provided with several customized features, such as an enlarged ejection port, tuned trigger action, bevelled magazine well, etc.

Llama pistols

The Spanish Basque company of Llama was founded in 1904 as the Gabilondo y Urresti and was situated in Guernica. After the First World War it moved to Elgoibar and the company name was changed to Gabilondo Y Compañía (Company). About a decade later the factory was moved to the Basque town of Vitoria. Gabilondo is the manufacturer of Ruby revolvers, Llama pistols and revolvers, and Star pistols. The name (pronounced as: "Li-jama) means "flame".

A number of Llama pistols are also manufactured under the brands Tauler and Múgica, mainly for the South American market. A number of models are derived from the trusted Colt 1911 and 1911-A1 pistol. The calibres vary from .22 LR up to .45 ACP. Some models were also made in calibre .38 Super especially for the American market. Some models are an exact copy of the Colt 1911, and others are a reduced version of that, like the Model XI-B with an overall length of 203mm instead of the standard Colt length of 216mm. A number of Llama Colt look-alikes have, just like the original, a grip safety at the backstrap of the frame. T

he balance between quality and price of the Llama handguns is very good. A long time before Colt introduced its automatic firing-pin safety in its 'Series 80' models, Llama had already installed this system in most of its models. Llama has several pistol types, based on the Colt 1911-A1 model:

Model	Calibre
X-A	.32 ACP (7.65mm)
III-A	.380 ACP (9mm Short)
Max I L/F	.45 ACP, .40 S&W, 9mm Para
Max I C/F	.45 ACP, .40 S&W, 9mm Para
IX-C	.45 ACP
IX-D	.45 ACP
XI-D	9mm Para
VIII-C	.38 Super

The Llama Model 82 pistol has a steel frame and slide, which is obvious from the weight: 1110g. Llama also made a lighter version, the Model 82-LM, with an alloy frame and a weight of 875g.
The Llama M82 has a falling-block locking action, derived from the well-known Walther P38 or Beretta 92 system. In this model no firing-pin safety is installed, but another device, namely, the magazine safety.
The extractor also serves as a loading indicator: if a cartridge is in the chamber, the extractor sticks out and a red dot is visible. The guide for the slide runs over the entire length of the top of the frame, which is advantageous for the gun's precision.

It is a rugged handgun, designed as a service pistol for army or police.
The Llama Omni pistol, introduced in 1983, was developed for the American market and was available in the calibres 9mm Para and .45 ACP. The most striking differences compared with the M82 are the rugged square slide and the square trigger guard.
The locking action is somewhat extravagant and works by a heavy lug situated around the barrel, for which system the well-tried Browning design was very definitely abandoned. There is also a new principle for the trigger system. At the trigger, two trigger bars have been fitted. The left trigger bar takes care of the firing in the single-action mode and with the right trigger bar a double-action shot can be fired. Llama ceased the production of the Omni only a few years later. In 1987, Llama introduced a match version of the military Model 82.
The Llama 87 'Shooting Competition' in calibre 9mm Para is specially designed for action shooting, such as practical pistol courses, falling plate, and bowling pin shooting. The pistol is provided with a double-action trigger action, external hammer, adjustable rear sight, a magazine catch on the left side of the frame, behind the trigger guard, a bevelled magazine well, and a trigger stop. The butt plate of the magazine is fitted with a rubber buffer plate.
The pistol has a tuned trigger and a two-chamber compensator.
At the end of 1993, two new sporting pistols were introduced, the standard Model M87 and a compensator model M87 with a three-chamber, factory-installed compensator. Both models have a two-tone finish: a blued slide and matt nickel-plated frame.

Llama M82

TECHNICAL SPECIFICATIONS:

Calibre	: 9mm Para
Trigger action	: double action
Magazine capacity	: 15 rounds
Locking mechanism	: falling-block system
Weight	: 1110g (LM model 875 g)
Length	: 209mm
Height	: 135mm
Barrel length	: 113mm
Trigger stop	: none
Sights	: fixed with three-dot low-light sights
Sight radius	: 151mm
External safety	: combined decock/safety catch
Internal safety	: slide safety, magazine safety, half-cock safety

FEATURES:

• slide catch	: on left side frame
• magazine catch	: on left side frame, behind trigger guard
• material	: steel (LM model has alloy frame)
• finish	: blued
• grips	: composition

Llama M87

TECHNICAL SPECIFICATIONS:

Calibre	: 9mm Para, 9x21 IMI .40 S&W
Trigger action	: double action
Magazine capacity	: 15 rounds
Locking mechanism	: falling-block system
Weight	: 1235g
Length	: 245mm (Compact)
Height	: 143mm
Barrel length	: 133mm
Trigger stop	: adjustable
Sights	: fixed of adjustable Millet rear sights
Sight radius	: 195mm
External safety	: ambidextrous decocking lever on slide, blocked firing-pin; safety catch on left side of frame, wich blocks trigger bar and back part of dual firing-pin
Internal safety	: slide safety

FEATURES:

• slide catch	: on left side frame
• magazine catch	: on left side frame, behind trigger guard (is reversable)
• material	: steel
• finish	: blued; two-tone finish (blue slide, matt nickel frame)
• grips	: rubber or wood

The Llama M87 has a compensator, fixed to the barrel, which also serves as a barrel weight.

Llama Model Max I L/F

TECHNICAL SPECIFICATIONS:

Calibre	: .45 ACP, .40 S&W, 9mm Para
Trigger action	: single action
Magazine capacity	: 7 rounds (.45); 8 rounds (.40), 9 rounds (9mm Para)
Locking mechanism	: Browning system
Weight	: 1150g
Length	: 216mm
Height	: 137mm
Barrel length	: 127mm
Trigger stop	: none
Sights	: fixed
Sight radius	: 150mm
External safety	: safety catch on left side frame
Internal safety	: slide safety, automatic firing-pin safety, grip safety

FEATURES:

• slide catch	: on left side frame
• magazine catch	: on left side frame, behind trigger guard
• material	: steel
• finish	: blued
• grips	: black neoprene

Llama Model VIII-C

TECHNICAL SPECIFICATIONS:

Calibre	: .38 Super
Trigger action	: single action
Magazine capacity	: 18 rounds
Locking mechanism	: Browning system
Weight	: 1200g
Length	: 216mm
Height	: 137mm
Barrel length	: 127mm
Trigger stop	: no
Sights	: fixed
Sight radius	: 150mm
External safety	: safety catch on left side frame
Internal safety	: slide safety, automatic firing-pin safety, grip safety

FEATURES:

• slide catch	: on left side frame
• magazine catch	: on left side frame, behind trigger guard
• material	: steel
• finish	: blued
• grips	: black rubber

Llama Model IX-C

TECHNICAL SPECIFICATIONS:

Calibre	: .45 ACP
Trigger action	: single action
Magazine capacity	: 13 rounds
Locking mechanism	: Browning system
Weight	: 1200g
Length	: 216mm
Height	: 137mm
Barrel length	: 127mm
Trigger stop	: none
Sights	: fixed
Sight radius	: 150mm
External safety	: safety catch on left side frame
Internal safety	: slide safety, automatic firing-pin safety, grip safety

FEATURES:

• slide catch	: on left side frame
• magazine catch	: on left side frame, behind trigger guard
• material	: steel
• finish	: blued
• grips	: black rubber

Llama Model IX-D and XI-D

TECHNICAL SPECIFICATIONS:

Calibre	: .45 ACP, 9mm Para
Trigger action	: single action
Magazine capacity	: 13 rounds (.45), 18 rounds (9mm Para)
Locking mechanism	: Browning system
Weight	: 1100g
Length	: 200mm
Height	: 137mm
Barrel length	: 114mm
Trigger stop	: no
Sights	: fixed
Sight radius	: 143mm
External safety	: safety catch on left side frame
Internal safety	: slide safety, automatic firing-pin safety, grip safety

FEATURES:

• slide catch	: on left side frame
• magazine catch	: on left side frame, behind trigger guard
• material	: steel
• finish	: blued
• grips	: black rubber

Llama Model X-A

TECHNICAL SPECIFICATIONS:

Calibre	: .32 (7.65 mm)
Trigger action	: single action

Magazine capacity : 8 rounds
Locking mechanism : blowback system
Weight : 625g
Length : 160mm
Height : 110mm
Barrel length : 86mm
Trigger stop : none
Sights : fixed
Sight radius : 110mm
External safety : safety catch on left side frame
Internal safety : slide safety, automatic firing-pin safety, grip safety

FEATURES:

- slide catch : on left side frame
- magazine catch : on left side frame, behind trigger guard
- material : steel slide, alloy frame
- finish : blued
- grips : composition

Llama Model III-A

TECHNICAL SPECIFICATIONS:

Calibre : .380 ACP (9mm Short)
Trigger action : single action
Magazine capacity : 7 rounds
Locking mechanism : blowback system
Weight : 625g
Length : 160mm
Height : 110mm
Barrel length : 86mm
Trigger stop : none
Sights : fixed
Sight radius : 110mm
External safety : safety catch on left side frame
Internal safety : slide safety, automatic firing-pin safety, grip safety

FEATURES:

- slide catch : on left side frame
- magazine catch : on left side frame, behind trigger guard
- material : steel slide, alloy frame
- finish : blued
- grips : composition

Llama revolvers

In recent decades the Spanish arms factory, Llama, has produced a wide range of revolvers, most of which had quite fanciful names like the Comanche, Super Comanche, Crusader, and Martial, in calibres ranging from .22 LR up to .44 Magnum. Llama regularly changed its programme under the pressure of heavy competition.

The recent range of products is, certainly in comparison with the former programme, considerably slimmer. Not only as regards the large-bore calibres but also as regards the available finishes. For instance, in 1991 Llama introduced a stainless-steel Super Comanche Silhouette revolver in calibre .357 Magnum with an 83/8in barrel, which vanished silently two years later. Until about 1976, Llama had a line of Martial Series revolvers. In 1978, the construction of these guns changed a little and they were marketed under the name of the Comanche Series. That same year Llama introduced the Comanche in calibre .44 Magnum with barrel lengths of 6_in and 8 3/8in. The production of this .44 Magnum revolver ceased in 1993.

The new Llama programme consists of a small series of double-action revolvers with a unique safety device. The hammer axis is eccentrically fitted and is not able to reach the firing-pin in the uncocked position. If the trigger is pulled, the hammer drops a little and can therefore reach the firing-pin. As soon as the trigger is released, the hammer rises again. The Llama revolvers have a very good price/quality ratio. The workmanship is fair to good. The recent revolver programme consists of the models Scorpio, a small 2in barrelled revolver in calibre .38 Special; the Martial, a very good revolver with ventilated barrel in calibre .38 Special and with barrel lengths of 3in, 4in and 6in; the Model XXVI (26) in calibre .22 LR; and the Comanche in calibre .357 Magnum with a 4in or 6in barrel. Llama discontinued revolver models in stainless steel, but a matt nickel-plated finish can be supplied on special order.

Llama Comanche

TECHNICAL SPECIFICATIONS:

Calibre	: .357 Magnum
Trigger action	: double action
Magazine capacity	: 6 rounds
Locking mechanism	: rear/front-side centre pin
Weight	: 1035g
Length	: 235mm
Height	: 140mm
Barrel length	: 102mm
Trigger stop	: none
Sights	: adjustable micrometer rear sight
Sight radius	: 150mm
External safety	: none
Internal safety	: eccentric hammer axis, cylinder blocks with cocked hammer

FEATURES:

• thumb piece	: on left side frame
• material	: steel
• finish	: blued
• grips	: wood

The Llama Comanche is also available with a 152mm (6in) barrel.

Llama Scorpio

TECHNICAL SPECIFICATIONS:

Calibre	: .38 Special
Trigger action	: double action
Magazine capacity	: 6 rounds
Locking mechanism	: rear/front-side centre pin
Weight	: 825g
Length	: 180mm
Height	: 126mm
Barrel length	: 51mm (2")
Trigger stop	: none
Sights	: fixed
Sight radius	: 100mm
External safety	: none
Internal safety	: eccentric hammer axis, cylinder blocks with cocked hammer

FEATURES:

• thumb piece	: on left side frame
• material	: steel
• finish	: blued
• grips	: wood

Llama XXVI

TECHNICAL SPECIFICATIONS:

Calibre	: .22 LR
Trigger action	: double action
Magazine capacity	: 6 rounds
Locking mechanism	: rear/front-side centre pin

Weight	: 1115g
Length	: 235mm
Height	: 139mm
Barrel length	: 102mm
Trigger stop	: none
Sights	: adjustable micrometer rear sight
Sight radius	: 150mm
External safety	: none
Internal safety	: eccentric hammer axis, cylinder blocks with cocked hammer

FEATURES:

• thumb piece	: on left side frame
• material	: steel
• finish	: blued
• grips	: wood

Llama Martial

TECHNICAL SPECIFICATIONS:

Calibre	: .38 Special
Trigger action	: double action
Magazine capacity	: 6 rounds
Locking mechanism	: back/front-side centre pin
Weight	: 1067g (4")
Length	: 235mm (4")
Height	: 130mm
Barrel length	: 76mm (3"); 102mm (4"); 152mm (6")
Trigger stop	: none
Sights	: adjustable micrometer rear sight
Sight radius	: 150mm (4")
External safety	: none
Internal safety	: eccentric hammer axis, cylinder blocks with cocked hammer

FEATURES:

• thumb piece	: on left side frame
• material	: steel
• finish	: blued
• grips	: wood

Manurhin revolvers

The name Manurhin is a combination of the names Manufacture, Mulhouse (a French town), and Rhin (the River Rhine). Originally the company was involved in the production of machinery, especially for producing ammunition. The history of this factory, as far as arms are concerned, goes back to just after the end of the Second World War.
The Allied forces captured the German region of Thuringia. In that area, in the town of Zella-Mehlis, there was a branch of the Walther company.
In accordance with the Treaty of Yalta, this "sector" was handed over to the Russians. In Yalta an agreement was reached between the American President Roosevelt, the British Prime Minister Churchill, and the Russian President Stalin, by which Europe was to be divided among the different super-powers. Walther was forced to abandon the factory and fled to the western sector. When Nazi Germany surrendered, one stipulation was that Germany was not to be allowed to produce arms. Because the demand for Walther pistols continued, an agreement was made with Manurhin, who produced these pistols under licence. In 1955 Germany regained its sovereignty and Walther was able to produce its own weapons once again. After this period, Manurhin concentrated on the manufacture of revolvers and, more recently, on special weapons for governments. This is especially the case with the MR-35 Punch, a combination of a pistol and a carbine, which can fire rubber bullets with a diameter of 35mm, for riot-control.
The range of revolvers at Manurhin consists of a series of police revolvers, named Defense et Gendarmerie (Defence and Police), and a series of match revolvers. The current name of the company is Manurhin Equipment.

Manurhin MR73 G Gendarmerie 3"

TECHNICAL SPECIFICATIONS:

Calibre	: .357 Magnum
Trigger action	: double action
Magazine capacity	: 6 rounds
Locking mechanism	: front/rear-side centre pin
Weight	: 910g
Length	: 205mm
Height	: 142mm
Barrel length	: 76mm
Trigger stop	: none
Sights	: adjustable micrometer rear sight
Sight radius	: 117mm

External safety : none
Internal safety : transfer bar

FEATURES:

- thumb piece : left on frame
- material : steel
- finish : blued
- grips : walnut

The MR73 Gendarmerie (Police) is available with a 3in or 4in barrel.

Manurhin MR73 Sport 6"

The gun shown here is a specially engraved MR 73 Sport model

TECHNICAL SPECIFICATIONS:

Calibre : .357 Magnum
Trigger action : double action
Magazine capacity : 6 rounds
Locking mechanism : front/rear-side centre pin
Weight : 1070g
Length : 283mm
Height : 142mm
Barrel length : 152mm
Trigger stop : none
Sights : adjustable micrometer rear sight
Sight radius : 193mm
External safety : none
Internal safety : transfer bar

FEATURES:

- thumb piece : left on frame
- material : steel
- finish : blued
- grips : walnut

Manurhin MR88 D Defense 3"

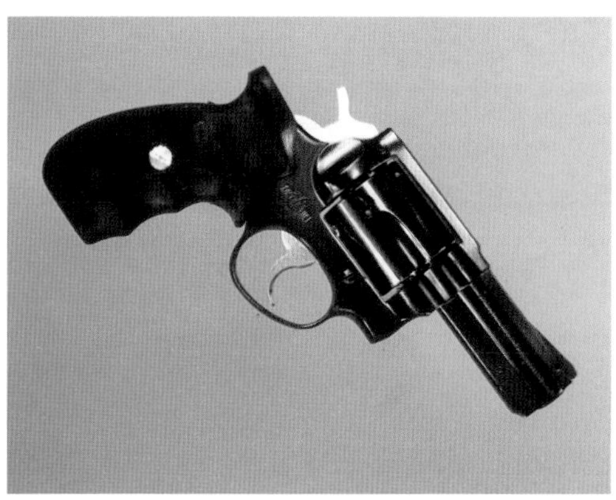

TECHNICAL SPECIFICATIONS:

Calibre : .357 Magnum
Trigger action : double action
Magazine capacity : 6 rounds
Locking mechanism : front/rear-side centre pin
Weight : 950g
Length : 206mm
Height : 142mm
Barrel length : 76mm
Trigger stop : none
Sights : fixed
Sight radius : 123mm
External safety : none
Internal safety : transfer bar

FEATURES:

- thumb piece : left on frame
- material : steel
- finish : blued
- grips : rubber

The MR88 revolver has three basic models, namely, the Defence model (D): blued finish with fixed rear sight; the Defence model (DX): stainless steel with fixed rear sight; and the Sport model (SX): stainless-steel sport revolver with micrometer rear sight.

Manurhin MR88 DX Defence Inox 4"

TECHNICAL SPECIFICATIONS:

Calibre	: .357 Magnum
Trigger action	: double action
Magazine capacity	: 6 rounds
Locking mechanism	: front/rear-side centre pin
Weight	: 1005g
Length	: 231mm
Height	: 142mm
Barrel length	: 102mm
Trigger stop	: no
Sights	: fixed
Sight radius	: 150mm
External safety	: none
Internal safety	: transfer bar

FEATURES:

• thumb piece	: left on frame
• material	: stainless steel
• finish	: stainless
• grips	: rubber

Manurhin MR88 SX Sport Inox 4"

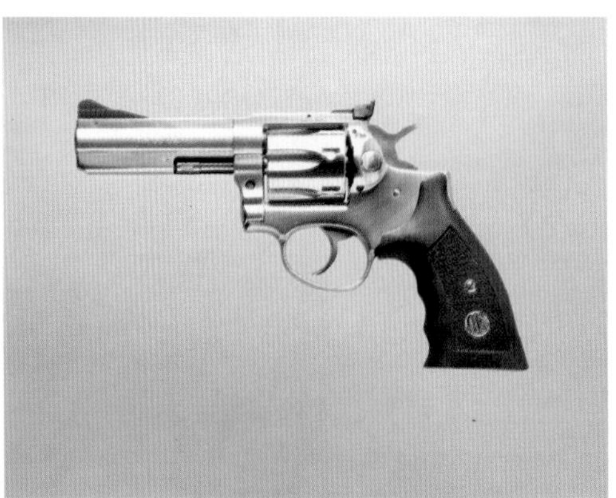

TECHNICAL SPECIFICATIONS:

Calibre	: .357 Magnum
Trigger action	: double action
Magazine capacity	: 6 rounds
Locking mechanism	: front/rear-side centre pin
Weight	: 1005g
Length	: 231mm
Height	: 142mm
Barrel length	: 102mm
Trigger stop	: no
Sights	: adjustable
Sight radius	: 150mm
External safety	: none
Internal safety	: transfer bar

FEATURES:

• thumb piece	: left on frame
• material	: stainless steel
• finish	: stainless
• grips	: walnut

Manurhin MR88 SX Sport Inox 5-1/4"

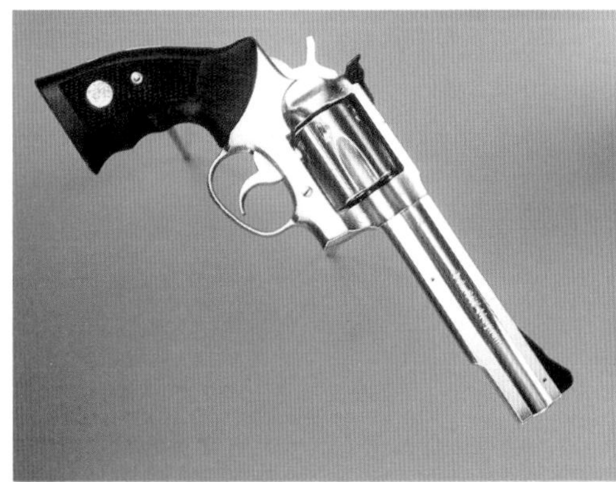

TECHNICAL SPECIFICATIONS:

Calibre	: .357 Magnum
Trigger action	: double action
Magazine capacity	: 6 rounds
Locking mechanism	: front/rear-side centre pin
Weight	: 1060g
Length	: 263mm
Height	: 142mm
Barrel length	: 133mm
Trigger stop	: no
Sights	: adjustable
Sight radius	: 182mm
External safety	: none
Internal safety	: transfer bar

FEATURES:

• thumb piece	: left on frame

• material	: stainless steel
• finish	: stainless
• grips	: walnut

Manurhin MR93 Sport 4"

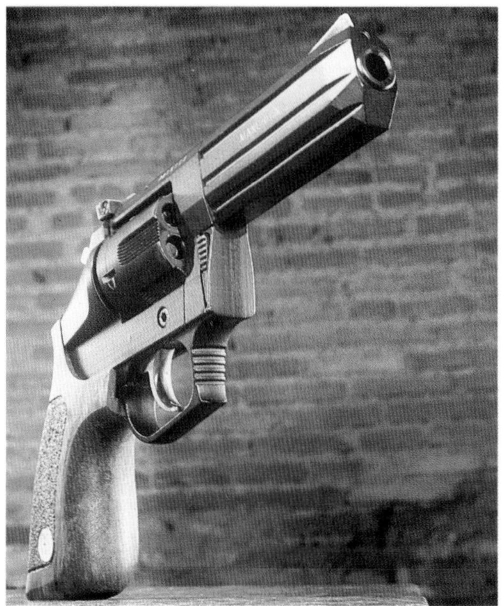

TECHNICAL SPECIFICATIONS:

Calibre	: .357 Magnum
Trigger action	: double action
Magazine capacity	: 6 rounds
Locking mechanism	: rear side centre pin, cylinder crane
Weight	: 1116g
Length	: 245mm
Height	: 142mm
Barrel length	: 102mm
Trigger stop	: none
Sights	: adjustable
Sight radius	: 150mm
External safety	: none
Internal safety	: transfer bar

FEATURES:

• thumb piece	: on cylinder crane
• material	: steel
• finish	: black coating
• grips	: walnut

The MR93 revolver has interchangeable barrels, similar to the Dan Wesson system.

Mauser/Luger pistols

Peter Paul Mauser, an arms manufacturer par excellence and an authority on the military arms market, decided in 1890 to compete for several contracts for a new army pistol. His factory manager, called Federle, had designed a system for a semi-automatic pistol, for which Mauser himself developed a matching cartridge. This cartridge was derived from the calibre 7.65mm Borchardt. Mauser had great success with his pistol and there are many variations of the model. Because the pistol was introduced in 1896, it was named C-96. Mauser kept improving the design and twenty-two model modifications are known from the period 1896–1934.

From 1912 to 1918 Mauser produced vast numbers of this pistol, especially for export in calibre 9mm Mauser. This model was named the Mauser military M12 or Mauser Bolo. In 1916 the C-96 was also manufactured in calibre 9mm Para. In the grip the number "9" was carved and coloured with red varnish. In the whole production period considerable numbers of C-96 pistols were exported to other countries, including Turkey, Italy, France, Siam, Austria, Persia, Finland, and Norway. Some Mauser C-96 models were equipped with a removable wooden carbine stock for long-range shooting. These models had a special ladder rear sight for ranges up to 450 or even 700m. Besides the name of Mauser, names of other trading companies, who ordered large quantities, are also stamped on these models, such as Westley Richards & Co., Stoeger Inc., Jeffery & Co., and Lengerke & Detmold. The Mauser C-96 was copied by the Spanish arms company Astra and several Chinese arms factories in calibre .45 ACP.

The Mauser C-96 pistol was also used as a personal defence gun by Winston Churchill. The production of the C-96 model ceased in 1930, in favour of the new model 1930, and the total production came to an end after the surrender of the German army in 1945.

Around the turn of the century, a great number of arms companies struggled in competition for large government orders. In Germany these were Mauser, Bergmann, and the American combine Borchardt-Bayard. Because the first semi-automatic pistols were regularly malfunctioning and a good calibre design was lacking, those big orders were not granted. George Luger, a German engineer, worked together with Borchardt to design a new army pistol. In 1898 the pistol was tested in the Swiss army trials, after which the calibre was changed, at the request of the Swiss, from 7.65mm

Borchardt to 7.65mm Para. In 1900 the Swiss army issued this pistol as a service gun, named Ordonnanz Pistole 1900 (Ordnance pistol 1900). This type is provided with a grip safety. In 1908, the German army placed a large order and the gun was issued to the German troops as the Model P08, first in calibre 7.65mm Para but later in calibre 9mm Para.
The unique lock action is achieved by means of a toggle bolt, which hinges upwards during the cycling of the gun. In the beginning this pistol was produced by DWM (Deutsche Waffen- und Munitionsfabrik – German Arms and Ammunition factory) in Berlin, but in 1930 the manufacture was taken over by Mauser.
The pistol was produced until 1942, after which Mauser had to switch to the production of the Walther P38, on orders of the Wehrmacht (the German army).

Many variations of the Luger P08 pistol are known. The P08 was sold to many countries, including The Netherlands, Russia, Sweden, Persia, Portugal, Morocco, and Bulgaria. The pistol was even tested in the US army trials in 1900 and 1907, but was turned down in favour of the Colt 1911 pistol. Several companies, Mauser included, still produce small series of Lugers in blued or even stainless finishes and in several different calibres from .22 LR up to .45 ACP. Mauser, for instance, introduces a special model almost every year to celebrate the International Arms Exhibition in Neurenberg, Germany.

Mauser P08

The Luger P08 pistol has a great many variations. The basic models are:

- Model P08 in calibre 7.65mm Para and 9mm Para.
- Model P08/20 in calibre 7.65mm Para and with a maximum barrel length of 102mm.
- Model 1917 with a 190mm barrel, detachable carbine stock and a thirty-two-round magazine.

TECHNICAL SPECIFICATIONS:

Calibre	: 7.65mm Para, 9mm Para
Trigger action	: single action
Magazine capacity	: 8 rounds
Locking mechanism	: Luger toggle system
Weight	: 835g
Length	: 230mm
Height	: 135mm
Barrel length	: 102mm
Trigger stop	: none
Sights	: fixed
Sight radius	: 205mm
External safety	: safety catch on left side frame, grip safety
Internal safety	: slide safety

FEATURES:

• slide catch	: not present
• magazine catch	: on left side frame, behind trigger guard
• material	: steel
• finish	: blued
• grips	: walnut

Mauser P08

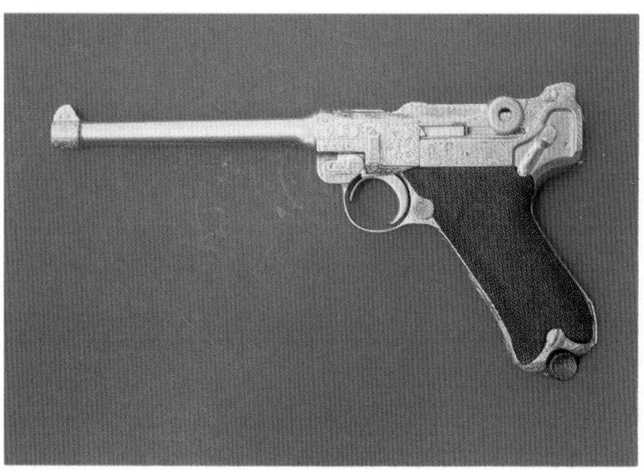

TECHNICAL SPECIFICATIONS:

Calibre	: 7.65mm Para, 9mm Para

Trigger action	: single action
Magazine capacity	: 8 rounds
Locking mechanism	: Luger toggle system
Weight	: 910g
Length	: 281mm
Height	: 135mm
Barrel length	: 152mm
Trigger stop	: none
Sights	: adjustable
Sight radius	: 255mm
External safety	: safety catch on left side frame
Internal safety	: slide safety

FEATURES:

• slide catch	: not present
• magazine catch	: on left side frame, behind trigger guard
• material	: steel
• finish	: matt chrome plated, working components 18K gold
• grips	: walnut

Mauser P08

Special commemorative model for the founders of the Mauser Company, Paul and Wilhelm Mauser. Portraits of both are engraved on the ivory grips.
On both sides of the frame is an engraving of the Mauser factory

TECHNICAL SPECIFICATIONS:

Calibre	: 7.65mm Para, 9mm Para
Trigger action	: single action
Magazine capacity	: 8 rounds
Locking mechanism	: Luger toggle system
Weight	: 910g
Length	: 280mm
Height	: 135mm
Barrel length	: 152mm
Trigger stop	: none
Sights	: fixed
Sight radius	: 255mm
External safety	: safety catch on left side frame, grip safety
Internal safety	: slide safety

FEATURES:

• slide catch	: not present
• magazine catch	: on left side frame, behind trigger guard
• material	: steel
• finish	: chrome plated
• grips	: ivory

Mauser P08

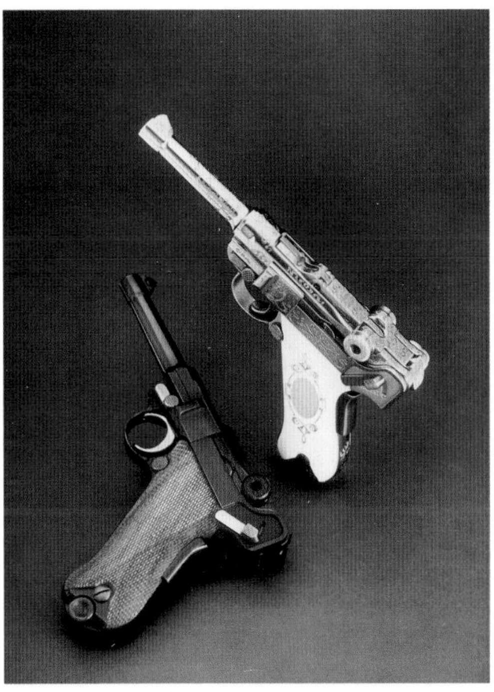

This picture shows the standard Luger/Mauser P08.

TECHNICAL SPECIFICATIONS:

Calibre	: 9mm Para
Trigger action	: single action
Magazine capacity	: 8 rounds
Locking mechanism	: Luger toggle system
Weight	: 835g
Length	: 230mm
Height	: 135mm

Barrel length	:	102 mm
Trigger stop	:	none
Sights	:	fixed
Sight radius	:	205 mm
External safety	:	safety catch on left side frame, grip safety
Internal safety	:	slide safety

FEATURES:

• slide catch	:	not present
• magazine catch	:	on left side frame, behind trigger guard
• material	:	steel
• finish	:	chrome plated
• grips	:	ivory with monogram inlay

Mauser P08

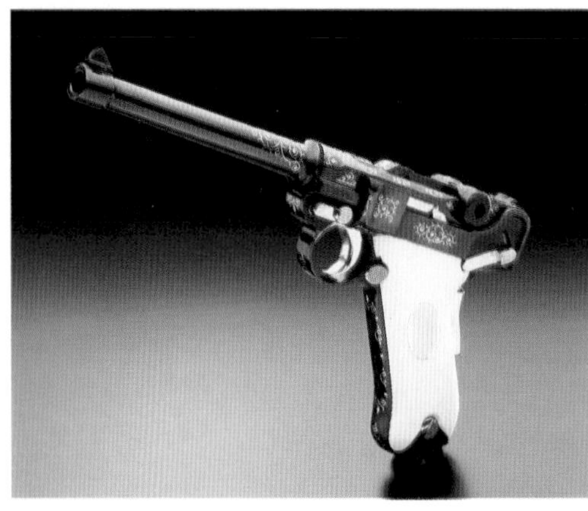

TECHNICAL SPECIFICATIONS:

Calibre	:	7.65mm Para, 9mm Para
Trigger action	:	single action
Magazine capacity	:	8 rounds
Locking mechanism	:	Luger toggle system
Weight	:	910g
Length	:	280mm
Height	:	135mm
Barrel length	:	152mm
Trigger stop	:	none
Sights	:	fixed
Sight radius	:	255mm
External safety	:	safety catch on left side frame, grip safety
Internal safety	:	slide safety

FEATURES:

• slide catch	:	not present
• magazine catch	:	on left side frame, behind trigger guard
• material	:	steel
• finish	:	blued, engraved with inlay of 18K gold; working elements 18 K gold plated
• grips	:	ivory with 18K gold inlay for monogram engraving

Mauser P08

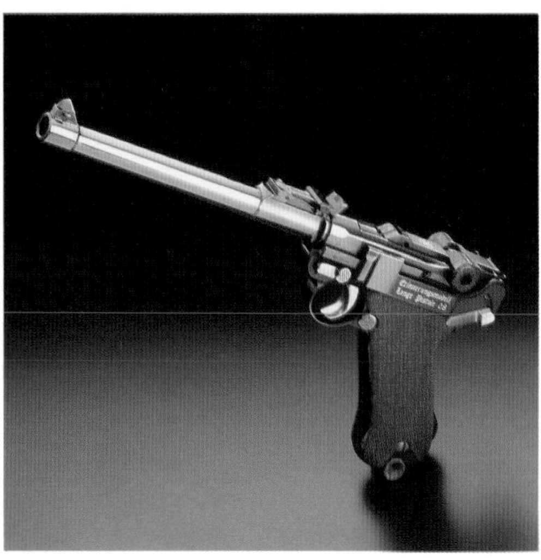

Only 250 guns of this special model are manufactured in one series

TECHNICAL SPECIFICATIONS:

Calibre	:	7.65mm Para, 9mm Para
Trigger action	:	single action
Magazine capacity	:	8 rounds
Locking mechanism	:	Luger toggle system
Weight	:	980g
Length	:	332mm
Height	:	135mm
Barrel length	:	203mm
Trigger stop	:	no
Sights	:	adjustable ladder rear sight (up to 800 m)
Sight radius	:	202mm
External safety	:	safety catch on left side frame, grip safety (early models)
Internal safety	:	slide safety

FEATURES:

• slide catch	:	not present
• magazine catch	:	on left side frame, behind trigger guard
• material	:	steel
• finish	:	blued
• grips	:	walnut

Mauser Model 80 SA pistol

TECHNICAL SPECIFICATIONS:

Calibre : 9mm Para
Trigger action : single action
Magazine capacity : 13 rounds
Locking mechanism : Browning-FN system
Weight : 990g
Length : 203mm
Height : 141mm
Barrel length : 119mm
Trigger stop : none
Sights : fixed
Sight radius : 163mm
External safety : safety catch on left side frame
Internal safety : slide safety, magazine safety

FEATURES:

- slide catch : on left side frame
- magazine catch : on left side frame, behind trigger guard
- material : steel
- finish : blued
- grips : walnut

Mauser Model 90 DA-pistol

TECHNICAL SPECIFICATIONS:

Calibre : 9mm Para
Trigger action : double-action
Magazine capacity : 14 rounds
Locking mechanism : Browning-FN system
Weight : 1000g
Length : 203mm
Height : 141mm
Barrel length : 119mm
Trigger stop : none
Sights : fixed
Sight radius : 163mm
External safety : decock/safety catch on left side slide
Internal safety : slide safety, magazine safety

FEATURES:

- slide catch : on left side frame
- magazine catch : on left side frame, behind trigger guard
- material : steel
- finish : blued
- grips : walnut

Mauser Model 90 DA Compact pistol

TECHNICAL SPECIFICATIONS:

Calibre : 9mm Para
Trigger action : double action
Magazine capacity : 14 rounds
Locking mechanism : Browning-FN system
Weight : 900g

Length	:	185mm
Height	:	141mm
Barrel length	:	100mm
Trigger stop	:	none
Sights	:	fixed
Sight radius	:	145mm
External safety	:	decock/safety catch on left side slide
Internal safety	:	slide safety, magazine safety

FEATURES:

• slide catch	:	on left side frame
• magazine catch	:	on left side frame, behind trigger guard
• material	:	steel
• finish	:	blued
• grips	:	walnut

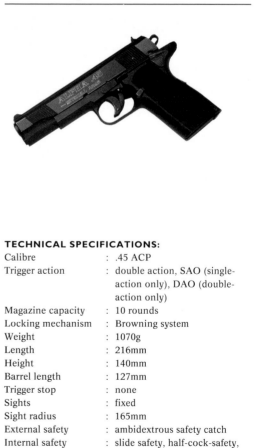

Mitchell handguns

The American Mitchell Arms Company was founded in 1984 by John Mitchell, the former manager of the High Standard arms factory, which went bankrupt in the beginning of 1984. Mitchell Arms is situated in Santa Anna in the State of California.

To begin with the company devoted itself to the production of assault rifles in calibre .22 LR, like the Colt M16, the Kalashnikov AK-47, and the French MAS. It also manufactured replicas of the Colt Single-Action Army (Peacemaker) in the calibres .44 Magnum and .45 Long Colt. It also traded in replicas of several large-bore blackpowder revolvers like Colts and Remingtons, which were bought from the well-known Italian arms factory Uberti. After the termination of the High Standard production, Mitchell saw the opportunity to produce the beloved High Standard small-bore pistols himself. Mitchell produces these famous models in stainless steel and in barrel lengths of 114mm (4_in) up to 184mm (7_in) with a matt stainless finish or in blued stainless steel. The unique rear-sight bridge, in particular, built over the slide of the pistol, can be found on the models Citation II, Trophy II, and Olympic II. Other models, like the Victor II, are provided with a wide and high ventilated barrel band, on to which the rear sight is built. Another well-known product is the Luger (or Mauser) P08 pistol in calibre 9mm Para in a stainless-steel finish. This model is produced on behalf of Mitchell by the American Aimco company in Houston, Texas. Furthermore, the company is engaged in the production and sale of all kinds of special versions of the Colt Model 1911-A1 pistol. The latest situation with respect to the High Standard match pistols is not quite clear, because since 1995 the High Standard pistols have been produced by another American company, the New England Arms.
Further, Mitchell offers an extensive range of grip plates, made of laminated wood, mahogany, Cocobolo wood, cherry wood, and special match grips with adjustable palm rest. He also produces a complete line of revolvers, all with the well-known Dan Wesson cylinder lock, which means that the cylinder locks into the frame with a catch on the cylinder crane. These revolvers are made in the calibres .38 Special and .357 Magnum, in all kinds of finishes and barrel lengths. The total range of Mitchell products is extensive.

Mitchell Alpha .45

TECHNICAL SPECIFICATIONS:

Calibre	:	.45 ACP
Trigger action	:	double action, SAO (single-action only), DAO (double-action only)
Magazine capacity	:	10 rounds
Locking mechanism	:	Browning system
Weight	:	1070g
Length	:	216mm
Height	:	140mm
Barrel length	:	127mm
Trigger stop	:	none
Sights	:	fixed
Sight radius	:	165mm
External safety	:	ambidextrous safety catch
Internal safety	:	slide safety, half-cock-safety, automatic firing-pin safety

FEATURES:

• slide catch	:	on left side frame
• magazine catch	:	on left side frame, behind trigger guard
• material	:	steel
• finish	:	blued
• grips	:	hard rubber

Mitchell High Standard Citation II

TECHNICAL SPECIFICATIONS:

Calibre	:	.22 LR
Trigger action	:	single action
Magazine capacity	:	10 rounds
Locking mechanism	:	blowback action
Weight	:	1300g
Length	:	295mm
Height	:	142mm
Barrel length	:	184mm
Sight radius	:	260mm
Trigger stop	:	fixed
Sights	:	adjustable rear sight on slide bridge
External safety	:	safety catch
Internal safety	:	slide safety, magazine safety

FEATURES:

• slide catch	:	on left side frame
• magazine catch	:	front bottom of grip
• material	:	stainless steel
• finish	:	matt stainless
• grips	:	walnut

Mitchell Gold .45

TECHNICAL SPECIFICATIONS:

Calibre	:	.45 ACP
Trigger action	:	single action
Magazine capacity	:	10 rounds
Locking mechanism	:	Browning system
Weight	:	1110g
Length	:	216mm
Height	:	136mm
Barrel length	:	130mm
Trigger stop	:	fixed
Sights	:	micrometer rear sight
Sight radius	:	170mm
External safety	:	ambidextrous safety catch on the frame, grip safety
Internal safety	:	slide safety, automatic firing-pin safety, half-cock safety

FEATURES:

• slide catch	:	on left side frame
• magazine catch	:	on left side frame, behind trigger guard
• material	:	stainless steel
• finish	:	matt stainless
• grips	:	hard rubber

Mitchell High Standard Olympic I.S.U. II

TECHNICAL SPECIFICATIONS:

Calibre	: .22 LR of .22 Short
Trigger action	: single action
Magazine capacity	: 10 rounds
Locking mechanism	: blowback system
Weight	: 1300g
Length	: 283mm
Height	: 142mm
Barrel length	: 172mm with integrated compensator
Sight radius	: 250mm
Trigger stop	: adjustable
Sights	: adjustable
External safety	: safety catch
Internal safety	: slide safety, magazine safety

FEATURES:

• slide catch	: on left side frame
• magazine catch	: front bottom of grip
• material	: stainless steel
• finish	: matt stainless
• grips	: walnut

Mitchell High Standard Sharpshooter II

TECHNICAL SPECIFICATIONS:

Calibre	: .22 LR
Trigger action	: single action
Magazine capacity	: 10 rounds
Locking mechanism	: blowback action
Weight	: 1250g
Length	: 250mm
Height	: 142mm
Barrel length	: 140mm
Sight radius	: 205mm
Trigger stop	: adjustable
Sights	: adjustable
External safety	: safety catch
Internal safety	: slide safety, magazine safety

FEATURES:

• slide catch	: on left side frame
• magazine catch	: front bottom of grip
• material	: stainless steel
• finish	: matt stainless
• grips	: walnut

Mitchell High Standard Sport King II

TECHNICAL SPECIFICATIONS:

Calibre	: .22 LR
Trigger action	: single action
Magazine capacity	: 10 rounds
Locking mechanism	: blowback action
Weight	: 1300g
Length	: 283mm
Height	: 142mm
Barrel length	: 172mm
Sight radius	: 250mm
Trigger stop	: fixed
Sights	: fixed
External safety	: safety catch
Internal safety	: slide safety, magazine safety

FEATURES:

• slide catch	: on left side frame
• magazine catch	: front bottom of grip
• material	: stainless steel
• finish	: matt stainless
• grips	: black rubber or walnut

Mitchell High Standard Victor II

TECHNICAL SPECIFICATIONS:

Calibre	: .22 LR
Trigger action	: single action
Magazine capacity	: 10 rounds
Locking mechanism	: blowback action
Weight	: 1210g

Length	: 216mm
Height	: 143mm
Barrel length	: 115mm
Sight radius	: 195mm
Trigger stop	: adjustable
Sights	: adjustable
External safety	: safety catch on left side frame
Internal safety	: slide safety, magazine safety
FEATURES:	
• slide catch	: none, slide stays open after last shot
• magazine catch	: front bottom of grip
• material	: stainless steel
• finish	: matt stainless
• grips	: walnut

Weight	: 1020g
Length	: 243mm
Height	: 149mm
Barrel length	: 102mm
Trigger stop	: none
Sights	: fixed
Sight radius	: 150mm
External safety	: cylinder blocks with cocked hammer
Internal safety	: transfer bar
FEATURES:	
• thumb piece	: on left side frame
• material	: steel
• finish	: blued
• grips	: walnut or rubber

Mitchell Guardian II 4"

TECHNICAL SPECIFICATIONS:

Calibre	: .38 Special
Trigger action	: double action
Magazine capacity	: 6 rounds
Locking mechanism	: rear-side centre pin, cylinder crane

Mitchell Guardian II 6"

TECHNICAL SPECIFICATIONS:

Calibre	: .38 Special
Trigger action	: double action
Magazine capacity	: 6 rounds
Locking mechanism	: rear-side centre pin, cylinder crane
Weight	: 1100g
Length	: 289mm
Height	: 149mm
Barrel length	: 152mm
Trigger stop	: none
Sights	: adjustable
Sight radius	: 205mm
External safety	: cylinder blocks with cocked hammer
Internal safety	: transfer bar
FEATURES:	
• thumb piece	: on left side frame
• material	: steel
• finish	: blued
• grips	: walnut

Mitchell Titan MK II 4"

TECHNICAL SPECIFICATIONS:

Calibre	: .357 Magnum
Trigger action	: double action
Magazine capacity	: 6 rounds
Locking mechanism	: back-side centre pin, cylinder crane
Weight	: 1010g
Length	: 243mm
Height	: 149mm
Barrel length	: 102mm
Trigger stop	: none
Sights	: fixed
Sight radius	: 150mm
External safety	: cylinder blocks with cocked hammer
Internal safety	: transfer bar
FEATURES:	
• thumb piece	: left side frame, on cylinder crane
• material	: steel
• finish	: blued
• grips	: walnut or rubber

Mitchell Titan MK III 6"

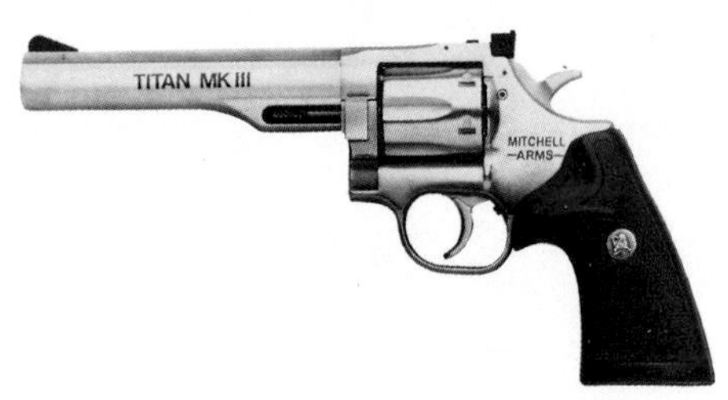

TECHNICAL SPECIFICATIONS:

Calibre	: .357 Magnum
Trigger action	: double-action
Magazine capacity	: 6 rounds
Locking mechanism	: rear-side centre pin, cylinder crane
Weight	: 1100g
Length	: 289mm
Height	: 149mm
Barrel length	: 152mm
Trigger stop	: nones
Sights	: adjustable
Sight radius	: 205mm
External safety	: cylinder blocks with cocked hammer
Internal safety	: transfer bar
FEATURES:	
• thumb piece	: left side frame, on cylinder crane
• material	: stainless steel
• finish	: matt stainless
• grips	: Pachmayr

Para-Ordnance

The Para-Ordnance Company from Ontario in Canada has been involved since the mid-1980s in improving the Colt Model 1911-A1 pistol. In 1988, a twelve-round magazine was developed for the 1911-A1, followed in 1990 by an M1911-A1 pistol with a magazine capacity of even fourteen rounds in calibre .45 ACP. Furthermore, all kinds of technical improvements were integrated into their pistols, such as an automatic firing-pin safety, three-dot low-light sights, and a combat-style trigger guard. Para-Ordnance also designed a special feeding ramp, which allows the dependable feeding of cartridges, even with lead bullets. The company developed special grip plates, so reducing the thickness of guns, even if double-row magazines are used. The guiding rails on top of the frame of the pistol have also been improved. The slide runs on two long guiding rails over the frame, in contrast to the old 1911-A1 design.

Para-Ordnance has three basic models of .45 ACP pistols – the P12, a compact pistol with a twelve-round magazine; then the P13, a slightly longer model with a thirteen-round magazine capacity and finally the P14 for fourteen rounds in calibre .45 ACP.

Furthermore, the company produces the P16, a sixteen-round 1911-A1 pistol in calibre .40 S&W and even a twenty round capacity in calibre .38 Super. In 1989 Para-Ordnance developed a special exchange kit for the Colt model 1911 and look- alikes. This kit consists of a steel frame with magazine, with which the magazine capacity of a .45 Colt pistol can be increased to fifteen rounds.

For shooters who fancy a model 1911-A1 with a large capacity and who want to rebuild their pistol into their own parcours pistol, Para-Ordnance makes an excellent choice. The workmanship of the handguns is high class, certainly in relation to the price. It is certainly not a coincidence that many special government units from all over the world have the Para-Ordnance in their armament.

Para-Ordnance P12

TECHNICAL SPECIFICATIONS:

Calibre	: .45 ACP
Trigger action	: single action
Magazine capacity	: 11 rounds
Locking mechanism	: Browning system
Weight	: 879g
Length	: 178mm
Height	: 127mm
Barrel length	: 89mm
Trigger stop	: none
Sights	: fixed three-dot rear sight
Sight radius	: 126mm
External safety	: safety catch on left side frame, grip safety
Internal safety	: slide safety, automatic firing-pin safety

FEATURES:

• slide catch	: on left side frame
• magazine catch	: on left side frame, behind trigger guard
• material	: steel, stainless steel or alloy frame
• finish	: blued or stainless
• grips	: black composition

The P12 is available in three different versions: P12.45R: alloy frame, weight 680g; P12.45E: steel with blued finish; and P12.45S, a stainless-steel version.

Para-Ordnance P13

TECHNICAL SPECIFICATIONS:

Calibre	: .45 ACP
Trigger action	: single action
Magazine capacity	: 13 rounds
Locking mechanism	: Browning system
Weight	: 1020g
Length	: 197mm
Height	: 133mm
Barrel length	: 108mm
Trigger stop	: none
Sights	: fixed three-dot rear sight
Sight radius	: 144mm
External safety	: safety catch on left side frame, grip safety
Internal safety	: slide safety, automatic firing-pin safety

FEATURES:

• slide catch	: on left side frame
• magazine catch	: on left side frame, behind trigger guard
• material	: steel or alloy frame
• finish	: blued
• grips	: black composition

The P13 is available in two different versions: the P13.45R with alloy frame, weight 794g; and the P13.45E, steel with blued finish.

Para-Ordnance P14

TECHNICAL SPECIFICATIONS:

Calibre	:	.45 ACP
Trigger action	:	single action
Magazine capacity	:	13 rounds
Locking mechanism	:	Browning system
Weight	:	1050g
Length	:	216mm
Height	:	146mm
Barrel length	:	127mm
Trigger stop	:	none
Sights	:	fixed three-dot rear sight
Sight radius	:	164mm
External safety	:	safety catch on left side frame, grip safety
Internal safety	:	slide safety, automatic firing-pin safety

FEATURES:

• slide catch	:	on left side frame
• magazine catch	:	on left side frame, behind trigger guard
• material	:	steel or alloy frame
• finish	:	blued
• grips	:	black composition

The P14 is available in three different versions: the P14.45R, with alloy frame, weight 794g; the P14.45E, steel with blued finish; and the P14.45S stainless-steel version.

Pardini match pistols

The Pardini Armi Company from Lido di Camaiore (Viareggio) in Italy was founded in the 1970s by the match-shooter, Giampiero Pardini. As a member of the Italian national team he had designed his own match pistol. This unique handgun became so popular that Pardini thought it was time to go into business. To begin with he built the so-called free-pistols for the 50m small-bore matches, but soon customers wanted him to produce semi-automatic pistols for every kind of international competition. He owes this success to his refusal to compromise in the manufacture of his guns. In order to secure the marketing and sales of his products, he began co-operating with the great Italian ammunition company, Fiocchi, in 1984. The result was the introduction of a complete line of Fiocchi- Pardini match pistols in 1985. Because Fiocchi had its own establishment in the USA, the Fiocchi of America Inc. in Springfield, Montana, the American market was wide open to him immediately. At the beginning of 1990 Pardini ended the association with Fiocchi, so from then on the pistols have again been Pardini's. With the exception of the barrels and bolts, all parts are produced in Pardini's own factory.

Pardini-Fiocchi MP pistol

TECHNICAL SPECIFICATIONS:

Calibre	: .32 S&W Long
Trigger action	: single action
Magazine capacity	: 5 rounds
Locking mechanism	: blowback system
Weight	: 1100g
Length	: 300 mm
Height	: 155 mm
Barrel length	: 123 mm
Trigger stop	: adjustable
Sights	: micrometer rear sight
Sight radius	: 220mm
External safety	: safety catch in trigger guard
Internal safety	: slide safety, magazine safety
FEATURES:	
• slide catch	: none
• magazine catch	: catch in trigger guard
• material	: steel slide, alloy frame
• finish	: blued
• grips	: walnut match grip with adjustable palm rest

Pardini-Fiocchi SPE-pistol

TECHNICAL SPECIFICATIONS:

Calibre	: .22 LR
Trigger action	: single action
Magazine capacity	: 6 rounds
Locking mechanism	: blowback action
Weight	: 1050g
Length	: 300mm
Height	: 155mm
Barrel length	: 123mm
Trigger stop	: adjustable
Sights	: micrometer rear sight
Sight radius	: 220mm
External safety	: safety catch in trigger guard
Internal safety	: slide safety, magazine safety
FEATURES:	
• slide catch	: none
• magazine catch	: catch in trigger guard
• material	: alloy frame, steel slide
• finish	: blued
• grips	: walnut match grip with adjustable palm rest

Rossi revolvers

The Brazilian arms company, Rossi, was founded in 1889 and is situated in Sao Leopoldo. The official company name is Amadeo Rossi SA. Until halfway through this century, Rossi concentrated mainly on the Latin American markets. In the 1950s it started an export line to the USA, mainly with cheap revolvers and carbines. The recent policy is different. Rossi is producing quality arms, equal to those of its competitors, and it exports them to more than seventy countries. The range of products contains more than sixty different revolver models and twenty-five different rifles and shotguns. In South America, Rossi is one of the main arms manufacturers and is on the top-ten list of arms makers of the world. Many of the Rossi revolvers fall into the category "defence handguns", which means a five-round revolver with a 51mm (2in) or 76mm (3in) barrel and fixed sights. But Rossi also has an excellent line of sports revolvers with micrometer rear sights,

with or without a heavy barrel, some with a ventilated barrel, and all of this in a blued or stainless finish.
For this book the most popular models have been chosen from the complete range of Rossi revolvers.

Rossi Model 712

TECHNICAL SPECIFICATIONS:

Calibre	: .357 Magnum
Trigger action	: double action
Magazine capacity	: 6 rounds
Locking mechanism	: front/rear-side centre pin
Weight	: 800g
Length	: 187mm
Height	: 130mm
Barrel length	: 64mm (2,5")
Trigger stop	: none
Sights	: adjustable
Sight radius	: 112mm
External safety	: none
Internal safety	: blocking bar, cylinder blocks with cocked hammer

FEATURES:

• thumb piece	: on left side frame
• material	: stainless steel
• finish	: matt stainless
• grips	: hard-rubber combat

Rossi Model 718

TECHNICAL SPECIFICATIONS:

Calibre	: .38 Special
Trigger action	: double action
Magazine capacity	: 6 rounds
Locking mechanism	: front/rear-side centre pin
Weight	: 1020g
Length	: 230mm
Height	: 138mm
Barrel length	: 102mm (4")
Trigger stop	: none
Sights	: adjustable
Sight radius	: 150mm
External safety	: none
Internal safety	: blocking bar, cylinder blocks with cocked hammer

FEATURES:

• thumb piece	: on left side frame
• material	: stainless steel
• finish	: matt stainless, Bull barrel
• grips	: hard-rubber combat or walnut target

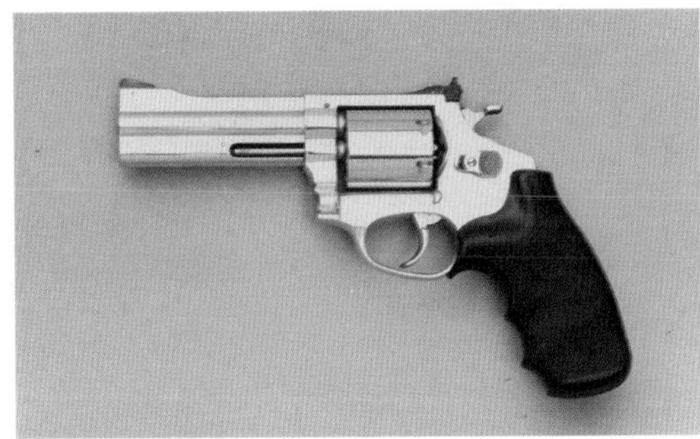

Rossi Model 763

TECHNICAL SPECIFICATIONS:

Calibre	: .357 Magnum
Trigger action	: double action
Magazine capacity	: 6 rounds
Locking mechanism	: front/rear-side centre pin
Weight	: 1125g
Length	: 280mm
Height	: 138mm
Barrel length	: 152mm (6")
Trigger stop	: none
Sights	: adjustable
Sight radius	: 195mm

External safety	: none
Internal safety	: blocking bar, cylinder blocks with cocked hammer

FEATURES:

• thumb piece	: on left side frame
• material	: stainless steel
• finish	: matt stainless with ventilated barrel
• grips	: hard-rubber combat or Brazilian hardwood

Rossi Model 845

TECHNICAL SPECIFICATIONS:

Calibre	: .38 Special
Trigger action	: double action
Magazine capacity	: 6 rounds
Locking mechanism	: front/rear-side centre pin
Weight	: 850g
Length	: 230mm
Height	: 138mm
Barrel length	: 102mm (4")
Trigger stop	: none
Sights	: fixed
Sight radius	: 140mm
External safety	: none
Internal safety	: blocking bar, cylinder blocks with cocked hammer

FEATURES:

• thumb piece	: on left side frame
• material	: stainless steel
• finish	: matt stainless
• grips	: hard rubber combat

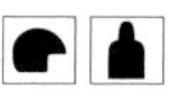

Rossi Model 87

TECHNICAL SPECIFICATIONS:

Calibre	: .38 Special
Trigger action	: double action
Magazine capacity	: 5 rounds
Locking mechanism	: front/rear-side centre pin
Weight	: 630g
Length	: 174mm
Height	: 124mm
Barrel length	: 51mm (2")
Trigger stop	: none
Sights	: fixed
Sight radius	: 92mm
External safety	: none
Internal safety	: blocking bar, cylinder blocks with cocked hammer

FEATURES:

• cilinderpal	: on left side frame
• material	: stainless steel
• finish	: matt stainless
• grips	: special Pachmayr

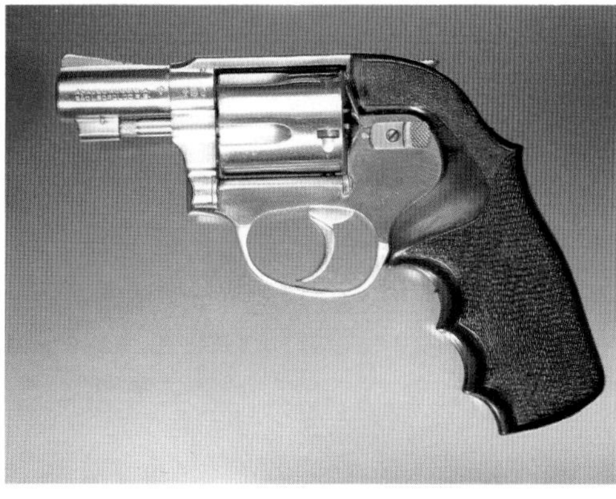

Rossi Model 873 Lady Rossi

TECHNICAL SPECIFICATIONS:

Calibre	: .38 Special
Trigger action	: double action
Magazine capacity	: 5 rounds
Locking mechanism	: front/rear-side centre pin
Weight	: 600g

Length	: 174mm
Height	: 123mm
Barrel length	: 51mm (2")
Trigger stop	: none
Sights	: fixed
Sight radius	: 92mm
External safety	: none
Internal safety	: blocking bar, cylinder blocks with cocked hammer

FEATURES:

• thumb piece	: on left side frame
• material	: stainless steel
• finish	: matt stainless
• grips	: Brazilian hardwood

Rossi Model 971

TECHNICAL SPECIFICATIONS:

Calibre	: .357 Magnum
Trigger action	: double action
Magazine capacity	: 6 rounds
Locking mechanism	: front/rear-side centre pin
Weight	: 850g
Length	: 230mm
Height	: 138mm
Barrel length	: 102mm (4")
Trigger stop	: none
Sights	: adjustable
Sight radius	: 150mm
External safety	: none
Internal safety	: blocking bar, cylinder blocks with cocked hammer

FEATURES:

• thumb piece	: on left side frame
• material	: steel
• finish	: blued
• grips	: hard rubber combat or hardwood target

Ruger

William B. Ruger was born on 21 June 1916 in Brooklyn, New York, the son of a lawyer. In his childhood he already showed great interest in the technology of firearms. Later he worked in Connecticut on the design of a semi-automatic version of the Savage lever-action carbine. The Savage Company was not particularly interested in this design. Even Ruger's attempts with Colt did not succeed. Finally, the US army showed some interest in the Savage redesign and Ruger was offered a job at the then State Arsenal, Springfield Armory. Ruger did not stay even a year, because he thought a public company did not offer enough opportunities. He moved to North Carolina and worked there on a design for a light machine-gun. This design caught the attention of another arms company, Auto Ordnance, manufacturers of the world-famous Thompson submachine-gun or "Tommy-gun". In 1940 Ruger was employed in the research department of the Auto Ordnance Company in Bridgeport, Connecticut.

The history of Sturm, Ruger & Company starts in 1948. In that year William B. Ruger and Alexander M. Sturm rented a storehouse in Southport in the State of Connecticut and started a small workshop. With the initial capital of $50,000 both young industrialists produced their first item at the beginning of 1949 - a semi-automatic small-bore pistol. After Alexander Sturm was killed in a tragic airplane accident, William Ruger continued the business alone. Out of respect for his dead associate, he changed the colour of their company logo from red to black. In 1953, Ruger introduced a small-bore revolver, the Single-Six, a single-action revolver, derived from the Colt Peacemaker. Ruger gauged the demand for such a handgun very well. He dealt with the production in a typical "Ruger way", which means that the manufacture has to be as simple as possible with as high a profit as possible. This Single-Six formed the basis of a complete line of single-action revolvers. The model stayed in production until 1973.

In 1956, Ruger introduced an alloy version and in 1959 the Single-Six was marketed in the calibre .22 WMR (Winchester Magnum Rimfire). The range of products was extended in 1964 with a Super Single-Six with adjustable rear sight. The first Blackhawk single-action revolver was launched in 1955 in

calibre .357 Magnum. This model was followed in 1956 by a Blackhawk in calibre .44 Magnum and in 1967 in calibre .30-M1 as well, the well-known carbine round. In 1971 Ruger introduced a Blackhawk model in the calibre .45 Colt, with an interchangeable cylinder in .45 ACP. The Bearcat single-action revolver in .22 LR was marketed in 1958. This model stayed in production until 1973 with a minor modification- a complete steel frame in 1971, called the Super Bearcat.
The Super Blackhawk made its debut in 1963. This single-action revolver was an extra-strengthened and embellished Blackhawk in the calibre .44 Magnum and with an adjustable rear sight.
The line of Ruger revolvers was further extended in 1971 with the Security Six, the Speed Six, and the Police Service Six, all double-action revolvers in calibres .357 Magnum and .38 Special. This basic model very soon turned out to be a box-office success. Other versions, like the stainless-steel finish, were marketed in 1975. In 1973 the New Model Single Six, New Model Blackhawk, and Super Blackhawk were introduced with a new firing-pin safety system, called the transfer bar. All old model single actions, produced and sold before 1973, could be adjusted free of charge. Stainless-steel finished versions of the New Model Single Six and New Model Blackhawk were introduced in 1974.
The Ruger Redhawk in calibre .44 Magnum came out in 1979. This revolver was originally only produced in stainless steel. In 1985, the Redhawk also became available in a blued finish. In 1982, Ruger found it time for a new small-bore pistol and introduced the Mark II Standard Automatic Pistol in calibre .22 LR. This handgun is, in fact, the older model Mark I with an extensive "face-lift". In 1985, the New Model Super Single Six in the then new calibre .32 H&R Magnum was introduced. In 1986, the single-action revolver line was extended with the start of the Ruger Bisley Single- Action revolvers in a blued finish in the calibres .22 LR, .32 H&R Magnum, .357 Magnum, .41 Magnum, .44 Magnum, and .45 Long Colt. In 1987, Ruger launched a number of new models once again with the Super Redhawk in .44 Magnum and the Ruger GP-100 as successor to the famous Security Six, in several versions.
That same year Ruger introduced its first 9mm Para pistol, the Ruger P-85, a fifteen-round army pistol that drew a lot of technical attention.
All gun parts Ruger did not consider as absolutely necessary for the functioning of the pistol were rigorously left out, such as catches, shafts, springs, etc. The frame was made of a coated alloy, called T-6, and is matt black coated like the rest of the gun.
The ambidextrous safety/decocking lever is situated on the slide. This model has been succeeded by other versions of the P-85, including the models P-89, KP-90, KP-91, KP-93, and the P-94 pistol in the calibres 9mm Para, .40 S&W, and .45 ACP.

Ruger MK I (Model T678)

TECHNICAL SPECIFICATIONS:

Calibre	: .22 LR
Trigger action	: single action
Magazine capacity	: 10 rounds
Locking mechanism	: blowback action
Weight	: 1190g
Length	: 276mm
Height	: 142mm
Barrel length	: 175mm
Trigger stop	: none
Sights	: adjustable
Sight radius	: 238mm
External safety	: safety catch
Internal safety	: slide safety
FEATURES:	
• slide catch	: bolt catch, left on frame
• magazine catch	: in heel of grip
• material	: steel
• finish	: blued
• grips	: black composition or walnut

Ruger MK II (Model MK512)

TECHNICAL SPECIFICATIONS:

Calibre	: .22 LR
Trigger action	: single action

Magazine capacity	: 10 rounds
Locking mechanism	: blowback system
Weight	: 1190g
Length	: 248mm
Height	: 142mm
Barrel length	: 140mm
Trigger stop	: no
Sights	: adjustable
Sight radius	: 200 mm
External safety	: safety catch
Internal safety	: slide safety
FEATURES:	
• slide catch	: bolt catch, left on frame
• magazine catch	: in heel of grip
• material	: steel
• finish	: blued
• grips	: black composition or walnut

Ruger MK II (Model KMK4)

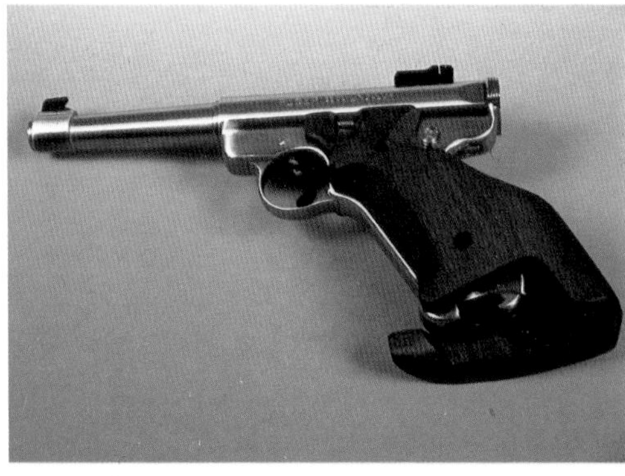

The pistol shown here has a special match grip with an adjustable palm rest.

TECHNICAL SPECIFICATIONS:

Calibre	: .22 LR
Trigger action	: single action
Magazine capacity	: 10 rounds
Locking mechanism	: blowback action
Weight	: 990g
Length	: 211mm
Height	: 142mm
Barrel length	: 121mm
Trigger stop	: none
Sights	: adjustable
Sight radius	: 175mm
External safety	: safety catch
Internal safety	: slide safety
FEATURES:	
• slide catch	: bolt catch, left on frame
• magazine catch	: in heel of grip
• material	: stainless steel
• finish	: matt stainless
• grips	: black composition or walnut

Ruger MK II (Model KMK10)

TECHNICAL SPECIFICATIONS:

Calibre	: .22 LR
Trigger action	: single action
Magazine capacity	: 10 rounds
Locking mechanism	: blowback action
Weight	: 1445g
Length	: 364mm
Height	: 142mm
Barrel length	: 254mm
Trigger stop	: none
Sights	: adjustable
Sight radius	: 323mm
External safety	: safety catch
Internal safety	: slide safety
FEATURES:	
• slide catch	: bolt catch left on frame
• magazine catch	: in heel of grip
• material	: stainless steel
• finish	: matt stainless
• grips	: black composition ot walnut

The Ruger MK II pistol is available in many versions. Barrel lengths are: 121mm (43/4in) standard barrel, 133mm (51/4in), 140mm (51/2in), 152mm (6in), 175mm (67/8in), and

254mm (10in). Standard models have a fixed rear sight, the Target models have an adjustable rear sight, and the Bull barrel versions have a thick match barrel. The models with the 254mm (10in) barrel are especially suited for small-bore silhouette shooting.

Ruger 22/45 (Model P512)

TECHNICAL SPECIFICATIONS:

Calibre	: .22 LR
Trigger action	: single action
Magazine capacity	: 10 rounds
Locking mechanism	: blowback system
Weight	: 1190g
Length	: 248mm
Height	: 142mm
Barrel length	: 140mm
Trigger stop	: none
Sights	: adjustable
Sight radius	: 205mm
External safety	: safety catch on left side frame
Internal safety	: slide safety

FEATURES:

• slide catch	: on left side frame
• magazine catch	: on left side frame, behind trigger guard
• material	: composition frame, steel barrel an receiver
• finish	: black frame blued barrel
• grips	: black composition

Ruger 22/45 (Model KP4)

TECHNICAL SPECIFICATIONS:

Calibre	: .22 LR
Trigger action	: single action
Magazine capacity	: 10 rounds
Locking mechanism	: blowback action
Weight	: 795g
Length	: 224mm
Height	: 142mm
Barrel length	: 121mm
Trigger stop	: none
Sights	: adjustable
Sight radius	: 186mm
External safety	: safety catch on left side frame
Internal safety	: slide safety

FEATURES:

• slide catch	: on left side frame
• magazine catch	: on left side frame, behind trigger guard
• material	: composition frame, stainless steel barrel and receiver
• finish	: black frame, matt stainless barrel
• grips	: black composition

Ruger New Model Single-Six Blue $5^1/_2$" (Model NR5F)

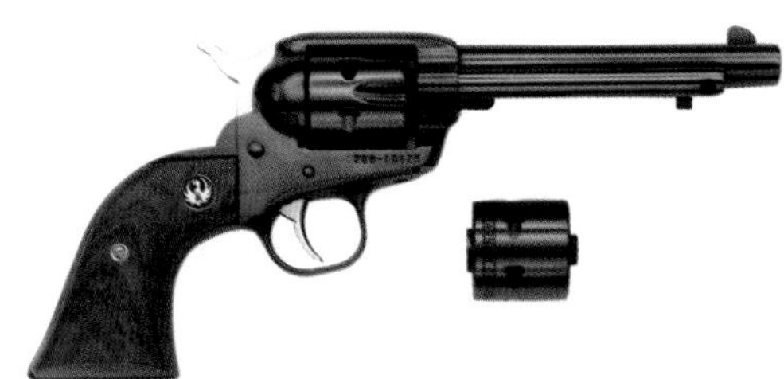

TECHNICAL SPECIFICATIONS:

Calibre	: .22 LR with extra cylinder .22 WMR

Trigger action	: single action
Cylinder capacity	: 6 rounds
Locking mechanism	: fixed cylinder
Weight	: 935g
Length	: 274mm
Height	: 140mm
Barrel length	: 140mm
Trigger stop	: none
Sights	: fixed
Sight radius	: 150mm
External safety	: none
Internal safety	: transfer bar, loading gate blocks with cocked hammer

FEATURES:

• thumb piece	: none
• material	: steel
• finish	: blued
• grips	: walnut

Ruger New Model Single-Six HG Stainless $5^1/_2$" (Model GKNR5F)

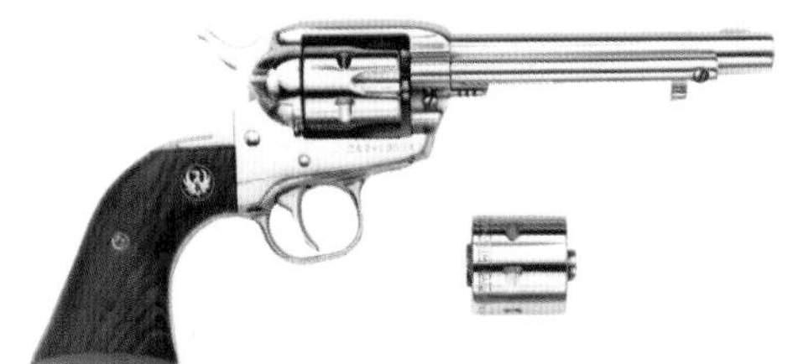

TECHNICAL SPECIFICATIONS:

Calibre	: .22 LR with extra cylinder .22 WMR
Trigger action	: single action
Cylinder capacity	: 6 rounds
Locking mechanism	: fixed cylinder
Weight	: 935g
Length	: 274mm
Height	: 140mm
Barrel length	: 140mm
Trigger stop	: none
Sights	: fixed
Sight radius	: 150mm
External safety	: none
Internal safety	: transfer bar, loading gate blocks with cocked hammer

FEATURES:

• thumb piece	: none
• material	: stainless steel
• finish	: high-gloss stainless
• grips	: walnut

Ruger New Super Bearcat Blue 4" (Model SBC4)

TECHNICAL SPECIFICATIONS:

Calibre	: .22 LR with extra cylinder .22 WMR
Trigger action	: single action
Cylinder capacity	: 6 rounds
Locking mechanism	: fixed cylinder
Weight	: 655g
Length	: 225mm
Height	: 140mm
Barrel length	: 102mm
Trigger stop	: none
Sights	: fixed
Sight radius	: 127mm
External safety	: none
Internal safety	: transfer bar, loading gate block

FEATURES:

• cilinderpal	: none
• material	: steel
• finish	: blued
• grips	: walnut

Ruger Blackhawk Vaquero Blue $4^1/_2$" (Model BNV455)

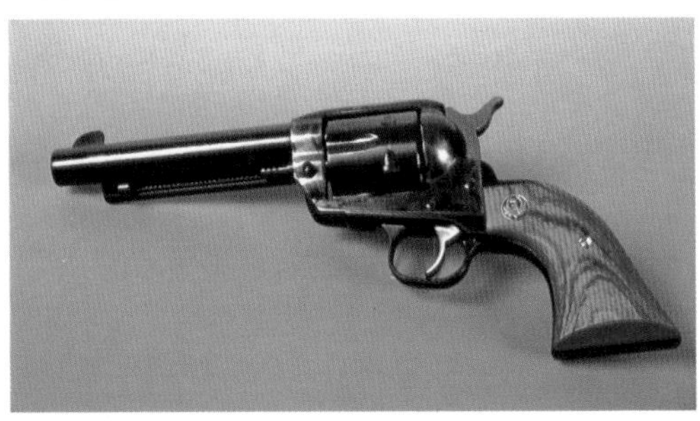

TECHNICAL SPECIFICATIONS:

Calibre	: .45 Long Colt
Trigger action	: single action

Cylinder capacity	:	6 rounds
Locking mechanism	:	fixed cylinder
Weight	:	1135g
Length	:	292mm
Height	:	130mm
Barrel length	:	140mm
Trigger stop	:	none
Sights	:	fixed
Sight radius	:	162mm
External safety	:	none
Internal safety	:	transfer bar, loading-gate block

FEATURES:

• thumb piece	:	none
• material	:	steel
• finish	:	blued with flame-hardened frame
• grips	:	rosewood

Ruger Blackhawk Vaquero Stainless $4^5/_8$" (Model KBNV44)

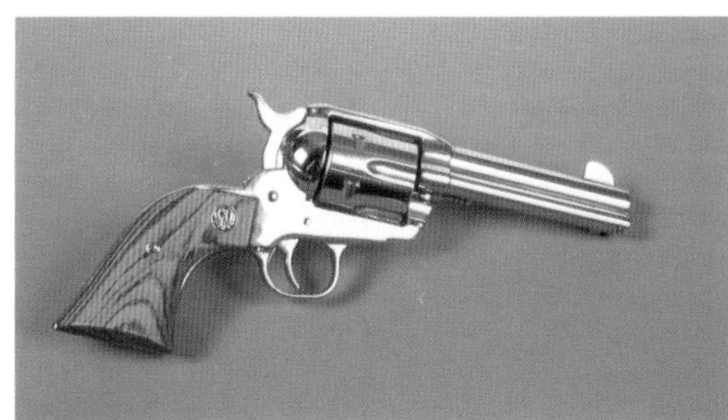

TECHNICAL SPECIFICATIONS:

Calibre	:	.45 Long Colt
Trigger action	:	single action
Cylinder capacity	:	6 rounds
Locking mechanism	:	fixed cylinder
Weight	:	1105g
Length	:	260mm
Height	:	135mm
Barrel length	:	118mm
Trigger stop	:	none
Sights	:	fixed
Sight radius	:	140mm
External safety	:	none
Internal safety	:	transfer bar, loading-gate block

FEATURES:

• thumb piece	:	not relevant
• material	:	stainless steel
• finish	:	stainless
• grips	:	rosewood

Ruger Blackhawk Blue $5^1/_2$" (Model BN455)

TECHNICAL SPECIFICATIONS:

Calibre	:	.45 Long Colt
Trigger action	:	single action
Cylinder capacity	:	6 rounds
Locking mechanism	:	fixed cylinder
Weight	:	1105g
Length	:	283mm
Height	:	140mm
Barrel length	:	140mm
Trigger stop	:	none
Sights	:	adjustable
Sight radius	:	200mm
External safety	:	none
Internal safety	:	transfer bar, loading-gate block

FEATURES:

• thumb piece	:	none
• material	:	steel
• finish	:	blued
• grips	:	walnut

Ruger Blackhawk Stainless $4^5/_8$" (Model KBN34)

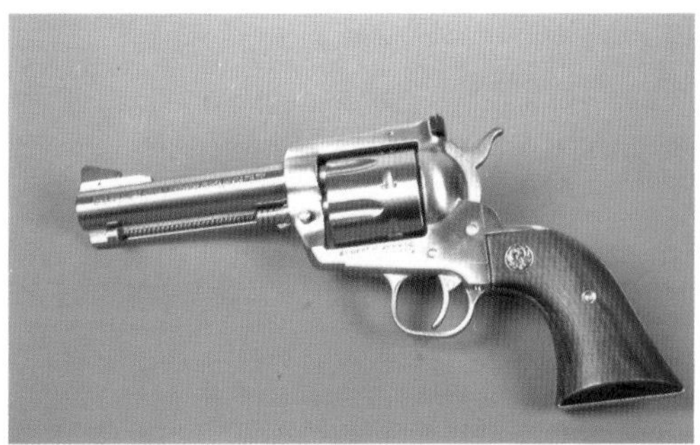

TECHNICAL SPECIFICATIONS:

Calibre	:	.357 Magnum
Trigger action	:	single action

Cylinder capacity	: 6 rounds
Locking mechanism	: fixed cylinder
Weight	: 1135g
Length	: 264mm
Height	: 140mm
Barrel length	: 118mm
Trigger stop	: none
Sights	: adjustable
Sight radius	: 163mm
External safety	: none
Internal safety	: transfer bar, loading-gate block

FEATURES:

• thumb piece	: not relevant
• material	: stainless steel
• finish	: stainless
• grips	: walnut

Ruger Blackhawk High-Gloss Stainless 4⁵/₈" (Model GKBN44)

TECHNICAL SPECIFICATIONS:

Calibre	: .45 Long Colt
Trigger action	: single action
Cylinder capacity	: 6 rounds
Locking mechanism	: fixed cylinder
Weight	: 1105g
Length	: 260mm
Height	: 140mm
Barrel length	: 118mm
Trigger stop	: no
Sights	: adjustable
Sight radius	: 165 mm
External safety	: none
Internal safety	: transfer bar, loading-gate block

FEATURES:

• thumb piece	: not relevant
• material	: stainless steel
• finish	: high-gloss stainless
• grips	: walnut

Ruger Blackhawk High Gloss Stainless 6¹/₂" (Model-GKBN36)

TECHNICAL SPECIFICATIONS:

Calibre	: .357 Magnum
Trigger action	: single action
Cylinder capacity	: 6 rounds
Locking mechanism	: fixed cylinder
Weight	: 1190g
Length	: 318mm
Height	: 140mm
Barrel length	: 165mm
Trigger stop	: none
Sights	: adjustable
Sight radius	: 215mm
External safety	: none
Internal safety	: transfer bar, loading-gate block

FEATURES:

• thumb piece	: not relevant
• material	: stainless steel
• finish	: high-gloss stainless
• grips	: walnut

Ruger Blackhawk Stainless 7¹/₂" (Model KBN45)

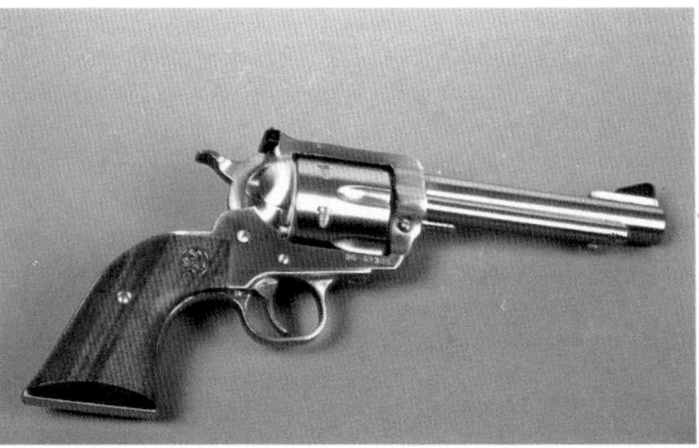

TECHNICAL SPECIFICATIONS:

Calibre	: .45 Long Colt
Trigger action	: single action

Cylinder capacity	: 6 rounds
Locking mechanism	: fixed cylinder
Weight	: 1160g
Length	: 333mm
Height	: 140mm
Barrel length	: 191mm
Trigger stop	: none
Sights	: adjustable
Sight radius	: 215mm
External safety	: none
Internal safety	: transfer bar, loading-gate block

FEATURES:

• thumb piece	: not relevant
• material	: stainless steel
• finish	: stainless
• grips	: walnut

Ruger Super Blackhawk High-Gloss Stainless 4⁵/₈" (Model GKS458N)

TECHNICAL SPECIFICATIONS:

Calibre	: .44 Magnum
Trigger action	: single action
Cylinder capacity	: 6 rounds
Locking mechanism	: fixed cylinder
Weight	: 1275g
Length	: 267mm
Height	: 136mm
Barrel length	: 118mm
Trigger stop	: none
Sights	: adjustable
Sight radius	: 175mm
External safety	: none
Internal safety	: transfer bar, loading-gate block

FEATURES:

• thumb piece	: not relevant
• material	: stainless steel
• finish	: high-gloss stainless
• grips	: walnut

Ruger Super Blackhawk Blue 10¹/₂" (Model S411N)

TECHNICAL SPECIFICATIONS:

Calibre	: .44 Magnum
Trigger action	: single action
Cylinder capacity	: 6 rounds
Locking mechanism	: fixed cylinder
Weight	: 1445g
Length	: 416mm
Height	: 136mm
Barrel length	: 267mm
Trigger stop	: none
Sights	: adjustable
Sight radius	: 320mm
External safety	: none
Internal safety	: transfer bar, loading-gate block

FEATURES:

• thumb piece	: not relevant
• material	: steel
• finish	: blued
• grips	: walnut

Ruger Super Blackhawk Stainless 10¹/₂" (Model KSN411N)

TECHNICAL SPECIFICATIONS:

Calibre	: .44 Magnum
Trigger action	: single action
Cylinder capacity	: 6 rounds
Locking mechanism	: fixed cylinder

Weight	: 1445g
Length	: 416mm
Height	: 136mm
Barrel length	: 267mm
Trigger stop	: none
Sights	: adjustable
Sight radius	: 320mm
External safety	: none
Internal safety	: transfer bar, loading-gate block

FEATURES:

• thumb piece	: not relevant
• material	: stainless steel
• finish	: stainless
• grips	: walnut

Ruger SP101 (Model KSP931)

TECHNICAL SPECIFICATIONS:

Calibre	: 9 mm Para
Trigger action	: double action
Cylinder capacity	: 5 rounds
Locking mechanism	: front/rear-side centre pin
Weight	: 765g
Length	: 220mm
Height	: 132mm
Barrel length	: 77mm
Trigger stop	: none
Sights	: fixed
Sight radius	: 112mm
External safety	: none
Internal safety	: transfer bar, cylinder blocks with cocked hammer

FEATURES:

• thumb piece	: on left side frame
• material	: stainless steel
• finish	: matt stainless
• grips	: rubber with walnut inlay or Xenoy grip

Ruger SP101 (Model KSP331X)

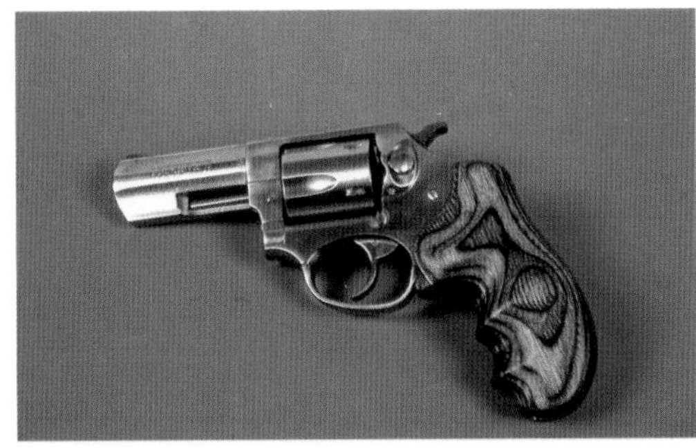

The revolver shown here has a so-called "phantasy stock", which is not standard

TECHNICAL SPECIFICATIONS:

Calibre	: .357 Magnum
Trigger action	: double action
Cylinder capacity	: 5 rounds
Locking mechanism	: front/rear-side centre pin
Weight	: 765g
Length	: 220mm
Height	: 132mm
Barrel length	: 77mm
Trigger stop	: no
Sights	: fixed
Sight radius	: 112mm
External safety	: none
Internal safety	: transfer bar, cylinder blocks with cocked hammer

FEATURES:

• thumb piece	: on left side frame
• material	: stainless steel
• finish	: matt stainless
• grips	: rubber with walnut inlay or Xenoy grip

Ruger GP100 Magna-Port (Model KGP141)

This model has slots cut at the muzzle end of the barrel, the so called Magna-Port compensator slots

TECHNICAL SPECIFICATIONS:

Calibre	: .357 Magnum
Trigger action	: double action
Cylinder capacity	: 6 rounds
Locking mechanism	: rear-side cylinder and cylinder crane
Weight	: 1160g
Length	: 242mm
Height	: 142mm
Barrel length	: 102mm
Trigger stop	: none
Sights	: adjustable
Sight radius	: 140mm
External safety	: none
Internal safety	: transfer bar, cylinder blocks with cocked hammer

FEATURES:

• thumb piece	: on left side frame
• material	: stainless steel
• finish	: matt stainless
• grips	: rubber with walnut inlay

Ruger GP100 (Model GP160)

The model shown here has slots cut at the muzzle end of the barrel, the so-called Magna-Port compensator slots

TECHNICAL SPECIFICATIONS:

Calibre	: .357 Magnum
Trigger action	: double action
Cylinder capacity	: 6 rounds
Locking mechanism	: rear-side cylinder and cylinder crane
Weight	: 1150g
Length	: 295mm
Height	: 142mm
Barrel length	: 152mm
Trigger stop	: none
Sights	: adjustable
Sight radius	: 190mm
External safety	: none
Internal safety	: transfer bar, cylinder blocks with cocked hammer

FEATURES:

• thumb piece	: on left side frame
• material	: steel
• finish	: blued
• grips	: rubber with walnut inlay

Ruger GP100 Stainless (Model KGP160)

TECHNICAL SPECIFICATIONS:

Calibre	: .357 Magnum
Trigger action	: double action
Cylinder capacity	: 6 rounds
Locking mechanism	: rear-side cylinder and cylinder crane
Weight	: 1220g
Length	: 295mm
Height	: 142mm
Barrel length	: 152mm
Trigger stop	: none
Sights	: adjustable
Sight radius	: 190mm
External safety	: none
Internal safety	: transfer bar, cylinder blocks with cocked hammer

FEATURES:

• thumb piece	: on left side frame
• material	: stainless steel
• finish	: matt stainless
• grips	: rubber with walnut inlay

Ruger Redhawk Stainless $5^{1}/_{2}$" (Model KRH445)

TECHNICAL SPECIFICATIONS:

Calibre	: .44 Magnum
Trigger action	: double action

Cylinder capacity : 6 rounds
Locking mechanism : front/rear-side centre pin
Weight : 1390g
Length : 280mm
Height : 146mm
Barrel length : 140mm
Trigger stop : none
Sights : adjustable
Sight radius : 181mm
External safety : none
Internal safety : transfer bar, cylinder blocks with cocked hammer

FEATURES:
- thumb piece : on left side frame
- material : stainless steel
- finish : matt stainless
- grips : walnut

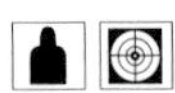

Ruger Redhawk $7^{1}/_{2}$" (Model RH44)

TECHNICAL SPECIFICATIONS:
Calibre : .44 Magnum
Trigger action : double action
Magazine capacity : 6 rounds

Locking mechanism : front/rear-side centre pin
Weight : 1530g
Length : 330mm
Height : 146mm
Barrel length : 191mm
Trigger stop : none
Sights : adjustable
Sight radius : 232mm
External safety : none
Internal safety : transfer bar

FEATURES:
- thumb piece : on left side frame
- material : steel
- finish : blued
- grips : walnut

Ruger Redhawk Stainless $7^{1}/_{2}$" (Model KRH44)

TECHNICAL SPECIFICATIONS:
Calibre : .44 Magnum
Trigger action : double action
Cylinder capacity : 6 rounds
Locking mechanism : front/rear-side centre pin
Weight : 1530g
Length : 330mm
Height : 146mm
Barrel length : 191mm
Trigger stop : none
Sights : adjustable
Sight radius : 232mm
External safety : none
Internal safety : transfer bar, cylinder blocks with cocked hammer

FEATURES:
- thumb piece : on left side frame
- material : stainless steel
- finish : matt stainless
- grips : walnut

Ruger Super Redhawk $7^1/_2$" (Model KSRH7)

TECHNICAL SPECIFICATIONS:

Calibre	: .44 Magnum
Trigger action	: double action
Cylinder capacity	: 6 rounds
Locking mechanism	: front/rear-side centre pin
Weight	: 1503g
Length	: 330mm
Height	: 150mm
Barrel length	: 191mm
Trigger stop	: none
Sights	: adjustable
Sight radius	: 241mm
External safety	: none
Internal safety	: transfer bar, cylinder blocks with cocked hammer

FEATURES:

• thumb piece	: on left side frame
• material	: stainless steel
• finish	: matt stainless
• grips	: rubber with walnut inlay

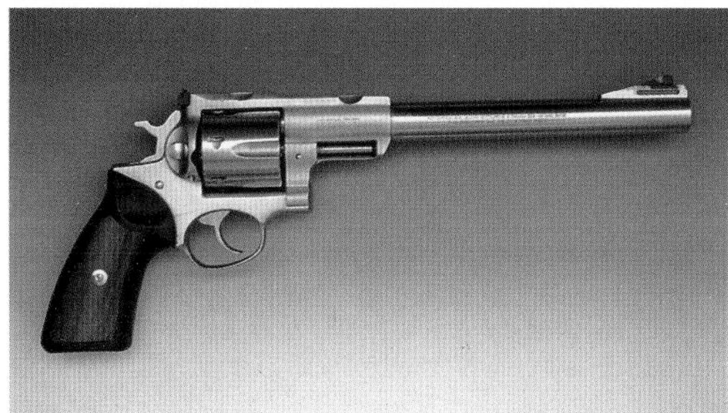

The extra-strong frame of the Super Redhawk has an integral scope-mounting system (patented). Scope rings are included.

Ruger P85 (Model P85)

TECHNICAL SPECIFICATIONS:

Calibre	: 9 mm Para
Trigger action	: double action
Magazine capacity	: 15 rounds
Locking mechanism	: Browning/SIG system
Weight	: 1077g
Length	: 199mm
Height	: 143mm
Barrel length	: 114mm
Trigger stop	: none
Sights	: fixed
Sight radius	: 155mm
External safety	: ambidextrous decock/safety catch on slide
Internal safety	: slide safety, automatic firing-pin safety

FEATURES:

• slide catch	: on left side frame
• magazine catch	: ambidextrous, behind trigger guard
• material	: steel slide, alloy frame
• finish	: blued
• grips	: blacke Xenoy composition

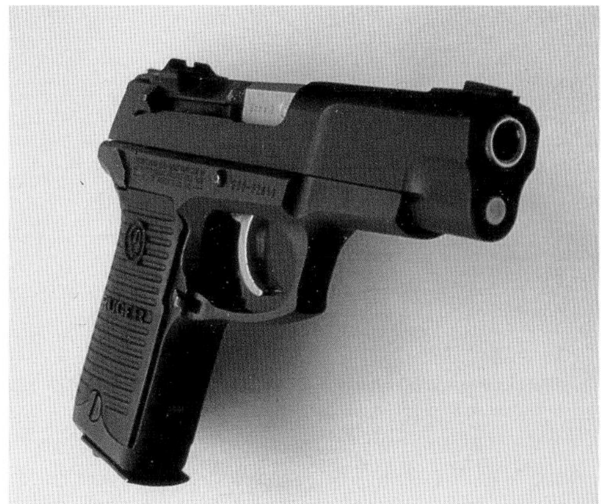

Ruger P90 (Model KP90)

TECHNICAL SPECIFICATIONS:

Calibre	: .45 ACP
Trigger action	: double action
Magazine capacity	: 7 rounds
Locking mechanism	: improved Browning system
Weight	: 960g
Length	: 198mm
Height	: 148mm

Barrel length	: 115mm
Trigger stop	: none
Sights	: fixed
Sight radius	: 145mm
External safety	: ambidextrous safety catch on slide
Internal safety	: slide safety, automatic firing-pin safety

FEATURES:

• slide catch	: on left side frame
• magazine catch	: ambidextrous, behind trigger guard
• material	: alloy frame, stainless steel slide
• finish	: two-tone: black frame, stainless slide
• grips	: black Xenoy

Ruger P91DC (Model P91DC)

TECHNICAL SPECIFICATIONS:

Calibre	: .40 S&W
Trigger action	: double action
Magazine capacity	: 11 rounds
Locking mechanism	: improved Browning system
Weight	: 900g
Length	: 200mm
Height	: 149mm
Barrel length	: 110mm
Trigger stop	: no
Sights	: fixed
Sight radius	: 146mm
External safety	: ambidextrous decocking lever on slide
Internal safety	: slide safety, automatic firing-pin safety

FEATURES:

• slide catch	: on left side frame
• magazine catch	: ambidextrous, behind trigger guard
• material	: alloy frame, stainless slide
• finish	: black frame, stainless slide
• grips	: black Xenoy

The Ruger P91 pistol is also available in a DAO version (Double-Action Only) under catalogue number KP91DAO.

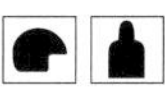

Ruger P93DC Compact (Model KP93DC)

TECHNICAL SPECIFICATIONS:

Calibre	: 9mm Para
Trigger action	: double action
Magazine capacity	: 15 rounds
Locking mechanism	: improved Browning system
Weight	: 880g
Length	: 185mm
Height	: 140mm
Barrel length	: 90mm
Trigger stop	: none
Sights	: fixed
Sight radius	: 130mm
External safety	: ambidextrous decocking lever on slide
Internal safety	: slide safety, automatic firing-pin safety

FEATURES:

• slide catch	: on left side frame
• patroonhouderpal	: ambidextrous, behind trigger guard
• material	: alloy frame, stainless steel slide
• finish	: black frame, stainless slide
• grips	: black Xenoy composition

The Ruger P93 pistol is also available with a DAO (Double-Action Only) trigger system, under catalogue number KP93DAO.

Ruger P94DC (Model KP94)

TECHNICAL SPECIFICATIONS:

Calibre	: 9mm Para
Trigger action	: double-action
Magazine capacity	: 15 rounds
Locking mechanism	: improved Browning system
Weight	: 935g
Length	: 191mm
Height	: 144mm
Barrel length	: 108mm
Trigger stop	: none
Sights	: fixed
Sight radius	: 135mm
External safety	: ambidextrous decocking lever on slide
Internal safety	: slide safety, automatic firing-pin safety

FEATURES:

• slide catch	: on left side frame
• magazine catch	: ambidextrous, behind trigger guard
• material	: alloy frame, stainless steel slide
• finish	: dark grey frame, stainless slide
• grips	: black Xenoy composition

Ruger P94 Laser (Model KP94L)

TECHNICAL SPECIFICATIONS:

Calibre	: 9mm Para
Trigger action	: double action
Magazine capacity	: 15 rounds
Locking mechanism	: improved Browning system
Weight	: 935g
Length	: 191mm
Height	: 144mm
Barrel length	: 108mm
Trigger stop	: none
Sights	: fixed
Sight radius	: 135mm
External safety	: ambidextrous safety catch on slide
Internal safety	: slide safety, automatic firing-pin safety

FEATURES:

• slide catch	: on left side frame
• magazine catch	: ambidextrous, behind trigger guard
• material	: alloy frame, stainless steel slide
• finish	: black frame with integrated laser, matt stainless slide
• grips	: black Xenoy composition

Safari Arms

The Matchmaster model of the M/S Safari Arms Company of Phoenix, Arizona, has been designed for parcours and combat shooters in such a way that extra investment in accessories is not needed.
The standard features of this gun are a Smith & Wesson rear sight (the "K" sight), a red-inlaid front post, a combat hammer, an ambidextrous safety catch, a square trigger guard, an enlarged ejection port, and special magazines. This pistol has a long barrel of 127mm (5in) and is available in a number of different finishes, such as a water-resistant Teflon coating, hard chrome plated, stainless steel, alloy frame (Armaloy), or blued and all high polished or sand blasted, or in two-tone finish in the combination blue/stainless. The most interesting part is the ergonomic grip of the gun with the sharply indented finger groove for the middle finger

(and, with recent models, for the ring finger too) under the trigger guard.

All Safari pistols are recognizable straight away because of this feature. Safari Arms has, apart from its own pistols, an extensive line of accessories for a large number of pistol brands and models: for instance, ambidextrous safety catches, magazine catches, special combat grip safeties, combat hammers and triggers, enlarged and extended slide catches (for the usual left side, but also for the right or ambidextrous). In 1983 Safari Arms marketed a limited commemorative edition of exactly 101 pistols (numbered from 1881 to 1981) – the Phoenix Centennial in calibre .45 ACP. This model is in honour of the town of Phoenix in Arizona, also the site of Safari Arms. The most interesting part of this commemorative handgun is the fact that the frame is made from the metal element beryllium. It is not known whether an example of this handgun is to be found in Europe, or indeed where the others are.

Safari Arms Matchmaster .45ACP

TECHNICAL SPECIFICATIONS:

Calibre	: .45 ACP
Trigger action	: single action
Magazine capacity	: 6 rounds
Locking mechanism	: Browning/Colt system
Weight	: 1135g
Length	: 220mm
Height	: 126mm
Barrel length	: 127mm
Trigger stop	: standard
Sights	: adjustable
Sight radius	: 134mm
External safety	: ambidextrous safety catch
Internal safety	: grip safety, half-cock safety

FEATURES:

• slide catch	: on left side frame, above trigger guard
• magazine catch	: on left side frame, behind trigger guard (reversible or ambidextrous as option)

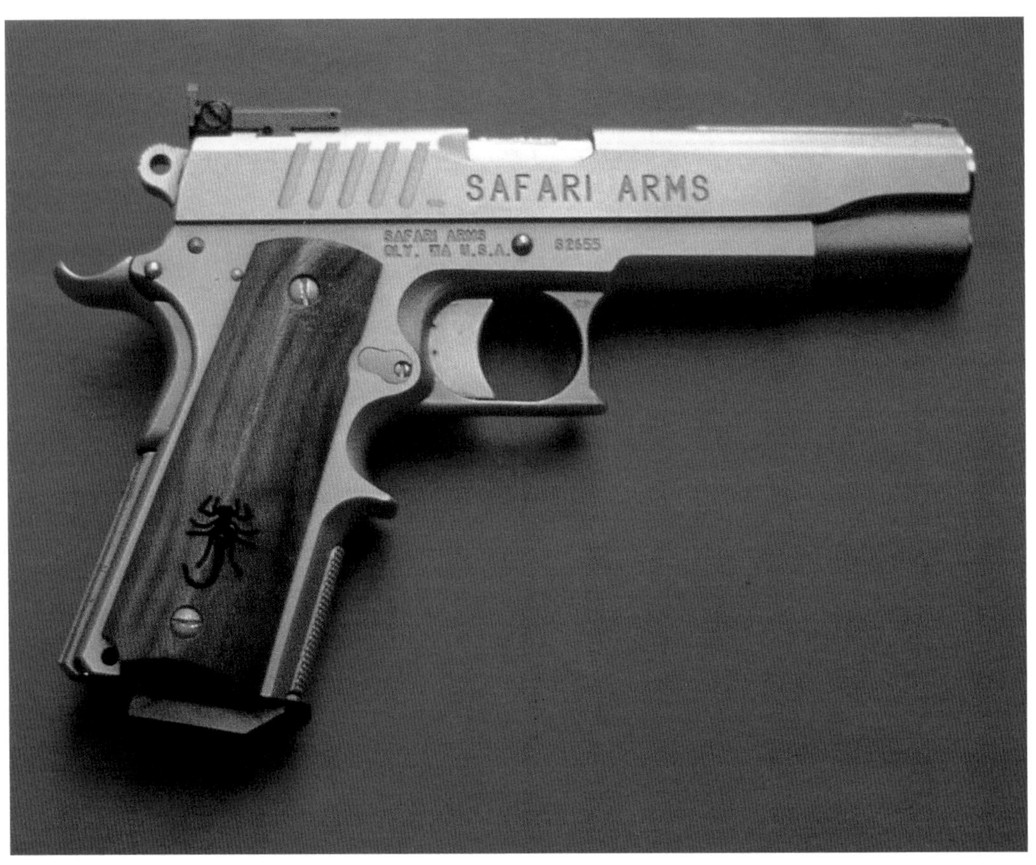

• material	:	stainless steel
• finish	:	in any chosen finish
• grips	:	Pachmayr or walnut

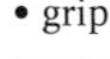  

Sako sport pistol

The Sako Arms factory in Finland has been producing excellent small-bore match pistols for several decades. The company's history in manufacturing arms goes back a long way. Sako has a famous tradition in the production of an extensive line of rifles and carbines in all common calibres from .22 LR up to .416 Remington.

The Sako Tri-Ace match pistol sets a very high standard of quality and is more than equal to its competitors, such as the Walther GSP, the Unique Des-69, and others. Sako offers exchange kits in the calibres .22 LR, .22 Short, and .32 S&W Long.

Sako Tri-Ace sportpistol

TECHNICAL SPECIFICATIONS:

Calibre	:	.22 LR (.22 Short, .32 S&W Long)
Trigger action	:	single action
Magazine capacity	:	5 rounds
Locking mechanism	:	blowback system
Weight	:	1320g (.22 Short: 1255g, .32 S&W Long: 1370g)
Length	:	283mm
Height	:	140mm
Barrel length	:	150mm
Trigger stop	:	adjustable
Sights	:	adjustable
Sight radius	:	225mm (.22 Short), 210mm (.22 LR/.32)
External safety	:	safety catch on left side frame
Internal safety	:	slide safety

FEATURES:

• slide catch	:	none (bolt can be manually secured)
• magazine catch	:	in heel of grip
• material	:	steel
• finish	:	blued
• grips	:	match with adjustable palm rest

SIG/Sig-Sauer pistols

The name of SIG (Swiss Industrial Company) has been associated with the arms business for more than 140 years. The company has a long tradition. It was founded in 1853 by Heinrich Moser, a watchmaker, Friedrich Peyer im Hof, a politician, and Conrad Neher-Stokar, a Swiss army officer. In the beginning they started with the production of trains in the town of Schaffhausen, but in 1860 they undertook the manufacture of guns, at the request of the Swiss army. In 1865 the arms factory was managed by Friedrich Vetterli, the same man who was responsible for the design of a military rifle, the Vetterli Model 1869. Since then the company has developed numerous weapons. In 1947, they designed a semi-automatic pistol, ordered by the Swiss army, issued to the forces under the name of Model SP-47/8. For the civilian market the pistol's name was changed to Sig P210.

The Sig P210 pistol has several versions. In 1971, the Sig company took over the Hämmerli sporting gun factory and in 1974 the German arms company, Sauer & Son, from Eckenforde. The latter takeover resulted in the emergence of a complete series of pistols, the Sig-Sauers. The Sig-Sauer design originated in 1975, when the Swiss army was looking for a replacement for their old model SP-47/8 service pistol.

As a result the Sig-Sauer P220 was designed, specifically for the military market. Another pistol model from that time is the P230, a compact eight-round handgun in calibre .380 ACP. This is a typical holster gun and available in matt-blue or stainless-steel finish. For this design the well-known decocking lever system from Sig was also used. A number of governments within Europe were shopping round in 1975 for a replacement for their army and police handguns, among others the then West Germany and France. Sig was hoping for big orders from those countries. In order to apply for the rigorous specifications for the German pistol trials, a completely new pistol model had to be designed, based on the successful P220 concept. In the mean time, Sig also sold the P220 to the Japanese army.

Because the US government was also investigating the possibility of replacing the old Colt 1911-A1 .45 ACP service pistol, Sig decided to develop yet another pistol model. The Americans wanted a large-capacity pistol. Sig's answer to this was the fifteen-round P226. Their efforts eventually did not pay off, because the Beretta M92 was chosen as the new service pistol for the US army. Because Sig was counting on this huge order, the disappointment must have been great. A small comfort was the order from the FBI in 1988, who ordered 15,000 pistols with a special three-dot Sig-Lite Tritium night sight for their special Hostage Rescue Teams. Furthermore, Sig sold a large number of P226 pistols to the FBI to replace the earlier issue of Smith & Wesson M1076 10mm Auto pistols. Sig also applied for the arms trials of the Royal Canadian Mounted Police and the British army.

The New Zealand forces have recently been issued with the P226 pistol. In 1983, the P226 became available on the commercial civilian market. To be able to satisfy the request for more compact pistol types for police purposes, Sig had to redesign their pistol once again. Besides, Sig wanted to stand up to the competition from Smith & Wesson, who were introducing their models 469/669 "mini-guns".

Other manufacturers were already on the market with compact designs or were developing such guns. The smaller Sig that finally appeared was the model P228, a shortened version of the P226 with a thirteen-round capacity, but the fifteen-round magazines of the P226 fitted too. Within the US army, Sig managed to gain a strong position after all, with the order for the P228 supplied to the military police. The newest Sig pistol is the P229, a compact model in the calibres .40 S&W, 9mm Para, and in the new calibre .357 SIG. This last calibre consists of a .40 S&W shell of which the case mouth is reduced with a bottleneck to the .357 diameter. Ammunition for this calibre is made by Federal.

SIG P210-5 Target Compensator

TECHNICAL SPECIFICATIONS:

Calibre	: 9mm Para
Trigger action	: single action
Magazine capacity	: 8 rounds (9mm Para)
Locking mechanism	: SIG Petter system
Weight	: 1150g
Length	: 245mm
Height	: 137mm
Barrel length	: 150mm
Trigger stop	: adjustable
Sights	: adjustable
Sight radius	: 202mm
External safety	: safety catch
Internal safety	: slide safety, half-cock safety, magazine safety

FEATURES:

• slide catch	: on left side frame
• magazine catch	: in heel of frame
• material	: steel
• finish	: blued
• grips	: walnut

SIG P210-6

TECHNICAL SPECIFICATIONS:

Calibre	: 9 mm Para, 7.65 mm Para, conversion kit for .22 LR
Trigger action	: single action
Magazine capacity	: 8 rounds (9mm Para)
Locking mechanism	: SIG/Petter system
Weight	: 980g
Length	: 215mm
Height	: 137mm
Barrel length	: 120mm
Trigger stop	: none
Sights	: adjustable
Sight radius	: 164mm
External safety	: safety catch
Internal safety	: slide safety, half-cock safety, magazine safety

FEATURES:

• slide catch	: on left side frame
• magazine catch	: in heel of frame
• material	: steel
• finish	: blued
• grips	: wood

For the P210-5 and P210-6 optional barrels are available in calibre 9mm Para in lengths of 150mm, 150mm specially for lead bullets, and 180mm.

Sig-Sauer P220

TECHNICAL SPECIFICATIONS:

Calibre	: 9mm Para, 7.65mm Para, .38 Super, .45 ACP and .22 LR
Trigger action	: double action
Magazine capacity	: 9 rounds (9mm Para); 7 rounds (.45 ACP)
Locking mechanism	: Petter/SIG/Browning system
Weight	: 750g
Length	: 198mm
Height	: 143mm
Barrel length	: 112mm
Trigger stop	: none
Sights	: windage adjustable; elevation exchangeable
Sight radius	: 160mm
External safety	: decocking lever
Internal safety	: slide safety, automatic firing-pin safety, slip safety on hammer

FEATURES:

• slide catch	: on left side frame
• magazine catch	: in heel of grip
• material	: alloy frame, steel slide
• finish	: blued
• grips	: walnut or synthetic

Sig-Sauer P225

TECHNICAL SPECIFICATIONS:

Calibre	: 9mm Para
Trigger action	: double action or DAO (double-action-only)
Magazine capacity	: 8 rounds
Locking mechanism	: Petter/SIG system
Weight	: 740g
Length	: 180mm
Height	: 131mm
Barrel length	: 98mm
Trigger stop	: none
Sights	: windage adjustable
Sight radius	: 145mm
External safety	: decocking lever (not with DAO model)
Internal safety	: slide safety, automatic firing-pin safety

FEATURES:

• slide catch	:	on left side frame
• magazine catch	:	on left side frame, behind trigger guard
• material	:	alloy frame, steel slide
• finish	:	blued
• grips	:	black synthetic or walnut

Sig-Sauer P226

TECHNICAL SPECIFICATIONS:

Calibre	:	9mm Para
Trigger action	:	double action of DAO (double-action only)
Magazine capacity	:	15 rounds
Locking mechanism	:	Petter/SIG system
Weight	:	885g
Length	:	196mm
Height	:	139mm
Barrel length	:	112mm
Trigger stop	:	none
Sights	:	windage adjustable
Sight radius	:	160mm
External safety	:	decocking lever (not with DAO model)
Internal safety	:	slide safety, automatic firing-pin safety, half-cock safety

FEATURES:

• slide catch	:	on left side frame
• magazine catch	:	on left side frame, behind trigger guard
• material	:	alloy frame, steel slide
• finish	:	blued
• grips	:	black synthetic

Sig-Sauer P226 Sport

TECHNICAL SPECIFICATIONS:

Calibre	:	9mm Para
Trigger action	:	double action
Magazine capacity	:	15 rounds
Locking mechanism	:	Petter/SIG system
Weight	:	885g
Length	:	196mm
Height	:	139mm
Barrel length	:	112mm
Trigger stop	:	none
Sights	:	windage adjustable
Sight radius	:	160mm
External safety	:	decocking lever
Internal safety	:	slide safety, automatic firing-pin safety, half-cock safety

FEATURES:

• slide catch	:	on left side frame
• magazine catch	:	on left side frame, behind trigger guard
• material	:	roestvrijsteel slide, alloy frame
• finish	:	matt stainlesse slide, blued frame
• grips	:	walnut target

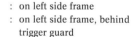

Sig-Sauer P228

TECHNICAL SPECIFICATIONS:

Calibre	:	9mm Para
Trigger action	:	double action or double-action only
Magazine capacity	:	13 rounds
Locking mechanism	:	Petter/SIG system
Weight	:	830g
Length	:	180mm
Height	:	136mm
Barrel length	:	98mm

Trigger stop	:	none
Sights	:	fixed, contrastvizier
Sight radius	:	145mm
External safety	:	decocking lever on left side frame (not present with DAO version)
Internal safety	:	automatic firing-pin safety, slide safety

FEATURES:

• slide catch	:	on left side frame
• magazine catch	:	on left side frame, behind trigger guard
• material	:	alloy frame, steel barrel and slide
• finish	:	blued
• grips	:	black synthetic

Sig-Sauer P229

TECHNICAL SPECIFICATIONS:

Calibre	:	.40 S&W, 9mm Para, .357 SIG
Trigger action	:	double action or DAO
Magazine capacity	:	12 rounds (.40); 13 rounds (9mm)
Locking mechanism	:	Petter/SIG system
Weight	:	905g
Length	:	180mm
Height	:	136mm
Barrel length	:	98mm
Trigger stop	:	none
Sights	:	windage adjustable
Sight radius	:	145mm
External safety	:	decocking lever (not present with DAO version)
Internal safety	:	slide safety, automatic firing-pin safety, half-cock safety

FEATURES:

• slide catch	:	on left side frame
• magazine catch	:	on left side frame, behind trigger guard
• material	:	alloy frame, steel or stainless-steel slide (SL)
• finish	:	P229 blued; P229 SL with stainless-steel slide
• grips	:	black synthetic

Sig-Sauer P230

TECHNICAL SPECIFICATIONS:

Calibre	:	.380 ACP (9mm Short)
Trigger action	:	double action
Magazine capacity	:	7 rounds
Locking mechanism	:	blowback action
Weight	:	470g
Length	:	165mm
Height	:	120mm
Barrel length	:	89mm
Trigger stop	:	none

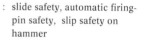

Sights	: fixed
Sight radius	: 112mm
External safety	: decocking lever
Internal safety	: slide safety, automatic firing-pin safety, slip safety on hammer

FEATURES:

• slide catch	: on left side frame
• magazine catch	: in heel of grip
• material	: alloy frame, steel slide
• finish	: blued
• grips	: walnut

Sig-Sauer P230 SL

TECHNICAL SPECIFICATIONS:

Calibre	: .380 ACP (9mm Short)
Trigger action	: double-action
Magazine capacity	: 7 rounds
Locking mechanism	: blowback action
Weight	: 470g
Length	: 165mm
Height	: 120mm
Barrel length	: 89mm
Trigger stop	: none
Sights	: fixed
Sight radius	: 112mm
External safety	: decocking lever
Internal safety	: slide safety, automatic firing-pin safety, slip safety on hammer

FEATURES:

• slide catch	: on left side frame
• magazine catch	: in heel of grip
• material	: alloy frame, stainless-steel slide
• finish	: stainless
• grips	: walnut

Smith & Wesson pistols

Most people associate the name of Smith & Wesson with revolvers. This American company, however, founded as such in 1857 and in British ownership since 1987, has since 1948 been producing semi-automatic pistols. At the end of that year the US army command decided to initiate research to replace the old Colt 1911-A1 .45 ACP service pistol. Smith & Wesson developed a semi-automatic single-action prototype, which was tested at the then State Arsenal, Springfield Armory. Shortly afterwards the Department of Defense decided to hang on to the old Colt. When in 1953 that same department decided to look around for

a replacement, Smith & Wesson tried to get hold of this huge order. Colt, however, was not asleep, so both companies had their prototype at the ready. Colt presented its Colt Commander Lightweight and Smith & Wesson had their Model 39, designed by Joseph Norman, the company's engineer. In this Model 39, Smith & Wesson applied the well-tried double-action system of the Walther P38. When the US Government decided to put the investigation for the replacement for the Colt service pistol on hold for an indefinite period, Smith & Wesson tried its luck on the civilian market with a version using an alloy frame. They introduced the M39 in double action in calibre 9mm Para and also the Model 44, a single-action version of the same design. The production of the Model 44 was abandoned in 1959. Only a small number of these pistols was made, because the public favoured the double-action M39.
In 1967, Smith & Wesson made a major step forward when the Illinois State Police Department issued the Model 39 as their service handgun. That was the signal for many more police departments gradually to replace their service sixguns with a semi-automatic pistol in calibre 9mm Para (or Luger, as this calibre is called in the USA).
In 1971, it became known that Smith & Wesson had another semi-automatic double-action 9mm Para pistol on the stocks, the Model 59. This new model had the same slide and barrel as the M39, but had a cartridge capacity of fourteen rounds. In fact, this first M59 is best described as a pistol with the top half of the M39, the frame and magazine of the FN Browning High Power, and the double-action trigger system of the Walther P38. It very soon became evident that the M59 was a winner. Most US police forces wanted to switch to the fourteen-shot DA pistol.
The M59 (and also the M39) is equipped with a safety/decock lever on the left side of the slide (with the newer models, ambidextrous), with which the firing-pin is blocked and the hammer decocked.
The first series M39 and M59 did not have the automatic firing-pin safety and the pistols were supplied with fixed sights. In 1978 several arms manufacturers were invited by the US Department of Defense to develop prototypes because it was decided to look for a replacement once again for the old Colt 1911-A1s and all kinds of .38 Special revolvers which were still in use with various army units. Smith & Wesson saw this as an opportunity to revise their entire 9mm pistol line. The production of the old M39 and M59 ceased in 1981, in favour of a new series of pistol models, namely the models 439 and 539, and the models 459 and 559.
The digit "4" before the model number indicates that the pistol has an alloy frame and the "5i" means the gun is totally made of steel. The 439 and 539 had wooden grip plates, whilst the "bigger brothers" were provided with black synthetic in order to make the grip less bulky. The rear sights were adjustable and the feeding ramp was made a bit longer and slanted in order to improve the feeding of cartridges with all kinds of bullet types. Because of this, the total length increased by 5mm. The new models were also provided with an automatic firing-pin safety and a modified extractor. In 1982, shortly after the introduction of the new 4 and 5 models, Smith & Wesson announced that these models were to be available in stainless steel at the beginning of 1983. The arms trade had been pressing S&W for such a finish for a long time. These models would have, according to the S&W tradition, the model names of 639 and 659, because the digit "6" represented the stainless finish.
The pistol series designated "third-generation pistols" in 1988 indicated that Smith & Wesson had introduced them as successors to the second-generation models. Besides new model numbers, these guns have a lot of new technology packed inside.
Smith & Wesson made a great effort with the development of this new pistol line. They started the AIP project (Autoloader Improvement Project) in which a great deal of research was carried out among many sports shooters and professional users of S&W pistols. The main differences between the old and new pistols are:

- a new kind of grip plate of synthetic Delrin, which completely wraps around the grip.
- the shape of the grip was redesigned (ergonomic), with a finger groove underneath the trigger guard in front of the grip.
- the trigger guard was enlarged.
- magazines with numbered holes to indicate the number of loaded cartridges.
- the magazines were provided with rubber butt plates.
- a flattened and enlarged magazine well for a quick change of magazines.

- the new magazines can be used in older models as well.
- new three-dot sights.
- ambidextrous safety catch on the slide.
- automatic firing-pin safety (derived from the previous models).
- magazine safety on some models (also derived from previous models).
- matt sand-blasted finish for blue and stainless-steel models.
- redesigned trigger action, by which the trigger bar, trigger spring, and sear were changed in order to smoothen the trigger action considerably, and
- a throated barrel for better fitting in the slide, so that a separate barrel bushing was superfluous.

At the beginning of 1990, Smith & Wesson introduced two new models, for which they reverted to an old and well-known designation, namely, the 'Lady Smith'. These small pistols were introduced as the models 3913 LS and 3914 LS and are derived from the new "compact line" of Smith & Wesson, the standard models 3913 and 3914. These pistols are provided with a Novak LoMount rear sight. The slides are made of steel and they have an alloy frame. The only difference between the LS finish and the standard one is the slightly changed angle of the grip, which makes it a better holster gun. The models 3913 and 3913 LS have a stainless-steel slide, while the models 3914 and 3914 LS are blued.
Mid-1990, Smith & Wesson came up with another surprise with the introduction of two pistols with a double-action only (DAO) trigger system, which means that every shot is fired in the double-action mode.
The numbering of these models consists of the last two digits "44", "53", "54", "56", or "86."
For example:

- Model 5903: a new type of M59 pistol with a stainless-steel slide and alloy frame.
- Model 5904: the same type of pistol, but with a blued slide and blued alloy frame.
- Model 5906: the same type, but with a stainless-steel slide and frame.
- Model 5946: the model 5906, but in DAO mode.

Another idea introduced by Smith & Wesson in mid-1990 was the possibility of providing all large-bore pistol models with a decock lever in the same style as the Walther P5 and P88 and the Sig-Sauer pistols. The first model in this design was the FBI finish of the M1006 in calibre 10mm Auto.
The newest model of Smith & Wesson is the Sigma pistol, or rather the Sigma Series. This handgun is, just like its competitors, built on a frame of high-impact synthetic material. It is available in the calibres .40 S&W and 9mm Para. The locking mechanism consists of an improved Browning type, where the massive block around the barrel chamber acts as a locking lug inside the ejection port of the slide.

Smith & Wesson Model 2206

TECHNICAL SPECIFICATIONS:

Calibre	: .22 LR
Trigger action	: single action
Magazine capacity	: 12 rounds
Locking mechanism	: blowback action
Weight	: 1106g
Length	: 229mm
Height	: 140mm
Barrel length	: 152mm
Trigger stop	: adjustable
Sights	: fixed or adjustable
Sight radius	: 192mm (6")
External safety	: safety catch on left side frame
Internal safety	: slide safety

FEATURES:

• slide catch	: on left side frame
• magazine catch	: mid-front of grip
• material	: stainless steel
• finish	: matt stainless
• grips	: black composition

Smith & Wesson Model 2206 Target

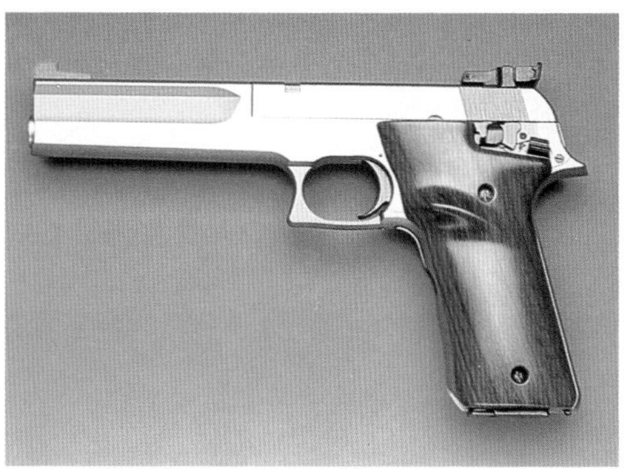

TECHNICAL SPECIFICATIONS:

Calibre	: .22 LR
Trigger action	: single action
Magazine capacity	: 12 rounds
Locking mechanism	: blowback action
Weight	: 1106g
Length	: 229mm
Height	: 140mm
Barrel length	: 152mm
Trigger stop	: adjustable
Sights	: adjustable Millet rear sight
Sight radius	: 192 mm
External safety	: safety catch on left side frame
Internal safety	: slide safety

FEATURES:

• slide catch	: on left side frame
• magazine catch	: mid-front of grip
• material	: stainless steel
• finish	: matt stainless
• grips	: walnut target or wood-grain polymer

Smith & Wesson Model 2213

TECHNICAL SPECIFICATIONS:

Calibre	: .22 LR
Trigger action	: single action
Magazine capacity	: 8 rounds
Locking mechanism	: blowback action
Weight	: 510g
Length	: 156mm
Height	: 112mm
Barrel length	: 76mm
Trigger stop	: none
Sights	: fixed
Sight radius	: 109mm
External safety	: safety catch on left side frame
Internal safety	: slide safety

FEATURES:

• slide catch	: on left side frame
• magazine catch	: mid-front of grip
• material	: alloy frame, stainless-steel slide
• finish	: M2213: matt stainless
• grips	: black polymer

Smith & Wesson Model 2214

TECHNICAL SPECIFICATIONS:

Calibre	: .22 LR
Trigger action	: single-action
Magazine capacity	: 8 rounds
Locking mechanism	: blowback action
Weight	: 510g
Length	: 156mm
Height	: 112mm
Barrel length	: 76mm

Trigger stop	:	none
Sights	:	fixed
Sight radius	:	109mm
External safety	:	safety catch on left side frame
Internal safety	:	slide safety

FEATURES:

• slide catch	:	on left side frame
• magazine catch	:	mid-front of grip
• material	:	alloy frame, steel slide
• finish	:	blued
• grips	:	black polymer

Smith & Wesson Model 3913

TECHNICAL SPECIFICATIONS:

Calibre	:	9mm Para
Trigger action	:	double action
Magazine capacity	:	8 rounds
Locking mechanism	:	Browning-S&W system
Weight	:	709g
Length	:	173mm
Height	:	134mm
Barrel length	:	89mm
Trigger stop	:	none
Sights	:	fixed
Sight radius	:	140mm
External safety	:	ambidextrous safety catch on slide
Internal safety	:	slide safety, firing-pin safety

FEATURES:

• slide catch	:	on left side frame
• magazine catch	:	on left side frame, behind trigger guard
• material	:	alloy frame, stainless-steel slide
• finish	:	matt stainless
• grips	:	black polymer

Smith & Wesson Model 3913 Lady Smith

TECHNICAL SPECIFICATIONS:

Calibre	:	9mm Para
Trigger action	:	double action
Magazine capacity	:	8 rounds
Locking mechanism	:	Browning-S&W system
Weight	:	709g
Length	:	173mm
Height	:	134mm
Barrel length	:	89mm
Trigger stop	:	none
Sights	:	fixed
Sight radius	:	140mm
External safety	:	safety catch on left side of slide
Internal safety	:	slide safety, firing-pin safety

FEATURES:

• slide catch	:	on left side frame
• magazine catch	:	on left side frame, behind trigger guard
• material	:	alloy frame, stainless-steel slide
• finish	:	matt stainless
• grips	:	light-grey polymer

Smith & Wesson Model 3914

TECHNICAL SPECIFICATIONS:

Calibre	:	9mm Para
Trigger action	:	double action
Magazine capacity	:	8 rounds
Locking mechanism	:	Browning-S&W system
Weight	:	709g
Length	:	173mm
Height	:	134mm
Barrel length	:	89mm

Trigger stop	: none
Sights	: fixed
Sight radius	: 140mm
External safety	: ambidextrous safety catch on slide
Internal safety	: slide safety, firing-pin safety
FEATURES:	
• slide catch	: on left side frame
• magazine catch	: on left side frame, behind trigger guard
• material	: alloy frame, steel slide
• finish	: blued
• grips	: black polymer

Smith & Wesson Model 3953

TECHNICAL SPECIFICATIONS:

Calibre	: 9mm Para
Trigger action	: double-action only
Magazine capacity	: 8 rounds
Locking mechanism	: Browning-S&W system
Weight	: 709g
Length	: 173mm
Height	: 134mm
Barrel length	: 89mm
Trigger stop	: none
Sights	: fixed
Sight radius	: 140mm
External safety	: none
Internal safety	: slide safety, firing-pin safety
FEATURES:	
• slide catch	: on left side frame
• magazine catch	: on left side frame, behind trigger guard
• material	: alloy frame, stainless-steel slide
• finish	: matt stainless
• grips	: black polymer

Smith & Wesson Model 4006

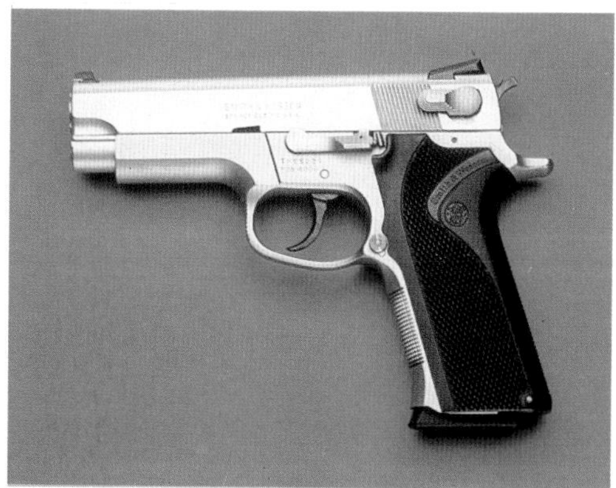

TECHNICAL SPECIFICATIONS:

Calibre	: .40 S&W
Trigger action	: double action
Magazine capacity	: 11 rounds
Locking mechanism	: Browning-S&W system
Weight	: 1091g
Length	: 191mm
Height	: 157mm
Barrel length	: 102mm
Trigger stop	: none
Sights	: fixed
Sight radius	: 168mm
External safety	: ambidextrous safety catch on slide
Internal safety	: slide safety, firing-pin safety
FEATURES:	
• slide catch	: on left side frame
• magazine catch	: on left side frame, behind trigger guard

• material	: stainless steel
• finish	: matt stainless
• grips	: black synthetic

Smith & Wesson Model 4013

TECHNICAL SPECIFICATIONS:

Calibre	: .40 S&W
Trigger action	: double action
Magazine capacity	: 8 rounds
Locking mechanism	: Browning-S&W system
Weight	: 765g
Length	: 180mm
Height	: 139mm
Barrel length	: 89mm
Trigger stop	: none
Sights	: fixed
Sight radius	: 138mm
External safety	: ambidextrous safety catch on slide
Internal safety	: slide safety, firing-pin safety
FEATURES:	
• slide catch	: on left side frame
• magazine catch	: on left side frame, behind trigger guard
• material	: alloy frame, stainless-steel slide
• finish	: stainless
• grips	: black polymer

Smith & Wesson Model 4043

TECHNICAL SPECIFICATIONS:

Calibre	: .40 S&W
Trigger action	: double-action only
Magazine capacity	: 11 rounds
Locking mechanism	: Browning-S&W system
Weight	: 794g
Length	: 191mm
Height	: 157mm
Barrel length	: 102mm
Trigger stop	: none
Sights	: fixed
Sight radius	: 168mm
External safety	: none
Internal safety	: slide safety, firing-pin safety
FEATURES:	
• slide catch	: on left side frame
• magazine catch	: on left side frame, behind trigger guard
• material	: alloy frame, stainless-steel slide
• finish	: matt stainless
• grips	: black polymer

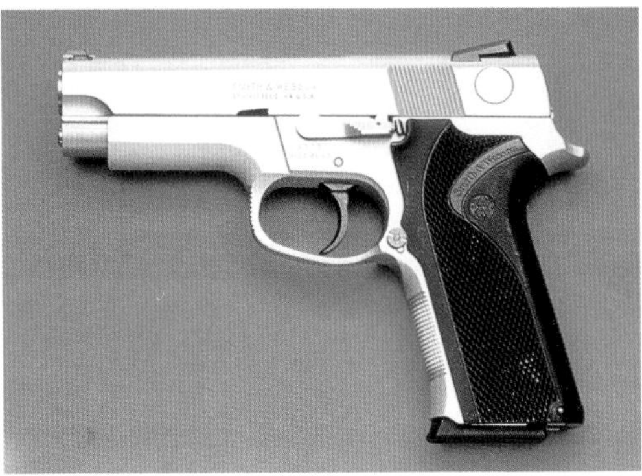

Smith & Wesson Model 4053

TECHNICAL SPECIFICATIONS:

Calibre	: .40 S&W
Trigger action	: double-action only
Magazine capacity	: 8 rounds

Locking mechanism	:	Browning-S&W system
Weight	:	765g
Length	:	180mm
Height	:	139mm
Barrel length	:	89mm
Trigger stop	:	none
Sights	:	fixed
Sight radius	:	138mm
External safety	:	none safety catch
Internal safety	:	slide safety, firing-pin safety

FEATURES:

• slide catch	:	on left side frame
• magazine catch	:	on left side frame, behind trigger guard
• material	:	alloy frame, stainless-steel slide
• finish	:	stainless
• grips	:	black polymer

Smith & Wesson M41 .22 LR

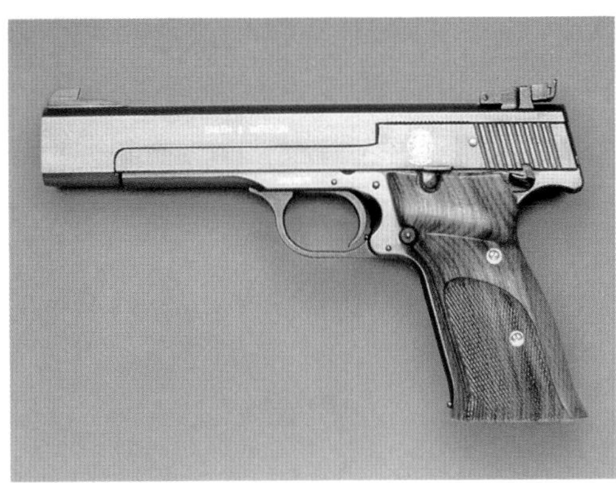

TECHNICAL SPECIFICATIONS:

Calibre	:	.22 LR
Trigger action	:	single action
Magazine capacity	:	12 rounds
Locking mechanism	:	blowback action
Weight	:	1247g
Length	:	230mm
Height	:	135mm
Barrel length	:	140mm (5-1/2"); 178mm (7")
Trigger stop	:	adjustable
Sights	:	adjustable Millet rear sight
Sight radius	:	200mm (7")
External safety	:	safety catch on left side of frame
Internal safety	:	slide safety, magazine safety

FEATURES:

• slide catch	:	on left side frame, above trigger guard
• magazine catch	:	on left side frame, behind trigger guard
• material	:	steel
• finish	:	blued
• grips	:	walnut

In 1947, two prototypes of this pistol were developed that were tested by the S&W pistol team at that time. However, it took until 1957 for the manufacture of this pistol to begin. That first production run was modest, with only 680 guns with a 73/8in barrel, on which a muzzle break was attached. Much to Smith & Wesson's surprise, this model was in great demand. In 1958, the production was increased to almost 10,000 pieces, but even that number was not enough to satisfy the market. In 1959, a second model, a lightweight version, was introduced, with a 5in barrel. That same year a less luxurious model was presented, the Model 46. It was specially made for target practice for the US airforce and had a 5in or 7in barrel without a muzzle break and with synthetic grips. Only about 4000 pistols were made of this model. In 1960, S&W introduced the Model 41-1, a calibre .22 Short model with an alloy slide. This model achieved little success and was only produced for a couple of years. In 1963, a 51/2in model with a heavy barrel came into production. It had a lengthened sight base for an extended sight radius. The construction of the rear sight itself was also changed. The same micrometric rear sight was used for another match pistol, the Model 52. One of the reasons for its success has been the opportunity to exchange barrels. By hinging down the trigger guard, the barrel is released from the frame and can be exchanged quickly for another type of barrel. Furthermore, the rear sight is not fixed to the slide, but to an extended sight base. The recycling slide runs underneath this base.

From 1987 onwards, three different models were introduced: a 7in barrel model without compensator, a 5in heavy barrel model, and a so-called "field model" for hunting small vermin.
In 1990, only the 51/2in and 7in models reappeared in the S&W programme, but in 1991 a 6in barrel model was introduced, which disappeared again the year after. You can imagine that these "special" models have great collectors' value.

Smith & Wesson Model 411

TECHNICAL SPECIFICATIONS:

Calibre	: .40 S&W
Trigger action	: double action
Magazine capacity	: 11 rounds
Locking mechanism	: Browning-S&W system
Weight	: 833g
Length	: 191mm
Height	: 142mm
Barrel length	: 102mm
Trigger stop	: none
Sights	: fixed
Sight radius	: 132mm
External safety	: safety catch on left side of slide
Internal safety	: slide safety, firing-pin safety

FEATURES:

• slide catch	: on left side frame
• magazine catch	: on left side frame, behind trigger guard
• material	: alloy frame, steel slide
• finish	: blued
• grips	: black polymer

Smith & Wesson Model 422

TECHNICAL SPECIFICATIONS:

Calibre	: .22 LR
Trigger action	: single action
Magazine capacity	: 12 rounds
Locking mechanism	: blowback system
Weight	: 652g
Length	: 229mm
Height	: 138mm
Barrel length	: 152mm
Trigger stop	: none
Sights	: fixed or adjustable
Sight radius	: 192mm
External safety	: safety catch on left side frame
Internal safety	: slide safety

FEATURES:

• slide catch	: on left side frame
• magazine catch	: mid-front of grip
• material	: alloy frame, steel slide
• finish	: blued
• grips	: black polymer

Smith & Wesson Model 4506

TECHNICAL SPECIFICATIONS:

Calibre	: .45 ACP
Trigger action	: double action
Magazine capacity	: 8 rounds
Locking mechanism	: Browning-S&W system
Weight	: 1148g
Length	: 216mm
Height	: 149mm
Barrel length	: 127mm
Trigger stop	: none
Sights	: fixed
Sight radius	: 166mm

External safety	: ambidextrous safety catch op slide
Internal safety	: slide safety, firing-pin safety

FEATURES:

• slide catch	: on left side frame
• magazine catch	: on left side frame, behind trigger guard
• material	: stainless steel
• finish	: matt stainless
• grips	: black polymer

In the third-generation pistols from Smith & Wesson, the Model 645, introduced in 1984, also had to undergo a number of important modifications. First of all a new trigger mechanism was developed through computer modelling, by which old complaints about the trigger characteristics were eliminated. From the prestigious programme, the AIP (Autoloader Improvement Project), Smith & Wesson learned that a lot of users found the trigger action of their pistols not flexible enough. In the computer studies it became apparent that, in the trigger action of the S&W pistols, there were some pressure-resistant areas, what could be called "humps". All the newer models, including the Model 4506, have this new trigger system.

The M4506 is available in different basic models, namely, with or without adjustable rear sight, and with a straight or curved backstrap to the grip. Furthermore, the pistol has a three-dot sight, a bevelled magazine well, and the magazines have rubber floor plates. The barrel bushing, already used in the M645, did not change, which means that the barrel is throated to such an extent that the fitting within the slide is almost without play. The precision of the gun has therefore been greatly increased.

Smith & Wesson Model 4516

TECHNICAL SPECIFICATIONS:

Calibre	: .45 ACP
Trigger action	: double action
Magazine capacity	: 7 rounds
Locking mechanism	: Browning-S&W system
Weight	: 964g
Length	: 191mm
Height	: 145mm
Barrel length	: 95mm
Trigger stop	: none
Sights	: fixed
Sight radius	: 145mm
External safety	: ambidextrous safety catch on slide
Internal safety	: slide safety, firing-pin safety

FEATURES:

• slide catch	: on left side frame
• magazine catch	: on left side frame, behind trigger guard
• material	: stainless-steel frame and slide
• finish	: stainless
• grips	: black polymer

Smith & Wesson Model 4566

TECHNICAL SPECIFICATIONS:

Calibre	: .45 ACP
Trigger action	: double action
Magazine capacity	: 8 rounds
Locking mechanism	: Browning-S&W system
Weight	: 1091g
Length	: 200mm
Height	: 153mm
Barrel length	: 108mm
Trigger stop	: none

Sights	:	fixed
Sight radius	:	156mm
External safety	:	ambidextrous safety catch on slide
Internal safety	:	slide safety, firing-pin safety

FEATURES:

• slide catch	:	on left side frame
• magazine catch	:	on left side frame, behind trigger guard
• material	:	stainless steel
• finish	:	matt stainless
• grips	:	black polymer

Smith & Wesson Model 4586

TECHNICAL SPECIFICATIONS:

Calibre	:	.45 ACP
Trigger action	:	double-action only
Magazine capacity	:	8 rounds
Locking mechanism	:	Browning-S&W system
Weight	:	1091g
Length	:	200mm
Height	:	153mm
Barrel length	:	108mm
Trigger stop	:	none
Sights	:	fixed
Sight radius	:	156mm
External safety	:	none
Internal safety	:	slide safety, firing-pin safety

FEATURES:

• slide catch	:	on left side frame
• magazine catch	:	on left side frame, behind trigger guard
• material	:	stainless steel
• finish	:	matt stainless
• grips	:	black polymer

Smith & Wesson Model 52 .38 Special WC

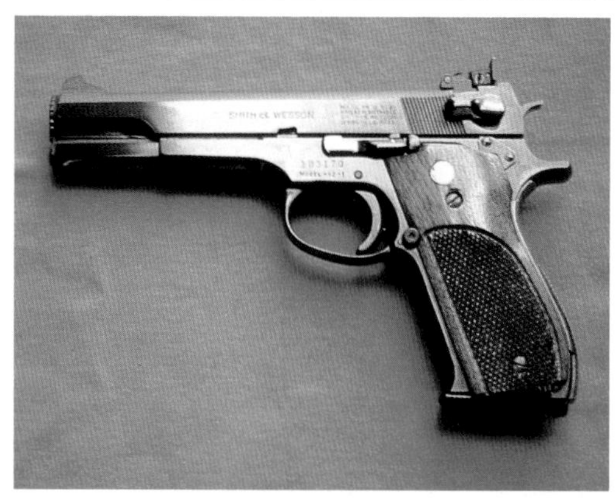

TECHNICAL SPECIFICATIONS:

Calibre	:	.38 Special WadCutter
Trigger action	:	single action
Magazine capacity	:	5 rounds
Locking mechanism	:	Browning-S&W system
Weight	:	1160g
Length	:	235mm
Height	:	146mm
Barrel length	:	127mm
Trigger stop	:	adjustable
Sights	:	S&W micro-rear sight
Sight radius	:	177mm
External safety	:	safety catch on left side of slide
Internal safety	:	magazine safety

FEATURES:

• slide catch	:	on left side frame
• magazine catch	:	on left side frame, behind trigger guard
• material	:	steel
• finish	:	blued
• grips	:	walnut

Smith & Wesson Model 5903/Model 5904

TECHNICAL SPECIFICATIONS:

Calibre	:	9mm Para
Trigger action	:	double action
Magazine capacity	:	15 rounds
Locking mechanism	:	Browning-S&W system
Weight	:	808g
Length	:	191mm
Height	:	139mm
Barrel length	:	102mm
Trigger stop	:	none

Sights	:	fixed
Sight radius	:	150mm
External safety	:	ambidextrous safety catch on slide
Internal safety	:	slide safety, firing-pin safety
FEATURES:		
• slide catch	:	on left side frame
• magazine catch	:	on left side frame, behind trigger guard
• material	:	M5903: alloy frame, stainless-steel slide; M5904: alloy frame, steel slide
• finish	:	M5903: stainless steel; M5904: blued
• grips	:	black polymer

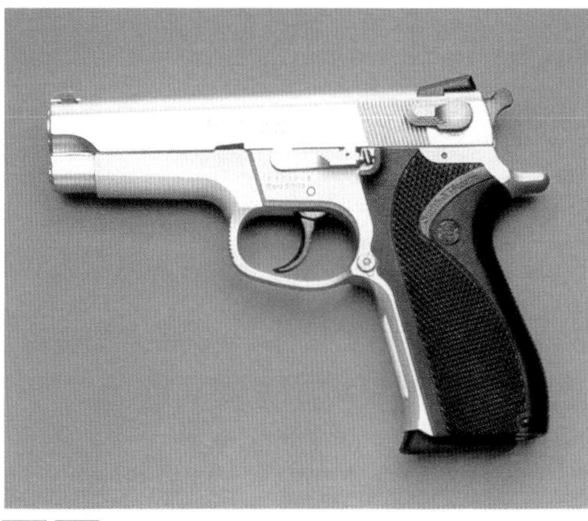

Smith & Wesson Model 5906

TECHNICAL SPECIFICATIONS:

Calibre	:	9mm Para
Trigger action	:	double action
Magazine capacity	:	15 rounds
Locking mechanism	:	Browning-S&W system
Weight	:	1063g
Length	:	191mm
Height	:	142mm
Barrel length	:	102mm
Trigger stop	:	none
Sights	:	fixed
Sight radius	:	152mm
External safety	:	ambidextrous safety catch on slide
Internal safety	:	slide safety, firing-pin safety
FEATURES:		
• slide catch	:	on left side frame
• magazine catch	:	on left side frame, behind trigger guard
• material	:	stainless steel
• finish	:	matt stainless
• grips	:	black polymer

Smith & Wesson Model 5946

TECHNICAL SPECIFICATIONS:

Calibre	:	9mm Para
Trigger action	:	double-action only
Magazine capacity	:	15 rounds
Locking mechanism	:	Browning-S&W system
Weight	:	1063g
Length	:	191mm
Height	:	142mm
Barrel length	:	102mm
Trigger stop	:	none
Sights	:	fixed
Sight radius	:	152mm
External safety	:	none
Internal safety	:	slide safety, firing-pin safety
FEATURES:		
• slide catch	:	on left side frame
• magazine catch	:	on left side frame, behind trigger guard

• material	:	stainless steel
• finish	:	matt stainless
• grips	:	black polymer

Smith & Wesson Model 622 4$^1/_2$"

TECHNICAL SPECIFICATIONS:

Calibre	:	.22 LR
Trigger action	:	single action
Magazine capacity	:	12 rounds
Locking mechanism	:	blowback system
Weight	:	624g
Length	:	191mm
Height	:	138mm
Barrel length	:	102mm
Trigger stop	:	none
Sights	:	fixed or adjustable
Sight radius	:	155mm
External safety	:	safety catch on left side frame
Internal safety	:	slide safety

FEATURES:

• slide catch	:	on left side frame
• magazine catch	:	mid-front of grip
• material	:	alloy frame, stainless-steel slide
• finish	:	matt stainless
• grips	:	black polymer

Smith & Wesson Model 622 6"

TECHNICAL SPECIFICATIONS:

Calibre	:	.22 LR
Trigger action	:	single action
Magazine capacity	:	12 rounds
Locking mechanism	:	blowback action
Weight	:	652g
Length	:	229mm
Height	:	138mm
Barrel length	:	152mm
Trigger stop	:	none
Sights	:	fixed or adjustable
Sight radius	:	192mm
External safety	:	safety catch on left side frame
Internal safety	:	slide safety

FEATURES:

• slide catch	:	on left side frame
• magazine catch	:	mid-front of grip
• material	:	alloy frame, stainless-steel slide
• finish	:	matt stainless
• grips	:	black polymer

Smith & Wesson Model 645

TECHNICAL SPECIFICATIONS:

Calibre	: .45 ACP
Trigger action	: double action
Magazine capacity	: 8 rounds
Locking mechanism	: Browning-S&W system
Weight	: 1060g
Length	: 220mm
Height	: 145mm
Barrel length	: 127mm
Trigger stop	: none
Sights	: adjustable
Sight radius	: 168mm
External safety	: safety catch on left side of slide
Internal safety	: slide safety, automatic firing-pin safety, magazine safety

FEATURES:

• slide catch	: on left side frame
• magazine catch	: on left side frame, behind trigger guard
• material	: stainless steel
• finish	: matt stainless , polished slide sides
• grips	: black polymer

Smith & Wesson Model 659

TECHNICAL SPECIFICATIONS:

Calibre	: 9mm Para
Trigger action	: double action
Magazine capacity	: 14 rounds
Locking mechanism	: Browning-S&W system
Weight	: 1134g
Length	: 194mm
Height	: 150mm
Barrel length	: 102mm
Trigger stop	: none
Sights	: fixed or adjustable
Sight radius	: 148mm
External safety	: decock/safety catch
Internal safety	: slide safety, magazine safety, automatic firing-pin safety

FEATURES:

• slide catch	: on left side frame
• magazine catch	: on left side frame, behind trigger guard
• material	: stainless steel
• finish	: stainless
• grips	: black polymer

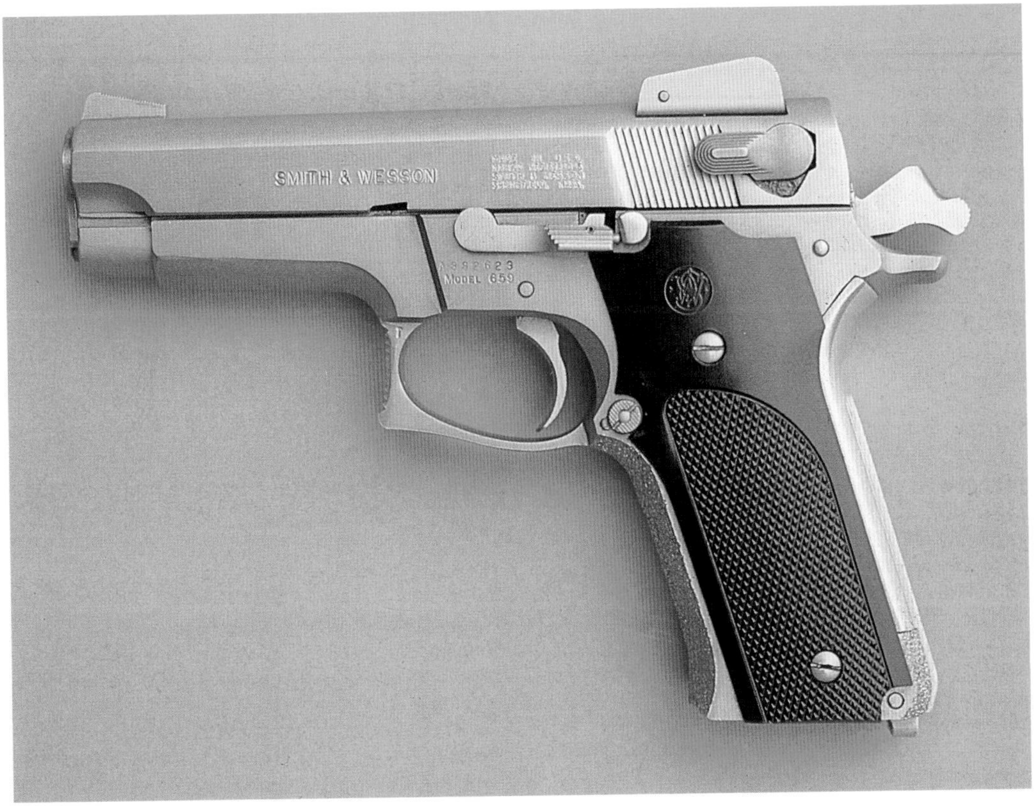

Smith & Wesson Model 6904

TECHNICAL SPECIFICATIONS:

Calibre : 9mm Para
Trigger action : double action
Magazine capacity : 12 rounds
Locking mechanism : Browning-S&W system
Weight : 751g
Length : 175mm
Height : 140mm
Barrel length : 89mm
Trigger stop : none
Sights : fixed
Sight radius : 144mm
External safety : ambidextrous safety catch on slide
Internal safety : slide safety, firing-pin safety

FEATURES:

- slide catch : on left side frame
- magazine catch : on left side frame, behind trigger guard
- material : alloy frame, steel slide
- finish : blued
- grips : black polymer

Smith & Wesson Model 6906

TECHNICAL SPECIFICATIONS:

Calibre : 9mm Para
Trigger action : double action
Magazine capacity : 12 rounds
Locking mechanism : Browning-S&W system
Weight : 751g
Length : 175mm
Height : 140mm
Barrel length : 89mm
Trigger stop : none
Sights : fixed
Sight radius : 144mm
External safety : ambidextrous safety catch on slide
Internal safety : slide safety, firing-pin safety

FEATURES:

- slide catch : on left side frame
- magazine catch : on left side frame, behind trigger guard
- material : alloy frame, stainless-steel slide
- finish : matt stainless
- grips : black polymer

Smith & Wesson Model 6946

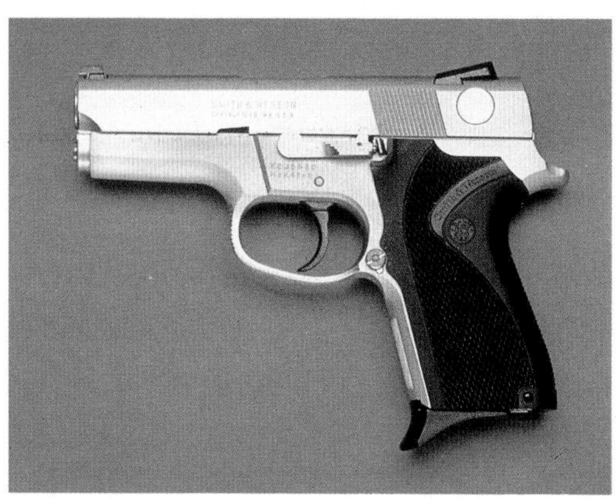

TECHNICAL SPECIFICATIONS:

Calibre : 9mm Para
Trigger action : double-action only
Magazine capacity : 12 rounds
Locking mechanism : Browning-S&W system
Weight : 751g
Length : 180mm
Height : 140mm
Barrel length : 89mm

Trigger stop	: none
Sights	: fixed
Sight radius	: 144mm
External safety	: none
Internal safety	: slide safety, firing-pin safety

FEATURES:

• slide catch	: on left side frame
• magazine catch	: on left side frame, behind trigger guard
• material	: alloy frame, stainless-steel slide
• finish	: matt stainless
• grips	: black polymer

Smith & Wesson Model 745

TECHNICAL SPECIFICATIONS:

Calibre	: .45 ACP
Trigger action	: single action
Magazine capacity	: 8 rounds
Locking mechanism	: Browning-S&W system
Weight	: 1065g
Length	: 219mm
Height	: 145mm
Barrel length	: 127mm
Trigger stop	: none
Sights	: adjustable
Sight radius	: 168mm
External safety	: combined decock/safety catch on slide
Internal safety	: slide safety, automatic firing-pin safety, magazine safety

FEATURES:

• slide catch	: on left side frame
• magazine catch	: on left side frame, behind trigger guard
• material	: stainless-steel frame, steel slide
• finish	: matt stainless frame, blued slide
• grips	: black synthetic (neoprene)

Smith & Wesson Model 910

TECHNICAL SPECIFICATIONS:

Calibre	: 9 mm Para
Trigger action	: double action
Magazine capacity	: 15 rounds
Locking mechanism	: Browning-S&W system
Weight	: 794g
Length	: 187mm
Height	: 137mm
Barrel length	: 102mm
Trigger stop	: none
Sights	: fixed
Sight radius	: 150mm
External safety	: safety catch on left side of slide
Internal safety	: slide safety, firing-pin safety

FEATURES:

• slide catch	: on left side frame
• magazine catch	: on left side frame, behind trigger guard
• material	: alloy frame, steel slide
• finish	: matt blued
• grips	: black polymer

Smith & Wesson Sigma Model SW40F/Sigma SW9F

TECHNICAL SPECIFICATIONS:

Calibre	: SW40F: .40 S&W; SW9F: 9mm Para
Trigger action	: double-action only

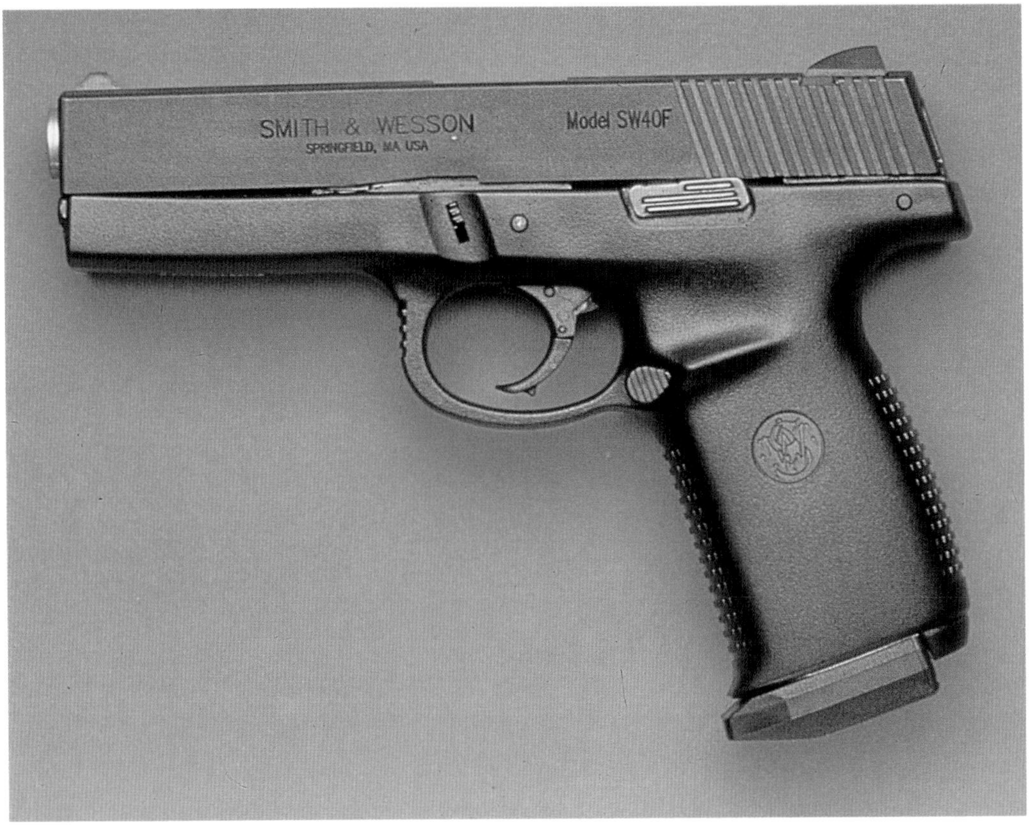

Magazine capacity	:	SW40F: 15 rounds; SW9F: 17 rounds (because of the recent American legislation, the magazine capacity of the newest version is limited to 10 rounds for the North American market only)
Locking mechanism	:	Browning-S&W system
Weight	:	737g
Length	:	197mm
Height	:	142mm
Barrel length	:	114mm
Trigger stop	:	none
Sights	:	fixed
Sight radius	:	165mm
External safety	:	none
Internal safety	:	slide safety, firing-pin safety
FEATURES:		
• slide catch	:	on left side frame
• magazine catch	:	on left side frame, behind trigger guard
• material	:	partly steel/polymers
• finish	:	matt black
• grips	:	integrated frame and grip

Smith & Wesson revolvers

In 1852, Daniel B. Wesson and Horace Smith decided to team up and start a small workshop for guns in the town of Norwich in the State of Connecticut. They won a gold medal during the Baltimore Exhibition in 1854 for their first attempt to make a handgun, capable of firing a united cartridge, which means bullet, powder, and ignition in one single unit. In June 1855, Smith and Wesson decided to sell their business to a group of businessmen, who later became known as the Volcanic Repeating Arms Company. One of those businessmen was the later well-known Oliver Winchester. Smith and Wesson applied themselves to the development of a revolver, to Wesson's design, which could fire metallic cartridges (Patent no. 11496, August 1854). When they wanted to start production, Wesson discovered that one of the parts of their new revolver had already been patented by Rollin White, namely, a completely drilled cylinder that could be loaded at the back. They approached White to avoid legal problems about the patent. For a fee of 25 cents per handgun, White agreed to his patent being used. The production started in 1856 in a workshop on Market Street in Springfield, Massachusetts. In the years that followed the company manufactured topbreak revolvers, now known as Model One First Issue, in the calibre .22 rimfire. Violation of the patent rights of Smith & Wesson were many. No less than twenty-five lawsuits were conducted by Smith & Wesson against the same number of offenders. In 1870, Smith & Wesson had a difficult time. Generally speaking, a patent was only valid for fifteen years, after which the whole market was free to use the design. The government belief was that a company should have had sufficient time in those fifteen years to recoup the costs of development and that further protection of the patent would be damaging for industry as a whole. Although the US Congress decided by law to extend the patent protection period, Smith & Wesson was refused such an extension in 1870 by the President, Ulysses S. Grant. Several theories have been put forward about this refusal. The most likely theories are given here. The first is that, during the Civil War, the then General Grant was dissatisfied with the way Smith & Wesson complied with its duty for delivery and suspected them more or less of sabotage. A second theory is that the US government would have had to pay huge patent fees to Smith & Wesson for the conversion of all army percussion revolvers to cartridge revolvers. In spite of this setback Smith & Wesson continued with further developments. The company bought a patent from W.C. Dodge to improve the cylinder bridge and pivoting system of their revolvers. They also bought a patent from Charles A. King for an ejection system. In 1869, Smith & Wesson introduced its .44 American revolver, four years before Colt marketed its .45 Peacemaker.

In Washington, the US Ordnance Department placed an order with Smith & Wesson in 1872 for the delivery of 6000 revolvers of the type .45 Schofield. That made a lot of work for the company, because they were already producing more than 200,000 revolvers of calibre .44 for a Russian order. They owed this order to the fact that the Grand-Sovereign Alexis of Russia was entertained in a royal manner on US soil. That included, among other events, great hunting trips with Buffalo Bill (Cody) where a wild, and probably the last, buffalo was killed. With a grand total of around 250,000 revolvers to produce, Smith & Wesson had a lot on their hands and had to neglect the domestic market. This situation was gratefully exploited by Colt to sell the Colt Peacemaker in vast quantities. Besides, the US government was lobbied to such an extent by Colt and Remington that, in 1876, the Ordnance Department decided to give a major army order to Colt for Peacemaker revolvers. Ironically, Smith & Wesson received, also in 1876, a gold medal during the International Centennial Exhibition in Philadelphia, as manufacturers of the best army revolver ever made. Because the revolver line of Smith & Wesson lacked pocket revolvers, the company decided in 1876 to fill that gap. In that year they introduced a five-shot .38 revolver that was instantly nicknamed 'Baby Russian', undoubtedly because of the strong resemblance to its big brother. After 1880 more modifications were introduced into the Smith & Wesson revolvers, for example, the curved trigger guard. That was the beginning of the distinct S&W profile, which is evident in the entire S&W revolver collection.

In 1877, they introduced a double-action .38 revolver. That same year Colt also marketed its first double-action revolver, so this could not have been a coincidence. In the years that followed numerous small modifications were introduced, including variations in barrel length and calibre, new calibres, spurless revolvers, swing-out cylinders, and the Smith & Wesson 'New Departure' revolver models, the so-called "lemon squeezers" with a grip safety in the backstrap of the grip. Almost all the characteristic technical attributes of the revolver were developed in those tempestuous years leading up to 1900. The Smith & Wesson revolver, Hand-Ejector Triple Lock Model, also called the New Century Model, was introduced in 1907. These revolvers were mainly built in calibre .44 S&W Special, but a small number were in calibre .45 Colt and other calibres, such as .38 S&W Special and .32 S&W Long. This revolver is still a favourite amongst match shooters and collectors. From this model the later famous army revolver Model 1917 was derived that, together with the Colt M1917, was issued as the standard army handgun in the First World War. Both are issued in the calibre .45 ACP with specially designed three-round half-moon clips.

Another type, derived from the New Century, was the small Model M-Lady Smith, a seven-shot hand-ejector revolver. Hand ejector in this connection is nothing more than the fact that the empty shells can be ejected by pushing with the hand against the ejection rod, after the cylinder is swung out. This simple mechanism is not very spectacular nowadays, but at that time it was the invention of the century in arms technology. In total about 26,000 Lady Smiths are produced in three different finishes. It is almost 145 years since Dan Wesson and Horace Smith engaged in the competition with Sam Colt. In the end the strain was too great for the family business, and Smith & Wesson has over the years been owned by several multinationals. To put it briefly – the family business was sold in 1965 to the Bangor Punta Corp., a well-known multinational in the arms trade. In 1984, the Lear Siegler Corp. purchased the Bangor Punta Corp., together with Smith & Wesson. Lear Siegler was taken over by Forstmann Little & Co. in 1986, who sold Smith & Wesson to the British company Tomkins Ltd, which in 1996 still owns the company.

Smith & Wesson Model 10/Model 64 Military & Police

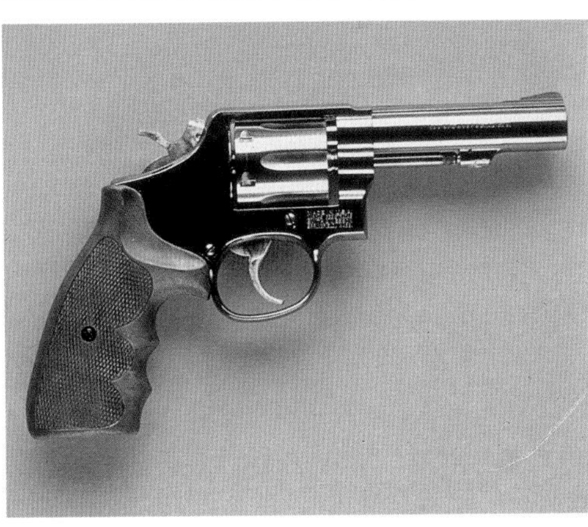

TECHNICAL SPECIFICATIONS:

Calibre	: .38 Special
Trigger action	: double action
Cylinder capacity	: 6 rounds
Locking mechanism	: front/rear-side centre pin
Weight	: 795g (M10-2"); 950g (4"-HB); 795g (M64-2"); 850g (3"-HB); 950g (4"-HB)
Length	: 175mm (2"); 202mm (3"); 237mm (4")
Height	: 132mm
Barrel length	: 51mm (2"), 76mm (3"), 102mm (4")
Trigger stop	: none
Sights	: fixed
Sight radius	: 145mm (4")
External safety	: cylinder blocks with cocked hammer
Internal safety	: blocking bar

FEATURES:

• thumb piece	: on left side frame
• material	: M10 steel; M64 stainless steel
• finish	: M10 blued; M64 matt stainless
• grips	: Uncle Mike's combat

Smith & Wesson Model 13/Model 65 .357 Military & Police

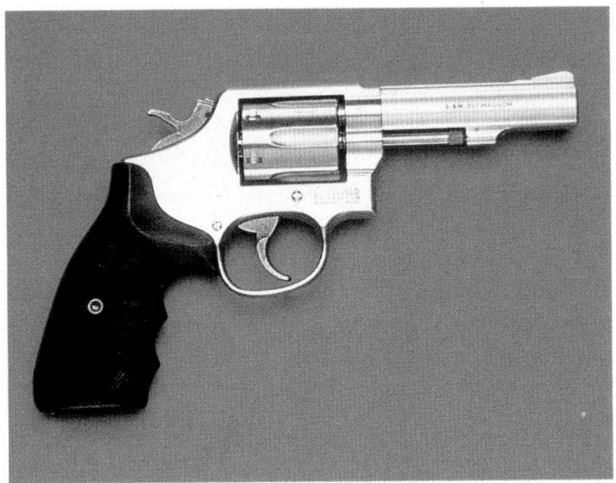

TECHNICAL SPECIFICATIONS:

Calibre	: .357 Magnum
Trigger action	: double action
Cylinder capacity	: 6 rounds
Locking mechanism	: front/rear-side centre pin
Weight	: 865g (3"-HB); 851g (4"-HB)
Length	: 202mm (3"-HB); 237mm (4"-HB)
Height	: 132mm
Barrel length	: 76mm (3"), 102 mm (4")
Trigger stop	: none
Sights	: fixed
Sight radius	: 140mm (4")
External safety	: cylinder blocks with cocked hammer
Internal safety	: blocking bar

FEATURES:

• thumb piece	: on left side frame
• material	: M13 steel; M65 stainless steel
• finish	: M13 blued; M65 matt stainless
• grips	: Uncle Mike's Combat

Smith & Wesson Model 14 .38 Masterpiece

TECHNICAL SPECIFICATIONS:

Calibre : .38 Special
Trigger action : double action
Cylinder capacity : 6 rounds
Locking mechanism : front/rear-side centre pin
Weight : 1332g
Length : 283mm
Height : 136mm
Barrel length : 152mm
Trigger stop : none
Sights : adjustable
Sight radius : 177mm
External safety : cylinder blocks with cocked hammer
Internal safety : blocking bar

FEATURES:

- thumb piece : on left side frame
- material : steel
- finish : blued
- grips : Hogue combat

Smith & Wesson Model 15/Model 67 Combat Masterpiece

TECHNICAL SPECIFICATIONS:

Calibre : .38 Special
Trigger action : double action
Cylinder capacity : 6 rounds
Locking mechanism : front/rear-side centre pin
Weight : 907g
Length : 237mm
Height : 139mm
Barrel length : 102mm
Trigger stop : none
Sights : adjustable
Sight radius : 149mm
External safety : cylinder blocks with cocked hammer
Internal safety : blocking bar

FEATURES:

- cilinderpal : on left side frame
- material : M15 steel; M67 stainless steel
- finish : M15 blued; M67 matt stainless
- grips : Uncle Mike's combat

Smith & Wesson Model 18 Combat Masterpiece

TECHNICAL SPECIFICATIONS:

Calibre : .22 LR
Trigger action : double action
Cylinder capacity : 6 rounds
Locking mechanism : front/rear-side centre pin
Weight : 960g
Length : 231mm
Height : 139mm
Barrel length : 102mm
Trigger stop : none
Sights : adjustable
Sight radius : 150mm

External safety : cylinder blocks with cocked hammer
Internal safety : blocking bar

FEATURES:

- thumb piece : on left side frame
- material : steel
- finish : blued
- grips : walnut target

Smith & Wesson Model 19 Combat Magnum

TECHNICAL SPECIFICATIONS:

Calibre : .357 Magnum
Trigger action : double-action
Cylinder capacity : 6 rounds
Locking mechanism : front/rear-side centre pin
Weight : 865g ($2^{1}/_{2}$"); 1021g (4"); 1106g (6")
Length : 191mm ($2^{1}/_{2}$"); 243mm (4"); 289mm (6")
Height : 149mm
Barrel length : 64mm ($2^{1}/_{2}$"); 102mm (4"); 152mm (6")
Trigger stop : none
Sights : adjustable
Sight radius : 115mm ($2^{1}/_{2}$")
External safety : cylinder blocks with cocked hammer
Internal safety : blocking bar

FEATURES:

- thumb piece : on left side frame
- material : steel
- finish : blued
- grips : Uncle Mike's combat or Goncalo Alves walnut

Smith & Wesson Model 27

TECHNICAL SPECIFICATIONS:

Calibre : .357 Magnum
Trigger action : double action
Cylinder capacity : 6 rounds
Locking mechanism : front/rear-side centre pin
Weight : 1293g (6")
Length : 287mm (6")
Height : 152mm
Barrel length : 102mm (4"), 152mm (6"), 213mm ($8^{3}/_{8}$")
Trigger stop : none
Sights : adjustable micrometer rear sight
Sight radius : 182mm
External safety : none
Internal safety : blocking bar

FEATURES:

- thumb piece : on left side frame
- material : steel
- finish : high polished blue
- grips : walnut Goncalo Alves target

The Smith & Wesson revolver Model 27 is a luxury model with a very highly polished deep-blue finish. The Model 28, the 'Highway Patrolman', has a plain finish and is only available with a 4in or 6in barrel. Both are heavy-frame revolvers with the so-called "N frame", also in use for the .41 and .44 Magnum Smith & Wesson revolvers. These guns last a lifetime, at least.

Smith & Wesson Model 28 Highway Patrolman

TECHNICAL SPECIFICATIONS:

Calibre : .357 Magnum
Trigger action : double action
Cylinder capacity : 6 rounds
Locking mechanism : front/rear-side centre pin

Weight	1293g (6")
Length	287mm (6")
Height	152mm
Barrel length	102mm (4"), 152mm (6")
Trigger stop	none
Sights	adjustable micrometer rear sight
Sight radius	182mm
External safety	none
Internal safety	blocking bar

FEATURES:

• thumb piece	on left side frame
• material	steel
• finish	matt blued
• grips	walnut or rubber

The Model 28, the 'Highway Patrolman,' has a plain police finish. The Model 27 is the luxury model. Both are heavy-frame revolvers with the so-called "N frame", also in use for the .41 and .44 Magnum Smith & Wesson revolvers.

Smith & Wesson Model 29 6"

TECHNICAL SPECIFICATIONS:

Calibre	.44 Magnum
Trigger action	double action
Cylinder capacity	6 rounds
Locking mechanism	front/rear-side centre pin
Weight	1332g
Length	289mm
Height	153mm
Barrel length	152mm
Trigger stop	none
Sights	adjustable
Sight radius	153mm
External safety	cylinder blocks with cocked hammer
Internal safety	blocking bar

FEATURES:

• thumb piece	on left side frame
• material	steel
• finish	blued
• grips	Hogue rubber or walnut target

Smith & Wesson Model 29 Silhouette

TECHNICAL SPECIFICATIONS:

Calibre	.44 Magnum
Trigger action	double action
Cylinder capacity	6 rounds
Locking mechanism	front/rear-side centre pin
Weight	1531g
Length	352mm
Height	153mm
Barrel length	213mm
Trigger stop	none
Sights	adjustable
Sight radius	255mm
External safety	cylinder blocks with cocked hammer
Internal safety	blocking bar

FEATURES:

• thumb piece	on left side frame
• material	steel
• finish	blued
• grips	Hogue Monogrip

Smith & Wesson Chiefs Special Model 37

TECHNICAL SPECIFICATIONS:

Calibre	: .38 Special
Trigger action	: double action
Cylinder capacity	: 5 rounds
Locking mechanism	: front/rear-side centre pin
Weight	: 385g
Length	: 160mm (2")
Height	: 122mm
Barrel length	: 51mm
Trigger stop	: none
Sights	: fixed
Sight radius	: 110mm
External safety	: cylinder blocks with cocked hammer
Internal safety	: blocking bar

FEATURES:

• thumb piece	: on left side frame
• material	: steel; Airweight model; alloy frame
• finish	: blued or nickel plated
• grips	: Uncle Mike's Boot

Smith & Wesson Model 442 Airweight

TECHNICAL SPECIFICATIONS:

Calibre	: .38 Special
Trigger action	: double action
Cylinder capacity	: 5 rounds
Locking mechanism	: front/rear-side centre pin
Weight	: 448g
Length	: 160mm
Height	: 105mm
Barrel length	: 51mm
Trigger stop	: none
Sights	: fixed
Sight radius	: 93mm
External safety	: cylinder blocks with cocked hammer
Internal safety	: blocking bar

FEATURES:

• thumb piece	: on left side frame
• material	: alloy frame, steel cylinder
• finish	: blued or nickel plated
• grips	: Uncle Mike's Boot

Smith & Wesson Model 586 Distinguised Combat Magnum 4"

TECHNICAL SPECIFICATIONS:

Calibre	: .357 Magnum
Trigger action	: double action
Cylinder capacity	: 6 rounds
Locking mechanism	: front/rear-side centre pin
Weight	: 1162g
Length	: 243mm
Height	: 161mm
Barrel length	: 102mm
Trigger stop	: none
Sights	: adjustable
Sight radius	: 152mm
External safety	: cylinder blocks with cocked hammer
Internal safety	: blocking bar

FEATURES:

• thumb piece	:	on left side frame
• material	:	steel
• finish	:	blued
• grips	:	Hogue combat

Smith & Wesson Model 586 4" Target

TECHNICAL SPECIFICATIONS:

Calibre	:	.357 Magnum
Trigger action	:	double action
Cylinder capacity	:	6 rounds
Locking mechanism	:	front/rear-side centre pin
Weight	:	1162g
Length	:	303mm
Height	:	161mm
Barrel length	:	102mm
Trigger stop	:	none
Sights	:	adjustable
Sight radius	:	152mm
External safety	:	cylinder blocks with cocked hammer
Internal safety	:	blocking bar

FEATURES:

• thumb piece	:	on left side frame
• material	:	steel
• finish	:	blued
• grips	:	walnut Goncalo Alves

Smith & Wesson Chiefs Special Model 60

TECHNICAL SPECIFICATIONS:

Calibre	:	.38 Special
Trigger action	:	double action
Cylinder capacity	:	5 rounds
Locking mechanism	:	front/rear-side centre pin
Weight	:	567g
Length	:	190mm
Height	:	122mm
Barrel length	:	76mm
Trigger stop	:	none
Sights	:	fixed
Sight radius	:	135mm
External safety	:	cylinder blocks with cocked hammer
Internal safety	:	blocking bar

FEATURES:

• thumb piece	:	on left side frame
• material	:	stainless steel
• finish	:	M60 matt stainless
• grips	:	Uncle Mike's combat

Smith & Wesson Chiefs Special Model 60 Lady Smith

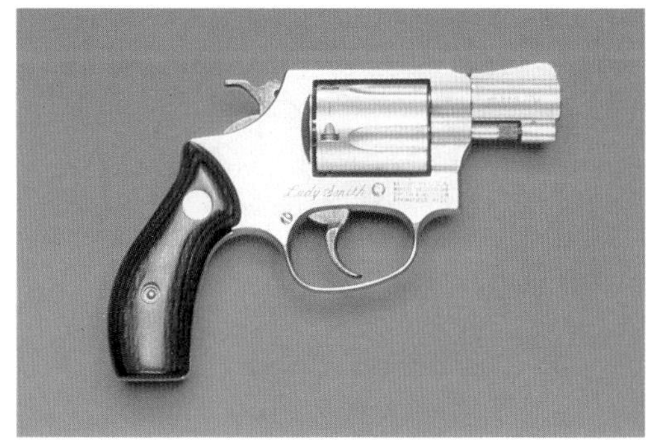

TECHNICAL SPECIFICATIONS:

Calibre	:	.38 Special
Trigger action	:	double action
Cylinder capacity	:	5 rounds
Locking mechanism	:	front/rear-side centre pin
Weight	:	567g

Length	: 160mm
Height	: 122mm
Barrel length	: 51mm
Trigger stop	: none
Sights	: fixed
Sight radius	: 110mm
External safety	: cylinder blocks with cocked hammer
Internal safety	: blocking bar
FEATURES:	
• thumb piece	: on left side frame
• material	: stainless steel
• finish	: stainless
• grips	: rosewood

Smith & Wesson Model 617 .22 Masterpiece

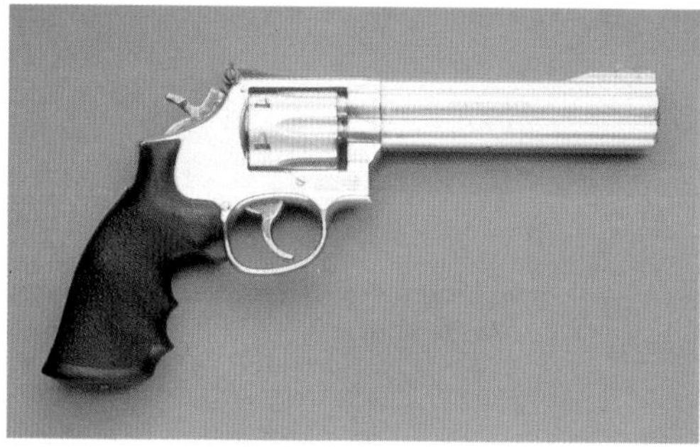

TECHNICAL SPECIFICATIONS:

Calibre	: .22 LR
Trigger action	: double action
Magazine capacity	: 6 rounds
Locking mechanism	: front/rear-side centre pin
Weight	: 1191g (4"); 1361g (6"); 1531g ($8^3/_8$")
Length	: 232mm (4"); 283mm (6"); 343mm ($8^3/_8$")
Height	: 142mm
Barrel length	: 102mm (4"); 152mm (6"); 213mm ($8^3/_8$")
Trigger stop	: none
Sights	: adjustable
Sight radius	: 176mm (6")
External safety	: cylinder blocks with cocked hammer
Internal safety	: blocking bar
FEATURES:	
• thumb piece	: on left side frame
• material	: stainless steel
• finish	: stainless
• grips	: Hogue combat

Smith & Wesson Model 625

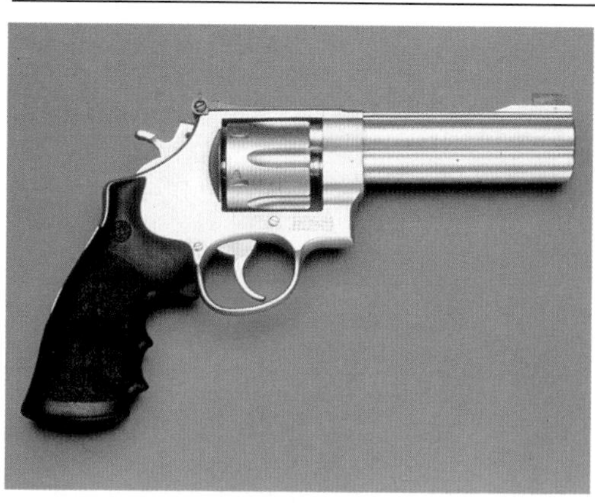

TECHNICAL SPECIFICATIONS:

Calibre	: .45 ACP
Trigger action	: double action
Cylinder capacity	: 6 rounds
Locking mechanism	: front/rear-side centre pin
Weight	: 1276g
Length	: 264mm
Height	: 152mm
Barrel length	: 127mm (5")
Trigger stop	: none
Sights	: adjustable
Sight radius	: 163mm
External safety	: cylinder blocks with cocked hammer
Internal safety	: blocking bar
FEATURES:	
• thumb piece	: on left side frame
• material	: stainless steel
• finish	: matt stainless
• grips	: Hogue combat

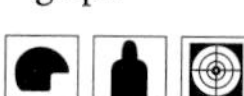

Smith & Wesson Model 629 4"

TECHNICAL SPECIFICATIONS:

Calibre	: .44 Magnum
Trigger action	: double action
Cylinder capacity	: 6 rounds
Locking mechanism	: front/rear-side centre pin
Weight	: 1247g
Length	: 244mm
Height	: 153mm
Barrel length	: 102mm
Trigger stop	: none
Sights	: adjustable
Sight radius	: 153mm
External safety	: cylinder blocks with cocked hammer
Internal safety	: blocking bar

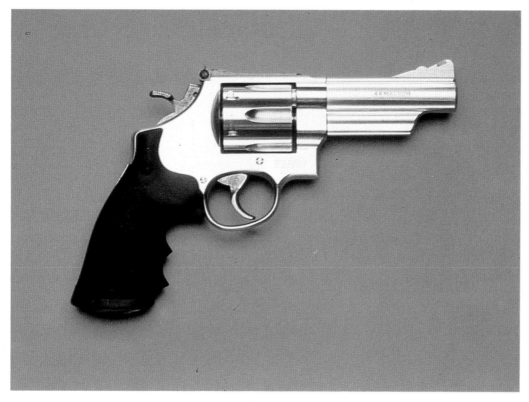

FEATURES:

- thumb piece : on left side frame
- material : stainless steel
- finish : matt stainless
- grips : walnut target or Hogue combat

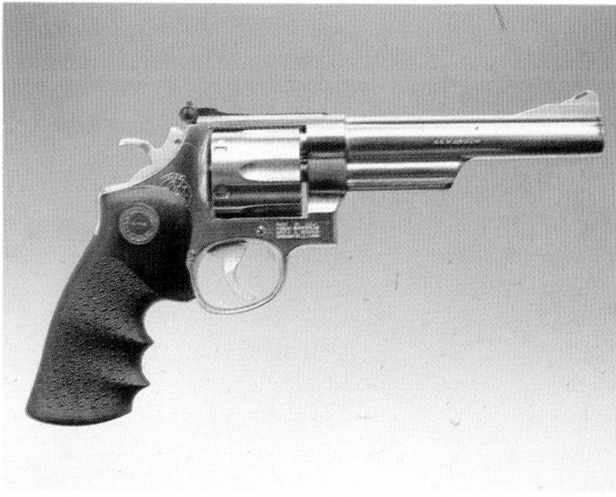

Smith & Wesson Model 629 6"

TECHNICAL SPECIFICATIONS:

Calibre	: .44 Magnum
Trigger action	: double action
Cylinder capacity	: 6 rounds
Locking mechanism	: front/rear-side centre pin
Weight	: 1332g
Length	: 289mm
Height	: 153mm
Barrel length	: 152mm
Trigger stop	: none
Sights	: adjustable
Sight radius	: 204mm
External safety	: cylinder blocks with cocked hammer
Internal safety	: blocking bar

FEATURES:

- thumb piece : on left side frame
- material : stainless steel
- finish : matt stainless
- grips : walnut target or Hogue combat

Smith & Wesson Model 629 CL

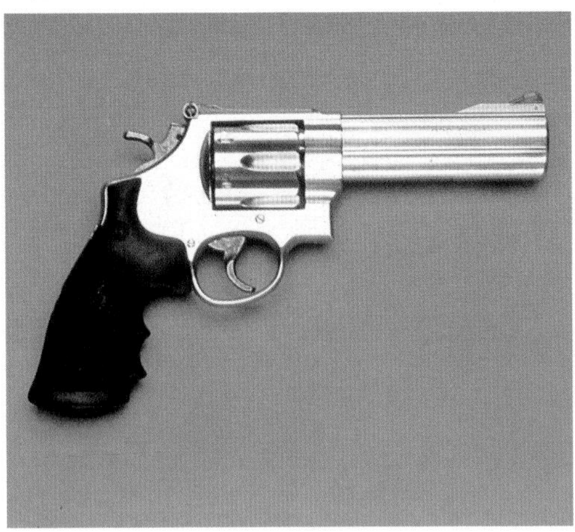

TECHNICAL SPECIFICATIONS:

Calibre	: .44 Magnum
Trigger action	: double action
Cylinder capacity	: 6 rounds
Locking mechanism	: front/rear-side centre pin
Weight	: 1446g
Length	: 267mm
Height	: 152mm
Barrel length	: 127mm
Trigger stop	: none
Sights	: adjustable
Sight radius	: 183mm
External safety	: cylinder blocks with cocked hammer
Internal safety	: blocking bar

FEATURES:

• thumb piece	: on left side frame
• material	: stainless steel
• finish	: matt stainless
• grips	: Hogue combat

  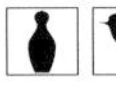

Smith & Wesson Model 629 CLDX

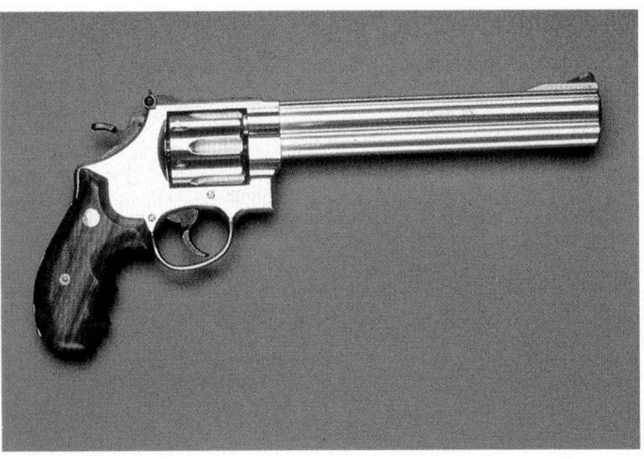

TECHNICAL SPECIFICATIONS:

Calibre	: .44 Magnum
Trigger action	: double action
Cylinder capacity	: 6 rounds
Locking mechanism	: front/rear-side centre pin
Weight	: 1531g
Length	: 352mm
Height	: 152mm
Barrel length	: 213mm
Trigger stop	: none
Sights	: adjustable
Sight radius	: 269mm
External safety	: cylinder blocks with cocked hammer
Internal safety	: blocking bar

FEATURES:

• thumb piece	: on left side frame
• material	: stainless steel
• finish	: matt stainless
• grips	: walnut combat

Smith & Wesson Model 63 .22 Kit Gun

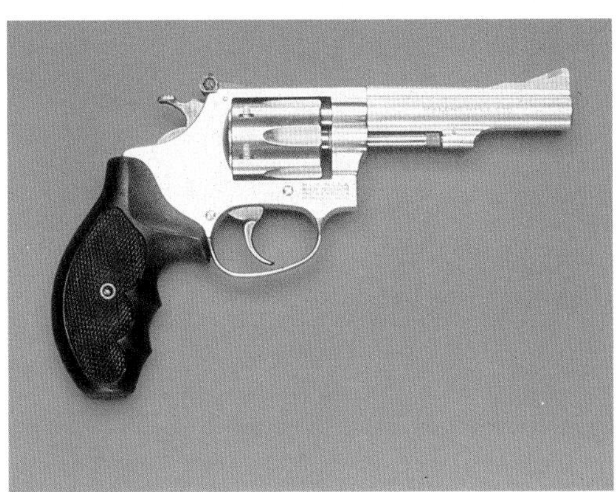

TECHNICAL SPECIFICATIONS:

Calibre	: .22 LR
Trigger action	: double action
Cylinder capacity	: 6 rounds
Locking mechanism	: front/rear-side centre pin
Weight	: 624g (2"); 695g (4")
Length	: 160mm (2"); 220mm (4")
Height	: 135mm
Barrel length	: 51mm (2"), 102mm (4")
Trigger stop	: none
Sights	: adjustable
Sight radius	: 145mm (4")
External safety	: cylinder blocks with cocked hammer
Internal safety	: blocking bar

FEATURES:

• thumb piece	: on left side frame

• material	: stainless steel
• finish	: matt stainless
• grips	: Uncle Mike's combat

Smith & Wesson Model 640

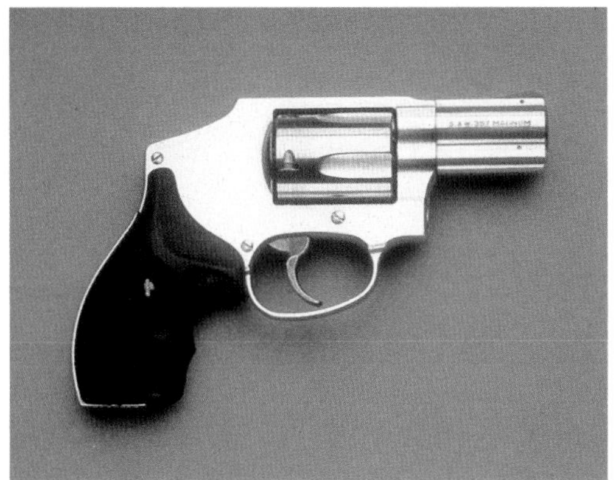

TECHNICAL SPECIFICATIONS:

Calibre	: .38 Special
Trigger action	: double action
Cylinder capacity	: 5 rounds
Locking mechanism	: front/rear-side centre pin
Weight	: 595g
Length	: 160mm
Height	: 105mm
Barrel length	: 51mm
Trigger stop	: none
Sights	: fixed
Sight radius	: 93mm
External safety	: cylinder blocks with cocked hammer
Internal safety	: blocking bar
FEATURES:	
• thumb piece	: on left side frame
• material	: stainless steel
• finish	: matt stainless
• grips	: Uncle Mike's Boot

Smith & Wesson Model 649/Model 38/Model 49 Bodyguard

TECHNICAL SPECIFICATIONS:

Calibre	: .38 Special
Trigger action	: double action
Cylinder capacity	: 5 rounds
Locking mechanism	: front/rear-side centre pin
Weight	: M38: 397g; M49/M649: 567g
Length	: 160mm
Height	: 110mm
Barrel length	: 51mm
Trigger stop	: none
Sights	: fixed
Sight radius	: 85mm
External safety	: cylinder blocks with cocked hammer
Internal safety	: blocking bar
FEATURES:	
• thumb piece	: on left side frame
• material	: M38: alloy; M49: steel; M649: stainless steel
• finish	: M38: blued or nickel plated; M49: blued; M649: matt stainless
• grips	: Uncle Mike's Boot

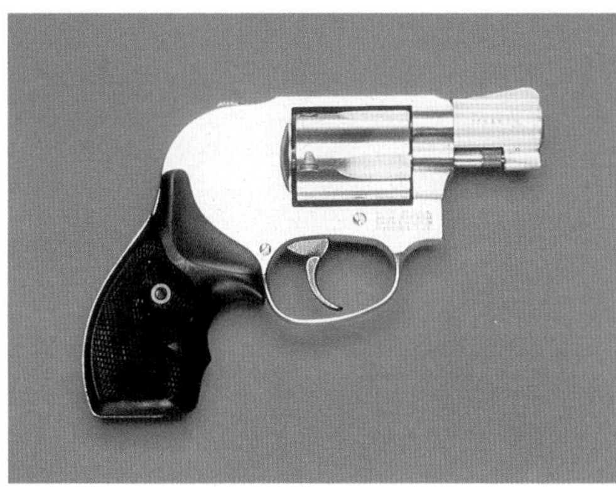

Smith & Wesson Model 65 Lady Smith

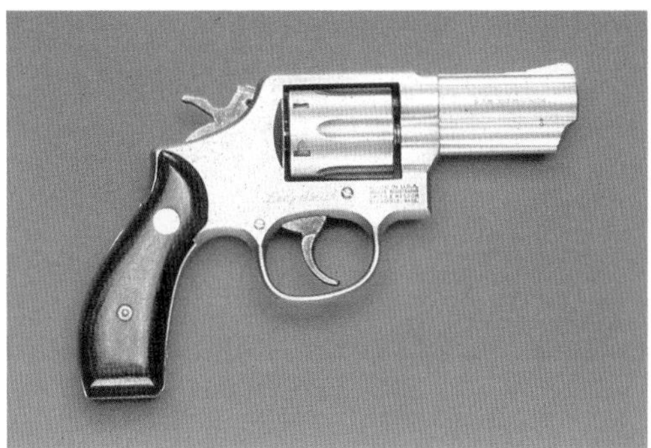

TECHNICAL SPECIFICATIONS:

Calibre	: .357 Magnum
Trigger action	: double action
Cylinder capacity	: 6 rounds

Locking mechanism	: front/rear-side centre pin
Weight	: 865g
Length	: 202mm
Height	: 132mm
Barrel length	: 76mm
Trigger stop	: none
Sights	: fixed
Sight radius	: 116mm
External safety	: cylinder blocks with cocked hammer
Internal safety	: blocking bar
FEATURES:	
• thumb piece	: on left side frame
• material	: stainless steel
• finish	: matt stainless
• grips	: rosewood

Smith & Wesson Model 651 .22 Kit Gun

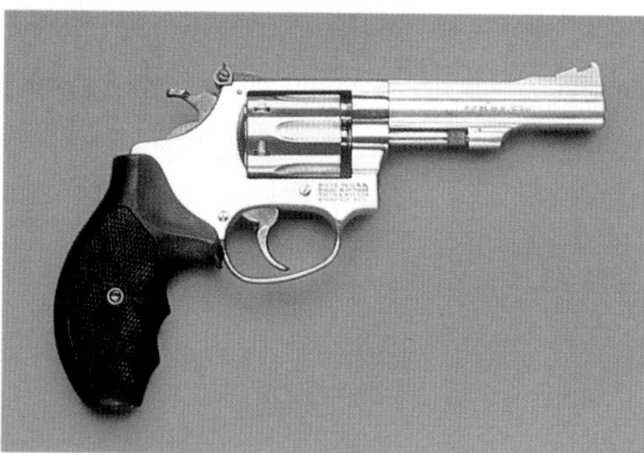

TECHNICAL SPECIFICATIONS:

Calibre	: .22 WMR
Trigger action	: double action
Cylinder capacity	: 6 rounds
Locking mechanism	: front/rear-side centre pin
Weight	: 695g
Length	: 220mm
Height	: 135mm
Barrel length	: 102mm
Trigger stop	: none
Sights	: adjustable
Sight radius	: 145mm
External safety	: cylinder blocks with cocked hammer
Internal safety	: blocking bar
FEATURES:	
• thumb piece	: on left side frame
• material	: stainless steel
• finish	: matt stainless
• grips	: Uncle Mike's combat

Smith & Wesson Model 657

TECHNICAL SPECIFICATIONS:

Calibre	: .41 Magnum
Trigger action	: double action
Cylinder capacity	: 6 rounds
Locking mechanism	: front/rear-side centre pin
Weight	: 1361g
Length	: 289mm
Height	: 154mm
Barrel length	: 152mm (6")
Trigger stop	: none
Sights	: adjustable
Sight radius	: 200mm
External safety	: cylinder blocks with cocked hammer
Internal safety	: blocking bar
FEATURES:	
• thumb piece	: on left side frame
• material	: stainless steel
• finish	: matt stainless
• grips	: Hogue combat

  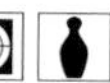

Smith & Wesson Model 66 Combat Magnum

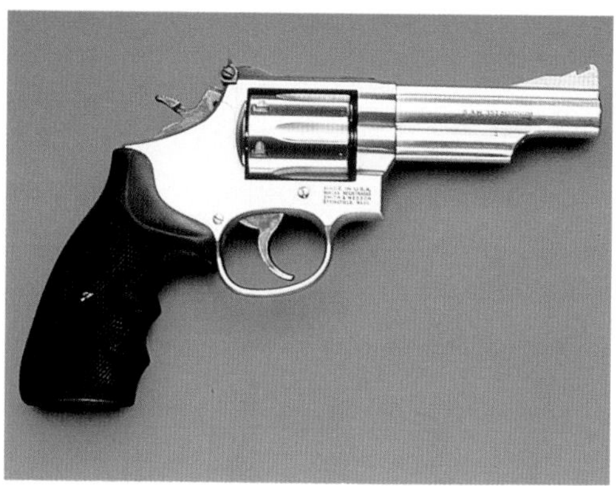

TECHNICAL SPECIFICATIONS:

Calibre	: .357 Magnum
Trigger action	: double action
Cylinder capacity	: 6 rounds
Locking mechanism	: front/rear-side centre pin
Weight	: 1021g
Length	: 243mm
Height	: 149mm
Barrel length	: 102mm
Trigger stop	: none
Sights	: adjustable
Sight radius	: 153mm
External safety	: cylinder blocks with cocked hammer
Internal safety	: blocking bar

FEATURES:

• thumb piece	: on left side frame
• material	: stainless steel
• finish	: matt stainless
• grips	: Uncle Mike's combat or Goncalo Alves walnut

Smith & Wesson Model 686 Distinguished Combat Magnum 2½"

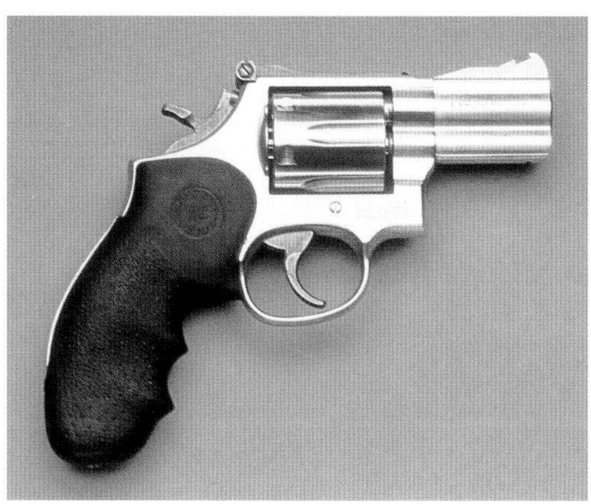

TECHNICAL SPECIFICATIONS:

Calibre	: .357 Magnum
Trigger action	: double action
Cylinder capacity	: 6 rounds
Locking mechanism	: front/rear-side centre pin
Weight	: 1006g
Length	: 191mm
Height	: 161mm
Barrel length	: 64mm
Trigger stop	: none
Sights	: adjustable
Sight radius	: 141mm
External safety	: cylinder blocks with cocked hammer
Internal safety	: blocking bar

FEATURES:

• thumb piece	: on left side frame
• material	: stainless steel
• finish	: matt stainless s
• grips	: Hogue combat

Smith & Wesson Model 686 Distinguished Combat Magnum 4"

TECHNICAL SPECIFICATIONS:

Calibre	: .357 Magnum
Trigger action	: double action
Cylinder capacity	: 6 rounds
Locking mechanism	: front/rear-side centre pin
Weight	: 1162g
Length	: 243mm
Height	: 161mm
Barrel length	: 102mm
Trigger stop	: none
Sights	: adjustable
Sight radius	: 152mm
External safety	: cylinder blocks with cocked hammer
Internal safety	: blocking bar

FEATURES:

• thumb piece	: on left side frame
• material	: stainless steel
• finish	: matt stainless
• grips	: walnut target

Smith & Wesson Model 686 Distinguised Combat Magnum 6"

TECHNICAL SPECIFICATIONS:

Calibre	: .357 Magnum
Trigger action	: double action
Cylinder capacity	: 6 rounds

Locking mechanism	: front/rear-side centre pin
Weight	: 1304g
Length	: 303mm
Height	: 161mm
Barrel length	: 152mm
Trigger stop	: none
Sights	: adjustable
Sight radius	: 203mm
External safety	: cylinder blocks with cocked hammer
Internal safety	: blocking bar

FEATURES:

• thumb piece	: on left side frame
• material	: stainless steel
• finish	: matt stainless
• grips	: Hogue combat

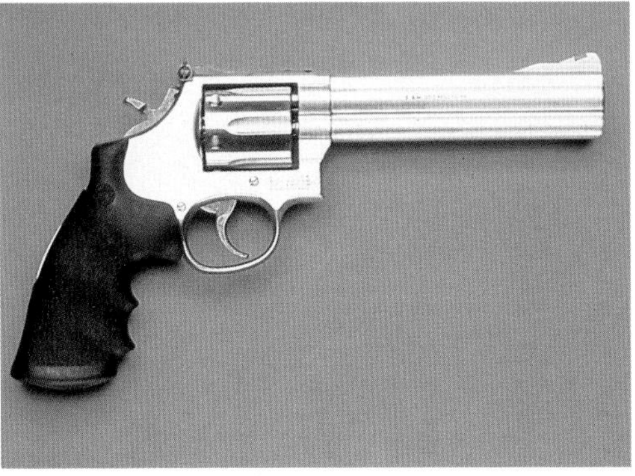

Smith & Wesson Model 686 Distinguished Magnum Target 6"

TECHNICAL SPECIFICATIONS:

Calibre	: .357 Magnum
Trigger action	: double action
Cylinder capacity	: 6 rounds
Locking mechanism	: front/rear-side centre pin
Weight	: 1304g
Length	: 303mm
Height	: 161mm
Barrel length	: 152mm
Trigger stop	: none
Sights	: adjustable
Sight radius	: 203mm
External safety	: cylinder blocks with cocked hammer
Internal safety	: blocking bar

FEATURES:

• thumb piece	: on left side frame
• material	: stainless steel
• finish	: matt stainless
• grips	: walnut Goncalo Alves target

Smith & Wesson Model 686 Distinguished Magnum Powerport 6"

TECHNICAL SPECIFICATIONS:

Calibre	: .357 Magnum
Trigger action	: double action
Cylinder capacity	: 6 rounds
Locking mechanism	: front/rear-side centre pin
Weight	: 1304g
Length	: 303mm
Height	: 161mm
Barrel length	: 152mm
Trigger stop	: none
Sights	: adjustable
Sight radius	: 180mm
External safety	: cylinder blocks with cocked hammer
Internal safety	: blocking bar

FEATURES:

• thumb piece	: on left side frame
• material	: stainless steel
• finish	: matt stainless met
• grips	: Hogue Monogrip

Sphinx

The Sphinx gun factory is quite a young firm, which specializes in high-tech pistols. The company is situated in Porrentruy in Switzerland. The corporation consists of the Müller AG company and the Sphinx group. The production of pistols is controlled by computerized equipment. The largest customers are governments of various countries, especially for the special AT 2000 Police pistol. Special police units, in particular, are equipped with this handgun. There is another production line for the manufacture of special match pistols, mainly fitted with special compensators and/or scopes, the so-called race guns.
The entire production is characterized by a very high degree of quality, which is, of course, reflected in the price one has to pay. The expression of quality "Swiss made" certainly applies to these pistols.

Sphinx AT 2000 Police Special

TECHNICAL SPECIFICATIONS:

Calibre : 9mm Para
Trigger action : double action
Cylinder capacity : 15 rounds
Locking mechanism : improved Browning/Sig system
Weight : 985g
Length : 184mm
Height : 138mm
Barrel length : 95mm
Trigger stop : none
Sights : fixed three-dot sights
Sight radius : 143mm
External safety : decocking lever on left side frame
Internal safety : slide safety, automatic firing-pin safety

FEATURES:

- slide catch : on left side frame
- magazine catch : on left side frame, behind trigger guard
- material : steel
- finish : matt black coating
- grips : black synthetic

Exchange kits are available for the calibres 9 x 21 IMI and .40 S&W.

Sphinx AT 2000 S

TECHNICAL SPECIFICATIONS:

Calibre : 9mm Para, 9x21mm IMI, .40 S&W
Trigger action : double action
Cylinder capacity : 15 rounds (9mm), 11 rounds (.40)
Locking mechanism : improved Browning/Sig system
Weight : 1030g
Length : 204mm
Height : 138mm
Barrel length : 115mm
Trigger stop : none
Sights : fixed three-dot sight
Sight radius : 163mm
External safety : ambidextrous decocking lever on left side frame
Internal safety : slide safety, automatic firing-pin safety

FEATURES:

- slide catch : on left side frame
- magazine catch : on left side frame, behind trigger guard
- material : stainless steel
- finish : matt stainless
- grips : black synthetic

Sphinx AT 2000 S Bi-Tone

TECHNICAL SPECIFICATIONS:

Calibre	: 9mm Para, 9x21mm IMI, .40 S&W
Trigger action	: double action
Magazine capacity	: 15 rounds (9mm), 11 rounds (.40)
Locking mechanism	: improved Browning/Sig system
Weight	: 1030g
Length	: 204mm
Height	: 138mm
Barrel length	: 115mm
Trigger stop	: none
Sights	: fixed three-dot sight
Sight radius	: 163mm
External safety	: ambidextrous decocking lever on left side frame
Internal safety	: slide safety, automatic firing-pin safety

FEATURES:

• slide catch	: on left side frame
• magazine catch	: on left side frame, behind trigger guard
• material	: stainless-steel frame, steel slide
• finish	: matt stainless frame, blued slide
• grips	: black synthetic

Sphinx AT 3000 S

TECHNICAL SPECIFICATIONS:

Calibre	: 9mm Para, 9x21mm IMI, .40 S&W
Trigger action	: single action
Magazine capacity	: 15 rounds (9mm), 11 rounds (.40)
Locking mechanism	: improved Browning/Sig system
Weight	: 1375g (inc. scope and mount)
Length	: 253mm
Height	: 138mm
Barrel length	: 135mm (inc. compensator)
Trigger stop	: fixed
Sights	: See-Thru-rear sight
Sight radius	: not relevant
External safety	: ambidextrous decock/safety catch op kast
Internal safety	: slide safety, automatic firing-pin safety

FEATURES:

• slide catch	: on left side frame
• magazine catch	: on left side frame, behind trigger guard
• material	: stainless-steel frame, steel slide
• finish	: matt frame, bluede slide
• grips	: black synthetic

Sphinx AT 380-M

TECHNICAL SPECIFICATIONS:

Calibre	: .380 ACP (9mm Short)
Trigger action	: double-action-only
Magazine capacity	: 10 rounds
Locking mechanism	: blowback system
Weight	: 710g
Length	: 155mm
Height	: 117mm
Barrel length	: 85mm
Trigger stop	: no
Sights	: fixed three-dot sights
Sight radius	: 124 mm
External safety	: safety catch on left side of slide

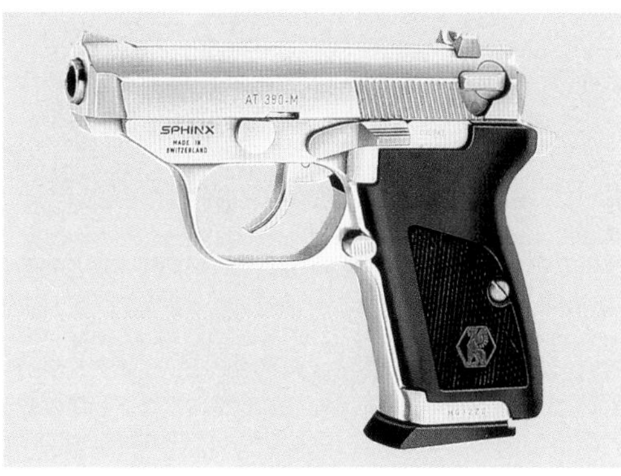

Internal safety	:	trigger is decocked after each shot

FEATURES:

• slide catch	:	on left side frame
• magazine catch	:	on left side frame, behind trigger guard
• material	:	alloy frame, steel slide
• finish	:	matt nickel (palladium)
• grips	:	black synthetic

Sphinx Grand Master

TECHNICAL SPECIFICATIONS:

Calibre	:	9mm Para, 9x21mm IMI, .40 S&W
Trigger action	:	single action
Magazine capacity	:	15 rounds (9mm), 11 rounds (.40)
Locking mechanism	:	improved Browning-Sig system
Weight	:	1550g (inc. scope and mount)
Length	:	253mm
Height	:	138mm
Barrel length	:	135mm (inc. compensator)
Trigger stop	:	fixed
Sights	:	Tasco ProPoint scope
Sight radius	:	not relevant
External safety	:	ambidextrous decock/safety catch on frame
Internal safety	:	slide safety, automatic firing-pin safety

FEATURES:

• slide catch	:	on left side frame
• magazine catch	:	on left side frame, behind trigger guard

• material : stainless-steel frame, steel slide
• finish : matt frame, blued slide
• grips : black synthetic

Sphinx Master

TECHNICAL SPECIFICATIONS:

Calibre	: 9mm Para, 9x21mm IMI, .40 S&W
Trigger action	: single action
Magazine capacity	: 15 rounds (9mm), 11 rounds (.40)
Locking mechanism	: improved Browning/Sig system
Weight	: 1250g
Length	: 253mm
Height	: 138mm
Barrel length	: 135mm (inc. compensator)
Trigger stop	: fixed
Sights	: micrometer rear sight
Sight radius	: 185mm
External safety	: ambidextrous decock/safety catch on frame
Internal safety	: slide safety, automatic firing-pin safety

FEATURES:

• slide catch : on left side frame
• magazine catch : on left side frame, behind trigger guard

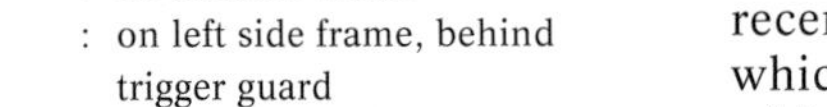

• material : stainless-steel frame, steel slide
• finish : matt frame, blued slide
• grips : black synthetic

  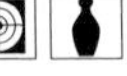

Springfield pistols

The US arms factory, Springfield Armory, formerly government owned, was the first manufacturer to produce the Colt M1911 pistol, apart from Colt. There are, however, two major differences: first, the inscriptions on the sides of the slide are not the same and, secondly, the front sight and slide are made out of one piece of steel. On the left side of the frame, behind the trigger guard, the company logo is stamped, a flaming grenade, which is also put on the back of the slide, behind the finger grooves. On the right side of the frame, just above the serial number, the logo of Springfield, an eagle, is pictured. After the Second World War Springfield ceased production of 1911s.

The original Springfield Armory, the US Government Arsenal, was situated in Massachusetts and was already founded by 1777. In 1968, this factory was abolished by the then Department of Defense Secretary, Robert S. MacNamarra. About three years later, a businessman from Texas bought the name of Springfield and its patents. The new Springfield did not survive the struggle and disappeared again in 1974.
Again some years later the next buyer, by the name of Robert Reese, appeared, who had a lot of experience as a wholesaler of guns. He saw possibilities in the old company and he moved it complete with name to Geneso in the State of Illinois, where he found a place in an old cattle-yard. He set to work, together with his three sons, and first of all produced a large series of M1As, a civil version of the US M14 army rifle. The recent Springfield gun line consists of a series of pistols, derived from the Colt Government:the M1A National Match .308 Winchester rifle; the M6 Scout Survival Carbine, a double-barrelled carbine in the calibres .22 LR/.410 shotgun; the most famous M1 Garand rifle in the calibres .30-06, .308 Win., and .270 Win.; a Beretta BM-59 army rifle in calibre .308 Win. built under licence; and the SAR-48, a copy of the Belgium FN-FAL rifle in calibre .308 Win. A recent pistol model is the Springfield Omega, which can cope with three different calibres with simple exchange kits. The Springfield 1911 A1 is a "Colt brother" look-alike, although some modifications have been made to its original design. First of all the feeding ramp has been widened. Because of this, the

feeding of cartridges with all kinds of bullets, especially lead bullets, is more reliable. Furthermore, the ejection port in the slide has been enlarged, which improves the gun's functioning. Springfield did not use the Colt modification in the "Series 70", the spring-tensioned barrel bushing. The Springfield has the old fixed-barrel bushing.

Springfield is not producing the M1911 A1 any more, but imports it from the Brazilian arms factory, Imbel in Itajuba. Imbel also produces the SAR-48 rifle for Springfield. Springfield builds several versions of the old Colt 1911 design, mainly with compensators, for special shooting events, such as parcours pistols and even some models we know as "pin guns" (for bowling pin shooting) and "race guns" (for falling plate and speed events).

Some models are built to special order in the Springfield Custom Shop. Springfield is also well known for special series, like the 'Desert Storm' and the 'Gulf Victory', both connected with the recent Gulf War in the Middle East. The Springfield collection is very extensive and consists of twenty-one different pistol models, all based on the original M1911 A1 pistol. Furthermore, Springfield has its Custom Shop where about ten different 1911 A1 pistol types are hand fitted. These special handguns can be customized to fulfil the wishes of the customer in any pistol calibre.

Springfield 1911 A1 Distiguished Custom Pistol

TECHNICAL SPECIFICATIONS:

Calibre	: .45 ACP, .38 Super
Trigger action	: single action
Magazine capacity	: 9 rounds
Locking mechanism	: Browning system
Weight	: ca. 1200g
Length	: 254mm
Height	: 139mm
Barrel length	: 143mm
Trigger stop	: adjustable
Sights	: adjustable
Sight radius	: 170mm
External safety	: safety catch on left side frame, grip safety
Internal safety	: slide safety, half-cock safety

FEATURES:

• slide catch	: on left side frame
• magazine catch	: on left side frame, behind trigger guard
• material	: stainless steel
• finish	: stainless
• grips	: walnut

Springfield Government Model 1911 A1

TECHNICAL SPECIFICATIONS:

Calibre	: 9mm Para
Trigger action	: single action

Magazine capacity	: 9 rounds
Locking mechanism	: Browning system
Weight	: 1110g
Length	: 219mm
Height	: 140mm
Barrel length	: 127mm
Trigger stop	: none
Sights	: fixed
Sight radius	: 159mm
External safety	: grip safety and safety catch
Internal safety	: half-cock-safety

FEATURES:

• slide catch	: on left side frame
• magazine catch	: left side frame, behind trigger guard
• material	: stainless steel
• finish	: matt stainless
• grips	: synthetic

Springfield MIL-Spec 1911 A1

TECHNICAL SPECIFICATIONS:

Calibre	: .45 ACP, .38 Super
Trigger action	: single action
Magazine capacity	: 9 rounds (.38 Super)
Locking mechanism	: Browning system
Weight	: 1009g
Length	: 219mm
Height	: 139mm
Barrel length	: 127mm
Trigger stop	: none
Sights	: fixed
Sight radius	: 159mm
External safety	: safety catch on left side frame, grip safety
Internal safety	: slide safety, half-cock safety

FEATURES:

• slide catch	: on left side frame
• magazine catch	: on left side frame, behind trigger guard
• material	: steel
• finish	: black parkerized
• grips	: black synthetic

Springfield PDP Defender 1911 A1

TECHNICAL SPECIFICATIONS:

Calibre	: .45 ACP
Trigger action	: single action
Magazine capacity	: 8 rounds
Locking mechanism	: Browning system
Weight	: 1134g
Length	: 228mm
Height	: 139mm
Barrel length	: 127mm
Trigger stop	: adjustable
Sights	: adjustable
Sight radius	: 162mm
External safety	: safety catch on left side frame, grip safety
Internal safety	: slide safety, half-cock safety

FEATURES:

• slide catch	: on left side frame
• magazine catch	: on left side frame, behind trigger guard
• material	: stainless-steel frame, steel slide
• finish	: blued slide, stainless frame
• grips	: black rubber

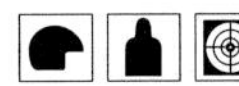 

Springfield PDP Factory Comp 1911 A1

TECHNICAL SPECIFICATIONS:

Calibre : .45 ACP, .38 Super
Trigger action : single action
Magazine capacity : 9 rounds
Locking mechanism : Browning system
Weight : 1134g
Length : 254mm
Height : 139mm
Barrel length : 143mm
Trigger stop : adjustable
Sights : adjustable
Sight radius : 172mm
External safety : safety catch on left side frame, grip safety
Internal safety : slide safety, half-cock safety

FEATURES:

- slide catch : on left side frame
- magazine catch : on left side frame, behind trigger guard
- material : steel
- finish : blued
- grips : walnut

Springfield Standard 1911 A1

TECHNICAL SPECIFICATIONS:

Calibre : .45 ACP, 9 mm Para and .38 Super
Trigger action : single action
Magazine capacity : 9 rounds (9 mm Para)
Locking mechanism : Browning system
Weight : 1009 gram (blue); 1111g (stainless steel); lightweight 811g
Length : 219mm
Height : 139mm
Barrel length : 127mm
Trigger stop : none
Sights : fixed
Sight radius : 159mm
External safety : safety catch on left side frame, grip safety
Internal safety : slide safety, half-cock safety

FEATURES:

- slide catch : on left side frame
- magazine catch : on left side frame, behind trigger guard
- material : steel, stainless steel or with alloy frame (lightweight)
- finish : blued, matt blued or stainless steel
- grips : walnut

Springfield/Drummen Race-gun

TECHNICAL SPECIFICATIONS:

Calibre : .45 ACP
Trigger action : single action
Magazine capacity : 9 rounds

Locking mechanism	:	Browning system
Weight	:	1134g
Length	:	254mm
Height	:	139mm
Barrel length	:	143mm
Trigger stop	:	adjustable
Sights	:	scope
Sight radius	:	not relevant
External safety	:	safety catch on left side frame, grip safety
Internal safety	:	slide safety, half-cock safety

FEATURES:

• slide catch	:	on left side frame
• magazine catch	:	on left side frame, behind trigger guard
• material	:	steel
• finish	:	blued
• grips	:	walnut

This particular pistol was built from the original model by the Dutch gunsmith, Maurice Drummen, in Nuth. Parts of the slide are cut away in places to reduce the weight.

Star

The company Echeverría, manufacturer of the Star pistols, was founded in 1906 in Eibar in northern Spain. Since then Star has produced a large number of pistol models, such as small-bore pistols and pocket pistols in the calibres .25 ACP, .32 ACP, and 9mm Short, and also army and police pistols in the calibres 9mm Short, 9mm Para, 9mm Largo, and .45 ACP. In the period 1906 to about 1919, Echeverría produced numerous pocket pistols under various brand names, including Izarra and Protector. In that time the brand-name Star was also used. Eibar, in Basque territory, was, together with the town Guernica, a well-known centre for production of and trade in weapons. Many names, well known at that time, have vanished, but the products still exist and are sometimes real collectors' items, worth a hundred times or more their original price. In 1919, the brand-name 'Star' was officially adopted, although earlier pistols were marketed with this name. The Star brand is still in existence today for a large assortment of specifically semi-automatic single-action pistols almost all derived from the Browning/Colt locking system. One of the first pistols (that strongly resembled the Colt 1911 and 1911-A1, both externally and technically) was the Star Model A from 1921. In those days, Star was known for its fast sequence of models.
The Star Model B was introduced in 1928. In the Second World War the Germans bought this pistol to remedy the shortage of handguns for their armies. Star also made several models with an attachable wooden carbine stock, which also served as a holster. These models were called "MB". The Model B served as the Spanish army pistol until 1985. After that it was replaced by the Star Model 28 and Model 30. The Star Model PD in calibre .45 ACP was introduced in 1975. This handgun is still in production.
The Star Model 28 was developed in 1976, specially for the US army trials for their new handgun. Star did not win this contest. In 1985 the Star was issued to the Spanish army and to the Spanish national police, the Guardia Civil. On the request of the Spanish army, the Model 28 was modified, after which the name was changed to Model 30M (Militar), Model 30P, and Model 30PK (shortened police models).
With the Star Model 43 (Firestar) the company followed the recent trend for compact service pistols. The Firestar was introduced in 1988 and has a slightly different design in comparison with its predecessors, like the Models 30M and 30PK. This is especially noticeable in the trigger action. For the Firestar, the single-action trigger was chosen. The gun is sold with two magazines. One has a flat floor plate, with a capacity of seven rounds, and one has a lengthened rubber bottom end, for eight rounds.
The Megastar pistol in the calibres .45 ACP and 10mm Auto was designed for use by police and army units. In this pistol the M43 Firestar technology has been continued. It is a pity that 1993, the year of its introduction, coincided with the introduction of a new trend in the arms business, namely, that of synthetic handguns. To be able to compete, Star introduced the Ultrastar in 1994 in the calibre 9mm Para. This compact pistol has a frame of high-impact synthetic material and a steel slide.

Star Model B

TECHNICAL SPECIFICATIONS:

Calibre	:	9mm Para

Trigger action	: single action
Magazine capacity	: 8 rounds
Locking mechanism	: Browning system
Weight	: 1065g
Length	: 216mm
Height	: 140mm
Barrel length	: 127mm
Trigger stop	: none
Sights	: fixed
Sight radius	: 147mm
External safety	: safety catch on left side frame
Internal safety	: slide safety, magazine safety, half-cock safety

FEATURES:

• slide catch	: on left side frame
• magazine catch	: on left side frame, behind trigger guard
• material	: steel
• finish	: blued
• grips	: walnut or synthetic

The Star Model B is derived from the Colt Model 1911-A1 pistol. The technical specifications given above are the same.for many slightly different models Star produced in the calibres 9mm Largo, .38 Super, and .45 ACP. Some Stars are made of steel, others have an alloy frame.

Steyr

The Austrian company, Steyr, dates from 1834, when Jozef Werndl founded a gun factory in the Austrian town of Steyr. Several pistol models were designed by Ritter (Knight) Ferdinand von Mannlicher, a German who lived in Austria. Steyr has a long tradition in weapons, especially for military guns. The most recent example of this is the most famous Steyr AUG (Armee Universal Gewehr) (Universal Army Rifle) rifle system, a basic construction which can be extended from sniper to machine-gun.

Steyr also made its name in the field of the pistol. One of the first army pistols, the Roth-Steyr Model 07, was designed in 1896 and issued to the cavalry of the Austrian-Hungarian army in 1907.

One of the newer designs, the GB-pistol, is fitted with a remarkable feature, and it is a pity that this pistol never attracted the public interest it deserves. The barrel of the gun is fitted with a gas-tap system. Halfway through the barrel two gas holes are drilled. When the bullet, after being fired, is driven through the barrel, a part of the gas pressure escapes through these gas holes. The escaping gas is guided into a special cylinder space between barrel and slide. The recoil impulse of the shot is retarded by the pressurized gas. After the bullet has left the barrel, the gas escapes through the barrel and the pistol will recycle. Steyr also has a compensator available as an option.

In 1994, a whole new design was introduced, the Steyr SPP (Special Police Pistol). The frame of this gun is made entirely from a special high-impact synthetic material, called IXEF-1313. The pistol looks exactly like a submachine-gun.

Steyr GB-pistol

TECHNICAL SPECIFICATIONS:

Calibre	: 9mm Para
Trigger action	: double action
Magazine capacity	: 18 rounds
Locking mechanism	: gas-retarded blowback action
Weight	: 845g
Length	: 216mm
Height	: 143mm
Barrel length	: 136mm
Trigger stop	: none
Sights	: fixed
Sight radius	: 162mm
External safety	: decocking lever on left side of slide
Internal safety	: slide safety, automatic firing-pin safety

FEATURES:

• slide catch	: ambidextrous on frame
• magazine catch	: on left side frame, behind trigger guard
• material	: steel
• finish	: matt blued
• grips	: black synthetic

The Steyr GB-pistol is no longer in production.

Steyr SSP

TECHNICAL SPECIFICATIONS:

Calibre	: 9mm Para
Trigger action	: double action
Magazine capacity	: 15 rounds (optional 30-round magazine)
Locking mechanism	: bolt-rotation system
Weight	: 1250g
Length	: 322mm
Height	: 166mm
Barrel length	: 130mm
Trigger stop	: none
Sights	: windage-adjustable micrometer rear sight; front post adjustable in elevation
Sight radius	: 190mm
External safety	: safety button above trigger guard
Internal safety	: slide safety, automatic sear block

FEATURES:

• slide catch	: none
• magazine catch	: on left side frame, behind trigger guard
• material	: synthetic stock, steel barrel and bolt
• finish	: matt black
• grips	: integrated synthetic stock/frame

Tanfoglio

The Italian company Tanfoglio from Gardone specializes in the production of special and high-tech pistols for particular forms of shooting. The pistols, in particular, fitted with all kinds of compensators, provide the mainstay of their manufacture. Furthermore, the company has an extensive series of special "custom" parts, with which the skilful gunsmith, amateur or professional, can work very well. Tanfoglio offers, for instance, seven kinds of barrel, five kinds of slide, three different hammers, six different compensators, four different triggers, and so on.
Most of their models are derived from the CZ-75 pistol, as far as the external shape is concerned. The custom department of the company will build any kind of pistol to any kind of specification from individual customers.

Tanfoglio Combat Stainless

TECHNICAL SPECIFICATIONS:

Calibre	: 9mm Para, 9x21 IMI .40 S&W, .38 Super Auto .45 ACP, 10mm Auto
Trigger action	: double action
Magazine capacity	: 16 rounds (9 mm Para)
Locking mechanism	: FN-Browning system
Weight	: 980g
Length	: 205mm
Height	: 129mm
Barrel length	: 115mm
Trigger stop	: adjustable
Sights	: fixed combat rear sight
Sight radius	: 136mm
External safety	: safety catch left side frame
Internal safety	: slide safety, automatic firing-pin safety

FEATURES:

• slide catch	: on left side frame
• magazine catch	: on left side frame, behind trigger guard
• material	: stainless steel
• finish	: matt
• grips	: walnut

Tanfoglio Joe Peters Special Racegun

TECHNICAL SPECIFICATIONS:

Calibre	: 9mm Para, 9x21 IMI .40 S&W, .38 Super Auto .45 ACP, 10 mm Auto
Trigger action	: single action
Magazine capacity	: 16 rounds (9mm Para)
Locking mechanism	: FN-Browning system
Weight	: 1020g
Length	: 215mm
Height	: 142mm
Barrel length	: 120mm
Trigger stop	: yes
Sights	: Pro-Point scope
Sight radius	: not relevant
External safety	: safety catch on left side frame
Internal safety	: slide safety, automatic firing-pin safety

FEATURES:

• slide catch	: on left side frame
• magazine catch	: on left side frame, behind trigger guard
• material	: stainless steel
• finish	: matt
• grips	: walnut

This pistol has been specially modified to a racegun by Joe Peters from Germany (Peters Stahl).

Taurus

Brazil is always associated with tropical rain forests, bird-spiders and strangle-snakes. The Portuguese language dates back to the time Brazil was a part of the Portuguese colonial empire. Brazil became an independent state in 1821 when Don Pedro was appointed as governor of Brazil by his father, John VI of Portugal. Later he was crowned as Emperor of Brazil. From then until 1889 Brazil was a monarchy. In that year there was a coup d'état, and the country became a federal republic, which it still is today. Apart from the rain forests, Brazil has an extensive industry, especially making weapons. The country plays a major role in supplying arms in Latin America. The Taurus factories, called Forjas Taurus SA, were founded in 1939 by German immigrants. The company has been producing revolvers for decades. In 1968, Taurus started an export business to the USA for revolvers under the name of Taurus, but they mainly produced and exported under several brand names, according to US import companies. In 1971, Taurus changed its policy and started to carve out a market share under its own brand name. That same year the company was taken over by an American multinational, Bangor Punta, the holding company to which Smith & Wesson belonged. In 1977, two Taurus directors, Luis Estima and Carlos Murgel, bought the company themselves. In 1980, Taurus bought the Beretta factory in Brazil, together with the complete assembly line for the Beretta Model 92 pistols. A branch of Beretta was established in Brazil to produce semi-automatic pistols and submachine guns for several South American armies. Brazil has in fact two large gun factories: Amadeo Rossi in Sao Paulo and Forjas Taurus in Porto Algre.

Taurus manufactures excellent double-action revolvers, based on the Smith & Wesson design, in calibres ranging from .22 LR to .44 Magnum. The semi-automatic pistols of Taurus, marketed with a prefix "PT," are derived from the Italian Beretta pistols. The locking mechanism of their large-bore pistols has a falling-block lock, like the handguns of Beretta, who in turn derived this system from the German Walther pistols. Apart from the normal weapon production, Taurus also has a so-called "Custom Shop", in which standard guns can be rebuilt or adapted to the wishes of each customer. The Custom Shop also makes small series of handguns to specific specifications. In this connection they build several series of large-bore revolvers, fitted with the Hybra-port system. This means that in the upper side of the barrel a number of little holes are drilled in line, to serve as a compensator to reduce the recoil and muzzle jump. Furthermore, they produce a version of the revolver model 80 as a course handgun. This revolver is also fitted with the Hybra-port system and several supports, attached to the barrel, for barricade shooting. The Custom Shop is also producing a special Combat pistol for the IPSC tournament. Altogether Taurus has a well-balanced line of handguns with an acceptable price-tag.

Taurus Model PT58

TECHNICAL SPECIFICATIONS:

Calibre	: .380 ACP (9mm Short)
Trigger action	: double action
Magazine capacity	: 10 rounds
Locking mechanism	: falling-block system
Weight	: 851g
Length	: 183mm
Height	: 127mm
Barrel length	: 102mm
Trigger stop	: none
Sights	: windage adjustable three-dot combat sight
Sight radius	: 136mm
External safety	: ambidextrous decocking lever
Internal safety	: slide safety, half-cock safety, load indicator, automatic firing-pin safety

FEATURES:

• slide catch	: on left side frame
• magazine catch	: on left side frame, behind trigger guard
• material	: steel or stainless steel
• finish	: blued or matt stainless
• grips	: Brazilian hardwood

Taurus Model PT908

TECHNICAL SPECIFICATIONS:

Calibre	: 9mm Para
Trigger action	: double action
Magazine capacity	: 8 rounds
Locking mechanism	: improved Browning system
Weight	: 850g
Length	: 179mm
Height	: 110mm
Barrel length	: 97mm
Trigger stop	: none
Sights	: fixed
Sight radius	: 130mm
External safety	: ambidextrous decocking lever on frame
Internal safety	: slide safety, slip safety on hammer, load indicator, automatic firing-pin safety

FEATURES:

• slide catch	: on left side frame
• magazine catch	: left side frame, behind trigger guard
• material	: steel or stainless steel
• finish	: blued or stainless
• grips	: black rubber (Santoprene II)

he Model PT910 is a larger, ten-round version in 9mm calibre, with a total length of 190mm.

Taurus Model PT92 AF

TECHNICAL SPECIFICATIONS:

Calibre	: 9mm Para
Trigger action	: double action
Magazine capacity	: 15 rounds
Locking mechanism	: falling-block system (Walther)
Weight	: 964g
Length	: 216mm
Height	: 138mm
Barrel length	: 125mm
Trigger stop	: none
Sights	: fixed
Sight radius	: 161mm
External safety	: ambidextrous decocking lever on frame
Internal safety	: slide safety, slip safety on hammer, load indicator, automatic firing-pin safety

FEATURES:

• slide catch	: on left side frame
• magazine catch	: on left side frame, behind trigger guard
• material	: steel or stainless steel
• finish	: blued or stainless
• grips	: Brazilian hardwood

Taurus Model PT92 AFS-D

TECHNICAL SPECIFICATIONS:

Calibre : 9mm Para
Trigger action : double action
Magazine capacity : 15 rounds
Locking mechanism : falling-block system (Walther)
Weight : 964g
Length : 216mm
Height : 138mm
Barrel length : 125mm
Trigger stop : none
Sights : fixed
Sight radius : 161mm
External safety : ambidextrous decocking lever on frame
Internal safety : slide safety,slip safety on hammer, load indicator, automatic firing-pin safety

FEATURES:

- slide catch : on left side frame
- magazine catch : on left side frame, behind trigger guard
- material : steel of stainless steel
- finish : blued of stainless
- grips : Brazilian hardwood

Taurus Model PT945

TECHNICAL SPECIFICATIONS:

Calibre : .45 ACP
Trigger action : double action
Magazine capacity : 8 rounds
Locking mechanism : falling-block system
Weight : 836g
Length : 180mm
Height : 140mm
Barrel length : 108mm
Trigger stop : none
Sights : windage adjustable three-dot combat sight
Sight radius : 140mm
External safety : ambidextrous decocking lever
Internal safety : slide safety, half-cock safety, load indicator, automatic firing-pin safety

FEATURES:

- slide catch : on left side frame
- magazine catch : on left side frame, behind trigger guard
- material : steel
- finish : blued
- grips : hard rubber

Taurus Model PT945 Stainless

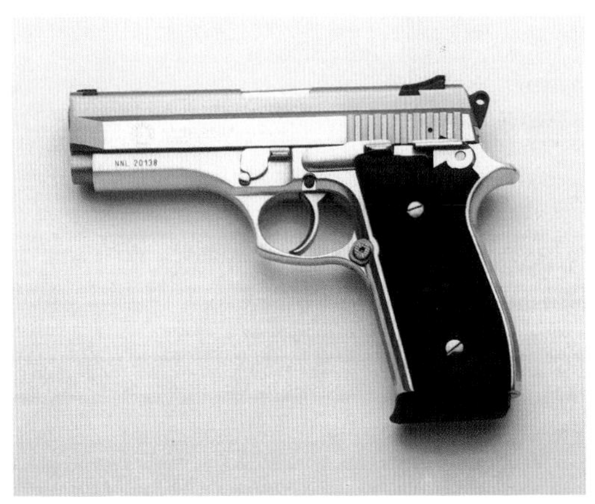

TECHNICAL SPECIFICATIONS:

Calibre : .45 ACP
Trigger action : double action
Magazine capacity : 8 rounds
Locking mechanism : falling-block system
Weight : 836g
Length : 190mm
Height : 140mm
Barrel length : 108mm
Trigger stop : none
Sights : windage-adjustable three-dot combat sight
Sight radius : 140mm
External safety : ambidextrous decocking lever
Internal safety : slide safety, half-cock safety, , automatic firing-pin safety

FEATURES:

- slide catch : on left side frame
- magazine catch : on left side frame, behind trigger guard
- material : stainless steel
- finish : matt stainless
- grips : hard rubber

Taurus Model PT99 AF

TECHNICAL SPECIFICATIONS:

Calibre	: 9mm Para
Trigger action	: double action
Magazine capacity	: 15 rounds
Locking mechanism	: falling-block system (Walther)
Weight	: 964g
Length	: 216mm
Height	: 140mm
Barrel length	: 125mm
Trigger stop	: none
Sights	: micrometer rear sight
Sight radius	: 162mm
External safety	: ambidextrous decocking lever on frame
Internal safety	: slide safety, slip safety on hammer, load indicator, automatic firing-pin safety

FEATURES:

• slide catch	: on left side frame
• magazine catch	: on left side frame, behind trigger guard
• material	: steel
• finish	: blued
• grips	: Brazilian hardwood

Taurus Model PT99 AFS Stainless

TECHNICAL SPECIFICATIONS:

Calibre	: 9mm Para
Trigger action	: double action
Magazine capacity	: 15 rounds
Locking mechanism	: falling-block system (Walther)
Weight	: 964g
Length	: 216mm
Height	: 140mm
Barrel length	: 125mm
Trigger stop	: none
Sights	: micrometer rear sight
Sight radius	: 162mm
External safety	: ambidextrous decocking lever on frame
Internal safety	: slide safety, slip safety on hsmmer, load indicator, automatic firing-pin safety

FEATURES:

• slide catch	: on left side frame
• magazine catch	: on left side frame, behind trigger guard
• material	: stainless steel
• finish	: matt nickel plated or stainless
• grips	: Brazilian hardwood

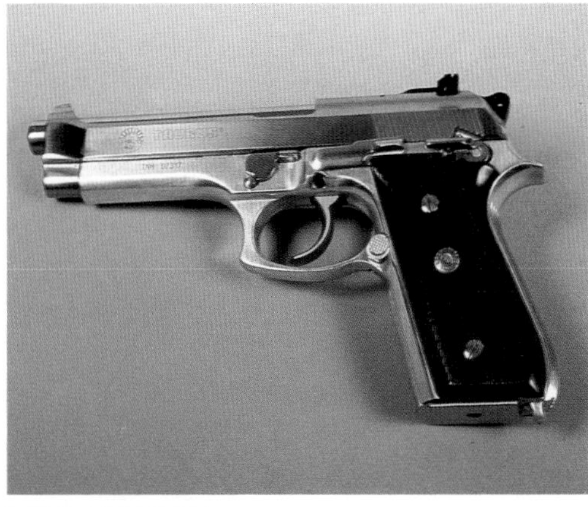

Taurus Model PT100

TECHNICAL SPECIFICATIONS:

Calibre	: .40 S&W
Trigger action	: double action
Magazine capacity	: 10 rounds
Locking mechanism	: falling-block system
Weight	: 990g
Length	: 216mm
Height	: 138mm
Barrel length	: 125mm
Trigger stop	: none

Sights : windage-adjustable three-dot combat sight
Sight radius : 161mm
External safety : ambidextrous decocking lever
Internal safety : slide safety, half-cock safety, load indicator, automatic firing-pin safety

FEATURES:

- slide catch : on left side frame
- magazine catch : on left side frame, behind trigger guard
- material : steel or stainless steel
- finish : blued or matt stainless stainless steel
- grips : Brazilian hardwood

Taurus Model PT101

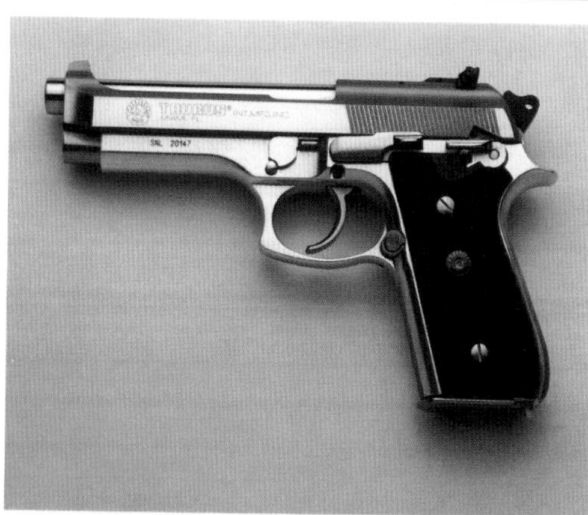

TECHNICAL SPECIFICATIONS:

Calibre : .40 S&W
Trigger action : double action
Magazine capacity : 11 rounds
Locking mechanism : falling-block system
Weight : 998g
Length : 216mm
Height : 140mm
Barrel length : 127mm
Trigger stop : none
Sights : adjustable three-dot combat sight
Sight radius : 162 mm
External safety : ambidextrous decocking lever
Internal safety : slide safety, half-cock safety, load indicator, automatic firing-pin safety

FEATURES:

- slide catch : on left side frame
- magazine catch : on left side frame, behind trigger guard
- material : steel or stainless steel
- finish : blued or matt stainless
- grips : Brazilian hardwood

Taurus Model 44

TECHNICAL SPECIFICATIONS:

Calibre : .44 Magnum
Trigger action : double §action
Magazine capacity : 6 rounds
Locking mechanism : front/rear-side centre pin
Weight : 1488g ($6^{1}/_{2}$" loop)
Length : 308mm
Height : 160mm
Barrel length : 102mm (4"), 165mm ($6^{1}/_{2}$"), 213mm ($8^{3}/_{8}$"). the two last barrel lengths have integrated compensators
Trigger stop : none
Sights : adjustable micrometer rear sight
Sight radius : 216mm
External safety : cylinder blocks with cocked hammer
Internal safety : transfer bar

FEATURES:

- thumb piece : on left side frame
- material : steel or stainless steel
- finish : blued or stainless
- grips : black rubber (Santoprene I)

Taurus Model 441

TECHNICAL SPECIFICATIONS:

Calibre : .44 Special
Trigger action : double action
Magazine capacity : 5 rounds
Locking mechanism : front/rear-side centre pin
Weight : 1148g (6" barrel)
Length : 320mm (6" barrel)

Height : 160mm
Barrel length : 76mm (3"), 102mm (4"), 152mm (6")
Trigger stop : none
Sights : adjust. micrometer rear sight
Sight radius : 202mm (6" barrel)
External safety : cylinder blocks with cocked hammer
Internal safety : transfer bar

FEATURES:

- thumb piece : on left side frame
- material : steel or stainless steel
- finish : blued or stainless
- grips : Brazilian hardwood

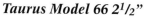

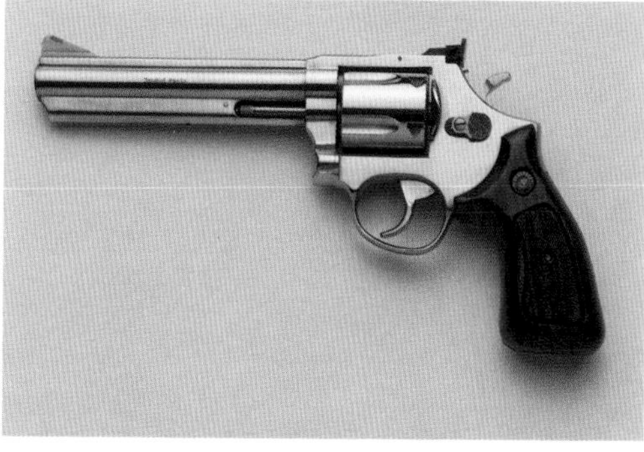

Taurus Model 66 2½"

TECHNICAL SPECIFICATIONS:

Calibre : .357 Magnum
Trigger action : double action
Magazine capacity : 6 rounds
Locking mechanism : front/rear-side centre pin
Weight : 945g
Length : 191mm
Height : 155mm
Barrel length : 64mm
Trigger stop : none
Sights : adjustable micrometer rear sight
Sight radius : 115mm
External safety : cylinder blocks with cocked hammer
Internal safety : transfer bar

FEATURES:

- thumb piece : on left side frame
- material : steel or stainless steel
- finish : blued or stainless
- grips : Brazilian hardwood

Taurus Model 66 4"

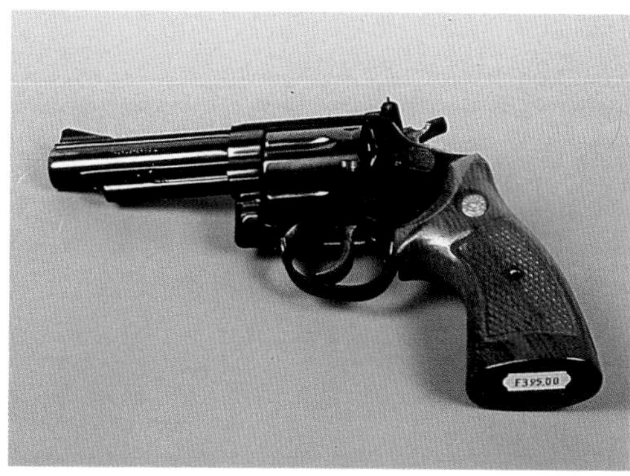

TECHNICAL SPECIFICATIONS:

Calibre : .357 Magnum
Trigger action : double action
Magazine capacity : 6 rounds
Locking mechanism : front/rear-side centre pin
Weight : 992g
Length : 240mm
Height : 155mm
Barrel length : 102mm
Trigger stop : none
Sights : adjust. micrometer rear sight
Sight radius : 153mm
External safety : cylinder blocks with cocked hammer
Internal safety : transfer bar

FEATURES:

- thumb piece : on left side frame
- material : steel or stainless steel
- finish : blued or stainless
- grips : Brazilian hardwood

Taurus Model 669

TECHNICAL SPECIFICATIONS:

Calibre : .357 Magnum

Trigger action	: double action
Magazine capacity	: 6 rounds
Locking mechanism	: front/rear-side centre pin
Weight	: 1050g (4"-barrel)
Length	: 240mm (4"-barrel)
Height	: 160mm
Barrel length	: 102mm (4"), 152mm (6")
Trigger stop	: none
Sights	: adjus. micrometer rear sight
Sight radius	: 180mm
External safety	: cylinder blocks with cocked hammer
Internal safety	: transfer bar

FEATURES:

• thumb piece	: on left side frame
• material	: steel or stainless steel
• finish	: blued or stainless
• grips	: Brazilian hardwood

Taurus Model 82

TECHNICAL SPECIFICATIONS:

Calibre	: .38 Special
Trigger action	: double action
Magazine capacity	: 6 rounds
Locking mechanism	: front/rear-side centre pin
Weight	: 964g (4" barrel)
Length	: 240mm
Height	: 160mm
Barrel length	: 76mm (3"), 102mm (4")
Trigger stop	: none
Sights	: fixed
Sight radius	: 150mm
External safety	: cylinder blocks with cocked hammer
Internal safety	: transfer bar

FEATURES:

• thumb piece	: on left side of frame
• material	: steel or stainless steel
• finish	: blued or stainless
• grips	: Brazilian hardwood

Taurus Model 96

TECHNICAL SPECIFICATIONS:

Calibre	: .22 LR
Trigger action	: double action
Magazine capacity	: 6 rounds
Locking mechanism	: front/rear-side centre pin
Weight	: 964g
Length	: 295mm
Height	: 160mm
Barrel length	: 152mm
Trigger stop	: adjustable
Sights	: adjustable
Sight radius	: 203mm
External safety	: cylinder blocks with cocked hammer
Internal safety	: transfer bar

FEATURES:

• thumb piece	: on left side frame
• material	: steel
• finish	: blued
• grips	: Brazilian hardwood

Thompson Contender

The American arms factory, Thompson Center Arms, is situated in Rochester in the State of New Hampshire. From the 1960s, Thompson has been producing the single-shot Center Contender pistol. Their advertising campaign with the slogan "The most versatile handgun available" is true to a large extent. Furthermore, it is significant that Thompson grants a lifetime warranty for his Contender pistols, which indicates their quality. Exchangeable barrels are available in more than twenty calibres. In fact, any kind of calibre can be produced by special order. In 1978, the Super Contender was introduced with a standard barrel of 14in.

The weapon had not only a longer barrel but also a longer rear sight and longer stock. In 1980, the Contender went through a kind of face-lift. Thompson redesigned the grip and fitted the pistols with a new kind of wood for the grip, or rather, stock. The Contender has four different barrel types, which are interchangeable. They are the conical 10in barrel, the 10in and 14in Bull barrel and the 10in barrel with ventilated rib, with special exchangeable shotgun chokes for the calibres .357 Hot Shot and .44 Hot Shot. These are, respectively, .357 Magnum or .44 Magnum cartridges with an enlarged bullet-type synthetic container, loaded with lead shot. The barrel of the Contender has the basculating system, which means that the barrel pivots around an axis, almost the same principle as that in a double-barrel shotgun. The barrel is unlocked by pushing the trigger guard to the front. The firing-pin has an interesting system. A bolt on the back of the hammer can switch the pistol from central fire to rimfire and back again. The complete weapon system is even more simple to explain: if you own a Contender bascule/stock, you can vary it endlessly with calibres for any chosen cartridge and with different barrels.

The Contender is designed for long-distance shooting. In North America handgun hunting is legal in most states, and the Contender was developed for that purpose. In recent decades, with the introduction of silhouette shooting, the Contender has gained much interest. Shooting at a metallic target at 400m is no exception at such matches. It is far beyond the purpose of this book to mention the complete list of available barrel calibres. Generally speaking, the Contender is sold in any calibre, ranging from .22 LR to .50 in any handgun or rifle calibre. Furthermore, the Contender is available in a blue and stainless-steel finish.

Thompson Center Contender

TECHNICAL SPECIFICATIONS:

Calibre	: from .22 LR to .500
Trigger action	: single action
Magazine capacity	: none, single shot
Locking mechanism	: basculating system
Weight	: ca. 1250g (depends on calibre and barrel length)
Length	: 343mm
Height	: 150mm
Breedte	: 35mm
Barrel length	: 254mm; (optional barrel lengths, inc. 14in- 355mm)
Trigger stop	: yes
Sights	: adjustable rear sight
Sight radius	: 215 mm
External safety	: safety catch on hammer
Internal safety	: automatic safety after basculation

FEATURES:

• slide catch	: not relevant
• magazine catch	: not relevant
• material	: steel or stainless steel
• finish	: blued or stainless
• grips	: walnut stock

Unique

The French brand Unique is produced by the Manufacture d'Armes des Pyrénées Françaises (Arms Manufacture of the French Pyrenees) in the city Hendaye in France. This company not only manufactures the Unique sport pistols but also produces rifles and carbines: for instance, the F-11, the small-bore (.22 LR) version of the very famous French FAMAS assault rifle, in use with the Foreign Legion. Furthermore, the company has a long tradition in the field of police pistols for the French government. With the exception of the following Unique DES sporting pistols, most Unique products are not very well known in northern Europe and on the American continent.

Unique DES/69

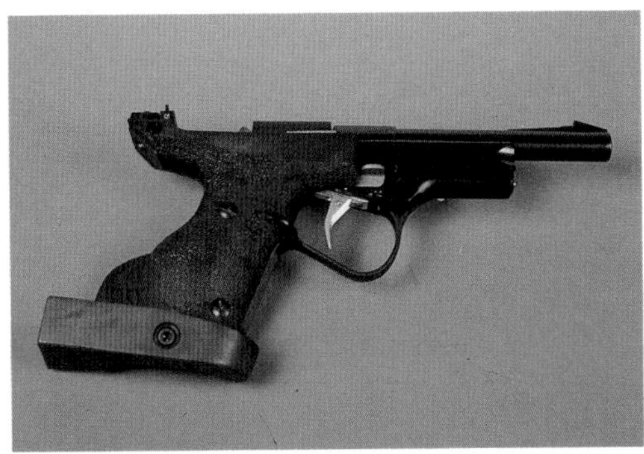

TECHNICAL SPECIFICATIONS:

Calibre	: .22 LR
Trigger action	: single action
Magazine capacity	: 5 rounds
Locking mechanism	: blowback action
Weight	: 1000g
Length	: 270mm
Height	: 145mm
Barrel length	: 150mm
Trigger stop	: totally adjustable
Sights	: adjustable micro rear sight
Sight radius	: 220mm
External safety	: safety catch on right side of frame
Internal safety	: slide safety

FEATURES:

• slide catch	: none, slide can be manually fixed in rear position
• magazine catch	: centre of left grip
• material	: steel
• finish	: blued
• grips	: walnut match with palm rest

Unique DES/69U

TECHNICAL SPECIFICATIONS:

Calibre	: .22 LR
Trigger action	: single action
Magazine capacity	: 5 rounds
Locking mechanism	: blowback action
Weight	: 1140g
Length	: 285mm
Height	: 140mm
Barrel length	: 150mm
Trigger stop	: totally adjustable
Sights	: adjustable micro rear sight
Sight radius	: 220mm
External safety	: safety catch on right side of frame
Internal safety	: slide safety

FEATURES:

• slide catch	: none, slide can be manually fixed in rear position
• magazine catch	: centre of left grip
• material	: steel
• finish	: blued
• grips	: walnut match with palm rest

This pistol can be fitted with different models of barrel weights.

Vektor pistols

The pistols from the Republic of South Africa discussed here are manufactured by the Lyttelton Company Ltd. South African gun factories are not very well known outside that continent. This situation can be largely put down to the economic boycott, owing to the international indignation at racial discrimination in that country. Movement of guns to and from South Africa was not permitted by most countries in the world. Countries that were able to trade with South Africa, like Austria and Israel, could buy South African products themselves, but were not allowed to sell these again on the international market. In the 1980s, the Clarbex Company Ltd from Wijnberg in South Africa introduced a semi-automatic pistol, the Varan PMX-90. The name Varan is taken from a very dangerous lizard from South America. After its introduction, nothing more has been heard of pistol or company. That is not the case with Vektor. Some Vektor models are clearly derived from the Beretta Model 92 pistol. That is especially the case with the locking action, which Beretta in its turn derived from the Walther P38. Another Vektor pistol, the CP1, has a locking system which is similar to the Heckler & Koch P7 handgun.

Since political changes have taken place in South Africa, great interest has arisen in the products of this country. In Europe vast quantities of the "Swartklip" ammunition are being sold. Furthermore, a number of South African gun manufacturers have an interesting range of rifles and carbines for hunting and sports. Other companies will no doubt soon follow suit.

Vektor CP1

TECHNICAL SPECIFICATIONS:

Calibre	: 9mm Para
Trigger action	: single-action
Magazine capacity	: 13 rounds
Locking mechanism	: gas-retarded blowback
Weight	: 720g
Length	: 177mm
Height	: 140mm
Barrel length	: 101mm (polygonal)
Trigger stop	: none
Sights	: fixed
Sight radius	: 136mm
External safety	: safety catch in front-side trigger guard
Internal safety	: slide safety, trigger safety (trigger in trigger system), automatic firing-pin safety

FEATURES:

• slide catch	: none, slide stays open after last shot
• magazine catch	: ambidextrous, behind trigger guard
• material	: steel slide, synthetic grip frame
• finish	: blacke coating
• grips	: integrated stock/frame

This futuristic-looking model can also be provided with a twelve-round magazine, which reduces the height to only 128mm.

Vektor SP1

TECHNICAL SPECIFICATIONS:

Calibre	: 9mm Para
Trigger action	: double action
Magazine capacity	: 15 rounds
Locking mechanism	: falling-block system (Walther)
Weight	: 995g
Length	: 210mm
Height	: 145mm
Barrel length	: 118mm
Trigger stop	: none
Sights	: fixed
Sight radius	: 156mm
External safety	: ambidextrous safety catch on frame
Internal safety	: slide safety, automatic firing-pin safety

FEATURES:

• slide catch	: on left side frame
• magazine catch	: on left side frame, behind trigger guard

• material : steel slide, alloy frame
• finish : blued
• grips : black synthetic

Vektor SP1 Sport

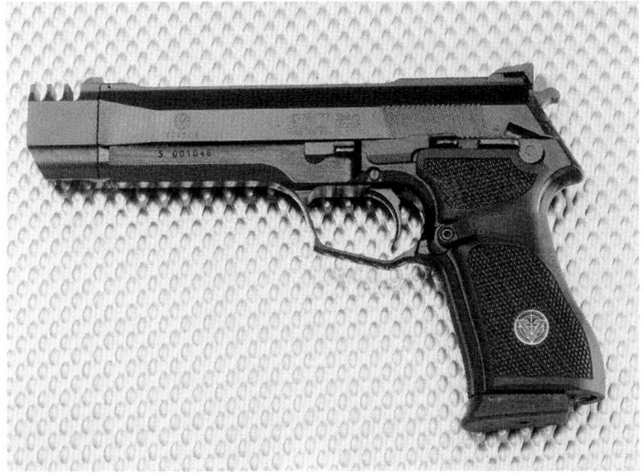

TECHNICAL SPECIFICATIONS:

Calibre : 9mm Para
Trigger action : switchable to double-action orsingle-action
Magazine capacity : 15 rounds
Locking mechanism : falling-block system (Walther)
Weight : 1080g
Length : 240mm (inc. compensator)
Height : 145mm
Barrel length : 125mm
Trigger stop : none
Sights : fixed combat sight
Sight radius : 183mm
External safety : ambidextrous safety catch on frame
Internal safety : slide safety, automatic firing-pin safety

FEATURES:

• slide catch : on left side frame
• magazine catch : on left side frame, behind trigger guard
• material : alloy frame, steel slide
• finish : blued
• grips : black synthetic

Vektor SP2

TECHNICAL SPECIFICATIONS:

Calibre : .40 S&W
Trigger action : double action
Magazine capacity : 11 rounds
Locking mechanism : falling-block system (Walther)
Weight : 995 gram
Length : 210mm
Height : 145mm
Barrel length : 118mm
Trigger stop : none
Sights : fixed
Sight radius : 156mm
External safety : ambidextrous safety catch on frame
Internal safety : slide safety, automatic firing-pin safety

FEATURES:

• slide catch : on left side frame
• magazine catch : on left side frame, behind trigger guard
• material : alloy frame, steel slide
• finish : blued
• grips : black synthetic

An exchange kit is available for calibre 9mm Para.

Walther pistols

The German Walther Company has existed for more than 100 years. In the course of time it developed a wide range of handguns for defence and sport purposes. A large number of old and prewar models are no longer in production. In 1929 the famous Walther PP pistol was developed, followed in 1931 by the model PPK. The latter became well known from the many James Bond movies, in which Sean Connery as secret agent "007" went after his opponents with this handgun. The PP model – PP is short for Polizei Pistole (Police Pistol) – served for a very long time with many police forces all over the world. It is still available in the calibres .32 ACP (7.65mm Browning) and .380 ACP

(9mm Short). According to present standards, the calibres lack sufficient stopping power for police purposes, at least with conventional ammunition. A smaller pocket-gun, derived from the PP/PPK series, is the TPH in the calibres .22 LR and .25 ACP (6.35mm). In the late 1930s, a large double-action 9mm Parabellum pistol was developed for the army. Because this handgun was issued to the German army in 1938, it was given the prefix P38. After the Second World War, the German army was issued with the same pistol once again, under the name of P1. In 1980 Walther introduced the model P5, specially designed for the police. This double-action pistol has no safety catch, but only a decocking lever, which also serves as a slide catch. The gun has the same locking principle as the P38, namely, the falling-block lock. In order to compete for government orders for new army and police handguns, the model P88 was introduced in 1987. Strangely enough, Walther abandoned the faithful falling-block principle for this model and switched to a variation of the Browning action. Beneath the chamber of the barrel a locking lug is attached and the chamber "block" itself functions as a lock-up inside the ejection port of the slide. Furthermore, this pistol is equipped with an ambidextrous combined decock and slide catch, like the P5 lever. With this model Walther competed for the handgun race of the US army in the latest pistol trials. It must have been a bitter disappointment for Walther that, of all the competitors, the Beretta Model 92-F was selected. After all, this Beretta is fitted with the well-proven (Walther) falling-block action. In the area of sporting pistols, Walther has an excellent reputation, particularly because of the Model GSP. Over the years this model has undergone several modifications.

Walther GSP .22 LR sport pistol

TECHNICAL SPECIFICATIONS:

Calibre	: .22 LR
Trigger action	: single action
Magazine capacity	: 5 rounds
Locking mechanism	: blowback action
Weight	: 1180g
Length	: 292mm
Height	: 150mm
Barrel length	: 115mm
Trigger stop	: totally adjustable trigger: trigger stop, tension creep, position of angle, release-point force, etc.
Sights	: micrometer rear sight
Sight radius	: 220mm
External safety	: none
Internal safety	: slide safety

FEATURES:

• slide catch	: ambidextrous on frame
• magazine catch	: under trigger guard
• material	: steel
• finish	: black coating
• grips	: special match stock with adjustable palm rest

Walther GSP Atlanta .22 LR sport pistol

TECHNICAL SPECIFICATIONS:

Calibre	: .22 LR
Trigger action	: single action
Magazine capacity	: 5 rounds
Locking mechanism	: blowback action
Weight	: 1180g
Length	: 292mm
Height	: 150mm
Barrel length	: 115mm
Trigger stop	: totally adjustable trigger:

trigger stop, tension creep, position of angle, release-point force, etc.

Sights : micrometer rear sight
Sight radius : 220mm
External safety : none
Internal safety : slide safety

FEATURES:

- slide catch : ambidextrous on frame
- magazine catch : under trigger guard
- material : steel
- finish : black coating
- grips : special match stock with adjustable palm rest

Walther GSP MV .22 LR sport pistol

TECHNICAL SPECIFICATIONS:

Calibre : .22 LR
Trigger action : single action
Magazine capacity : 5 rounds
Locking mechanism : blowback action
Weight : 1180g
Length : 292mm
Height : 150mm
Barrel length : 115mm
Trigger stop : totally adjustable trigger: trigger stop, tension creep, position of angle, release-point force, etc.
Sights : micrometer rear sight
Sight radius : 220mm
External safety : none
Internal safety : slide safety

FEATURES:

- slide catch : ambidextrous on frame
- magazine catch : under trigger guard
- material : steel
- finish : matt nickel plated
- grips : special match stock with adjustable palm rest

Walther GSP .32 S&W L sport pistol

TECHNICAL SPECIFICATIONS:

Calibre : .32 S&W Long
Trigger action : single action
Magazine capacity : 5 rounds
Locking mechanism : blowback action
Weight : 1280g
Length : 284mm
Height : 150mm
Barrel length : 107mm
Trigger stop : totally adjustable trigger: trigger stop, tension creep, position of anngle, release-point force, etc.
Sights : micrometer rear sight
Sight radius : 220mm

External safety : none
Internal safety : slide safety

FEATURES:

- slide catch : ambidextrous on frame
- magazine catch : under trigger guard
- material : steel
- finish : black coating
- grips : special match stock with adjustable palm rest

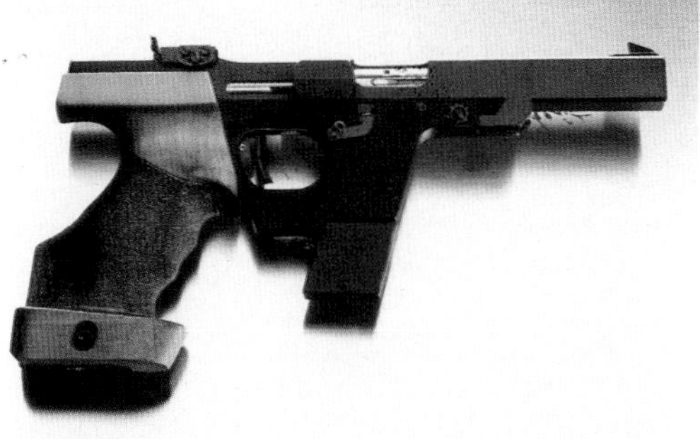

Walther GSP MV .32 S&W L sport pistol

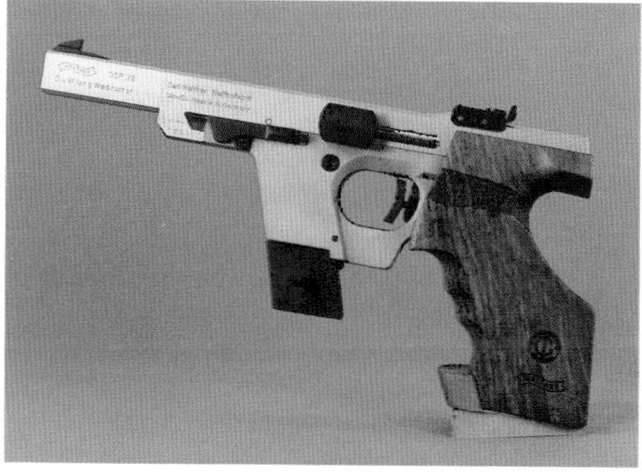

TECHNICAL SPECIFICATIONS:

Calibre	: .32 S&W Long
Trigger action	: single-action
Magazine capacity	: 5 rounds
Locking mechanism	: blowback action
Weight	: 1280g
Length	: 284mm
Height	: 150mm
Barrel length	: 107mm
Trigger stop	: totally adjustable trigger: trigger stop, tension creep, position of angle, release-point force, etc.
Sights	: micrometer rear sight
Sight radius	: 220mm
External safety	: none
Internal safety	: slide safety

FEATURES:

- slide catch : ambidextrous on frame
- magazine catch : under trigger guard
- material : steel
- finish : matt nickel plated
- grips : special match stock with adjustable palm rest

Walther OSP 2000 sport pistol

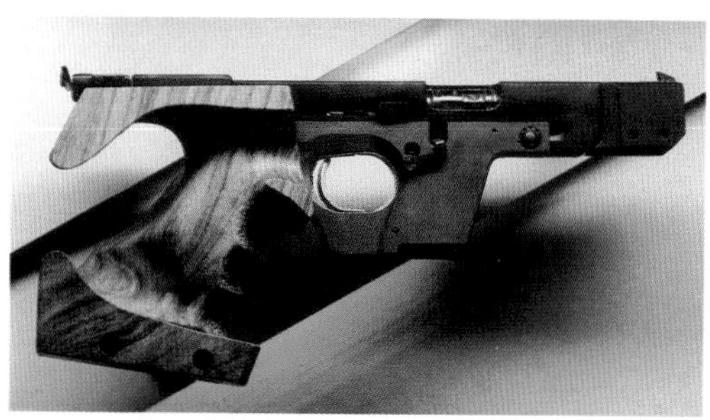

TECHNICAL SPECIFICATIONS:

Calibre	: .22 Short
Trigger action	: single action
Magazine capacity	: 5 rounds
Locking mechanism	: blowback action
Weight	: 1160 gram
Length	: 298 mm
Height	: 142 mm
Barrel length	: 85 mm
Trigger stop	: totally adjustable trigger: trigger stop, tension creep, position of angle, release-point force, etc.
Sights	: micrometer rear sight
Sight radius	: 274mm
External safety	: none
Internal safety	: slide safety

FEATURES:

- slide catch : ambidextrous on frame
- magazine catch : under trigger guard
- material : steel
- finish : black coating
- grips : special match stock with adjustable palm rest

Walther P38

TECHNICAL SPECIFICATIONS:

Calibre	: 9mm Para

Trigger action	:	double action
Magazine capacity	:	8 rounds
Locking mechanism	:	falling-block system
Weight	:	800g
Length	:	216mm
Height	:	137mm
Barrel length	:	125mm
Trigger stop	:	none
Sights	:	windage adjustable
Sight radius	:	178mm
External safety	:	combined decock/safety catch on left side slide
Internal safety	:	slide safety, automatic firing-pin safety

FEATURES:

• slide catch	:	on left side frame
• magazine catch	:	in heel of grip
• material	:	steel slide, alloy frame
• finish	:	blued/black coating
• grips	:	black synthetic

Several other versions of this model were produced over the years, such as the P38K (Kurz = Short), the P4, and the model PP Super in calibre 9mm Ultra (9 x 18mm), and even, later on, the Walther P5.

Walther P5

TECHNICAL SPECIFICATIONS:

Calibre	:	9mm Para
Trigger action	:	double action
Magazine capacity	:	8 rounds
Locking mechanism	:	Walther falling-block system
Weight	:	795g
Length	:	180mm
Height	:	129mm
Barrel length	:	90mm
Trigger stop	:	fixed
Sights	:	windage adjustable
Sight radius	:	134mm
External safety	:	decocking lever on left side of frame
Internal safety	:	slide safety, automatic firing-pin safety

FEATURES:

• slide catch	:	on left side frame (combined with decocking lever)
• magazine catch	:	in heel of grip
• material	:	steel slide and barrel, alloy frame
• finish	:	matt-black coating
• grips	:	synthetic

The Walther P5 is also available in a compact version with a total length of 170mm.

Walther P88 Compact

TECHNICAL SPECIFICATIONS:

Calibre	:	9mm Para
Trigger action	:	double action
Magazine capacity	:	14 rounds
Locking mechanism	:	Browning /SIG system
Weight	:	820g
Length	:	181mm
Height	:	134mm
Barrel length	:	100mm
Trigger stop	:	adjustable
Sights	:	windage adjustable
Sight radius	:	140mm
External safety	:	combined ambidextrous safety/decocking lever on slide
Internal safety	:	slide safety, automatic firing-pin safety

FEATURES:

• slide catch	:	on left side frame
• magazine catch	:	ambidextrous, behind trigger guard
• material	:	alloy frame, steel slide

• finish	black coating
• grips	black synthetic

The P88 Compact is also available in a Police version with only a decocking lever on the slide. It is otherwise identical to the P88 Compact.

Walther P88 Competition

TECHNICAL SPECIFICATIONS:

Calibre	9mm Para
Trigger action	double action
Magazine capacity	14 rounds
Locking mechanism	Browning/Sig system
Weight	800g (4"barrel); 885g (5"barrel)
Length	181mm (4"barrel); 206mm (5"barrel)
Height	135mm
Barrel length	100mm (4"); 125mm (5")
Trigger stop	adjustable
Sights	windage adjustable
Sight radius	140mm
External safety	combined ambidextrous safety/catch on slide
Internal safety	slide safety, automatic firing-pin safety

FEATURES:

• slide catch	on left side frame
• magazine catch	on left side frame, behind trigger guard
• material	alloy frame, steel slide
• finish	black coating
• grips	walnut

Walther PP

TECHNICAL SPECIFICATIONS:

Calibre	.380 ACP (9mm Short)
Trigger action	double action
Magazine capacity	8 rounds
Locking mechanism	blowback action
Weight	660g
Length	170mm
Height	109mm
Barrel length	98mm
Trigger stop	none
Sights	fixed
Sight radius	120mm
External safety	combined decock/safety catch on slide
Internal safety	slide safety, automatic firing-pin safety

FEATURES:

• slide catch	none
• magazine catch	on left side frame, above trigger guard
• material	steel
• finish	blued
• grips	black synthetic

Walther PPK/Walther PPK/S

TECHNICAL SPECIFICATIONS:

Calibre	: .32 ACP (7.65mm) .380 ACP (9mm Short)
Trigger action	: double action
Magazine capacity	: 7 rounds (7.65mm); 6 rounds (9mm Short)
Locking mechanism	: blowback action
Weight	: 590g
Length	: 155mm
Height	: 100mm
Barrel length	: 83mm
Trigger stop	: none
Sights	: fixed
Sight radius	: 107mm
External safety	: combined decock safety catch on slide
Internal safety	: slide safety, automatic firing-pin safety

FEATURES:

• slide catch	: none
• magazine catch	: on left side frame, above trigger guard
• material	: steel
• finish	: blued
• grips	: black synthetic

The model PPK/S is also available in stainless steel.

Walther TPH Jubilee Model

TECHNICAL SPECIFICATIONS:

Calibre	: .22 LR, .25 ACP (6.35mm)
Trigger action	: double action
Magazine capacity	: 6 rounds
Locking mechanism	: blowback action
Weight	: 325g
Length	: 135mm
Height	: 93mm
Barrel length	: 71mm (.22 LR); 73mm (6.35 mm)
Trigger stop	: none
Sights	: fixed
Sight radius	: 98mm
External safety	: decock/safety catch on slide
Internal safety	: slide safety

FEATURES:

• slide catch	: none
• magazine catch	: in heel of grip
• material	: steel slide, alloy frame

- finish : matt nickel-plated engraved slide; blue frame
- grips : engraved walnut

This commemorative model is supplied in a walnut case

Walther TPH Stainless

TECHNICAL SPECIFICATIONS:

Calibre	: .22 LR
Trigger action	: double action
Magazine capacity	: 6 rounds
Locking mechanism	: blowback action
Weight	: 395g
Length	: 135mm
Height	: 93mm
Barrel length	: 71mm
Trigger stop	: none
Sights	: fixed
Sight radius	: 98mm
External safety	: decock/safety catch on slide
Internal safety	: slide safety

FEATURES:

- slide catch : none
- magazine catch : in heel of grip
- material : stainless steel
- finish : matt stainless
- grips : black synthetic

Dan Wesson revolvers

The history of the American Dan Wesson Arms Company is linked with that of Smith & Wesson. To begin with, Dan Wesson worked in the Smith & Wesson factory, which was founded by his grandfather. Wesson left when the company was taken over by the multinational Bangor Punta in the 1960s. He started his own company, the Dan Wesson Arms Company in Monson in the State of Massachusetts. When he died in 1978 the company started to decline. In 1979, it was taken over and, partly because of the recession in the arms industry, difficult times began for the company. The son of the founder, Seth Wesson, stayed at work in the business until 1983. In 1990, Dan Wesson Arms became involved in a suspension of payment. At that time Seth Wesson decided, together with some company employees, to take control. In January 1991, the company was once again in the hands of the Wesson family, under the name of Wesson Firearms Company, and it took up residence in Palmer, Massachusetts. At first they started with the production of .38 Special and .357 Magnum revolvers, but gradually this line expanded to the old, well-tried concept of revolvers from light to very heavy. The keyword of the Wesson revolvers is the exchangeability of barrels. Per calibre there is a wide range of barrels and barrel shrouds from 2_in up to 15in. The barrel is quite easily unscrewed from the frame and replaced by a barrel of another length. Dan Wesson is the only manufacturer that offers revolvers in the so-called "Pistol-Pac" outfit. This is a small briefcase in which a Dan Wesson revolver is packed, together with one, two, or more exchange barrels. The barrel shrouds, too, are available in different models, such as the massive shroud with integrated barrel weight, or without such an extra weight, with or without ventilation rib, and all in stainless steel or deep-blue molybdenum steel. Furthermore, the front post sight is easily exchanged for one of a different colour. Because the barrel of a Dan Wesson revolver is threaded at the back (in the frame) and at the muzzle end (with the muzzle nut in the barrel shroud), a very high precision can be achieved. This is noticeable especially at the longer ranges, and that is the main reason why many silhouette shooters, for distances from 50 to 200m, favour Dan Wesson revolvers. The international rankings show that 60–80% of the shooters in the top twenty shoot with Dan Wesson revolvers.

Another speciality is the tapered "choke" of the barrel. This means that the barrel itself tightens a little (some 1/100mm) towards the muzzle end that the contact between the bullet and the rifling within the barrel remains good, despite the high speed of the bullet. The cylinder of a Dan Wesson revolver has a lock-up on the cylinder crane as well as at the rear end of the cylinder, in the centre of the extractor, with a spring-tensioned ball. The recent production line includes revolvers in the calibres .22 LR, .22 WMR, .32 H&R Magnum, .38 Special, .357 Magnum, .357 SuperMag (Maximum), .41 Magnum, .44 Magnum, .45 Long Colt, and .445 SuperMag. The types of barrel shrouds are as follows:

- Standard – without barrel weight.
- Ventilated – without barrel weight, with ventilation rib on the barrel shroud.
- Vent-Heavy – with barrel weight and ventilation rib.

Dan Wesson Model 15-2 and 715

TECHNICAL SPECIFICATIONS:

Calibre : .357 Magnum
Trigger action : double action
Cylinder capacity : 6 rounds
Locking mechanism : rear-side cylinder, cylinder crane
Weight : 1190g (6" VH)
Length : 285mm (6")
Height : 146mm
Barrel length : 64mm ($2^{1}/_{2}$"); 102mm (4"); 152mm (6"); 203mm (8"); 254mm (10"); 38 mm (15")
Trigger stop : adjustable
Sights : micrometer rear sight
Sight radius : 157mm
External safety : cylinder blocks with cocked hammer
Internal safety : transfer bar

FEATURES:

• thumb piece : left side on cylinder crane
• material : 15-2: steel; 715: stainless steel
• finish : blued or stainless
• grips : walnut, synthetic, or Pachmayr

Dan Wesson 22 VH

TECHNICAL SPECIFICATIONS:

Calibre : .22 LR and .22 WMR
Trigger action : double action
Cylinder capacity : 6 rounds
Locking mechanism : rear-side cylinder, cylinder crane
Weight : 1330g (6" VH)
Length : 285mm (6")
Height : 146mm
Barrel length : 64mm ($2^{1}/_{2}$"), 102 mm (4"), 152mm (6"), 203mm (8")
Trigger stop : adjustable
Sights : micrometer rear sight
Sight radius : 157 mm
External safety : cylinder blocks with cocked hammer
Internal safety : transfer bar

FEATURES:

• thumb piece : left side on cylinder crane
• material : 22: steel; 722: stainless steel
• finish : blued or stainless
• grips : walnut, synthetic, or Pachmayr

Dan Wesson SuperMag

TECHNICAL SPECIFICATIONS:

Calibre : .357 SuperMag, .445 SuperMag
Trigger action : double action
Cylinder capacity : 6 rounds
Locking mechanism : rear-side cylinder, cylinder crane
Weight : 1845g (8")
Length : 365mm (8")
Height : 165mm
Barrel length : 152mm (6"), 203mm (8") 254mm (10")

Trigger stop	: adjustable
Sights	: micrometer rear sight
Sight radius	: 295mm (8")
External safety	: cylinder blocks with cocked hammer
Internal safety	: transfer bar
FEATURES:	
• thumb piece	: left side frame on cylinder crane
• material	: stainless steel
• finish	: stainless
• grips	: walnut, rubber or Pachmayr

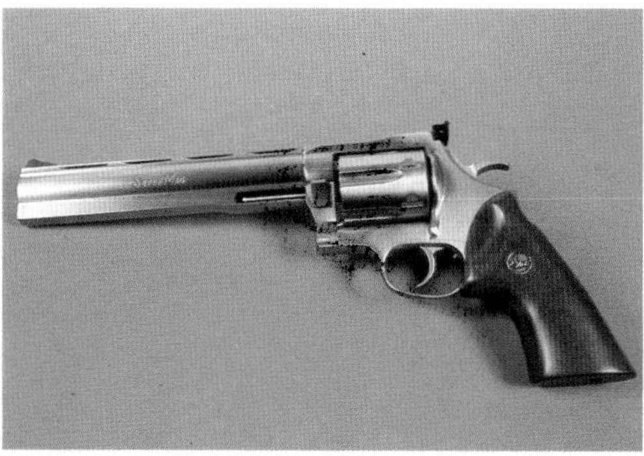

Wildey

The Wildey pistol, with its typical gas-assisted locking system, was developed in 1975 by Wildey J. Moore. The basic principle of this system was derived from the Karl Gustav rifle. A lot of problems were experienced with deliveries to the gunshops to begin with, mainly because Wildey depended on contractors for several parts. Up to now there have been production problems and the company disappeared from the market several times. Apart from the unique locking system, this pistol also has a gas control, with which the repeating action of the gun can be adapted to the power of the cartridge. Especially for reloaders of ammunition, this system has a lot to offer. This gun is used in North and South America for handgun hunting. This pistol is above all favoured for silhouette shooting. It gained publicity through the movie Death Wish III, in which Charles Bronson shoots all bad guys "out of their shoes". A lot of variations of the Wildey are known, of which the technical details are almost the same as the details of the standard model. Furthermore, Wildey is famous for the variation in barrel lengths, which can be changed in seconds. As far as calibre is concerned, Wildey has been producing pistols in several calibres, such as the 9mm Winchester Magnum and the .475 Wildey-Magnum of the 'Survival Model' of 1989. Wildey also produced pistols in all kinds of "wildcat" calibres, such as the .357 Peterbilt, a calibre which was developed by Wildey's engineer, Peter Hylenski.

Wildey Magnum

TECHNICAL SPECIFICATIONS:	
Calibre	: .45 Winchester Magnum
Trigger action	: double action
Magazine capacity	: 7 rounds
Locking mechanism	: Wildey-gas-assisted bolt lock
Weight	: 1980g
Length	: 356mm
Height	: 162mm
Barrel length	: 254mm
Trigger stop	: none
Sights	: adjustable
Sight radius	: 330mm
External safety	: safety catch on left side frame
Internal safety	: slide safety, slip safety on hammer, magazine safety
FEATURES:	
• slide catch	: on left side frame
• magazine catch	: in heel of grip
• material	: stainless steel
• finish	: matt stainless
• grips	: walnut

Bibliography

Title	*Author/Publisher*
American Centerfire Handguns	Trzoniec
American Handgunner	FMG
Armas	Hobby Press SA
Armas y Municiones	Gun Press SA
Arms Info 9 mm Para Pistolen	Vervloet & Hartink
Arms Info Colt 1911 Pistolen	Vervloet & Hartink
Combat Digest	Boger
Combat Handguns	Harris Publ. Inc.
Combat .45 Auto	Wilson
Das Pistolenbuch	Walter
Deutsches Waffen Journal	Schwend Verlag
Faustfeuerwaffen	König
Feuerwaffen für Sammler	Steinwedel
Firearms	Myatt
Firearms History	Hogg
Frankonia Jagd Katalog	Frankonia Jagd
Gewehre, Pistolen und Revolver	Müller
Guns	Publishers Development
Guns & Ammo	Petersen Publ. Comp.
Gun Annual	Modern Day Period.
Gun Digest	DBI Books Inc.
Guns & Gunsmiths	North & Hogg
Guns Illustrated	DBI Books Inc.
Gun Journal	Charlton Publ. Inc.
Guns & Shooting	Aceville Publ. Ltd.
Guns of the World	Tanner e.v.a.
Gun World	Gallant Charger Publ.
Handboek voor de herlader	A.S.I. / Hartink
Handloading for Handgunners	Nonte Jr.
Hornady Handbook of Catridge Rel.	Hornady
Illustrated book of Pistols	Wilkinson
Internationales Waffen Magazin	Orell Füssli Verlag
Internationaler Waffen Spiegel	Civil Arms Verlag
Kaliber	Magnum Uitgeverij
Law Enforc. Handgun Digest	Lewis
Man/Magnum	SA Man 1982 (Pty) Ltd.
Metallic Cartridge Reloading	Matunas
Military Small Arms	Hogg & Weeks
Modern Law Enforc. Weapons & Tactics	Clapp
9 mm Handguns	Grennel & Clapp
Petersen Handguns	Petersen Publ. Comp.
Pistole und Revolver	Henning
Pleasure of Guns	Rosa & May
Revolvers & Pistolen	Myatt
Sam	NVTU De Schakel
Sam	S.I. Publicaties
Schiessen mit Pistole & Revolver	König
Schusswaffen tunen und testen	Heymann
Schweizer Waffen Magazin	Orell Füssli Verlag
Shooter's Bible	Stoeger Publ. Comp.
Shooting Times	PJS Publ. Inc.
Small Arms	Myatt
Small Arms of the World	Smith & Smith
Technik von Faustfeuerwaffen	König
Visier	Pietsch and Scholten
Vuurwapens van 1840 tot heden	Lenselink
Waffen Digest	Motorbuch Verlag
Waffen Lexikon	Lampel & Mahrholdt
Waffen Revue	Schwend Verlag
Waffen Sammeln	König & Hugo
WM Waffenmarkt Jahrbuch	GFI Verlag GmbH

Index

Acknowledgements

The author and publisher would like to thank the following persons and companies for their co-operation. Without them this book could not have been written nor would is have been complete.

- AKAH: Albrecht Kind GmbH & Co. (Les Baer), PO Box 310283, D-51617 Gummersbach (D)
- AMT/IAI, 6226 Santos Diaz Street, Irwindale CA 91702 (USA)
- J.A. Angyal, deputy-police and sports shooter from Groot-Ammers (NL)
- T. van den Anker from Sliedrecht, policeman and arms collector (NL)
- Anschütz GmbH, Jagd- und Sportwaffenfabrik, Daimlerstrasse 12, D-7900 Ulm/Donau (D)
- A.S.I. Uitgeverij, Postbus 2279, 8203 AG Lelystad (NL)
- Astra Sport, C/ La vega, 48300-Guernica-Vizcaya (ESP)
- Auto-Ordnance Corporation, Williams Lane, West Hurley NY 12491 (USA)
- Benelli Armi SA, Via della Stazione 50, I-61029 Urbino (I)
- Pietro Beretta, 25063 Gardone V.T. (Brescia) (I)
- C.J. van den Berg from Langerak, policeman and sports shooter (NL)
- Bersa SA, Castillo 312, 1704 Ramos, Mejia, (Argentina)
- Bold-Action Zwijndrecht BV (arms dealer and importer), Lindeweg 115, Zwijndrecht (NL)
- Calico, 405 East 19th Street, Bakersfield CA 93305 (USA)
- Caspian Arms Ltd., Hardwick VT 05843 (USA)
- Casull/Freedom Arms, P.o. box 158, Wyoming 83120, (USA)
- Ceska Zbrojovka A.s., 688 27 Uhersky Brod Czech Republic
- Colt's Manufcturing Company Inc. (Freebairn & Co.), Hartford CT 06144-1868 (USA)
- CZ (Ceska Zbrojvka A.S., 688-27 Uhersky Brod, Tsjechië
- Van Dam Arms Trade, Zuideinde 46, 2421 AK Nieuwkoop (NL)
- Erma Werke GmbH, Postfach 1269, D-85202 Dachau (D)
- Feinwerkbau Westinger & Altenburger GmbH, Neckarstrasse 43 D-7238 Oberndorf am Neckar (D)
- FN-Browning S.A., Parc Industriel des Hauts Sarts, B-4400 Herstal, (B)
- Frankonia Jagd, D-97064 Würzburg (D)
- Glock GmbH, P.O. Box 50, A-2232 Deutz Wagram (A)
- Grizzly / L.A.R. Manufacturing Inc., 4133 West Farm Road – 8540 South, West Jordan, Utah 84084 (USA)
- Hämmerli Ltd, Target Arms, CH-5600 Lenzburg (CH)
- Miriam Hartink, daughter of the author, high-school girl, computer expert, secretary, support, and trusted companion (NL)
- High Standard Manufacturing Co. Inc., 264 Whitney Street Hartford CT 06105-2270 (USA)
- Helmut Hofmann GmbH, Postfach 60, D-97634 Mellrichstadt (D)
- IMI/TAAS-ISRAEL Industries Ltd, (Israel Militry Industries) P.o. Box 1044, Ramat Hasharon 47100, Israel
- Kel-Tec CNC Industries Inc., Cocoa-Florida (USA)
- Eduard Kettner, D-50602 Köln (D)
- Korth Feuerwaffen GmbH, Robert Boschstrasse 4, D-23909 Ratzeburg (D)
- Llama Gabilondo y Cia, Prado 6 E-01005 Vitoria, Spain
- Magnum Research Inc., 7110 University Ave.NE Minneapolis MN 55432 (USA)
- Manufacture d'Armes des Pyrénées Francaises, P.o. box 420 64700 Hendaye (F)
- Manurhin, Manufacture de Machines du Haut-Rhin SA (Manurhin), 15 Rue de Quimper, F-68060 Mulhouse (F)
- Mauser Werke Oberndorf, Postfach 1349 78722 Oberndorf am Neckar (D)
- Mikx Groningen (wapen-groothandel), P.o. box 2, 9700 AA Groningen (NL)
- Mitchell Arms Inc., 3400 W. MacArthur Blvd. #1, Santa Ana, CA 92704 (USA)
- Tech. Bureau Muller, P.o. box 219, 6800 AE Arnhem (NL)
- Para-Ordnance Manufacturing Co. Inc., 3411 McNicoll Ave. Scarborough, Ontario M1V 2V6 (CND)
- Armas Amadeo Rossi SA, Sao Leopoldo – RS, Brazil
- J. Roukema, arms technician and sports shooter from Papendrecht (NL)
- Shooting Club The Magnum Brotherhood of Nieuwpoort (NL)
- Sharps Shotters Club Zuid-Holland-Zuid te

Nieuwpoort (NL)
- SIG Schweizerische Industrie Gesellschaft CH-8212 Neuhausen am Rheinfall (CH)
- Smith & Wesson, P.O. Box 2208, Springfield, Mass 01102 (USA)
- Sphinx Engineering SA, Ch. des Grandes-Vies 2, CH-2900 Porrentruy (CH)
- Springfield Armory, 420 West Main Street, Geneso, IL 61254 (USA)
- Steyr-Daimler-Puch AG, Mannlicherstrasse 1, A-4400 Steyr (A)
- Sturm, Ruger & Company Inc, Lacey Place Southport, CT 06490 (USA)
- Fratelli Tanfoglio SpA, 45 Via Valtrompia, 25063 Gardone V.T. (Brescia) (I)
- Taurus Europe / Helmut Hofmann GmbH, Postfach 60, D-97634 Mellrichstadt (D)
- Thompson / Center Arms, P.o. Box 2426 Rochester, New Hampshire 03867 (USA)
- A. Tolenaars uit Wijngaarden, policeman, sports shooter and hunter without conceit (NL)
- J.A.F. Verdick from Langerak, war-veteran and sports shooter (NL)
- F. Vervloet from Heerlen, collegue-writer and publisher (NL)
- Carl Walther GmbH Sportwaffenfabrik, P.o. Box 4325, D-7900 Ulm (D)
- Hermann Weihrauch KG, (Arminius) P.o. Box 20, D-8744 Mellrichstadt (D)
- Wildey Inc., 83 Old Route 7, Brookfield CT 06804 (USA)
- Winchester Europe Division, Paris, 31 Av. du General Leclerc, 92012 Boulonge Billancourt (F)

and others, omitted in error.